Solutions to Ethical and Legal Problems in Social Research

QUANTITATIVE STUDIES IN SOCIAL RELATIONS

Consulting Editor: Peter H. Rossi

UNIVERSITY OF MASSACHUSETTS
AMHERST, MASSACHUSETTS

In Preparation

Peter H. Rossi, James D. Wright, and Andy B. Anderson (Eds.), HAND-BOOK OF SURVEY RESEARCH

Paul G. Schervish, THE STRUCTURAL DETERMINANTS OF UNEM-PLOYMENT: Vulnerability and Power in Market Relations

Toby L. Parcel and Charles W. Mueller, ASCRIPTION AND LABOR MARKETS: Race and Sex Differences in Earnings

Irving Tallman, Ramona Marotz-Baden, and Pablo Pindas, ADOLESCENT SOCIALIZATION IN CROSS-CULTURAL PERSPECTIVE: Planning for Social Change

Published

Robert F. Boruch and Joe S. Cecil (Eds.), SOLUTIONS TO ETHICAL AND LEGAL PROBLEMS IN SOCIAL RESEARCH

J. Ronald Milavsky, Ronald C. Kessler, Horst H. Stipp, and William S. Rubens, TELEVISION AND AGGRESSION: A Panel Study

Ronald S. Burt, TOWARD A STRUCTURAL THEORY OF ACTION: Net-work Models of Social Structure, Perception, and Action

Peter H. Rossi, James D. Wright, and Eleanor Weber-Burdin, NATURAL HAZARDS AND PUBLIC CHOICE: The Indifferent State and Local Politics of Hazard Mitigation

Neil Fligstein, GOING NORTH: Migration of Blacks and Whites from the South, 1900–1950

Howard Schuman and Stanley Presser, QUESTIONS AND ANSWERS IN ATTITUDE SURVEYS: Experiments on Question Form, Wording, and Context

Michael E. Sobel, LIFESTYLE AND SOCIAL STRUCTURE: Concepts, Definitions, Analyses

William Spangar Peirce, BUREAUCRATIC FAILURE AND PUBLIC EX-PENDITURE

Bruce Jacobs, THE POLITICAL ECONOMY OF ORGANIZATIONAL CHANGE: Urban Institutional Response to the War on Poverty

The list of titles in this series continues on the last page of this volume

Solutions to Ethical and Legal Problems in Social Research

Edited by

ROBERT F. BORUCH

Department of Psychology
Northwestern University
Evanston, Illinois

JOE S. CECIL

Federal Judical Center
Washington, D.C.

ACADEMIC PRESS 1983

A Subsidiary of Harcourt Brace Jovanovich, Publishers

New York   London

Paris San Diego San Francisco São Paulo Sydney Tokyo Toronto

ACADEMIC PRESS, INC.
111 Fifth Avenue, New York, New York 10003

United Kingdom Edition published by
ACADEMIC PRESS, INC. (LONDON) LTD.
24/28 Oval Road, London NW1 7DX

LIBRARY OF CONGRESS CATALOG CARD NUMBER: 83-2697

ISBN 0-12-118680-6

PRINTED IN THE UNITED STATES OF AMERICA

83 84 85 86   9 8 7 6 5 4 3 2 1

Contents

3
Reducing the Hazards of Human Experiments
through Modifications in Research Design   49
HANS ZEISEL

4
Statistics and Ethics in Surgery and Anesthesia   65
JOHN P. GILBERT, BUCKNAM MCPEEK, and FREDERICK MOSTELLER

5
Ethical Issues in the Prediction
of Criminal Violence   83
JOHN MONAHAN

6
Randomized Social Experiments and the Law   97
MARSHALL J. BREGER

7
The Signed Form—Informed Consent?   145

CHARLES W. LIDZ and LOREN H. ROTH

8
Randomization and Consent in
the New Mexico Teleconferencing Experiment:
Legal and Ethical Considerations   159

JEROME R. CORSI

9
The Efficient Conduct of
Social Science Research and
Administrative Review Procedures   171

LAUNOR F. CARTER

14

Statutory Approaches to Ensuring
the Privacy and Confidentiality of
Social Science Research Information:
The Law Enforcement Assistance
Administration Experience   263

THOMAS J. MADDEN and HELEN S. LESSIN

15

Proposed Legislation to Improve Statistical and
Research Access to Federal Records   273

LOIS ALEXANDER

16

Solutions to Legal and Ethical Problems
in Applied Social Research:
Perspective and Prospects   293

ROBERT F. BORUCH

List of Contributors

Numbers in parentheses indicate the pages on which the authors' contributions begin.

LOIS ALEXANDER (273), Office of Research and Statistics, Social Security Administration, Washington, D.C. 20009

ROBERT F. BORUCH (293), Department of Psychology, Northwestern University, Evanston, Illinois 60201

MARSHALL J. BREGER (97), State University of New York at Buffalo, Law School, Buffalo, New York 14260

LAUNOR F. CARTER[1] (171), Systems Development Corporation, Santa Monica, California 90406

JEROME R. CORSI[2] (159), Department of Political Science, University of Denver, Denver, Colorado 80208

TORE DALENIUS (237), Department of Applied Mathematics, Brown University, Providence, Rhode Island 02912

JOHN P. GILBERT[3] (65), Office of Information Technology, Harvard University, Cambridge, Massachusetts 02138

[1]*Present address:* Pacific Palisades, California 90272.
[2]*Present address:* J. R. Corsi Incorporated, Denver, Colorado 80206.
[3]Deceased.

TERRY E. HEDRICK (213), U.S. General Accounting Office, Washington, D.C. 20548

HELEN S. LESSIN (263), Law Enforcement Assistance Administration, U.S. Department of Justice, Washington, D.C. 20530

CHARLES W. LIDZ (145), Western Psychiatric Institute and Clinic, University of Pittsburgh, Pittsburgh, Pennsylvania 15213

THOMAS J. MADDEN (263), Kaye, Scholer, Fierman, Hays and Handler, Washington, D.C. 20005

BUCKNAM MCPEEK (65), Department of Anesthesia, Massachusetts General Hospital, and Harvard University, Cambridge, Massachusetts 02138

JOHN MONAHAN (83), School of Law, University of Virginia, Charlottesville, Virginia 22901

FREDERICK MOSTELLER (65), Health Policy and Management, School of Public Health, Harvard University, Boston, Massachusetts 02115

ROBERT L. NELSON (213), American Bar Foundation, Chicago, Illinois 60637

HENRY W. RIECKEN (1), School of Medicine, University of Pennsylvania, Philadelphia, Pennsylvania 19104

LOREN H. ROTH (145), Western Psychiatric Institute and Clinic, University of Pittsburgh, Pittsburgh, Pennsylvania 15213

ELEANOR SINGER (183), Center for the Social Sciences, and Editor, *Public Opinion Quarterly*, Columbia University, New York, New York 10027

JOSEPH STEINBERG (249), Survey Design, Inc., Silver Spring, Maryland 20901

LEE E. TEITELBAUM (11), School of Law, University of New Mexico, Albuquerque, New Mexico 87131

HANS ZEISEL (49), School of Law, University of Chicago, Chicago, Illinois 60637

Preface

This volume addresses some of the conflicts between our society's need for information and the ethical or legal restrictions governing its acquisition. A book title can only hint at what is to come; we offer potential solutions to these conflicts, and we discuss those solutions that are available. However, to be an entirely accurate account, the title would have to be expanded in two rather awkward ways. First, it would show that in some circumstances the solutions offered are imperfect, diminishing some problems while raising others. We believe, however, that there is value in permitting researchers and others to choose those problems they wish to confront. Second, the title would indicate our abiding interest in applied social research and the standards this research must satisfy. Although the problems considered are not unique to field research involving social programs, it is in this context that most of these problems are considered.

The progenitor for this and several other volumes is *Social Experimentation: A Method for Planning and Evaluating Social Programs* (1974)—a volume sponsored by the Social Science Research Council. This earlier book identifies classes of problems that arise when researchers collect systematic information about the effects of social programs, problems of science, ethics, law, and the organizational context in which the research takes place. Several subsequent volumes, such as *Experimental Testing of Social Policy* (1975), *Assuring the Confidentiality of Social Research* (1979), and *Reanalyzing Program Evaluation* (1981) explore some of those issues. This volume focuses in greater detail on the ethical and legal issues, offering solutions that may have not received sufficient attention.

Frequently, these solutions have been overlooked because the problems occur in one discipline while the solutions are found in another. The primary purposes of this book are to overcome these barriers and to clarify the interdisciplinary nature of the problems and solutions. This task was furthered considerably by a conference on this topic, sponsored by the National Science Foundation. The conference offered a unique opportunity for applied researchers to consider these problems in the company of methodologists, federal program managers, attorneys, statisticians, and even judges. By collecting this work in a single volume, we hope to make these strategies more accessible to social researchers, project managers, and observers of social research who seek to reconcile data collection with the legal and ethical values of the society.

The chapters in this volume offer solutions that may be characterized as procedural, statistical, or legal in nature. Both technical and nontechnical solutions are offered; we have attempted to present the technical material in a way that is accessible to readers with little prior training in statistics, law, or social research. Most of these chapters were presented at the conference of the National Science Foundation. Two of the chapters have been published elsewhere and are included with this collection to ensure that they receive the broad audience they deserve.

Grants from the National Science Foundation (NSF DAR 7820374 and ARP 77-00349) supported the development of this volume. We are very grateful to Frank Scioli and Arthur Konopka, of the former Division of Applied Research of the National Science Foundation, for their suggestions and encouragement. As always, Lucina Gallagher and Ethelyn Bond of our staff have been conscientious, productive, and pleasant company. Finally, the individual authors of this volume deserve credit for their extraordinary patience and understanding. It is a pleasure to acknowledge these debts.

1

Solutions to Ethical and Legal Problems in Social Research: An Overview

HENRY W. RIECKEN

Never in the history of social research have so many parties from outside the research community itself taken an interest in how social research is conducted, especially with respect to legal and ethical issues. Their concerns are as diverse as the perspectives they bring to bear upon the act of inquiry; and, as we shall see, there are a substantial number and variety of interested parties. The various parties espouse different values, which sometimes conflict. The purpose of this book is to examine some of the dilemmas raised by these conflicting values, purposes, and perspectives and some of the solutions that have been proposed, designed, and implemented by social scientists attempting to cope with the dilemmas.

The purpose of this introductory chapter is to sketch the principal components of these ethical and legal dilemmas. In order to be brief as well as comprehensive it is necessary to avoid examining any particular component in depth. Subsequent chapters will probe into problems and solutions in each of the major areas with which the book is concerned: privacy and confidentiality of information collected from or about individuals in identifiable form; the design and execution of social experiments in which participants (subjects) are randomly assigned to treatments; the ethical dilemmas of longitudinal studies that

1

involve predicting the future conduct of subjects; the efficacy of informed consent; and the effectiveness of review boards in agencies that support social research; or in institutions that conduct it, for the purpose of keeping surveillance over research procedures.

These topics were chosen for several reasons. The legal and ethical problems that have arisen in each area have an important impact upon applied social research and, accordingly, upon the formulation of public policy. The current controversies in each area have involved a wide variety of interested parties who do not quite speak one another's technical language; accordingly, they have sometimes talked at cross-purposes and sometimes just talked past one another. Although the legal and ethical dilemmas are far from simple, there are practical solutions for some of them, and there is work currently going on that can be expected to suggest solutions for unresolved dilemmas.

It is important to comment on what is excluded by choosing these themes. These themes focus on research that, by and large, involves a social scientist–investigator who is securing information directly from individuals by interview, questionnaire, or observation, or from archival records that contain information about identifiable individuals. Some types of social research are not so oriented, and their particular ethical or legal dilemmas are not addressed in this book. For example, a good deal of research in political science is concerned with how the government does its business, whether that be the conduct of foreign policy, the detection of law violation, or the granting of licenses and franchises. Access to information, confidentiality (in some cases "secrecy"), and other legal and ethical issues are involved, but detailed information about numbers of identifiable individuals is not of great importance to such research. Likewise, much of institutional economic research is excluded from the focus of this conference, again because such research does not usually involve the information nexus of investigator and individual respondent.

What kinds of social research are included in the scope of the book? Concretely, the range is enormous. It includes the major social experiments, such as the Negative Income Tax, Housing Allowance, and Health Insurance Experiments, smaller-scale experiments on the effects of income subsidies for parolees, medical care by nurse practitioners, or dietary protein supplements for children in less developed countries. Even experiments that do not collect data about identifiable individuals can have other ethical or legal problems, including questions of fairness to or safety of groups or treatments that are inherently unequal, possibly ineffective, or potentially damaging.

Many program evaluation studies fall within the scope of interest of this book, usually because they rely on individually identifiable data. When evaluations do not collect personal data and do not involve an experimental design, they avoid serious legal or ethical problems. So, too, do most one-time social surveys, such as public opinion or pre-election polls, consumer or marketing studies, as long as there is no need or intention to link the survey to other data about the individuals surveyed—such as archival material or follow-up surveys. One-time isolated surveys usually do not *require* identification of respondents or the collection of data through which the identity can be deduced. Sometimes individual identifiers are sought from survey respondents in order to facilitate efforts to increase the response rate and/or detect biases in the sample, but individual identifiers are not indispensable for this purpose.

In general, the research of most concern is the kind that collects information about individual respondents that permits them to be identified, and/or research that deliberately (and usually randomly) exposes individuals to some treatment regimen for the purpose of discovering the effects of that treatment. The reason for collecting individual identifiers is not that the social scientist wishes to know who the individual respondent is, in the ordinary sense of "to know." Nor are scientists ordinarily interested in disclosing the information they collect about an individual; they do not seek the information in order to make an administrative, judicial, or other determination about the individual. The social scientist only wants a simple, dependable way of matching a piece of information collected by one procedure on one occasion with a (similar or different) piece of information collected *about the same individual* by another procedure or on a different occasion. Any dependable matching method would be equally acceptable in principle to the social scientist. An arbitrary serial number, a unique alias, or fingerprints would all accomplish the purpose, though with varying difficulty, uncertainty, and cost. Social surveys usually collect names and addresses of respondents—for these are the simplest, most dependable, and cheapest identifiers to collect. They are also, unfortunately, the most useful for nonresearch purposes and, hence, most conducive to pressures to corrupt confidentiality.

The special interest of social scientists in experimental designs and novel treatments is subtle. In justifying an experiment, a sine qua non is that the efficacy, and indeed the effects, of a particular treatment or procedure are unknown. There must be a sufficient area of uncertainty to ensure the possibility of discovery. An "experiment" whose outcome is a foregone conclusion is child's play, deception, or foolishness. Yet, almost by definition, a procedure whose effects are uncertain in

nontrivial ways must involve some risks for those who undergo it—
even if the risk is only disappointment. Social scientists try to maximize discovery while minimizing risk when they design experiments,
but they do not always meet a sympathetic understanding of their purposes, or a concurrence with their judgments on the part of other interested parties.

Who are these interested parties? What is the nature of their interest?
It is easy to identify half a dozen or so, and this list may not be exhaustive.

The parties with the most direct interest, of course, are researcher
and respondent, who seek, on the one side, to maximize the amount of
information obtained and, on the other, to minimize the disclosure of
information that may result in harm, loss, or other damage. In fact, little
is known about the wishes and the fears, the attractant and the re-
pellent forces, acting upon participants in research, and there is much
groundless supposition about why individuals agree or refuse to take
part in research. One important feature of the direct relationship between investigator and respondent is the degree to which an inquiry
invades the privacy of a respondent. *Privacy* can be thought of as a state
of the person, in contrast to *confidentiality*, a state of the information.
Privacy refers to an individual's unwillingness to disclose some personal information to anyone for any purpose. Confidentiality refers to
the desire of an individual to restrict the recipients of personal information or the purposes to which it may be put. For example, patients may
be willing to tell a physician how much alcohol they drink in order to
inform a diagnosis or treatment of an illness, but insist on the *confidentiality* of that information, especially with respect to an insurance company. On the other hand, the same patient might well regard the physician's questions about fantasies as an invasion of *privacy*. The issue of
privacy is virtually restricted to the direct relationship between researcher and respondent and is almost wholly an ethical issue unless
the inquiry is accompanied by a real or imagined power of compulsory
process. Social research almost never has real power to compel an
answer (the decennial census is probably the limiting instance), but
some respondents, especially children, inmates of institutions, the
poor, and the very ignorant, may believe that the investigator has the
power (if not the right) to invade their privacy. For the most part,
however, privacy is an ethical and, importantly, a psychological problem about which, unhappily, rather little is known. There have been
some attempts to measure the boundaries of personal privacy, but the
task is difficult and results so far have been meager. For example, the
American Civil Liberties Union reported a study of "privacy in the

workplace," in which they asked employees whether an employer had ever asked for information that the employee thought should not have been required. Only about 15% of the respondents answered affirmatively, giving examples such as questions about religious affiliation, methods of birth control used, and the marital and financial status of parents. Whether the remaining 85% had not encountered such inquiries or did not consider them an invasion of their privacy is unclear. This problem remains on the agenda of behavioral research.

Once removed from the center of the research action is a group of interested parties who are predominantly concerned with the results of social research (rather than with its process). Perhaps the most important are legislative bodies such as the U.S. Congress or state legislatures acting through investigative committees, or, in the case of the Congress, through the General Accounting Office (GAO). The interests of investigative committees are quite broad, but they have often focused on suspicion of political conspiracy or criminal activity. Thus, a congressional investigation sought access to the research records of the Woodlawn community project, a community action program that used the youth gang social structure to recruit manpower trainees. The question of whether federal funds were being used to support gang activities apparently was the basis for the subpoena.

The GAO has usually been interested in detecting fraud or misuse of government funds, but it has also sought to audit the quality of research results, especially where they might be expected to have an important impact on the formulation of public policy. Thus, the GAO asserted its responsibility to review the data collected by a contractor about individuals and households participating in the Housing Allowance Experiment sponsored by the Department of Housing and Urban Development. It is clear the GAO was interested in the soundness of the design and adequacy of its execution as well as in whether participating households' incomes had been accurately and honestly established.

Judicial agencies are, of course, interested in the detection and prosecution of criminal violations. The district attorney of Mercer County, New Jersey, subpoenaed the records of the Negative Income Tax (NIT) Experiment in order to determine whether some of its participating families were guilty of "welfare fraud"—drawing conventional welfare payments through the county while accepting NIT payments. Judicial interest is believed not to be limited to fraud, however, judging by the special legal protections that have been granted to research records about persons being treated for narcotics addiction and persons arrested for driving while intoxicated.

Judicial interest in research records is not limited to criminal pro-

ceedings. As long as 20 years ago, civil suits over trademark infringe-
ment brought survey researchers into conflict with lawyers and, ultimately, judges. In one of the best-known cases, a midwestern
manufacturer of a soft drink brought suit against a competitor for having adopted a brand name that plaintiff claimed was easily confused
with his product. Plaintiff had tried to establish his claim through a
survey that seemed to show that the public did, in fact, have trouble
distinguishing between the two brands. Lawyers for the defense demanded the names of the persons surveyed in order to check their
testimony through cross-examination. The survey agency refused to
provide the names on the grounds that confidentiality had been promised. Defense counsel then moved to have the evidence from the survey
disqualified.

Another party at interest is the sponsoring agency, on whose behalf
the research is being conducted. Its interests may parallel those of the
GAO, for presumably the agency wants to get value for the money
spent. It is, if anything, even more interested than the GAO in the
adequacy of both design and execution of the research and, consequently, the validity of its results. For these reasons, the sponsoring
agency may wish to look over the researcher's shoulder, so to speak, as
he goes about his work, and this motive may threaten confidentiality.
In other respects, sponsoring agencies may take the side of the respondent against the interest of the social researcher. It was almost 20
years ago, well before institutionalizing the practice of reviewing research plans to protect subjects, that the National Institutes of Health
began subjecting behavioral research questionnaires and other procedures to staff review prior to granting approval for their use. This
instance of an agency taking responsibility to protect subjects' privacy,
welfare, or whatever is perhaps singular, but it indicates the extent to
which a sponsor of research can act to maintain propriety or, perhaps,
to stave off anticipated public criticism.

The institutional review board (IRB) was the outcome of a complex
confluence of diverse public sentiments ranging from professional concern about the ethicality of deceiving subjects in certain types of psychological experiments to a widespread outrage among laymen over
medical experiments that injected live cancer cells into the bodies of
elderly patients in a chronic disease hospital. The IRB is so placed in
the research stream that it ordinarily poses no threat to the confidentiality of data. Since it is concerned with the adequacy of procedures
proposed to protect subjects, it is usually the adversary of the investigator. The IRB may ask investigators to make provision for more secure
management of their records, or to dispense with identifiers or destroy
them before they are entirely comfortable with unidentifiable data. It

may urge them to collect data by a less intrusive (or by a less concealed) procedure, or insist that their procedures for obtaining informed consent reveal more of their purpose than they think wise. The IRB may judge an experimental treatment to be much more dangerous than the investigator believes, or it may rule that certain categories of human subjects may not be exposed to allegedly hazardous research procedures because these subjects are incapable of voluntary and informed consent.

At the outer fringe of the crowd around the research ring stand the public interest groups, like the American Civil Liberties Union, whose concern extends well beyond social research, extending, as we have seen, from questions of privacy in employment practices to the confidentiality of procedures used by credit bureaus and insurance companies and to access to information from government agencies. The public interest groups have tended to center on confidentiality of data and protection of subjects in experiments, though some have pronounced an interest in, as they see it, the potential for damage to individuals from longitudinal research that attempts to predict or forecast future behavior, especially deviant behavior. The danger, as they see it, lies in publicly labeling the individual and thus creating a self-fulfilling prophecy.

The various parties with interests in the research process and its products press their claims for attention on the basis of a number of fundamental social values that they hold to be self-evident. Almost everyone believes in First Amendment rights, in the free flow of information, in the right of citizens to find out what their government is doing, in freedom of scientific inquiry, and in the legitimacy of investigation and collection of information for the purpose of enforcing laws and seeing that justice is done. On the other side is the right of individuals to be left alone, to be free of harassment and snooping prompted by idle curiosity, and their right to control, to some degree, what is known about them by whom. Whether the right to privacy is a property right or a more personal one is not clear, and its legal basis seems cloudy, but it is a value that is increasingly widely endorsed in contemporary America.

The possibility of conflict between these two major social values is obvious. Clearly, there must be some accommodation between them in any concrete instance. Facts and circumstances must help to determine how the balance is struck, as well perhaps as additional value considerations. The way such additional values play a part can be seen in such examples as testimonial privilege, where, it is held in law, spouses cannot be compelled to testify against each other and information transactions between physician and patient, lawyer and client, priest and penitent may claim immunity from compulsory process. But other classes of communication—notably for present purposes, communications between social researcher and respondent—do not enjoy testimonial privilege. Under most circumstances research records may be obtained for evidence by subpoena, given adequate legal justification, whether or not the investigator has promised confidentiality to the respondent. The issue of legal protection of research records is complex, but the balance between values of confidentiality and public access to information seems heavily weighted toward the latter in disputes involving criminal actions.

There is perhaps less direct conflict between other major values bearing on social research, although there may be differences of opinion about their bearing upon specific situations. The need to ensure the safety of human subjects in experiments is rarely challenged. Even when an experimental procedure is undertaken for the purpose of benefiting the subject personally, the obligation to minimize risk to the individual is recognized. Reasonable people may disagree about the riskiness of any procedure, but they rarely dispute, in principle, the need to minimize risk.

Furthermore, the obligation to protect subjects is consistent with the notion of equal protection under law, which is sometimes invoked to challenge the legitimacy of randomly assigning participants to treatments in an experiment. The research investigator regards randomization as an essential technical feature, without which causal inference is jeopardized, whereas the civil libertarian looks upon "blind chance" as an irrational and unfair method of distributing or withholding a benefit—that is, the active treatment. The social researcher would reply, of course, that this view begged the experimental question. It is precisely because the worth of the experimental treatment is in doubt that the experiment is justified. It is only by giving and withholding the treatment randomly that its qualification as a benefit can be clearly established. The value conflict here is between some version of equity, though not the only reasonable version, and the validity of inferences about the efficacy of an intervention. Social researchers have appealed to the analogy of a lottery in trying to explain the notion of randomization, and evidence suggests that most potential participants in an experiment agree that it is a fair procedure.

It is only relatively recently that social research has been faced with the demand to obtain the informed consent of prospective participants in the process. The protection of participants is the value invoked, though it is not always clear what they are to be protected from— annoyance, risk, invasion of personal privacy, or the intrinsic discomfort of learning that they have been deceived, at least, uninformed about having been observed or studied. Whether truly informed consent is possible under some conditions, and whether it serves uniformly as a protection as well as more than occasionally as an unintended deterrent to participation—these are issues over which conflict has occurred. Yet the major conflict between informed consent and social research turns around the probability that individuals may conduct themselves differently when they know they are being observed or studied than when they do not. For research that depends on eliciting spontaneous and characteristic behavior without stimulating favorable self-presentation, the values represented by informed consent are in direct conflict with the value of obtaining valid research results.

Finally, the widely shared value of accountability appears in two guises. The more familiar is the accountability of an agency sponsoring research for the way in which its funds have been spent. A complementary accountability is, of course, the investigators' discharge of their contractual responsibility to the agency, including honest performance of the various research tasks. There is a second kind of accountability, namely, the researcher's accountability to scientific peers and the well-recognized scientific obligation to disclose enough data and details of procedure to permit competent colleagues to review and judge one's performance. This well-established scientific convention buttresses the social value of dependable knowledge, especially when it is intended for use in the formulation of public policy. The social benefits of knowledge are to be balanced against any personal costs of participating in research, but the knowledge must be open to competent scrutiny of its validity.

Having presented the ethical and legal problems of contemporary social research, as well as having attempted to identify the principal actors in the struggle over these problems, their interests, and the values they hold, I hope to have set the stage for the principal topic of this book, namely, the available feasible solutions, or approaches to solution of these problems.

The chapters that follow will provide detailed examinations of these solutions—their advantages and drawbacks, suitability to various research purposes, evidence for effectiveness and ethicality. Although it is clear that we are better able to deal with some concerns than with others, the commitment to deal with legal and ethical considerations is impressive. I hope that this volume will both encourage the use of current approaches and stimulate others to provide advances from our current position.

2

Spurious, Tractable, and Intractable Legal Problems: A Positivist Approach to Law and Social Science Research

LEE E. TEITELBAUM

Much recent discussion of social science research has displayed a grave concern for "legal" and "ethical" issues. This concern quite rightly apprehends that questions of goal, strategy, and technique must be answered in the social contexts of their operation. Frequently, however, legal and ethical matters are treated as "issues" in a global sense: that is, as more or less undifferentiated problem areas affecting categories of research wherever and however conducted. There is also some inclination to treat legal and ethical issues as if they are interchangeable or as if they form parts of a single entity—a kind of "legal–ethical complex."

The utility of such approaches depends on the nature of one's interest. If the idea is to reconcile social science with jurisprudence and moral philosophy, global discussion is an appropriate way to proceed. And, doubtless, genuine and profound concern of this sort exists. There is, however, another concern of social scientists that is no more jurisprudential than that of doctors, businessmen, and plumbers: to know whether conflict exists between legal rules and the programs or activities they wish to carry out. Their interest is with law in its positivist sense—that is, with determining the risk that public force will be brought to bear against their activities and against them.

SOLUTIONS TO ETHICAL
AND LEGAL PROBLEMS
IN SOCIAL RESEARCH

The following discussion addresses legal problems from this positivist perspective. For this purpose, generalized reference to "legal problems" is singularly unhelpful. Inquiry focuses rather on the existence of particular rules of law that may attach legal consequences to the execution of a specific research activity, create liability for consequences that activity may produce, or require the researcher to do certain things because of the activity or information gained during its operation. In this view, a legal right or obligation consists of "nothing but a prediction that if a man does or omits certain things he will be made to suffer in this or that way by judgment of the court [Holmes, 1897:457–458]."

A positivist approach not only implies specific attention to the kinds of laws that affect a given research activity but requires separation of legal issues from judgments concerning the moral correctness of that activity (that is, "ethics"). We are interested in predicting the consequences of behavior by reference to the dictates of law rather than those of conscience. A bad man, as Justice Holmes long ago observed, has quite as much reason as a good one for wishing to avoid an encounter with public force (1897:459), and law for him is the same as it is for the saint. The difference, of course, is that a saint may choose not to do things that the law allows because some other authority says he ought not. Attention to the distinction between legal and ethical norms is important, not only because it is helpful to be clear about the limits of the law but also because confusion in that regard obscures what may be the real reasons for hesitation in acting—objections traceable to notions of decent behavior, equality of treatment, or the like, but not to legal command. As a result, matters that should be carefully considered as problems of professional ethics are hidden because of their identification with an external source of constraint.

The Characteristics of a Positivist Approach to Legal Problems

It is worthwhile to consider the characteristics of this positivist view of law. An example drawn from a non–social science area of activity will be used, both to provide a vehicle for identifying these characteristics and to demonstrate that the problems of social science researchers are, from this perspective, much the same as those of other kinds of entrepreneurs.

For purposes of discussion, *legal problems* will be defined as situations in which some statutory, common law, or constitutional rule affects the conduct of research. Although this is not the place to develop a sophisticated typology of such problems, it is useful to distinguish among three gross classes: problems that are spurious, those that are genuine but tractable, and those that are intractable. Spurious problems are those that, from a legal perspective, are not problems at all. Suppose, for example, that I wish to sell fireworks. In approaching that activity, I am likely to want to know whether there is some law prohibiting some or all persons from doing so, and if so, whether I am among the persons restricted in this respect. If reference to statutory and case authority reveals no licensing or other laws that declare that fireworks may not be sold, or if the relevant law regulates the sale of fireworks only in respect of certain classes of persons (for example, felons) to which I clearly do not belong, I have no legal "problem," or (if I have begun my inquiry by viewing this as a problem) the problem can properly be described as spurious. For purposes of this discussion, then, a spurious legal problem is one in which no law regulates the activity in a way that affects the particular program in question. It is a fear without basis.

A tractable legal problem differs from one that is spurious in that there is indeed some body of law that affects the questioned activity. However, steps can be taken within that law that either satisfy the requirements it imposes or make its barrier tolerable as a practical matter. To return to the fireworks vendor, the law may say that "any person of good character [defined as a person not convicted of a felony] shall be issued a license for selling fireworks upon payment of a $1,000 license fee." The license fee requirement imposes a barrier to my entrance into this enterprise, but it may be a tractable one. If I either have or can raise $1000 that I am willing to invest in this way, my legal problem is soluble by completing whatever administrative requirements obtain and by paying the fee. Similarly, I may learn that if I do sell fireworks, there exists a potential for liability on my part in consequence of harm done by defective items that I sell. I face, then, a legal problem in the sense that a rule of law imposes on me a risk of financial harm. If, however, adequate insurance is available, or if by incorporating my business I can limit my liability to the assets of the business and avoid the risk of recovery against my personal wealth, the problem is a tractable one to the extent I am willing to accept some measure of cost (insurance premiums) and/or risk (loss of the value of my investment in the business).

Finally, there are some legal problems that are intractable—legal rules create insurmountable barriers to the activity in question. If an ordinance regulating sale of fireworks declares that only persons not convicted of a felony may engage in that business and I have been convicted of such a crime, there is no lawful way in which I can sell fireworks. True, I may decide to sell fireworks anyway, but in doing so I have not relieved the legal problem—I have simply decided to act lawlessly.

Determination of the kind of legal problem faced by any actor will involve a close analysis of all those rules that may operate upon the specific activity under the precise circumstances of its implementation and with a view toward its potential effects. This implies, in the first place, a multifaceted view of law. Complex areas of activity are compartmentalized, at least initially, into specific legal issues. The fireworks vendor wishes to know not only whether he or she may engage in that activity and if so, under what conditions, but also what liability may be incurred in that activity and what, if anything, can be done in order to control those risks.

Inquiry into the legal issues presented by a complex activity is therefore broad-ranging; it is at the same time very specific. The person seeking to sell fireworks is interested in licensing laws only to the extent that they affect him or her. This person will not be concerned with the laws governing hairdressers or plumbers, except to the extent that like rules or interpretations may be expected in connection with the sale of fireworks. Moreover, this particularistic inquiry is jurisdiction-specific. The fireworks vendor is not interested in the laws of any jurisdiction other than the one that will affect his or her enterprise. It is of no moment that other states or towns have laws that will prohibit the vendor from selling fireworks as long as the locality in which he or she proposes to act does not have those laws.

This, then, is the perspective we will bring to bear on the conduct of social science research. Plainly, the idea is not to resolve all or even very many legal questions, but rather to indicate that the questions are specific rather than general and that the existence of problems depends on the particular activity, the methodology employed, the place in which it is undertaken, and, perhaps, even the identity of the investigator. In the following sections, we will examine several kinds of research activity in order to illustrate both the typology used and the positivist approach to legal problems in social science research.

Confidentiality of Data:
A Case Study in Positivist Analysis

The problems associated with acquisition and maintenance of information from persons who might be harmed by its disclosure provide a useful case study of the positivist approach. Our concern will be not with proposed long-term solutions, such as shield laws, which have been thoroughly considered elsewhere (Nejelski and Peyser, 1976), but with identifying rules of law that may now predictably affect a researcher in possession of such harmful information.

THE CASE STATED

Suppose that a researcher is engaged in a study of "hidden" crime—that is, crime that has gone undetected or unsolved by the authorities. The principal instrument to be used is a questionnaire, which will ask whether respondents have committed crimes for which they have never been prosecuted and if so, the nature of those crimes. The investigator apprehends that this study may reveal the commission of very serious crimes, including murder,[1] and therefore promises in the questionnaire that the information received in the course of study "will be maintained in confidence and used only in statistical reports in which subjects will not be identified."[2]

This not-so-hypothetical situation may stand for a number of other research settings in which damaging information is solicited or received. A study of a police department might reveal incriminating information about police and underworld figures alike; research involving the "life-style" of prostitutes will place the investigator in a position to know both of past crimes and of the certain commission of crimes in the future (Nejelski and Lerman, 1971:1089; Nejelski, 1976:1, 13). In these instances, as in the case stated earlier, the researcher possesses evidence of criminal activity that might well be of interest to prosecutors, grand juries, and the general public. At the same time, the researcher's professional interest lies in not disclosing this information.

The legal questions facing investigators in these settings can be stated with deceptive simplicity: Are they required to disclose information concerning activities of these kinds on their own initiatives (that is, without waiting for a subpoena or other form of compulsion)? Are they required to respond to demands for disclosure, even if they need not volunteer information? And, if either of these is true and they

[1]Although studies of undetected crime deal typically with relatively minor offenses, in at least one such study 4 homicides and 75 forcible rapes were reported by respondents (Wolfgang, 1976:25, 27).

[2]This statement is an adaptation of one used by the Harvard Law School Center for Criminal Justice in a methadone evaluation project. Quoted in Nejelski and Lerman (1971:1085, 1098, n. 39).

comply, will they then be liable to the subjects who are harmed by their disclosures?

Rules Concerning Disclosure on One's Own Initiative

It has been suggested that "having obtained information about criminal offenses from specific, known and identified subjects of a research project, the researchers stand in a posture a [sic] harboring information, if not hiding individuals or abetting escape [Wolfgang, 1976:29]." In this posture, it is said, investigators may be guilty of crimes if they continue to "harbor" the information. This will be true, but only if there are rules that require a person in possession of information incriminating another to disclose that information to appropriate authorities.

Three possible theories of liability have been suggested: that researchers who keep secret evidence of crimes committed by others are accessories after the fact to those crimes; that they are guilty of the separate crime of misprision of felony; and that they are guilty of the crime of obstruction of justice (Wolfgang, 1976:29–30). These are all grounds for concern. However, the kind of legal problems they actually involve requires specific analysis of the elements of these crimes and consideration of the extent to which these crimes are recognized by local laws.

Accessorial liability

Every jurisdiction provides that persons who render certain kinds of aid to known felons will under some circumstances be associated with those felons' crimes and themselves be criminally liable. However, not every form of behavior that may aid a criminal will implicate another person with the former's crime. At common law (and presently in many jurisdictions), an accessory after the fact is one who (a) knew of the commision (b) of a felony by another, and (c) gave that felon aid personally for the purpose of hindering arrest or punishment.[3] All of these elements, which may differ in interpretation from state to state, must be satisfied for accessorial liability to exist.

Kind of Crime. At common law, and still in most jurisdictions, one can only be an accessory after the fact to a felony.[4] Accordingly, accomplice liability will not attach to aid to a misdemeanant, even if the aid is

---

[3]W. LaFave & A. Scott, Jr., Criminal Law 522 (1972).
[4]*Id.* at 522, 525.

overt and obviously intended to assist the criminal escape just punishment. If, therefore, a researcher receives evidence that a subject has committed the crimes of prostitution or possession of marijuana, he or she must first examine the law of the jurisdiction in which the offense was committed to determine (a) if accessorial liability extends only to felonies; and (b) the penal category into which these crimes fit. Assuming that possession of marijuana is a misdemeanor, which is often true with respect to small amounts, and that prostitution is similarly treated, these research subjects have not committed the kind of offense that could give rise to accessorial liability after the fact. Accordingly, liability as an accessory after the fact for such crimes is a spurious legal problem in those states.

In other states (such as Illinois), accessory statutes have extended liability to assistance rendered to misdemeanants as well as felons.[5] What is a spurious legal problem in, for example, New Mexico, may therefore be genuine in those states if the researcher's conduct constitutes the kind of aid prohibited by accessory laws.

Rendition of Assistance. Even if the crime reported to the researcher is a felony under applicable law, or the jurisdiction extends liability to misdemeanor cases, the question remains whether an investigator's failure to notify authorities is the kind of assistance that will make him or her an accessory after the fact. In most jurisdictions, personal assistance—implying some kind of affirmative conduct—is ordinarily required, and it must be rendered "for the purpose of hindering the felon's apprehension, conviction or punishment." The most common rule is that "mere failure to give information of a crime will not, in the absence of other acts of comfort or assistance, constitute one an accessory after the fact."[6] In states following this general (and indeed almost unanimous) rule, preservation of confidentiality by researchers cannot alone make them accessories to the crimes of respondents. In the main, therefore, accessorial liability for researchers receiving information of criminal misconduct must be regarded as a spurious issue, whatever the crime.

Misprision of felony

The crime that formally comes closest to the situation of our hypothetical researcher is misprision of felony. In its original form, this crime was committed by failure to report a known felon, thereby im-

---

[5]See Ill. Rev. Stat. ch. 38, §§ 31–4, 31–5 (1977).
[6]Levering v. Commonwealth, 132 Ky. 666, 117 S.W. 253, 257 (1909). See W. LaFave & A. Scott, Jr., Criminal Law 523 (1972).

posing on anyone with knowledge of another's felony a duty to disclose that information to some proper authority.[7] Of course, a researcher would fear no criminality in respect of misdemeanors disclosed by respondents, but receipt of a confession by a research subject concerning a rape or murder might create "knowledge" sufficient to trigger a duty to report. It is not wholly clear that receipt of such information would suffice; the subject's admission could be inaccurate, and the researcher ordinarily has no independent knowledge that the crime reported was in fact committed by anyone. Nevertheless, liability for misprision at common law is at least possible.

However, this potential arises only if misprision of felony remains a crime in the jurisdiction where the researcher operates. It is doubtful that this offense was often prosecuted even in England,[8] and in jurisdictions that have entirely codified their criminal laws, misprision is commonly omitted, except with respect to treason.[9] Even where common law crimes are recognized apart from statutory compilation,[10] some courts have reached the conclusion that misprision is not part of the common law adopted from England, partly on the basis that the crime had already fallen into desuetude in the mother country and there was, accordingly, nothing to adopt. The nature of the duty imposed itself seems to account for this pattern of abandonment. As Chief Justice Marshall observed long ago, in holding that misprision was not part of the common law adopted by the colonies: "It may be the duty of a citizen to accuse every offender, and to proclaim every offence which comes to his knowledge; but the law which would punish him in every case, for not performing this duty, is too harsh for a man."[11]

In many jurisdictions, therefore, misprision of felony is a spurious legal issue for researchers, either because the crime has never been recognized or because it has been abandoned. Indeed, this may be the case even where the table of contents of the criminal code reveals an entry under "Misprision." For example, the federal criminal code, which primarily deals with interstate crime and offenses on a federal reservation, incorporates a section entitled "Misprision of Felony," but the elements of the crime defined therein differ from those at common law. The federal act reaches only a person who "*conceals* and does not . . . make known" the felony to an appropriate authority.[12] As in-

[7]R. Perkins, Criminal Law 514 (2d ed. 1969).

[8]*Id.*; W. LaFave & A. Scott, Jr., *supra* note 6, at 526.

[9]See, for example, Mich. Comp. Laws Ann. § 750.545(b) (1968).

[10]In some states, codification of the criminal law is not intended to exclude recognition in that jurisdiction of crimes that were recognized at common law.

[11]Marbury v. Brooks, 20 U.S. 556, 575–576 (1822).

[12]18 U.S.C. § 4 (1976) (emphasis added).

terpreted, "concealment" is a necessary element of the crime and requires an affirmative step by the person with knowledge, such as suppression of evidence of the felony.[13] And although the meaning of the positive act requirement is not entirely clear, it has been held that mere silence will not suffice.[14] Accordingly, the construction placed on the federal statute reveals that, although labeled "misprision," the law places a fundamentally different duty on a citizen who possesses knowledge of serious crime than did the common law. The obligation it imposes is not to interfere with the ordinary processes of justice, rather than to come forward with information. So interpreted, the law of misprision becomes virtually identical with that governing accessories after the fact. The importance of this change is suggested by our experience under the National Prohibition Act, which made felonious the sale of liquor. Had misprision reached silence alone, the freedom of an entire generation would have been endangered. As it happened, however, the statute was interpreted to mean that even the buyer's failure to disclose sale of liquor would not constitute misprision of felony.[15]

What protected the speakeasy patron should also protect the social science investigator who maintains silence with respect to federal crime or crime on a federal reservation. An analogous line of interpretation has been applied to a few state statutes, making an affirmative act necessary for misprision. In all of these jurisdictions, as well as in those that have abandoned the crime entirely, misprision represents a spurious legal problem. However, reference to local law is still necessary. Just as it is improper to conclude that the crime of misprision exists in one state because it exists in others, so it is wrong to say that because most jurisdictions have expressly or implicitly abandoned a responsibility to come forward with knowledge of a felony, every state has done so. Ohio, for one, enacted a statute in 1975 making it unlawful for a person with knowledge of a felony to fail to report that information to law enforcement authorities.[16] This law does not seem to have been interpreted by the courts. However, the risk of its employment cannot

---

[13]Neal v. United States, 102 F.2d 643 (8th Cir. 1939), *cert. denied*, 312 U.S. 679 (1940).

[14]Bratton v. United States, 73 F.2d 795 (10th Cir. 1934). See United States v. Farrar, 38 F.2d 515 (D. Mass. 1930), *aff'd*, 281 U.S. 624 (1930).

[15]United States v. Farrar, 38 F.2d 515 (D. Mass. 1930), *aff'd*, 281 U.S. 624 (1930).

[16]Ohio Rev. Code Ann. § 2921.22 (1980 Supp., p. 48) (Page). See also State v. Conquest, 152 N.J. Super. 382, 377 A.2d 1239 (1977). In Vermont, it appears, misprision requires a motive "in some form evil as respects the administration of justice." State v. Wilson, 80 Vt. 249, 67 A. 533, 534 (1907). Failure to report without an intent to help the felon escape will not constitute misprision; whether the existence of such a desire will make silence punishable is hard to say and, in any event, requires an unlikely state of mind for the researcher.

be denied; nor can its interpretation be predicted with confidence. Accordingly, the social science investigator in Ohio may confront a genuine legal issue.

Even here, however, the legal problem may be authentic but tractable. Knowledge of both the felony and the identity of the felon appears to be essential to liability for misprision. A link-file system, in which the investigator does not know the identity of respondents to particular questionnaires (see, e.g., Astin and Boruch, 1970:615) seemingly would insulate one from knowledge of the identity of the felon and, therefore, from any duty to come forward. Custodians of the linking file would, for their part, have no reason to know that any one of the names or numbers in the files represented a felon or which of them did so. They might, as well, be located in a jurisdiction that has abandoned misprision.

Another technical device that might be of value relies on a randomized response method (Riecken and Boruch, 1974:264–265). Subjects are asked to roll a die and, if it turns up "one," to report commission of a predetermined crime, whether or not that was a true response. Accordingly, researchers cannot "know" that any given answer to the questionnaire is accurate. All they know is the probability of candor on the part of any given respondent, which might be insufficient to constitute knowledge of the kind contemplated by statute. If it be said that researchers have by such devices intentionally placed themselves in positions not to know, that creates legal problems only if they are required to avoid ignorance in this respect. No basis for such a legal obligation is readily apparent.

Of course, these or other strategies for responding to the law of misprision bear costs. A link-file system may be a relatively complicated or expensive procedure for an otherwise modest project, and randomized response techniques import methodological problems that would not otherwise exist (Riecken and Boruch, 1974:265). Finally, there may also be both risk and financial cost in persuading trial and appellate courts that these techniques were effective for the purpose— avoidance of circumstances giving rise to a legal duty of disclosure. This "risk," it should be said, is really multiple, since a trial court may find a duty to disclose and sanction the researcher for contempt while he or she is appealing (perhaps successfully) the initial decision. Nevertheless, such strategies merit consideration as possible solutions to a legal problem.

Obstruction of justice

It may appear that failure to come forward with evidence of crime (here, the subject's confession) will constitute the amorphous offense of obstruction of justice.[17] Although obstruction may embrace such various activities as attempting to influence a juror, preventing an officer from performing duties, dissuading a witness from testifying, lying to a grand jury, or suppressing evidence, it seemingly does not reach silence alone. The essence of the crime lies in the commission of acts that impede, rather than in omission to aid, the administration of justice. And in some states obstruction of justice is not recognized as a separate offense.[18]

A more difficult question arises with respect to destruction of questionnaires containing incriminating information. Although this step has been urged for purposes of protecting informants (Nejelski and Lerman, 1971:1097–1098), it is, in a literal sense, destruction of evidence. Specific reference to local law is necessary in this connection. Assuming, however, that we are still concerned only with duties arising without compulsion from grand juries or other agencies, even such acts commonly will not create liability under, for example, statutes resembling the federal law. Federal courts have held that "a pre-requisite for a conviction for obstruction of justice . . . is the pendency of some sort of judicial proceedings which equates to an 'administration of justice.'"[19] Moreover, not all investigations amount to "the due administration of justice." Grand jury proceedings constitute such a stage of the justice system, but FBI investigations, for example, may not.[20] Finally, the pendency of proceedings must be known to the person in possession of the information for destruction to amount to obstruction of justice. In the most likely case, where the investigator destroys the questionnaire before any proceedings have begun (or even been considered), justice has not been obstructed.

In other jurisdictions, however, the requirement of pendency of proceedings may not exist. An Illinois decision, for example, holds that it is possible to thwart a prosecution not yet begun,[21] a view that—taken to its extreme—would require maintenance of any evidence in perpetuo. In that case, it should be said, the evidence destroyed was evidence directly flowing from the crime (blood-stained clothing of the defendant), and there is also some suggestion that the person prosecuted for destroying evidence must have a specific intent to prevent prosecution (rather than some more innocent motive). However, the weight associated with these distinctions is impossible to state with

[17]It has been observed that any punishable misdeed tending to distort or impede the administration of law that is not itself a distinct crime is usually called "obstruction of justice." R. Perkins, Criminal Law 494 (2d ed. 1969).

[18]See, for example, Agnew v. Parks, 343 P.2d 118 (Cal. App. 1959).

[19]United States v. Walasek, 527 F.2d 676, 678 (3d Cir. 1975).

[20]United States v. Ryan, 455 F.2d 728, 733 (9th Cir. 1972).

[21]People v. Sumner, 40 Ill. App. 3d 832, 354 N.E.2d 18 (1976).

certainty, and the risk of liability must be acknowledged as genuine in these states.

The Problems of Compelled Disclosure

Disclosure on one's own initiative—that is, absent specific legal command—is only rarely a genuine legal problem for the researcher who, in any event, is disinclined to compromise research subjects. It may happen, however, that some judicial or legislative body, or even a civil litigant, learns of the research program and sees in it a convenient vehicle for discovery of information. This is by no means a purely theoretical concern. The efforts made by state prosecutors and a congressional committee to obtain data from the New Jersey negative income tax experiment have been thoroughly documented (Kershaw and Small, 1972). In Massachusetts, a grand jury subpoena was used in an effort to secure information from Samuel Popkin concerning expressed attitudes on the Vietnam War obtained in the course of his research. Popkin's refusal to comply with the subpoena resulted in his imprisonment for contempt.[22] Indeed, a report of the American Political Science Association Confidentiality in Social Science Research Data Project indicated that, as of 1975, "some two dozen scholars have been subpoenaed in recent years, or indirectly threatened with a subpoena, in efforts to obtain research data [Carroll and Knerr, 1975:258–259]." And, occasionally, parties in civil litigation with reason to think that a researcher's notes or data will be helpful in presentation of their case have also sought to use the subpoena power to compel disclosure.[23]

Compelled disclosure by subpoena is, in the main, a legitimate legal problem for the researcher. The power of grand juries and congressional committees to compel presentation of testimony and production of documentary evidence is undeniably extensive. Even if researchers think there is some basis for refusal to comply, they must promptly respond to subpoenas by motions to quash or analogous steps challenging the validity of the order to produce; it cannot safely be ignored and challenged at some later time.[24] Moreover, the grounds for objecting to a subpoena are characteristically narrow. Under the Federal Rules of

---

[22]The Popkin affair has been discussed in a variety of places, including Carroll (1973), and the report of the American Political Science Association's Committee on Professional Ethics and Academic Freedom (1973b). The former source also lists a variety of incidents involving issuance of subpoenas to researchers (pp. 268, 277).

[23]For example, Richards of Rockford, Inc. v. Pacific Gas & Electric Company, 22 Fed. R. Serv. 2d 321 (N.D. Cal., May 21, 1976).

[24]See, for example, Fed R. Crim. P. 17(c).

Criminal Procedure, for example, a subpoena may be quashed if it is "unreasonable or oppressive."[25] The latter notion, "oppressiveness," by and large goes to the scope of the order to produce, forbidding demands for production of unduly large numbers of documents gathered over too many years.[26] This defense will rarely be available, except in the largest research projects with immense amounts of data that cannot easily be sorted. The requirement that a subpoena be "reasonable" generally requires that the documents subpoenaed or questions asked a witness be relevant to the investigation of the grand jury or to the issues before a trial court.[27] In this connection, it should also be appreciated that relevance, at least for grand jury purposes, is an expansive notion. The evidence need not itself be admissible at trial; it is usually sufficient that the information bear in some way on the subject matter of the investigation.[28] Nor need the inquiry have already established the existence of a particular crime or its perpetrator. The purpose of grand jury proceedings is frankly investigatory, and jurors may act upon tips, rumors, evidence offered by the prosecutor, or their own personal knowledge.[29] Although it has been said that the jury may not use its power to conduct a "fishing expedition,"[30] the limits thereby implied have not been clearly articulated. Thus it seems that knowledge of any data revealing unpunished crime, however it came to the grand jury's attention, might justify issuance of a subpoena to produce evidence of these offenses.[31]

Congressional subpoena power is also broad, restricted only by requirements that (a) Congress have the power to investigate the matter in question; (b) the committee issuing the subpoena have the proper grant of authority from Congress to conduct an investigation; and (c) the materials or testimony compelled by pertinent to the investigation and within the scope of the committee's grant of authority.[32] Whether these conditions are satisfied will, obviously, depend on particular circumstances, but as long as the information is relevant to the investigation and the committee has not exceeded its grant of authority, the subpoena will be valid and enforceable by contempt.

---

[25]Id.

[26]United States v. Gurule, 437 F.2d 239 (10th Cir. 1970).

[27]United States v. Joyner, 494 F.2d 501, 506–507 (5th Cir. 1974); In re Grand Jury Proceedings, 486 F.2d 85, 93 (3d Cir. 1973).

[28]In re Morgan, 377 F. Supp. 281 (S.D.N.Y. 1974).

[29]United States v. Dionisio, 410 U.S. 1, 15 (1973).

[30]United States v. Moore, 423 F. Supp. 858, 860 (S.D.W.Va. 1976).

[31]See Branzburg v. Hayes, 408 U.S. 665 (1972).

[32]Bergman v. Senate Special Committee on Aging, 389 F. Supp. 1127, 1130 (S.D.N.Y. 1975).

It will be unusual for a civil litigant to find social scientists' research data useful, but the unusual sometimes happens. In a case involving a suit against a utility company for breach of contract, a researcher was served a subpoena ordering him to produce notes he had made during research on decision making at the defendant utility.[33] The research included interviews with company employees given under a promise of confidentiality, some of which might have contained information concerning the breach upon which plaintiff was suing and been of value to the plaintiff's case. Generally, parties to an action may issue a subpoena for production of evidence in the hands of witnesses who are not parties to the action.[34] In this case, disclosure of the scholar's research notes was ultimately denied, but entirely on discretionary grounds. A trial judge is vested with broad discretion in supervising pretrial discovery, and in this instance the court found that the interests of the plaintiff were outweighed by those of the researchers in keeping their pledge of confidentiality. This result is like that sometimes, but not uniformly, reached in connection with efforts to discover information possessed by reporters, and the court explicitly relied on that analogy in undertaking the process of balancing the interests favoring and opposing disclosure in this case. At the same time, the court did not hold that the public interest in protecting confidential relationships between academic researchers and their sources rises to the stature of a constitutional privilege, leaving open (as is also true for reporters) the possibility that, on other facts, the balance may be struck in favor of requiring disclosure of confidential information.[35]

If the much-discussed researcher's privilege were created, these problems would disappear, since a subpoena is essentially a demand to produce *unprivileged* information. In a jurisdiction that adopts such a privilege, therefore, the problem would indeed be spurious, and some shield statutes designed to protect media representatives might be interpreted to cover researchers as well.[36] This seemingly will require legislative action, since there is considerable reason to think that no

[33]Richards of Rockford, Inc. v. Pacific Gas & Electric Company, 22 Fed. R. Serv. 2d 321 (N.D. Cal. May 21, 1976).

[34]Fed. R. Civ. P. 45.

[35]See, for example, In the Matter of Myron Farber and the *New York Times* Co., 78 N.J. 259, 394 A. 2d 330 (1978), *cert. denied sub. nom. New York Times* v. New Jersey, 439 U.S. 997 (1978).

[36]The Delaware statute explicitly extends to scholars. Del. Code Ann. tit. 10, §§ 4320–4323 (1975). The Oregon shield law, although specifically addressed to "Newsmen," protects the confidentiality of sources used by any person "engaged in any medium of communication to the public." Or. Rev. Stat. §§ 44.510–44.520 (1977).

broad constitutionally based or judicially developed immunity from testifying or producing evidence will soon be recognized.[37]

Absent such a privilege for research data, it must be asked if there are procedures that might avoid the legal problems presented by a valid subpoena. One such device is relatively simple: elimination of identifying information before the initiation of legal proceedings. What the investigator is able to divulge will not prejudice research subjects, and a subpoena cannot require a person to disclose that which does not exist. This strategy, however, requires planning and foresight. Once the subpoena has been lawfully issued, destruction of material covered by the subpoena will probably amount to destruction of evidence and contempt of the authority commanding production.

If maintenance of identifying information is important for some further purpose, or if the research involves use of a source of information that cannot be destroyed, a more complex strategy might be considered. The first step lies in creation of a link-file system, in which identifying information and research data are separated into different files, and a third file containing linking information is created (Astin and Boruch, 1970). This last file is the only means of matching the subject's identity with his or her responses to the questionnaire. The link file is then deposited elsewhere, out of the possession of the researcher.

Taken only this far, the link-file system will probably not relieve a researcher of the responsibility imposed by subpoena. Although witnesses may not be compelled to produce material that they neither control nor possess,[38] the concept of "control" is broad. Inspection can be ordered if the party to whom the request is made has the legal right to obtain the document, even though this person does not have a copy at the time of subpoena.[39] The same is true of documents to which persons subpoenaed have practical access—that is, they can gain possession of them as a practical matter.[40] Moreover, if persons under command have "control" of the information demanded, they will be required to produce it even though the documents in question are themselves beyond the jurisdiction of the court.[41]

[37]See Branzburg v. Hayes, 408 U.S. 665 (1972), refusing to recognize a First Amendment privilege for reporters "to refuse to answer the relevant and material questions" presented in connection with grand jury subpoena.

[38]This is plainly true of subpoenas under the Federal Rules of Civil Procedure, 9 C. Wright & A. Miller, Federal Practice and Procedure: Civil § 2454, at 425 (1971). The subpoena power created by the rules of criminal procedure are closely patterned on civil rules. 8 J. Moore, Federal Practice: Rules of Criminal Procedure § 17.07.

[39]8 C. Wright & A. Miller, Federal Practice and Procedure: Civil § 2210, at 621 (1970).

[40]Herbst v. Able, 63 F.R.D. 135 (S.D.N.Y. 1972).

[41]8 C. Wright & A. Miller, Federal Practice and Procedure: Civil § 2210, at 624 (1971).

At least one authority, apparently anticipating this difficulty, has suggested placement of the link file in a computer facility in a foreign country (where matching runs are to be made) and—presumably to remove "control" of the link file from the researcher—has further recommended that the foreign repository agree by contract to refuse delivery of the link file to anyone, including the researcher (Astin and Boruch, 1970; Nejelski and Lerman, 1971:1097, n. 37).[42] This may, indeed, allow investigators to say in good faith that they cannot disclose the link file because they lack control over it. Although, of course, they still will be required to turn over data in their possession, these data will be of little or no value to a grand jury or congressional committee.

Unfortunately, no legal experience with such a system seems to exist. It is, for reasons that will be discussed later, arguable that a contract relinquishing control over the data will be viewed as illegal if its primary purpose is avoidance of the obligation to comply with a subpoena. If, however, other reasons of data security exist, which they doubtless do (Nejelski and Lerman, 1971:1097, n. 37), the contract may not be considered void as against public policy, since hindrance of subpoena powers is only a collateral effect, and not the purpose, of the agreement. Moreover, even a finding that the agreement with the foreign depository is void under local law may not justify the conclusion that the link file is within the "control" of the researcher. The foreign depository may well take the position that it will not turn over the file absent a court order, and if this is so, researchers have control only to the extent that they are able to prosecute successfully a legal action against the depository and have a judgment enforced in the latter's courts. To find "control" in these circumstances is a considerable extension of that doctrine, and one that courts may not be willing to accept. Without, however, a body of judicial decisions concerning closely analogous situations, firm conclusions concerning the effectiveness of this device must be withheld. And, of course, so complicated a set of protections may be practically unavailable for projects without substantial funding.

Liability for Disclosure Pursuant to Public Duty

Researchers who possess incriminating evidence, as we have just seen, may be required to disclose that evidence upon subpoena. In these circumstances, it should be asked, will investigators face liability

---

[42]Placement in a foreign country is necessary if a federal subpoena is used, but not always so if the authority in question is a state agency.

from subjects whose criminality or fraud they have revealed? At least three possible bases for such liability exist. The respondent may seek a tort recovery based on breach by the investigator of a duty not to invade his or her privacy by publishing (that is, disclosing in any way) the information. Alternatively, the subject might claim that a contract between the subject and the researcher existed and included a promise of confidentiality that was breached by disclosure pursuant to subpoena. Finally, the subject may claim that the researcher acquired the sensitive information by a misrepresentation concerning its confidentiality.

Invasion of privacy

At first glance, it may seem that investigators are responsible for an invasion of a subject's privacy when they disclose to an outside party the content of a questionnaire. This much is certainly true: There has been a publication of information that the respondent presumably expected to remain confidential and which he or she would not have revealed but for that expectation. Nevertheless, liability on the researcher's part is unlikely to exist, assuming that disclosure was in response to a subpoena or other form of legal compulsion.

The initial barrier to liability lies in a rule of privilege that immunizes conduct that in other circumstances would be actionable. In general, communications made by a witness in connection with legal proceedings are absolutely privileged—that is, unconditionally protected by the law.[43] This is true of defamatory statements by a witness[44] and of those that invade the privacy of a person about whom testimony is given.[45] It does not matter that the statement is offered voluntarily and not in response to a specific question, or even that the statement turns out to be irrelevant to the case at hand.[46] Accordingly, disclosure of information—even affecting the most intimate facts of a person's life—will be privileged and not subject to legal redress if given in connection with judicial proceedings, broadly defined. Moreover, the privilege extends to relevant information disclosed in the course of legislative proceedings or in communications preliminary to such proceedings.[47]

Liability for statements given in connection with pending (or even seriously proposed) grand jury, trial, or legislative investigative proceedings seems, therefore, a spurious legal issue. And even if disclosure of a respondent's crime occurred without compulsion or with-

[43]Restatement (Second) of Torts § 588 (1977) (hereinafter cited as Restatement, Torts).
[44]Id.
[45]Id. § 652(F).
[46]Id. § 588, Comment c.
[47]Id. §§ 590(A), 652(F).

out connection to such a proceeding, it is by no means clear that an action could be brought. In general, an invasion of privacy occurs when publicity is given to private facts, the disclosure of which would be objectionable to the normal person (see Prosser, 1960). Initially, it is necessary to determine whether commission of an unpunished crime is a "private fact" of the kind that should be protected by law. It has been suggested, on the one hand, that "deviant and abnormal behavior" would probably be so considered (Nejelski and Lerman, 1971:1124). On the other hand, a significant body of case law points in the other direction.

Berry v. National Broadcasting Company, for example, involved an invasion of privacy action arising out of publication of facts concerning the plantiff's slaying of another. In denying relief to the plaintiff, the court observed: "It is clear that as to the issue of privacy, Mr. Berry's act of shooting Norman Little Brave removed Mr. Berry's right to privacy as to that incident and matters relevant to it. Clearly, killing another person is a matter of public interest."[48] Even more closely in point is a case with the atavistic name of *Earp v. City of Detroit*,[49] in which two police detectives interviewed Earp about wiretapping activities, having promised confidentiality for anything they were told. During the interview, the plaintiff admitted having engaged in such activities, which the police officers promptly reported to his employer, Michigan Bell Telephone. After the telephone company fired plaintiff, he brought an action for invasion of privacy predicated upon the detectives' breach of confidence. The court denied recovery to plaintiff, concluding:

> The information given Bell [the employer] was not of a private nature. Clearly it was not something one would want to get around but it concerned a matter of public interest. . . .
>
> Here the confidential information that Earp gave to the police was not of such a nature that he was entitled by law to require all who knew of it to say nothing.[50]

The rationales for these decisions rest on one or more of the elements of the action of invasion of privacy itself. In the first place, it may be that disclosure of the fact of past criminality, particularly if unpunished, cannot properly be viewed as "offensive" to a reasonable person, however outraged the subject may actually be. Or it may be that the courts are applying the common law and constitutional notion that

[48]480 F.2d 428, 431 (8th Cir. 1973).
[49]167 N.W.2d 841 (Mich. App. 1969).
[50]*Id.* at 848.

any interest in privacy must in some circumstances yield to a greater interest in publicity concerning matters of legitimate public concern.[51] The decision in the Berry case seems indeed to rest explicitly on that basis, and certainly serious crime that is yet unpunished would seem generally to fall into the category of issues of legitimate public interest. Perhaps the same could not be said for minor instances of misbehavior, particularly those that transpire in private,[52] but at some point "deviant and abnormal" behavior becomes a source of justifiable community concern.

Breach of contract

The subject may, in the alternative, pursue a lawsuit against the researcher on the theory that there was a contract between them that included an agreement by the latter not to disclose the subject's confidence and that has been breached. It may be claimed that the promise was express (as in the hypothetical case stated earlier, where the questionnaire recited that the information received would be held in confidence and would be used only in statistical reports without identification of respondents), or that confidentiality was implicitly promised as part of the researcher–subject relationship.

Whether there is a breach of contract depends, in a positivist view, on whether the researcher created an expectation on the subject's part that will be enforced. This is partly a matter of language since, in the main, what one expects or may reasonably expect is a function of what one is told. The central question is, however, one of expectation rather than of verbal formulas, and the relationship of the parties, the nature of the activity, and other circumstances may be relevant in determining what the parties understood their arrangement to be and the legal effect it will be given.

Words, therefore, cannot be assumed to have an a priori meaning, even that which the researcher originally had in mind. Take, for example, the hypothetical assurance set out earlier: "Information received in the course of this study will be maintained in confidence and used only in statistical reports in which subjects will not be identified." Even so simple a recital creates a lawyer's sandbox. At least four interpretations of this assurance, each plausible (although not equally so) under various circumstances, might be reached by a court, with various legal consequences.

Most simply, it may be concluded that the researcher promised only

---

[51]Restatement, Torts § 652 (D), Comment d.
[52]Id. Comment b.

to publish the data received in aggregate form and to follow usual practice for access to the questionnaires. So interpreted, the assurance says nothing about refusal to disclose data in the face of a valid subpoena, and if the court finds that the promise was intended to be so limited by the researcher and that the subject either did understand or should reasonably have understood it to be so limited, there will be no breach since there was no promise.

Under other circumstances, however, the court might find that the researcher promised silence, come what may, or that a research subject could reasonably have understood him or her to so promise. This situation could arise from the preceding assurance (particularly if, for example, uttered in response to a question by the subject concerning compelled disclosure) or, even more likely, from further declarations, such as "I will not comply with any subpoena" or, less plainly, "Nobody will ever find out who completed these questionnaires." On such an interpretation, disclosure pursuant to subpoena would breach a promise by the researcher. However, that breach may not give rise to liability, since the promise may not be one that is enforceable at law. A "contract" to kill someone, although fitting the form for contracts generally (that is, the parties exchanged promises and consideration for those promises), obviously will not be enforced by a court because to do so violates a strong public policy against agreements to kill. It is, in short, desirable that such a promise be broken. By the same token, a promise not to respond to legal compulsion in presenting evidence violates the public policy reflected in the subpoena power itself. As a leading treatise on contract law observes: "A bargain the purpose of which is the stifling of a prosecution is in all cases contrary to public policy and illegal even though it may not itself be a crime. . . . It is true whether the prosecution has or has not been started at the time the bargain is made."[53] Obviously, the only way in which a researcher could be said to have breached a contract is in failing to honor an express or implied promise not to respond to a subpoena or cooperate with an investigation. If, as seems likely, such a promise is illegal and unenforceable, liability based upon its breach presents a spurious legal problem.[54]

[53]6A A. Corbin, Contracts § 1421, at 355 (1962). For a case following this rationale, see Baker v. Citizens Bank of Guntersville, 208 So. 2d 601 (Ala. 1968).

[54]It may be concluded that the investigator's promise of confidentiality was not actionable because circumstances rendered performance of the promise impossible, which in turn constitutes a valid defense to an action based on breach of agreement. Although one ordinarily thinks in terms of natural disaster as making performance impossible, it is clear that judicial order or decree secured by some third person may also operate as a

Yet a third interpretation of the researcher's promise might, however, be enforced and result in liability. Particularly where highly incriminating information is sought and/or specific concern by subjects has been expressed, the assurance quoted earlier could plausibly be taken as a promise by the researcher to use reasonable care in protecting the data. This promise might in turn include use of reasonably available techniques for preserving the confidentiality of informants' identities, insistence upon issuance of a lawful subpoena before delivery of harmful information, and (perhaps) determination of the validity of the subpoena itself through appropriate legal process. Failure in any of these respects would constitute breach of a promise of care, and the public policy considerations that nullify agreements to flout a court order would not necessarily imply nullification of a promise to take *lawful* steps to preserve information and to ensure that its disclosure is legally required. This apparently genuine legal problem may, however, be resolved by adequate forethought and planning. If devices for preserving confidentiality are explored and, where reasonably available, employed, and if the validity of any subpoena is ascertained appropriately, no breach will have occurred even should disclosure ultimately be required.

Finally, and most remotely, an imaginative lawyer for the subject might construe the assurance in question, or some other statement by the researcher, as a warranty of confidentiality or promise to indemnify the subject for any harm resulting from disclosure of information. A casual comment such as "I promise no harm will come to you from participating in this study" could conceivably produce such an interpretation and, with it, at least the possibility of an obligation to compensate the subject for damages such as loss of wages. We are, at this point, well beyond the boundaries of existing authority but, perhaps, not those of analogy and innovation. The antidote to liability here, if it exists, must lie in practical matters and, in particular, the careful use of language by the researcher. It is one thing to promise care in preserving data and quite another to say something that can reason-

---

defense of that kind. 6 A. Corbin, Contracts § 1346, at 430 (1962). However, this is a weaker defense than illegality of the promise, since it will be available only if the legal intervention is not viewed as caused by the researcher and if no means of avoiding such interference with performance was reasonably available. To the extent that devices for insulating the data from subpoena by, for example, a link-file system were available and not used (see discussion *supra* notes 38–42), at least a formal claim of causal connection could be advanced. That is not to say that causation would be found, but only that some risk exists that does not obtain under the doctrine of illegality.

ably be understood as a promise to hold the subject harmless. If the latter is avoided, no liability on this last theory would exist.

Misrepresentation and deceit

The research subject may seek relief not on the grounds of broken promise or invasion of privacy by the researcher but on a theory of misrepresentation: That is, that the researcher, in obtaining the incriminating information, was guilty of a representation of some factual matter that he or she knew or should have known was false and that was justifiably relied upon by the subject. In this area, the law is less clearly charted than is true of the preceding theories and, consequently, conclusions about the spuriousness and tractability of the problems presented must in some instances remain tentative. Moreover, much (indeed, almost everything) will depend on the precise circumstances of each case—and particularly on what exactly was said by the investigator and what exactly he had in mind at the time that he said it.

As suggested above, the tort of misrepresentation is predicated upon a representation of fact that the declarant knew or should have known was false and that was justifiably relied upon by the plaintiff to his or her detriment.[55] First, there must be a representation of *fact*, rather than a promise.[56] This representation is ordinarily in the form of an assertion that something is true, although misrepresentation may also take the form of an incomplete statement that is known or believed to be misleading.[57] An assurance that "Mommy won't punish you if you tell the truth" is a misleading invitation if one knows perfectly well that Daddy will.

Second, the misrepresentation must be made with a culpable state of mind. The most obvious case is when the person making the misrepresentation knows or believes the matter not to be as he or she says it is. However, liability may also be imposed when the declarant has neither knowledge nor belief in the truth of a matter asserted as fact. Thus, a reckless misrepresentation of fact—where one knows one has no *basis* for saying that something is true (even though one does not *know* it to be false)—may also suffice for liability.[58]

There must also be reasonable reliance by the subject upon the representation. Ordinarily this presents no problem, but there are instances

[55]Restatement, Torts § 525.

[56]Statements phrased in terms of opinion may amount to a representation of fact under some circumstances. See W. Prosser, Torts 720–724 (4th ed. 1971).

[57]Restatement, Torts § 529.

[58]*Id.* § 527.

in which no reasonable person would have believed the representation of fact, and, consequently, liability will be denied.[59] Finally, reliance upon the misrepresentation must result in some compensable form of harm to the deceived.

With these elements generally in mind, it may be useful to consider examples of what researchers might say to a subject whom they are soliciting to participate in a hidden crime (or some similar) study, with a view toward identifying the circumstances in which they may be held guilty of misrepresentation.

In the first example, the researcher says to the subject, "I promise not to reveal any information you give me to anyone except in statistical form and without any identifying information." At the time, the researcher is sincere, but he or she subsequently decides to reveal the information in identifiable form to a grand jury.

Ordinarily, there could be no fraud in this instance. An action for misrepresentation must be based upon a statement of *fact* by the researcher. A promise is not such a statement, because it is neither true nor false at the moment it is made. The subject's complaint here is not that anything was misrepresented at the time the statement was made, but rather that the researcher broke a promise. The remedy for noncompliance with a promise is breach of contract rather than fraud, and liability on this theory, as we have seen, is unlikely to be imposed.

If a researcher's disclosure is the result of unanticipated circumstances (he or she did not foresee the risk of subpoena) or change of heart, no fraud has occurred. Suppose, however, that the researcher's state of mind upon uttering the assurance in question was this: "I will tell subjects that I promise to keep their confidences, but I will disclose what they tell me upon subpoena." Under these circumstances, there may be a misrepresentation of fact. What has been misrepresented is not the researcher's future behavior, but his or her present state of mind, which, as the unappetizing phrase goes, is quite as much a "fact" as the state of one's digestion.[60] Accordingly, if researchers' assurances can be taken as statements that they do not *intend* to disclose information, whatever the circumstances, and their intentions were in fact different from that which they asserted to exist, a misrepresentation of fact occurred.

There is, in this preceding situation, both a misrepresentation of a fact and a culpable state of mind—the researchers *knew* their intentions were not what they said they were. It is doubtless also the case that the

[59] W. Prosser, Torts 715–718.
[60] Restatement, Torts § 530, Comment a.

subject relied in fact on that misrepresentation; it is hard otherwise to imagine why the subject would have revealed guilt. However, that reliance must also be "justifiable," in the sense that a reasonable person would have relied under the circumstances. Plainly, this is a matter upon which courts may differ. On the one hand, "unreasonableness" can be a narrow category. One treatise writer asserts that this quality requires the placement of faith, by a person of normal intelligence and experience, in a statement that "any such normal person would recognize at once as preposterous,"[61] and an English judge likened it to the judgment "of a moron in a hurry [Levine, 1978:14]." Perhaps, on the other hand, courts or juries *would* find preposterous researchers' assurances that they intend to flout the law and face imprisonment to protect their sources. Ironically, however, the latter conclusion is seriously undermined by formal declarations of various bodies, including the American Political Science Association, to the effect that it is not only reasonable but also ethically necessary for social science researchers to engage in just such conduct.[62] Reliance on an expressed intention to engage in contumacious behavior may well seem, therefore, "justifiable."

But what of the policy concerns, referred to earlier, that largely insulated researchers from liability for invasion of privacy and breach of contract? Some courts do indeed bar an action for misrepresentation when the underlying intention is one that should not be enforced or recognized in any way.[63] This position is obviously related to the policy forbidding enforcement of promises that are illegal or violate public policy. And, in these jurisdictions, liability under this set of facts is a spurious problem.

However, most courts distinguish actions founded on breach of a promise from those relying on misrepresentation of an existing fact, extending liability in the latter case.[64] This distinction, perhaps on its face jesuitical, is a defensible one. There is no policy against failing to perform an illegal promise; indeed, its breach is in a real sense desirable. There is, however, good reason to discourage intentional or reckless misrepresentations, which induce the deceived to suffer an other-

---

[61]W. Prosser, Torts 716 (4th ed. 1971).

[62]The American Political Science Association's Committee on Professional Ethics and Academic Freedom (1973a) states that the scholar "has a professional duty not to divulge the identity of confidential sources of information . . . whether to governmental or non-governmental officials or bodies, even though . . . he or she runs the risk of suffering some sort of penalty."

[63]W. Prosser, Torts 729–730 (4th ed. 1971).

[64]*Id.* at 730.

wise avoidable harm. Thus, imposition of liability in this circumstance serves a valid purpose, independent of the nature of the misrepresentation.

It may be, therefore, that the research subject could prove a culpable misrepresentation of fact, reasonably relied upon and, in some jurisdictions, not protected by policy. There remain only the issues of damage and causation. Formally, at least, damage could be stated: Subjects who are prosecuted and imprisoned lose at least the wages they would earn absent conviction, costs incident to the trial, and the like. If, moreover, the deception was deliberate or wanton—as may be the case here—the prospect of punitive damages must be considered. At this point we venture into the unknown. No case awarding damages on such facts readily comes to hand, and there is reason to doubt that courts will find the incidents of lawful imprisonment compensable. In a sense, the subjects have not lost anything to which they were entitled. However, noncompensability cannot be declared with conviction; thus, liability may or may not be a spurious issue.

It appears, therefore, that in some jurisdictions there will be no liability for misrepresentation but that in others a genuine legal problem exists for researchers who foresee and intend to comply with subpoenas but lead their subjects to believe the contrary. The question of the tractability of this problem in those jurisdictions leads to another formulation of the researcher's declaration.

In our second example, the farsighted researcher decides to utter the literal truth and places the following at the top of the questionnaire:

> This information will be published only in statistical form and you will not be identified in any report. You should know, however, that although every effort will be made to keep this information completely confidential, there is some risk of compelled disclosure pursuant to lawful order of a court or other agency.

This advice, one would think, surely removes any legal liability and equally surely removes the availability of data at least concerning serious criminality (Wolfgang, 1976:25, 28–29). It cannot, therefore, render the legal problem tractable as a practical matter.

In our third example, a somewhat less explicit recital, such as that employed by the Harvard Law School Center for Criminal Justice in connection with a methadone evaluation project, might be considered: "The information will only be used in statistical reports where you [will not] be identified. Every effort will be made to keep this material completely confidential [quoted in Nejelski and Lerman, 1971:1098, n. 39]." A number of interesting questions arise. The first is whether subjects would understand the risk of compelled disclosure to the courts or would simply view this as a promise of care in data protection. The second is whether if they understood the risk, they would cooperate, and, conversely, whether it is fair to assume that all respondents who answered the questionnaire did in fact appreciate the risk of subpoena. This is not necessarily to say that the advice given will not satisfy the requirements of accurate representation. It may well do so. However, it could also be claimed that the statement is misleading because in inviting attention to one relatively slight risk (data security), it distracts attention from the far more critical risk of subpoena. If this was the designed effect, or an effect that should have been foreseen, then there may be a misrepresentation of fact, leading us back to the previous discussion to determine the risk of liability.

The most practical avenue for making this class of problems tractable is to design the study in such a way as to minimize the value of the information to investigative agencies. The Harvard methadone project, for example, added to the advice quoted earlier the following instruction: "To further protect you, we ask that you do not give us any specific information about any crime you may have participated in for which you have not as yet been arrested. Just answer the questions generally, but as honestly as possible [quoted in Nejelski and Lerman, 1971:1098, n. 39]." Absent specific information, the usefulness of an admission to a court or prosecuting attorney is considerably reduced. And, if disclosure of other identifying information can be avoided—by not asking for names, destroying identifications before demand, or using an effective link-file system—the practical risk to respondents is virtually nonexistent. Consequently, misrepresentation is rendered unnecessary by the design of the research itself.

Problems in Selection of Research Projects

The areas of law discussed in the preceding sections—largely contracts and torts—are essentially local in the sense that they are created, interpreted, and revised at the state level. It may seem that the particularistic inquiry we have pursued is more appropriate there than in areas where uniformity of application is compelled by the national character of the laws. This may appear especially true with respect to constitutional doctrine, which cannot be "jurisdiction-specific" and which may apply to any area of activity.

However, even federal legislation and constitutional doctrine ultimately come into play in the context of particular fact situations.

Whether any particular activity is authorized by statute or protected by the Constitution will depend upon what is undertaken, by whom, in what way, and with what effect. We are concerned, therefore, with the same kind of enterprise discussed in the previous sections of this chapter: a prediction of how courts will act in response to some particular act or omission on the part of the researcher. The following discussion will consider briefly the positivist approach in the setting of constitutional doctrine.

Constitutional issues commonly arise in connection with the choice or design of the research project itself. True, neither the Constitution nor other bodies of law ordinarily direct that certain areas remain unstudied. They may, however, say that certain things cannot be done at all or cannot be done in ways that, from a research perspective, are desirable in terms of validity. In particular, the due process clause of the Fourteenth Amendment requires that "rights" once established— whether by common law, statute, or the Constitution itself—may not be denied except through lawful process. Moreover, this clause has been interpreted to protect certain kinds of rights against restriction even by lawful procedures without some adequate justification for their denial.[65] There must, therefore, exist some substantive rationality to governmental interference with private behavior or existing entitlements. The equal protection clause adds to this a further but related requirement: that even if a law imposes burdens or confers benefits that may properly be employed, those burdens or benefits must be allocated in such a way that persons who are similarly situated for purposes of the law are treated equally. This clause is also designed to ensure rationality in governmental activity. By way of illustration, a claimant denied benefits under a welfare program may raise two separate contentions against the department charged with administering the program. The first is that one is entitled by the welfare law to the benefits in question, denial of which therefore violates due process. The second is that if the law does not create a right to those benefits for the claimant, he or she is in the same position (e.g., needy) as others who are entitled to them under the statute; therefore the law offends the equal protection clause.

Whether a particular research activity runs afoul of these doctrines will depend on what the research plan seeks to do for or to its subjects

---

[65]This line of authority is usually called "substantive due process." Although its importance has formally been diminished since the 1930s, there is no doubt that substantive due process claims are currently presented under such labels as rights to privacy or autonomy and are frequently upheld. See, for example, Roe v. Wade, 410 U.S. 113 (1973).

and the manner in which it is carried out. The most frequent questions involving constitutional limitations on research arise when an experimental design involves administration of a treatment to some but not all persons, and this kind of research will prove the focus for examining the scope of these limitations. Such an experiment will present genuine legal issues if some constitutional doctrine says either that no person may be treated in one of the proposed modes (that is, the treatment contemplated for the experimental or control group improperly denies the subject some right) or that differential treatment of persons similarly situated (which will designedly be true for experiment and control groups) is impermissible. In considering the application of due process and equal protection notions to this kind of research, it is useful to distinguish between projects that seek to confer benefits on subjects and those that impose burdens, and between those that are privately conducted and those in which the state participates in some way.

PRIVATELY CONDUCTED RESEARCH CONFERRING BENEFITS

It should initially be observed that there is no obligation on private persons or agencies to help everyone in need. If I individually, or the Elks Club collectively, decide to confer some benefit on others, we may choose our recipients on any basis, however selective or even idiosyncratic. By the same token, if private researchers are adequately funded to provide legal aid or income subsidies,[66] that they act selectively or that they knowingly withhold services or funds from persons as needy as those they help present no legal issue. Constitutional guarantees of due process and equal protection are addressed only to governmental agencies[67] and, absent sufficient official participation to justify a conclusion that the government really is involved,[68] no constitutional rule prohibits differential treatment. This is not to say, of course, that nonlegal constraints may not operate. Researchers may be deeply troubled by the requirement that in order to keep control and experimental groups constant, they must deny food to the hungry or lawyers to those whose

[66]This assumes, contrary to present reality, that the funding is entirely from private sources. Federal agency funding creates issues of state involvement, which will be discussed later in the chapter.

[67]The equal protection clause of the Fourteenth Amendment is addressed only to states, and the Fifth Amendment due process clause, which has been interpreted to contain an equal treatment element, binds only congressional action.

[68]What constitutes such involvement is, to put it euphemistically, a developing area of the law. See, generally, Glennon and Nowak (1976).

liberty is at risk. These considerations of decency and fairness must, however, be evaluated according to some framework other than law, which is silent in this regard.

PRACTICAL LIMITATIONS ON THE PRIVATE MODE OF OPERATION

For private researchers, therefore, constitutional considerations present a spurious legal problem. This private (and constitutionally unregulated) mode of research is available, however, only under limited circumstances. The status of "private researcher" itself may only obtain for investigators who are in no way dependent upon the government. If they are housed at a state university or dependent upon public grants, that status may be compromised, although categorical statements in this regard are unsafe.

Moreover, private research is ordinarily feasible only where researchers are in positions of conferring benefits. This is so for the obvious practical reason that private actors must rely upon the cooperation of their subjects, which is unlikely to eventuate when participation is perceived to involve a net detriment.[69] In turn, the investigator will be in a position to offer benefits only when the law has not already created an entitlement to the matter in question. Suppose that social scientists, wishing to study the impact of counsel on juvenile court clients, find that representation is now available by statutory and constitutional command to all children charged with delinquency. Or suppose that, seeking to ascertain the impact of copayment plans on consumption of Medicaid services, they learn that current plans make benefits available without any copayment requirement. Under these circumstances, research that seeks to divide juvenile court clients or welfare recipients into experimental and control groups with respect to these "benefits" requires imposition of a burden—deprivation of legal assistance or denial of medical services without copayment—which the subjects would not suffer without the experiment. Plainly, such a program cannot be conducted privately. It does not matter that 15 years ago lawyers were not available to children or that Medicaid legislation could have been written to require copayment. Once a good or service is provided by law, it can be denied only by law, and governmentally

---

[69]Of course, a small research-imposed detriment (lack of sleep) might be overbalanced by financial compensation or even the honor of participation, creating a net benefit in the eyes of the participant. This is unlikely, however, to be true as one moves into more serious areas of social activity.

sanctioned deprivation squarely implicates the due process and equal protection clauses of the federal Constitution.[70]

Where benefits are offered, it is often also necessary that the benefit be available only from the investigator and not from any source. Should researchers wish to investigate, for example, the effects of providing counsel to juvenile court clients, assignment of the latter to experimental (represented) and control (unrepresented) groups may provide the best design for the study. However, if lawyers are readily available from the public defender's office, the risk of attrition in the control group could be unacceptably high.[71] Nor can the researcher, acting privately, deny the control group members access to that or any other alternative source of legal assistance.

Finally, governmental participation may be a practical requirement of research conferring benefits as well as that involving burdens. If the benefits can be provided only by the state because the expense is great or the distribution mechanism is within governmental control, the enterprise involves official action and is subject to constitutional requirements. Although conferral of benefits would not ordinarily create a due process problem, it might well raise issues of equal protection at the instance of those who are similarly situated with regard to the benefit but are denied access to it.

GOVERNMENTALLY SUPPORTED OR SANCTIONED RESEARCH

Where governmental support or sanction is required, researchers may face a genuine legal problem. The applicability of constitutional provisions does not, however, necessarily imply prohibition of activity. The due process clause, for example, requires that claims recognized by

---

[70]The Supreme Court has repeatedly made it clear that an entitlement created by law must be accorded constitutional protection as an aspect of liberty or property, even if there was no independent constitutional duty to create that entitlement. States are not, for example, required by federal constitutional command to provide public schooling or welfare benefits, but if they do, neither may be denied without some constitutionally adequate form of procedure, nor may they be given to some but not all of the population similarly situated with respect to the purposes of the law establishing the benefits. See Goss v. Lopez, 419 U.S. 565 (1975) (requiring hearings prior to expulsion from public school); Goldberg v. Kelly, 397 U.S. 254 (1970) (welfare hearings); United States Department of Agriculture v. Moreno, 413 U.S. 528 (1973) (equal protection in eligibility for food stamps).

[71]For an instance of the problems created by attrition and its methodological treatment, see Stapleton and Teitelbaum (1972).

law be limited only as that law allows; it does not forbid all restrictions on liberty or entitlements. By the same token, equal protection doctrine prohibits irrational classification among persons but does not require that all persons—or even all persons similarly situated—be treated alike or not at all. Rather, it demands that differentiation among persons be sufficiently justified by some legitimate purpose reflected in the law imposing differential treatment. It will ordinarily suffice that the classification used bear some rational relationship to (that it rationally tend to advance) a legitimate state purpose.[72] Higher degrees of justification are sometimes demanded, but only where the state action either burdens a "fundamental liberty"[73] or depends upon a "suspect classification."[74]

The most severe due process problems arise when research seeks to evaluate the effect of a program already in existence. Suppose, for example, one wished to study whether provision of certain welfare benefits would produce certain consequences for the target population. If those benefits have not yet been made available, due process would not hinder the research; no legal entitlement to the benefits exists on any person's behalf, and none is therefore denied. Even if the program is administered with governmental support to some but not all potential recipients, no due process issue should arise.

Once the benefits have already been provided, however, there is an entitlement, which can be denied only as the law permits. Ordinarily, statutes creating rights—as well as constitutionally based claims—contain only limited conditions under which those rights may be denied, and frequently this can be done only when the claimant is ineligible for the right itself. Welfare recipients ordinarily can be deprived of benefits only if they do not meet statutory or departmental criteria for receipt of

[72]See, for example, City of New Orleans v. Dukes, 427 U.S. 297 (1976); Rinaldi v. Yeager, 384 U.S. 305 (1966).

[73]A state seeking to limit exercise of a fundamental liberty (a class determined by Supreme Court decision and including such interests as privacy in respect of one's body, the right to travel interstate, and the franchise) must demonstrate a "compelling" and not merely a legitimate interest in the regulation. If the limitation operates only as to a group of persons, the differential treatment must also be necessary (or nearly so) to the accomplishment of that interest. See, for example, Planned Parenthood of Central Missouri v. Danforth, 428 U.S. 52 (1976).

[74]A suspect classification is one that ought not ordinarily be used. Like "fundamental liberty," it is a Court-created category and includes race and national origin. Sex, although not a suspect classification, can be used as a basis for differentiation only upon a showing of significant justification and therefore occupies a middle ground. See Craig v. Boren, 429 U.S. 190 (1976).

benefits. Where this is true, the due process clause presents an intractable legal problem for any research that seeks to use control and experimental groups regarding the benefits in question. Applicable law provides no basis for denying eligible persons access to those benefits, and those who are ineligible for them are by definition in a different position from recipients.

Occasionally, however, legislation creating benefits incorporates some basis for excluding otherwise eligible persons from those benefits, thus creating the possibility of experimentation within an existing program. The most visible instance of this strategy is found in the "demonstration project" provision of the Social Security Act, which gives broad power to the secretary of the Department of Health and Human Services to authorize state agencies to carry out projects at variance with ordinary requirements.[75] The only applicable statutory standard is a requirement that any experimental, pilot, or demonstration project be "likely to assist in promoting the objectives [of the Social Security Act plan, which is the subject of the experiment]."[76] Pursuant to this provision, experiments requiring copayment by groups of Medicaid recipients[77] and registration for training and employment by certain families receiving Aid for Families with Dependent Children (AFDC)[78] have been undertaken and upheld against legal attack by lower federal courts.

Plainly, the demonstration project provision makes possible research involving diminution of its subjects' entitlements, which could not be undertaken without such legal authority. The limits of that authority, correlatively, constitute the conditions of tractability for problems of research involving the imposition of burdens. Ascertainment of these limits, both as a statutory and as a constitutional matter, requires careful analysis of the precise nature of the imposition proposed, its relationship to the purpose of the Social Security Act program in question, the extent to which the research is likely to produce reliable and valid information about the functioning of the Social Security Act program,[79] and the various effects that the research might have on partici-

[75]The relevant provision is Section 1115 of the Social Security Act, 42 U.S.C. § 1315 (1976).

[76]Id.

[77]California Welfare Rights Organization v. Richardson, 348 F. Supp. 491 (N.D. Cal. 1972).

[78]Aguayo v. Richardson, 352 F. Supp. 462 (S.D.N.Y. 1972), aff'd, 473 F.2d 1090 (2d Cir. 1973).

[79]See Aguayo v. Richardson, 352 F. Supp. 46 (S.D.N.Y. 1972) (discussing the adequacy of research design in response to claim of arbitrariness).

pants.[80] Moreover, there must be full compliance with statutory requirements connected with the demonstration project provision (or any other enabling legislation).[81] This is not the place to examine all of these conditions of tractability in detail,[82] but simply to observe that they are considerable and demand careful planning by each project that seeks to act under such authority.

But what, it may be asked, about the equal protection clause? Even if the law does not yet provide the benefits in question or if the statute conferring benefits allows experimentation, the government is nevertheless treating similarly situated persons unequally by, for example, excusing copayment by some but not by others equally in need of services. This objection would be well taken if the purpose of the law were to provide benefits to needy persons; a scheme that treated similarly needy persons in different ways would offend the equal protection clause. If the aim of the program is not, however, to provide goods or services already determined to be appropriate, but rather to determine the appropriateness of their provision, the result may well be different. The essential inquiry, as we have seen, is whether a classification of persons rationally advances the underlying purpose of the law. Where the purpose is to learn how a given event or condition will, on the whole, affect the population exposed to it, experimentation may be permitted under circumstances that would be prohibited once the event or condition had been implemented. Tussman and tenBroek (1949) recognized some 30 years ago that:

> The "piecemeal" approach to a general problem, permitted by under-inclusive classifications, appears justified when it is considered that legislative dealing with such problems is usually an experimental matter. It is impossi-

[80]See Bay Bridge Diagnostic Laboratory, Inc. v. Dumpson, 400 F. Supp. 1104 (E.D.N.Y. 1975), enjoining experiments throughout New York City concerning Medicaid services, partially on the basis that "the City's plan might restrict a Medicaid patient's freedom of choice of medical services, result in possible inadequate laboratory evaluations to the detriment of patients, cause doctors serving Medicaid patients to compromise their medical ethics, and force a large number of laboratories out of business." Id. at 1110. However, the experiment was allowed to go forward in one borough of the city.

[81]It may not be enough, for example, to solicit the agreement of the secretary, unless other requirements have been met. See, for example, Crane v. Mathews, 417 F. Supp. 532 (N.D. Ga. 1976), enjoining a copayment plan on the basis that the project applicants failed to obtain a certification by the HEW Institutional Review Board that it had reviewed the project, determined whether human subjects were placed at risk, and approved the project.

[82]For a more extensive discussion of experiments under the Social Security Act, see Capron (1975) and Breger (1978).

ble to tell how successful a particular approach may be, what dislocations
might occur, what evasions might develop, what new evils might be generated. . . . Administrative expedience must be forged and tested. Legislators,
recognizing these factors, may wish to proceed cautiously, and courts must
allow them to do so [pp. 341, 349].

The governmental purpose here—acquisition of knowledge concerning
proposed legislation or activity—may rationally be advanced by
providing the goods or services in question to some but not all of the
potential recipients and comparing the conditions or behavior of group
members. Indeed, failure to create control and experimental groups of
similarly situated persons might significantly detract from accuracy of
knowledge and hence from the general purpose of the inquiry.

It is, of course, still true that individuals similarly situated are
treated unequally under the law calling for experimentation. However,
disparate treatment is not only rationally related but also perhaps essential to accomplishment of that program. An equal protection challenge must now be based on the proposition that governments may not
discriminate, even for the sole purpose of experimentation, among persons who are for every other purpose similarly situated. Although the
answer to this argument has not been clearly provided, certainly a case
can be made—as Tussman and tenBroek indicate—for recognizing the
importance of official action that is directed entirely or primarily to
acquisition of knowledge and for the legitimacy of strategies rationally
related to that end.[83]

The foregoing discussion may also help in considering the occasional suggestion that experimentation through random selection of
control and experimental groups cannot satisfy the requirement of a
rational relationship between classification and governmental purpose
because random choice is by its nature a nonrational and arbitrary
method of selection. It is indeed true that random choice does not
provide a rational basis for choosing one person over another; indeed, it
supposes that any member of one group could equally well fall into the
other. Where the legislative or governmental purpose requires selection
of persons for treatment or nontreatment on an individual basis, it
would follow that use of a procedure that eliminates individual characteristics as determinants for treatment is irrational. This would be the

---

[83]It may, however, be required that all persons similarly situated with respect to the
experimental issue be treated equally in terms of access to the experimental program,
unless some adequate reason—such as administrative convenience—exists for excluding
them. For example, a study concerning welfare benefits might have to include all equally
needy persons in the population from which experimental recipients will be selected.

case where a welfare law provides benefits for persons determined to be "needy" in a certain way; that law presupposes that each applicant's needs be determined and measured against the statute creating the entitlement. It might also be the case where sentencing of offenders is involved if, statutorily or by constitutional requirement, the law requires that sentences be given according to the "needs" or "deserts" of each convicted person.[84] A program that selected prisoners for incarceration or release by lot rather than individual behavior or circumstances would surely be an irrational device in light of that purpose.

On the other hand, random selection for treatment is an entirely rational and indeed peculiarly desirable method of choosing groups that are comparable to one another. If the controlling purpose of the legislation is to find out the effects of some proposed program, creation of comparable control and experimental groups may well be an appropriate and indeed the preferred approach from a methodological perspective. To the extent that randomized choice ensures comparability of these groups, it too would be a rational strategy to employ. Assuming, therefore, that the goal of a governmental program is to evaluate proposed welfare benefits rather than to administer benefits already determined to be desirable, random choice of control and experimental groups would seem an appropriate way to accomplish the goal. And, if sentencing for a particular crime or to a particular degree need not be individualized as either a statutory or a constitutional matter, random choice of convicted persons for incarceration or community treatment to ascertain the relative effectiveness of those sanctions might likewise be legally defensible.[85]

[84]In Lockett v. Ohio, 438 U.S. 586 (1978), the Supreme Court held that "individualized decision is essential in capital cases." *Id.* at 605. In doing so, however, the Court emphasized that capital punishment is "profoundly different from all other penalties" and expressly noted that in noncapital cases "the established practice of individualized sentences rests not on constitutional commands but public policy enacted into statutes." *Id.* at 604–605.

[85]As note 84, *supra*, indicates, the Supreme Court has apparently indicated that individualization of sentences is required by the Eighth Amendment only in connection with the death penalty. The level of justification for investigation of relative sentencing efficacy may, however, be great if not insuperable where the penalty is very grave, although not capital. There may also be constitutional limitations under the Eighth Amendment (prohibiting cruel and unusual punishment) or the due process clause where the penalty to be imposed is disproportionate to the offense proved. See Gregg v. Georgia, 428 U.S. 153, 173 (1976) (plurality opinion) (Eighth Amendment requires that "punishment . . . not be grossly out of proportion to the severity of the crime"); Weems v. United States, 217 U.S. 349 (1910).

Conclusion

The intent of this discussion has been a modest one. The idea was not to address jurisprudential questions such as the place of social science research in society, but to show that, as things now stand, the field social scientist is like anyone else in society: restricted by rules of law in certain areas of activity but free in others. And, like every other social actor, the rules with which the scientific investigator must conjure are specific to the kind of activity and often to the location in which it is carried out. Persons seeking to sell fireworks only need a license if the laws of *their states* so require; investigators need be concerned only with a duty to disclose information on their own initiatives if the laws of *their states* impose such an obligation through crimes like misprision of felony. If no such laws exist, neither fireworks vendors nor field researchers need fear judicial intervention in their careers. And, even if laws do address some activity, there may be available, within that law, steps that mitigate the bars or impositions it presents. These, too, are identifiable only upon specific consideration of what the law (speaking through courts) requires under particular factual circumstances.

Not only jurisprudence but also "ethics" has fallen outside the scope of this discussion. The reasons for this exclusion may now be clearer than they were at the outset. Initially, it was suggested that ethics draws upon a different body of authority than law, at least in its positivist sense, and this is surely true. Many activities allowed by legal rule may be distasteful by reference to other bodies of rules. This is true equally for social scientists who do not think it right to withhold benefits from needy persons for experimental purposes when they could serve the entire population and for the landlord who chooses not to evict a starving tenant for nonpayment of rent. These are instances of disparity between law and ethics, which may arise in any occupation or activity. To these should be added the observation that there may be not only disparity but conflict between law and ethics. Whereas the former ordinarily obliges researchers to disclose confidential information received from their subjects, ethics—at least those of the American Political Science Association—obliges them not to do so. The civil disobedience urged by this organization doubtless can find philosophical justification, but it cannot be called *lawful* in the sense that we have used that term. Accordingly, separation of law and other sources of judgments concerning the correctness of behavior is, for present purposes, essential to clarity and accuracy.

It should not require mention that nothing said in this chapter is intended to suggest that jurisprudence and ethics generally are "irrelevant." Rather, they are relevant to a different level of inquiry than has been essayed here. And, perhaps, the positivist approach is ultimately useful even for this further level of concern by making clear the nature of the problems presented by social science research under existing law.

Acknowledgments

The author wishes to express deep appreciation to his colleagues Frederick Hart and Joseph Goldberg for their helpful comments on portions of this chapter, and to Kathleen Ayres-Hurley and Francesca MacDowell for their assistance at all stages of its preparation.

References

American Political Science Association, Committee on Professional Ethics and Academic Freedom
    1973a "Advisory Opinion No. 13." August 16, 1973. *Political Science Quarterly* 6:451.
    1973b "Report." *Political Science Quarterly* 6:340–342.
Astin, A. W., and R. F. Boruch
    1970 "A link file system for assuring confidentiality in longitudinal studies." *American Educational Research Journal* 1:615–624.
Breger, M.
    1978 "Legal issues raised by randomized social experiments." Paper presented at Conference on Solutions to Ethical and Legal Problems in Applied Social Research, February.
Capron, A.
    1975 "Social experimentation and the law." Pp. 127–163 in A. Rivlin and P. Timpane (eds.), *Ethical and Legal Issues of Social Experimentation*. Washington, D.C.: Brookings Institution.
Carroll, J.
    1973 "Confidentiality of social science research sources and data: The Popkin case." *Political Science Quarterly* 6:268–280.
Carroll, J., and C. Knerr
    1975 "A report of the APSA Confidentiality in Social Science Research Data Project." *Political Science Quarterly* 8:258–261.
Glennon, R., and J. Nowak
    1976 "A functional analysis of the Fourteenth Amendment 'state action' requirement." *Supreme Court Review 1976:* 221–261.
Holmes, O. W.
    1897 "The path of the law." *Harvard Law Review* 10:457–478.
Kershaw, D., and J. Small
    1972 "Data confidentiality and privacy: Lessons from the New Jersey negative income tax experiment." *Public Policy* 20:257–280.

Levine, B.
  1978   "The man who missed the Clapham omnibus." *The Times* (London), October
         31, p. 14.
Nejelski, P.
  1976   "Conference summary." Pp. 1–23 in P. Nejelski (ed.), *Social Research in Con-
         flict with Law and Ethics.* Cambridge, Mass.: Ballinger Publishing Co.
Nejelski, P., and P. Lerman
  1971   "A researcher–subject testimonial privilege: What to do before the subpoena
         arrives." *Wisconsin Law Review:* 1971:1085–1148.
Nejelski, P., and H. Peyser
  1976   "A proposed researcher's shield statute: Text and summary of commentary."
         Pp. 163–171 in P. Nejelski (ed.), *Social Research in Conflict with Law and
         Ethics.* Cambridge, Mass.: Ballinger Publishing Co.
Prosser, W.
  1960   "Privacy." *California Law Review* 48:383–423.
Riecken, H. W., and R. F. Boruch (eds.)
  1974   *Social Experimentation: A Method for Planning and Evaluating Social Inter-
         vention.* New York: Academic Press.
Stapleton, W., and L. Teitelbaum
  1972   *In Defense of Youth: A Study of the Role of Counsel in American Juvenile
         Courts.* New York: Russell Sage.
Tussman, J., and J. tenBroek
  1949   "The equal protection of the laws." *California Law Review* 37:341–381.
Wolfgang, M.
  1976   "Ethical issues of research in criminology." Pp. 25–34 in P. Nejelski (ed.),
         Social Research in Conflict with Law and Ethics. Cambridge, Mass.: Ballinger
         Publishing Co.

3

Reducing the Hazards of Human Experiments through Modifications in Research Design[1]

HANS ZEISEL

The controlled experiment is an indispensable instrument in our search for knowledge. Yet experimentation with human beings will forever be a precarious enterprise. First, controlled experiments are by definition discriminatory—some people receive the experimental treatment while others are excluded from it, and either the treatment or its withholding may involve the risk of harm; second, legal rules and binding social norms set limits on such experimentation; last, there are limits to the cooperation from those who are expected to participate.

These difficulties become apparent when some supervisory body is asked to pass on the propriety of an experiment, or when the consent is sought of those who are to be experimented with.

Provided no law is violated, our mores sanction almost any experiment if participation is voluntary, after full disclosure of all its implications. But this principle is announced more easily than it is implemented. There are questions as to what full disclosure is, first as to what must be disclosed, and, more importantly, as to what must be understood by the participating subject; and there are questions as to what voluntary cooperation is.[2]

[1]This chapter is reproduced with permission from *Annals of the New York Academy of Sciences, 169* (1970): 475–486.

[2]See, generally, the papers by Edsall (1969), Freund (1969), Jaffee (1969), and Jonas (1969) in *Daedalus* 98.

SOLUTIONS TO ETHICAL
AND LEGAL PROBLEMS
IN SOCIAL RESEARCH

ISBN 0-12-118680-6

In any event, if consent is required, the participants to the experiment cease, as a rule, to be a cross section of the population and become, instead, a self-selected group. For many types of experiments, especially medical ones, this will be a minor disadvantage. But for some experiments, this self-selection may become a serious limitation and require remedial attention.

From the experimenter's point of view, consent, however essential, is likely to interfere with the best research design. In the first place, it may create self-consciousness and expectations that could bias the experiment. To counteract these effects, consent is preferably sought for a blind experiment, where the subjects know they are part of the experiment but do not know whether they are receiving the experimental treatment or the placebo that looks like it.[3] For good measure, then, the experimenter also is blindfolded, so that neither the subject nor the scientist knows before the end of the experiment which subjects have received the experimental treatment.

Many experiments (for instance, all those designed to test the effectiveness of communications, the retention of information, and change in attitudes) would become impossible if consent were required. In such situations, bypassing of disclosure and consent is often justified by the harmlessness of this type of experiment, as in Hovland, Lumsdaine, and Sheffield (1949) research, for example.[4] Partial disclosure may be an acceptable compromise (Simon, 1969): One discloses, for instance, the experimental procedure, without disclosing its ultimate purpose.[5] Special problems are created by experiments (Festinger and Carlsmith, 1959; Kelman, 1968) where a purposefully incomplete or outright misleading disclosure is part of the design.[6]

In general, then, consent will pose a problem if the experiment poses

[3]Not only nonactive pills that look and taste like the real drug but also food baskets that differ only in their content of cholesterol are being used.

[4]See, for example, the early experiments in Hovland et al. (1949). To be sure, judgments as to what is harmless may differ, as the scars of the University of Chicago Jury Project prove. Back in the 1950s, upon invitation by a trial judge in Wichita, Kansas, and with the consent of counsel, the project had placed a tape recorder in the jury room without the jury's knowledge. Although no law was violated, and although identity of the trial had been carefully masked and the effort was clearly limited to a few trials, public opinion disapproved almost unanimously (see Kalven and Zeisel, 1966).

[5]See, for instance, Simon (1967), where real jurors were asked to deliberate on tape-recorded trials that contained a number of experimental variations. The jorors learned only of their general task, but nothing of the experimental variations on the various tapes.

[6]The small-group experiments in Festinger and Carlsmith (1959) involve a progression of nondisclosure and active deceptions. Concerning the problem itself, see the comments of a thoughtful psychologist in Kelman (1968).

one (Zeisel, Kalven, and Bucholz, 1957). Whether these problems are always as grave as they seem is questionable.[7] In any event, this is not the question I shall pursue here. Rather, this chapter will review the methods by which these problems can be alleviated through technical changes in the experimental design: by reducing the expected discrimination and the risk of harm, by avoiding legal or contractual barriers, and by reducing the nature of the required cooperation.

The essence of all controlled experimentation is the random division between those who are to receive the treatment and those who are to be excluded from it. Random division—that is, selection by chance—has several precious advantages. It permits development of an appropriate measure of error, an essential gauge for appraising the value of the experiment. It is also the best device for making the experimental group and the control group as much alike as possible, prior to the treatment.[8]

When the treatment resources are scarce, so that not everybody in need can be treated, random division, because of its impartiality, will be also the morally tolerable mode of allocation. It will not always be tolerable, however, because this very impartiality may fail to single out the people who need the experimental curative drug, for instance, more urgently than others. The problem arises in this fashion: If a new drug is to be tested, one could restrict application to those who have the ailment in its most acute and dangerous form. But one might also want to include marginal forms of the ailment in order to study the drug's effectiveness over a broader spectrum. One of the early studies of the effectiveness of the drug streptomycin in the treatment of tuberculosis involved some of these problems. When the tests were designed, the drug was still in short supply; during the time they were carried out, the drug became more widely available. Nevertheless, the supply was still not sufficient to treat all tuberculosis patients in the Veterans Administration, where the study was carried out. Thus, a selection had to be made, and in some cases the selection was made by lot and not limited to the most severe cases. As a result, much more was learned about the effectiveness of the drug in some situations, but also about its failure in others.

Random selection should not raise any problems if the experimenter

---

[7]For the field of law, this point was argued in Zeisel et al. (1957).

[8]This attempt at equalization can be improved, of course, by stratification; that is, by ensuring that certain proportions (e.g., men and women, old and young) are equal in both groups. In the end, however, random selection within each subgroup is essential to taking care of all the unknown and uncontrolled proportions in the population that is to be sampled.

has no indication of whether the treatment will prove effective and when the risk involved in either direction is relatively small.

But where neither the scarcity of resources nor the small size of the risk mitigates the discriminatory aspects of experimentation, random selection will raise difficulties. I shall discuss now some of the devices by which, through redesign of the experiment, some of these difficulties can be reduced, if not removed. Most of these devices exact their price by reducing the power of the experiment. At times this reduction will be minimal; at times it may be so serious that it will offset whatever is gained in feasibility. The problem is to find the proper balance.

The first, because most obvious, among these devices is simply to keep the number of people who are exposed to the risky treatment at a minimum. The most important step here is always to have competent statistical counsel as to the minimal number of subjects necessary for the experiment to reveal an effect if one in fact exists. The other commonsense consideration in this context is to look at the probable universe of all experiments aiming at the same purpose, and to coordinate them both nationally and internationally. Drug tests are too often repeated, when proper coordination could keep repetition at a desirable minimum.[9] The task, however, is more difficult than it appears; it is not always easy to obtain consensus on design and interpretation, even within the more homogeneous confines of one country.

The second and very much a commonsense device is to make the experimental treatment the one that is expected to have favorable effects, even if the basic question goes to the effects of the unfavorable treatment. To find out whether smoking causes cancer, it will not do to suggest starting or increasing smoking. The experiment must be reversed, to test the effect of a reduction in smoking. The situation will be rare in which this change in the *direction* of the change will affect the significance of the experiment.

If it is not known at the outset which of the alternative treatments is superior, and if there is no need to curtail the experimental time period, a so-called sequential design may help keep the necessary number of unfavorable treatments at a minimum. One of these procedures is nicknamed "play-the-winner," after the often observed practice of gamblers who put their money on numbers or constellations that had won on the

---

[9]"A well-designed international collaborative and cooperative study in which the new drug could be tested on specified but much smaller number of human subjects could suffice for all." Citing the example of the United States and United Kingdom Cooperative Rheumatic Fever Study, D. D. Rutstein urges that "an international agency . . . explore the possibility of rapid, efficient international drug testing [1969:536]."

previous throw (Zelen, 1969; Cornfield, Halperin, and Greenhouse, 1969).[10]

Perhaps one should mention here one other variant of sequential design—not a very sophisticated one, but one that might greatly reduce the experimental risk: It involves simply experimentation in sequence with exponentially expanding samples, beginning with a small-scale experiment. If the results seem satisfactory, one would move on to an experiment on an intermediate scale and allow mass experiments only in the third stage (Meier, 1957).

The fifth device—now a standard safety valve in all medical double-blind tests—allows, in a way, tampering with the original design in situations where the effects of the experiment become visibly dangerous or harmful. If an experimentee shows symptoms of dangerous effects, the experimenter is allowed to open the envelope for this particular person in order to find out which treatment he or she had received and so be able to counteract the negative effects of the experiment. The price in knowledge that must be paid for this gain in human well-being is clear: Cutting off the development of symptoms at an earlier point could be misleading if the effects oscillate and the ultimate good effect is hidden behind a temporary negative one.

If, on the other hand, there is a strong advance intimation that the experimental treatment is likely to be superior, the temptation will be great to dispense with a simultaneously established control group and rely instead either on a baseline derived from groups that are assumed to be equivalent to control groups, or on computed baselines.

To begin with, one might compare the effect of the innovation simply against the traditionally established level. This type of evaluation was implied in the acceptance of Pasteur's classic rabies vaccination experiment. When a peasant boy who had been bitten by a rabid dog was vaccinated by Pasteur and survived, this was sufficiently dramatic proof of the cure's effectiveness. And in due course, it was indeed established that Pasteur's vaccine reduced the fatality rate of rabies bites from 9% to .5% (see, for instance, the entries for Pasteur and rabies in the Encyclopaedia Britannica). In our times, the effectiveness of penicillin in cases of pneumococcal meningitis provided a similar dramatic example of an experiment for which old control figures were clearly sufficient.

The method can be useful even in less dramatic situations. Thus, a comparison was recently made of the histories of high-risk cardiac

[10]The sequential design has limited application because it often tends to terminate the study before adequate precision for generally useful interpretation is obtained.

cases who had changed to a low-cholesterol diet, with the histories of such high-risk cases, found in a variety of earlier studies, that had made no such change.

In principle, this is a permissible procedure.[11] In practice, such comparisons are endangered by hidden traps. The question is always whether these prior "natural" control groups are truly comparable: Was the "high-risk" definition of the earlier cases the same as that for the later ones? Have the diagnostic means advanced, so that the "high risk" is now discovered earlier and hence will produce people with longer life expectancy, and so forth?

One subspecies of this bypassing of a special control group is a design where all individuals receive the treatment but receive it at different time periods. In this way, the last individuals to be treated can serve as control groups to be compared with the first ones who received the treatment. Again there is a potential price to pay, if the time difference happens to affect the relationship; suppose, for instance, the virulence of a bacterial strain has changed in the interval.

Finally, there are experimental designs that do not use any control groups but use computed baselines instead. They assume a variety of patterns. One of these has been called "regression discontinuity design" (Campbell, 1968). It allows for selecting for treatment any special group (e.g., according to highest merit or greatest need) and evaluates the validation criterion (success, mortality, etc.) for the treated group as against what the expectation would have been without the treatment. The expectation is provided by some regression line that is either extrapolated beyond its normal range or based on the full range of some prior, untreated cases. If, for the treated data, the regression of the criterion on the independent variable deviates from the untreated or extrapolated regression function, the difference is attributed to the treatment. Examples of this approach can be found in the area of evaluating differential penal treatments, where the recidivism expectation, based on known and normal regression functions, is compared with the actual recidivism rate of a treated group (see, for instance, Mannheim and Wilkins, 1955; Wilkins, 1955; and Grygier, 1966). Another effort of this kind sought to establish that nuclear testing had increased infant mortality in the United States. The mortality trend, which had been declining until 1950, following a straight regression line, registered from 1950 on a reduced rate of decline (Sternglass, 1969). This example

---

[11]The present experimental use of L-Dopa, a new drug for Parkinson's disease, is another example in this category. It is given only in cases where all other treatments have failed, and there is no control group.

shows, as well as any other, the precarious character of inferences of this sort. The assumptions that have to be correct to ensure the correctness of the inference are numerous and, worse, unknown. Nevertheless, often the analyst does not have more than nonrandomly selected data, and to find out how to make the best of them is a very important enterprise indeed.

The devices mentioned so far aim at reducing the risks of harm that may at times stand in the way of desirable experimentation. But there are other obstacles. The law, binding legal commitments, or simply our social mores might make certain experiments impossible. Suppose one wanted to learn whether the award of a merit fellowship had any effect on the future career of the students who receive it. To determine this, one would have to give the fellowships to only half the students who merited them and withhold them from the other half, a procedure that would be clearly impossible.

One could, however, conduct such an experiment in a slightly different setting. Suppose everybody above grade 100 is entitled to the fellowship. Then, of course, everybody above 100 must receive it. But it would be possible to conduct the experiment among students who received grades, let us say, between 100 and 90. In this group, then, half of the students would get the fellowship and the other half would not. Since here nobody was entitled to receive one, there is no discrimination. The price for such a shift consists of limiting the potential knowledge to the 90–100 range; if that group should react differently from the above-100 group, one would be misled (Campbell, 1968). This, then, is another device for making an otherwise impossible experiment possible. It consists of moving the controlled experiment from the legally or socially proscribed range.

Sometimes the only possible way of overcoming a legal barrier is to dilute the design by replacing some real traits of the experiment through mock features. At one time, for instance, we wanted to conduct experiments with juries in order to learn how different types of juries would treat the same type of case. The law, of course, would never permit trying the same case twice. We had to resort, therefore, to mock trials; that is, to a procedure in which a case was transmitted from a tape recording to a series of experimental juries. Everything else in the experiment was real. Real jurors were selected from the general jury room by a real judge, who would tell them that by listening to and deciding this tape-recorded case, they would render the court a service for which they would be paid as if they had served on a real jury. The problem, of course, was whether the decisions in these mock trials would reasonably correspond to decisions in real trials. The elaborateness of the jury deliberations, their naturalness and seriousness, left little doubt about the realism of these experiments. In some cases, these mock juries would deliberate and fight through many tiresome hours, as only real juries do; and some juries would actually hang in angry deadlock (Simon, 1969).

This method of overcoming obstacles will, of course, have no application to something like drug tests, but one can easily see its usefulness in certain psychological or social experiments.

Then there are studies that, if carried out along normal designs, would run into insuperable difficulties because the subjects, for one reason or another, are likely to refuse cooperation. In such situations it may happen that the sensitive data needed for the experiment may have been collected by some governmental agencies and could be obtained from them with safeguards against improper disclosure.

An attempt was made, for instance, to study various methods of improving honesty in the filing of income tax returns. Three randomly selected groups of income earners were exposed to three different treatments: With one group, conversations were held that emphasized the dire consequences of tax cheating, penalties and criminal prosecution; with the second group, the topic was treated more leniently, with stress on its being a civic duty to be honest about taxes because, in the end, the well-being of the community depended on such honesty; the third group, serving as control group, was not treated at all.

There was, of course, only one way of measuring the effect of these subtly varying approaches: through the tax returns of these people before and after the experimental treatment. Any effort to obtain these returns from the subjects themselves would have failed. In this situation, the Internal Revenue Service had no difficulty in making available certain statistics from the tax returns of these three groups, for both the time prior to and after the experimental treatment, without betraying the confidence to which such a public agency is obligated. The point is that the data were released not in terms of individual cases but in terms of averages for large groups of people, from which no possible inference could be drawn to the individuals in those groups (Orleans and Schwartz, 1967).[12] Thus a very sophisticated experiment was made possible without violating the privacy duty of the governmental agency.[13]

---

[12]The experiment had some flaws, but its basic design was ingenious.

[13]Government cooperation would be also the only resource for making studies possible that are more vital than the one just cited. Every so often, after the satisfactory conclusion of all required tests, a drug is released for general use. But most of the time,

Finally, there are situations in which, paradoxically, the partial surrender of the experimental control may be the only way to safeguard the controlled character of the experiment. The device, which has been called the indirect experiment, is best explained by way of two examples from Zeisel (1969).

In many of our courts, whenever somebody files a claim the judge will summon the litigants and their lawyers to a conference, prior to trial, in which he or she attempts to settle the case or, if this is not possible, to prepare it for the actual trial. It has been widely thought among the judiciary that this pretrial conference helps in the settlement of cases and, consequently, in the reduction of the overgrown trial load of our courts (Rosenberg, 1964). In the course of our studies of court procedures, we came to doubt this belief, and the state courts of New Jersey decided to conduct a controlled experiment to test the issue.[14] Ideally, in this experiment all filed claims should have been divided randomly into two groups; the cases in the one group should be called for pretrial, those in the other should have no pretrial. Eventually, one would compare the proportion of settlements in one group with the corresponding proportion in the other. The court, however, thought that in this form the experiment would pose legal difficulties, because it deprived one group of litigants of the right to pretrial. The objection was overcome through a slight modification in the design. Instead of contrasting obligatory pretrial with obligatory absence of pretrial, the experiment contrasted obligatory pretrial with *optional* pretrial; the cases in the control group would be pretried only if at least one of the litigants demanded it. By this shift, no litigant was deprived of the right to pretrial, yet the controlled character of the experiment was preserved because the two groups—obligatory versus optional—were still randomly selected.

To be sure, the shift reduced the power of the experiment. For one,

---

these tests do not extend over more than what one might call the middle range of time. For understandable reasons, tests for longtime effects are hardly ever insisted upon. But this is no reason for not conducting such long-run tests, except that they again can be conducted successfully only with government help. What with the great mobility of our citizenry, only the federal government, with the help of state agencies, could undertake to follow up a group of treated patients and their control group over a long period of time, possibly over their lifetimes.

[14]A similar problem arose in an interesting experiment aimed at testing the possible superiority of driver reeducation over a straight penalty for drivers guilty of careless driving. Here a random sample of those found guilty was offered the alternative of undergoing an intensive course of driving reeducation. As to the legal "equal protection" aspects of such a procedure, see Zeisel et al. (1957).

the experiment would fail if all or most litigants in the optional group would request pretrial—a condition over which the experimenter had no control. As it happened, only about half of the cases in the experimental group requested it; hence the experimental and the control group were sufficiently different. The experiment happened to reveal that this shift to optional pretrial did not reduce the proportion of cases settled prior to trial,[15] and the courts of New Jersey therefore promptly adopted a rule that made the former obligatory pretrial optional.

There was, of course, a price to be paid for this partial surrender of control. The experiment did not allow the experimenter to learn what the effect of complete abolition of pretrial would be; there was no legitimate way of inferring from this experiment that the settlement ratio of the cases that did opt for pretrial would have remained unchanged had they been deprived of the pretrial conference.

My second example of an indirect experiment is the field experiments designed to explore the effects of high-cholesterol diet and smoking on cardiac disease. This experiment also makes use of our first device, of reversing the experimental treatment in the favorable direction; the experimental treatment consists not of high-cholesterol diet and more smoking but of a low-cholesterol diet and reduced or given up smoking. But even with this reversal such direct experimentation would prove unfeasible, except in closed institutions, and even there it would be rather difficult to withdraw all cigarettes from a randomly selected group of inmates while allowing them to the others. Hence the experiment had to be indirect: After individuals were randomly assigned to the experimental group, they had to be *persuaded* to change their diet and smoking habits. If persuasion succeeded to a sufficient degree, one could compare cardiac morbidity and mortality in the three experimental groups with that in the control group, which was left to its normal diet and smoking habits.

Note that although this type of experiment, strictly speaking, again falls short of the ultimate proof that high-cholesterol diet and smoking affect cardiac incidents, for all practical purposes the experiment will suffice. In a pragmatic sense, it is sufficient to learn whether a partly successful effort to persuade people to reduce their cholesterol level and cigarette consumption results in reducing cardiac ailments.

The limitation of such an indirect experiment derives from the fact that the people who accept the treatment and thus select themselves might have, to begin with, a different cardiac expectation than the

[15]Cases settled prior to trial were as follows: control group, obligatory pretrial, 76%; and experimental group, optional pretrial, 78%.

people who do not accept the treatment, and therefore one does not learn how the latter would react. One way of counteracting such patterns of self-selection is to invoke group persuasion and group discipline, so that all or most people in a fairly diversified group would accept the treatment. One might, for instance, recruit employees of a banking system that has a great many branch offices. Some branches would then be randomly selected for treatment, and an effort would be made to persuade all employees in those offices to give up smoking or change their diets.[16] If one then achieves near success in some of the groups, one is entitled to assume that the self-selection disturbance has been reduced.

These, then, are some of the ways in which appropriate redesign of an experiment may alleviate the difficulties that unavoidably accompany experiments with human subjects. Some are designed to reduce the risk for the participating subjects, others to accommodate legal rules or other binding commitments, and still others merely to obtain data that normally would be unavailable. But such redesign will seldom do more than reduce the difficulty, and usually there will be a price to pay, in terms of the reduced power of the experiment. To some extent, the moral problem will remain. For the researcher, the adage of the half-loaf that is better than no loaf at all will have to suffice. In the long run, however, we shall have to cope with the basic difficulties if we want to continue to learn about ourselves through experimentation.

As matters stand, there is little public support for participation in human experiments. We do not hesitate to give our full admiration to the occasional doctor–hero who decides to become the first patient for his or her own new cure. On the whole, however, our image of the hero in our time is not the civil hero but the soldier or the daredevil astronaut. One would like to look forward to a moral climate in which the person who helps the advancement of science and thereby the well-being of humanity is promoted to the rank of hero and, perhaps, even stands at the head of the line.

There are at least two reasons that keep the moral support for human experimentation at a low level. Part of the trouble derives from the vicious circle that now exists with respect to the main participants in medical experiments. They are now primarily recruited from the temporary or permanent inmates of public institutions, our Veterans Ad-

---

[16]We might note here, more generally, that random assignment for experimental purposes does not always mean assignment of individuals; at times the random assignment may be limited to clusters of individuals such as particular hospitals or communities, or, as in the earlier example, branch offices of a chain organization.

ministration hospitals, our mental institutions, and, often, our prisons.[17] This means that it is mainly the underprivileged of our society who perform these services, which thereby have acquired some negative prestige. It would help if such service would become more democratic by extending it systematically to the upper economic strata also.[18]

The undemocratic distribution of subjects is also the reflection of a deeper malaise, the pervasive uncertainty as to whether the potential sacrifice is worthwhile. Again and again we learn of experiments that are not (Ringaber, 1969).

The ultimate impropriety, of course, is attained when an experiment involves a considerable invasion of privacy and even risk of harm, yet is so poorly designed that this infliction is useless in any event. In such situations a human experiment that would be of doubtful propriety if properly designed becomes altogether indefensible.

The report of such an experiment (Owens and Krieger, 1968) recently crossed my desk. Its purpose was to test the effectiveness of what is politely called an aversive treatment cure in reducing aggressive behavior of psychopathic prisoners. It is an enlarged version of the "if you do this, you will be spanked" syndrome of the rat that receives an electric shock each time it makes a forbidden move.

To qualify as a subject, the prisoner had to have a record either of having committed repeated assaults, constituting a constant threat to others, or of being a threat to himself by a record of self-mutilation, suicide attempts, or sniffing toxic substances.[19] The treatment was drastic. Every participating prisoner was told that each time he indulged in one of the designated behaviors, he would receive an injection that had rather unpleasant consequences, but that he would receive no injections if he refrained from the designated misbehavior (p. 5).

The injection involved a drug called amectine (Succinylcholine).[20] The injection creates "complete muscular paralysis including tempo-

---

[17]Prisoners are often accorded penal benefits for such cooperation. I wonder whether it would not be better to offer to give them money that will help them on their way when they leave prison rather than to connect experimenting with the penal process itself.

[18]The polio field trials of 1954 were a case in point. A straightforward appeal to the public succeeded in persuading a large number of people to subject themselves to a randomized trial in which people willingly risked the event that their child might be given a placebo vaccination. What probably helped here, though, was the even then low expectation of acquiring the disease.

[19]The report says, "Nearly all could be characterized as angry young men [Owens and Krieger, 1968:7]."

[20]Whether intravenously or intramuscularly is not clear; on page 3 in Owens and Krieger (1968) one method is mentioned, and on page 5, the other.

rary respiratory arrest . . . for approximately two minutes [p. 6]." The experimenters had little doubt about the nature of that experience; they refer to it as a "frightening consequence." Frightening it must have been, because when the subjects were later asked, "How would you describe the experience?" 32% said, "like dying," 7% said, "like when drowning," and 41% simply said, "scary" or "terrible."[21]

The experimental treatment then consisted of the threat of the anectine injection and carrying it out if one of the designated acts was committed. The experimenters, "to further emphasize the contractual nature of the treatment program," requested "the patients . . . to sign a statement of consent." The nature of this consent is noteworthy. In the subsequent interview by the evaluators, who wrote the report, 51% of those who had signed up answered the question "Why did you sign up for Anectine treatment?" with "Involuntary." And to relieve any remnant of doubt about the character of that consent, the report adds: "On five patients, consent was not received from the patient himself, but was granted by the institution's Special Treatment Board [p. 5]."

Thus, this study puts into focus all the problems that surround the obtaining of consent from subjects that are prisoners to begin with and mental cases to boot. As to the scientific theory that underlies this aversive treatment experiment, I shall say nothing, since I am not an expert, although I am aware that many psychiatrists would have doubts. I am prepared to assume instead that this treatment held high promise of cure of otherwise hopeless behavior.

We now come to the last and most crucial aspect of the experiment, its research design: Was it designed so that it could reliably test the effectiveness of the treatment? Remember the nature of a controlled experiment in its simplest form: Have one of two randomly selected, and therefore comparable, groups exposed to the treatment that is withheld from the other, the control group. In this case, it would have meant first determining the group of qualified subjects (those with records of aggressive behavior) and then signing up a random half of that group for potential treatment, leaving the other half as the control group. Eventually, one would see whether the treated half would show a decrease in aggressive behavior as compared with the control group.

The experimenters, however, did nothing of the kind, probably relying on the mistaken notion that it would suffice to compare those who

---

[21]"The use of the oxygen mask [apparently to prevent suffocation] during the treatment was theorized [sic] to contribute to certain deep symbolic aspects . . . the omnipotent, beneficient parent figure who holds the power of life and death [sic] [Owens and Krieger, 1968:4]."

received the injection with those who did not receive it because they refrained from misbehaving. This is indeed the comparison they made afterward.[22] But this comparison is misleading, since those who heeded the warning and those who were unable to heed it were clearly not comparable random halves prior to the experiment.[23]

Thus, instead of beginning with two originally equal groups, one of which is treated and the other not, that experiment began with two clearly unequal groups—as revealed by their differential ability to heed the warning—both of which were exposed to the experimental treatment; a nonexperiment, if there ever was one.

It is studies such as these that bring into sharpest focus all the problems that attend experimentation with human subjects: the need for weighing the expected results against the harm the treatment may cause; the limits of voluntary consent from subjects whose understanding and freedom of action is limited; and, most importantly, the essential need for the best research design that can (under the circumstances) evaluate the experimental treatment. Without such design, all is wasted.

Acknowledgments

The author wishes to thank Paul Meier of the University of Chicago, who, in this case, by counsel and advice, has far surpassed the customary generous level of reading a colleague's manuscript, and Jeremiah Stamler of Northwestern University, who was kind enough to read the manuscript critically and from whose discussions with the author the examples of cardiac experiments emerged.

[22]The number of infractions were shown in a table in Owens and Kreiger (1968: 12) as follows:

Time period	Treated group	Untreated group
Prior to treatment	95	48
After treatment	67	37
Decline	−29%	−23%

[23]If handled correctly, the result would have been a controlled indirect experiment (see Zeisel, 1969) instead of what in fact was a nonexperiment. The evaluators try to make up for this irremediable flaw in the design by noting that the total group of signed-up patients showed "27 percent decrease in . . . disciplinary infractions. Since no other . . . influence has impinged upon this group as a whole, there is no reason to believe that these . . . changes are due to any influence other than aversive therapy [Owens and Kreiger, 1968:12]." But to prove this surmise should have been precisely the burden of a correctly designed experiment.

References

Campbell, D. T.
    1968   "Reforms as experiments." Pp. 233–261 in F. G. Caro (ed.), Readings in Evaluation Research. New York: Russell Sage.
Cornfield, J., M. Halperin, and S. W. Greenhouse
    1969   "An adoptive procedure for sequential clinical trials." Journal of the American Statistical Association 64:759–770.
Edsall, G.
    1969   "A positive approach to the problem of human experimentation." Daedalus 98:463.
Festinger, L., and J. M. Carlsmith
    1959   "Cognitive consequences of forced compliance." Journal of Abnormal and Social Psychology 58:203–210.
Freund, P. A.
    1969   "Introduction" to the issue "Ethical Aspects of Experimentation with Human Subjects." Daedalus 98:viii.
Grygier, T.
    1966   "The effect of social action: Current prediction methods and two new models." British Journal of Criminology 6:269–293.
Hovland, C. I., A. A. Lumsdaine, and F. D. Sheffield
    1949   "Experiments on mass communication." In Studies in Social Psychology in World War II. Vol. 3. Princeton, N.J.: Princeton University Press.
Jaffee, L. L.
    1969   "Law as a system of control." Daedalus 98:406–426.
Jonas, H.
    1969   "Philosophical reflections on experimenting with human subjects." Daedalus 98:219–247.
Kalven, H., and H. Zeisel
    1966   The American Jury. Boston: Little, Brown.
Kelman, H. C.
    1968   A Time to Speak: On Human Values in Social Research. San Francisco: Jossey-Bass.
Mannheim, T., and L. T. Wilkins
    1955   Prediction Methods in Relation to Borstal Training. London: HM Stationery Office.
Meier, P.
    1957   "Safety testing of poliomyelitis vaccine." Science 125:1067–1075.
Orleans, S., and R. D. Schwartz
    1967   "On legal sanction." University of Chicago Law Review 34:274–300.
Owens, D., and R. Kreiger
    1968   "An aversive treatment program with extreme acting out in a psychiatric facility for criminal offenders." Mimeograph. California Department of Corrections.
Ringaber, W.
    1969   "Prison drug and plasma projects leave fatal trail." New York Times, July 29.
Rosenberg, M.
    1964   The Pretrial Conference and Effective Justice. New York: Columbia University Press.
Rutstein, D. D.
    1969   "The ethical design of human experiments." Daedalus 98:523–541.

Simon, R. J.
   1967   *The Jury and the Defense of Insanity.* Boston: Little, Brown.
Sternglass, E. J.
   1969   "Infant mortality and nuclear tests." *Bulletin of Atomic Scientists* 28:18.
Wilkins, L. T.
   1955   "Some developments in prediction methodology in applied social research."
          British Journal of Sociology 6:348–363.
Zeisel, H.
   1969   "The indirect experiment." *Law and Society* 3:504–508.
Zeisel, H., H. Kalven, and B. Bucholz
   1957   *Delay in the Court.* Boston: Little, Brown.
Zelen, M.
   1969   "Play the winner rule and the controlled clinical trial." *Journal of the American
          Statistical Association* 64:131–146.

4

Statistics and Ethics in Surgery and Anesthesia[1]

JOHN P. GILBERT
BUCKNAM MCPEEK
FREDERICK MOSTELLER

Ethical issues raised by human experimentation, especially in medicine, have been of increasing concern in the last half of the twentieth century. Except for issues of consent and capacity to consent, ethical concerns raised by controlled trials center about the fact that individuals are being subjected, randomly, to different treatments. Two arguments are raised, and in each the patients are seen to be losers. The first argument is an expression of the fear that the trial, by withholding a favorable new therapy, imposes a sacrifice on the part of some of the patients (the control group). The second argument raises the opposite concern that by getting an untested new therapy, some patients (those in the experimental group) are exposed to additional risk. To a large extent, both arguments imply that investigators know in advance which is the favorable treatment.

Some empirical evidence on these issues can be obtained by examining how potential new therapies are evaluated and what the findings

[1]This chapter is reproduced with permission from *Science* 198 (1977): 684–689, Copyright 1977 by the American Association for the Advancement of Science. This work was facilitated by National Institutes of Health grant Gm 15904 to Harvard University, by the Miller Institute for Basic Research in Science, University of California, Berkeley, and by National Science Foundation grant SOC75–15702 A01.

65

SOLUTIONS TO ETHICAL
AND LEGAL PROBLEMS
IN SOCIAL RESEARCH

ISBN 0-12-118680-6

are. How often do new therapies turn out to be superior when they are tested, and how much better or worse than the standard treatment is a new therapy likely to be? We have investigated such questions for surgery and anesthesia.

The Sample of Papers

For an objective sample we turned to the National Library of Medicine's Medical Literature Analysis and Retrieval System (MEDLARS). For almost 15 years, this computerized bibliographic service has provided exhaustive coverage of the world's biomedical literature. Articles are classified under about 12,000 headings, and computer-assisted bibliographies are prepared by cross tabulating all references appearing under one or more index subjects. For example, all articles indexed under prostatic neoplasms, prostatectomy, and postoperative complications might be sought.

We obtained our sample from the MEDLARS system by searching for prospective studies and a variety of surgical operations and anesthetic agents, such as cholecystectomy, hysterectomy, appendectomy, and halothane.[2] The papers appeared from 1964 through 1973.

We found 46 papers that satisfied our four criteria: The study must (a) include a randomized trial with human subjects; (b) have at least 10 people in each group; (c) compare surgical or anesthetic treatments; and (d) be written in English, because of our own language limitations. All the papers we found, by the MEDLARS search, that met these criteria are included in the sample. Although this sample is neither a strictly random sample nor a complete census of the literature of the period covered, the method does largely exclude personal biases in selection.

These papers evaluated two types of therapy. One type is designed to cure the patient's primary disease. An example is the trial of radiation therapy in addition to surgery for the treatment of cancer of the lung

---

[2]For a discussion of MEDLARS, see Day (1974). Indexing is done by specially trained abstractors at the National Library of Medicine. The MEDLARS contents vary over time as additions are made to correct omissions. Our initial search turned up 36 randomized clinical trials. These are listed in Gilbert, McPeek, and Mosteller (1977: app. 9–1, pp. 145–154). A repeat search, approximately 18 months later, done according to the same search instructions, revealed 13 additional randomized clinical trials, as follows: Haverstadt and Leadbetter (1968), Smith (1968), Lambie, Barbier, Dhall, and Matheson (1970), Brisman, Parks, and Haller (1971), Roddick and Greenelaw (1971), Rosenberg, Graham, DeDombal, and Goligher (1971), Brehmer and Madsen (1972), Harris et al. (1972), Pinto (1972), Haller et al. (1973), Laros, Zatuchni, and Andros (1973), Noone, Randell, Stool, Hamilton, and Winchester (1973), and Rothermel, Wessinger, and Stinchfield (1973).

(Miller, Fox, and Tall, 1969). The second type of therapy is used to prevent or decrease the rate of an undesirable side effect of the primary therapy. Examples are the various trials of anticoagulants to decrease the incidence of thromboembolism after operations on the hip. Because we felt that these two types of therapies might differ in the distributions of improvements we wished to study, as indeed they seemed to, we have recorded them separately using the terms *primary* and *secondary* therapies, respectively. Although each of our sample papers has provided important information concerning the treatment of a specific disease or condition, prognosis, complications, the natural history of disease, and the like, we have concerned ourselves only with the comparison of effectiveness between competing therapies.

We have classified each therapy either as an innovation or as the standard treatment to which the innovation was being compared. Although this distinction is usually clear, in a few instances some readers might disagree with our decisions. We took the position of the investigators, who usually indicated which therapies they regarded as the standards for comparison. Some papers report trials where several innovations were tested against one standard, or one innovation was sometimes tested against several standards, or the comparison was made for several distinct types of patients. To prevent one paper from having an undue effect on the total picture, no more than two comparisons were taken from any one paper, the choice being based on the importance of the comparisons for the surgery. When two comparisons were used, each was weighted one-half. When several papers reported the same investigation, we used the most recent one.

Comparisons of Innovations and Standards

To give a rough qualitative idea of how the innovations (1) compared with the standards (S), we have classified the outcomes by "highly preferred to" (>>), "preferred to" (>), and "about the same as" (=), in Table 4.1. In the first set designated =, the innovation was regarded as a success because it did as well as the standard and did not have other disadvantages, such as high cost, dangerous side effects, or the requirement of extra skill or training in its administration. Thus, it offers the surgeon an extra therapy when the standard may have drawbacks.

In the second set designated =, the investigators seemed indifferent to the equality; in the third set, the innovations were regarded as a disappointment because of undesirable features. The preferences reported reflect closely the views of the original investigators.

About 49% of the innovations were successful when compared to

Table 4.1

Qualitative Comparisons between Innovations (1) and Standards (S), Stratified by Primary and Secondary Therapies[a]

Preference	Primary	Secondary	Total	Percentage
1 >> S	1	5	6	13
1 > S	4	4½	8½	18
1 = S (success)	2½	6	8½	18
1 = S (indifferent)	1½	1	2½	5
1 = S (disappointment)	6	5	11	23
S > 1	3	4	7	15
S >> 1	1	2½	3½	7
Total	19	28	47[b]	(99)

[a] Where a paper had two comparisons, each was weighted one-half.
[b] One paper contributed to both the primary and the secondary columns.

their matched standards, and 13% were highly preferred. Among pairs of primary therapies, the innovation was highly preferred in 5%, and among pairs of secondary therapies the innovation was highly preferred in 18% of the comparisons. Indeed, the totals of the two extreme categories were smaller in the primary comparisons than in the secondary—10.5% as compared with 27%.

The overall impact of the data in Table 4.1 is to suggest that, when assessed by randomized clinical trials, innovations in surgery and anesthesia are successful about half the time. Since innovations brought to the stage of randomized trials are usually expected by the innovators to be sure winners, we see that in the surgery and anesthesia area the evidence is strong that the value of the innovation needs empirical checking.

Quantitative Comparisons

In addition to the qualitative comparisons of Table 4.1, we want to compare the performance of the innovation more quantitatively with the standard. For those primary therapies where survival gives a suitable measure of performance, we examine the distribution of the difference in survival percentages (1 minus S). For the secondary therapies, we compare the percentages of patients not getting a specific complication such as abdominal infection or thrombosis. (Where we have used two complications in one study, each has been weighted one-half, as in Table 4.1.) If we merely take the observed differences, they are subject to variation over and above the true differences because of sampling error due to the finite samples used in the experiments. To adjust for these sampling errors, we use an empirical Bayes procedure, as described in the Appendix. Efron and Morris (1973a) describe the general idea through an instructive sports example: If we observed the batting averages for their first 50 times at bat for 200 major league batters, we might find them ranging from .080 to .450, yet we know that major league averages for a season ordinarily run about .200 to .350 these days. The excess spread comes from the sampling error based on only 50 times at bat rather than on the season's total experience. To adjust this, we can shrink the results toward the center of the distribution (roughly .275). How this is done is explained by Efron and Morris (1973a, 1973b) and more simply by them in a later paper (1977). The explanation is given in detail for the present situation in Gilbert, McPeek, and Mosteller (1977).

After the shrinking is carried out, we can estimate the distribution of the true gains or losses associated with the innovation by methods discussed in the Appendix and in Gilbert, McPeek, and Mosteller, (1977). In Figure 4.1, we give the estimated cumulative distribution for the true gains of secondary innovations. The graph suggests that about 80% of the innovations offer gains between −10% and +30%. In about 24% of the studies, gains of at least 20% occur. In about 10% of the studies, gains of more than 30% occur. About 12% of the time losses of more than 10% occur. The sharp dip just to the right of zero improvement in Figure 4.1 could, in a replication, move a few percentage points to the left or right of its present position. We have to emphasize that the cumulative is based essentially on a sample of 24 papers (not all sec-

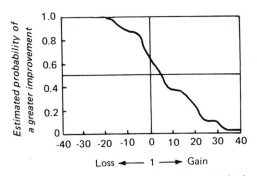

Figure 4.1. Secondary therapies: estimated cumulative distribution of true gains (reduction in percentage with a particular complication).

ondary papers in Table 4.1 could be used here), but each paper is worth rather less than one whole observation of the difference because of the sample sizes in the investigations. If the sample sizes were infinite, we would not have the shrinking problem, and each paper would provide a full observation.

Gains or losses of modest size, such as 10%, although extremely valuable, are hard to detect on the basis of casual observation. We need careful experimentation and good records to identify such gains and losses. To get an idea of how hard it is to detect a difference of 10%, say that between 55% and 45%, it may help to know that two samples of size about 545 are required to be 95% sure of detecting the difference, by a one-sided test of significance at the 5% level. To be 50% sure requires samples of 135. Such large trials were rare in our samples.

Nonrandomized Controlled Trials

In addition to the randomized clinical trials, 11 less well controlled trials seemed appropriate for reporting. Results are shown in Table 4.2 in a manner similar to that used in the randomized trials. By and large, the distribution leans more favorably toward innovations than does that seen in Table 4.1. A tendency for nonrandomized trials to favor innovations is frequently noted. Although speculation is easy, the reasons for this are unclear. Although in general a randomized trial provides stronger evidence than a corresponding nonrandomized trial, there are occasions where a nonrandomized trial may be convincing. A nonrandomized study of abdominal stab wounds seems especially instructive because it provides strong evidence favoring a new policy. The hospital's standard policy had been to perform a laparotomy (sur-

Table 4.2
Summary for Controlled Nonrandomized Trials

Preference	Primary	Secondary	Total
1 >> S	2	3	5
1 > S	1	1	2
1 = S (disappointment)		2	2
S > 1		1	1
S >> 1		1	1
Total	3	8	11

gical exploration of the abdominal cavity) on all patients with abdominal stab wounds. In 1967, the hospital instituted a change in policy, the results of which Nance and Cohn (1969) report. The new policy demanded exploration only when the attending surgeon judged it necessary. (A patient might be observed for a period and then explored.)

The investigators give a record of (a) the substantial number of complications (25%) emerging from routine laparotomy when, in retrospect, the patient had not required surgical repair for the stab wound; (b) the recovery without complications in the approximately 8% of patients who declined or otherwise passed by the former administrative rule of always performing a laparotomy; and (c) evidence that delay before exploration under the old policy was not associated with an increase in the complication rate. These observations suggest that omitting the laparotomy for selected patients might be good practice.

Some might have said, on the basis of the data presented in a,b, and c, that the proposed new policy of judgmental surgical decisions would be clearly preferable to routine laparotomy. Nevertheless, such inductive leaps have often failed in other attractive circumstances, sometimes because the new policy loses some advantages that the old one had, or falls prey to the fresh problems that may arise when any policy is totally changed. Changing from set policy to the regular use of judgmental surgical decisions plus keeping records provided an inexpensive type of quasi-experiment. The method has a grave weakness because the time period is not common to the differently treated groups, and, therefore, causes other than the change in treatment may produce at least part of the observed differences.

For the stab wounds, the need for a randomized clinical trial is not now compelling for the hospital partly because, in addition to the logic and data of a, b, and c, discussed earlier, the final quasi-experiment produced a large improvement. Although the percentage requiring repair of the stab wound was about the same under the old and new policies (30% as compared to 28%), the overall complication rate dropped substantially from 27% to 12%. One fear was that the unexplored group would produce a proportion of very severe complications. The evidence goes the other way. Among those not explored, the number without complications remained at zero even though the number not explored rose from 38 to 72 patients, and the percentage explored fell from 92% to 40%. The average length of hospitalization over all patients dropped from 7.9 to 5.4 days. Had the effect been small, one might still be concerned whether possible biases and other changes could have given misleading results. All told, the evidence favoring the new policy seems persuasive for this hospital.

John P. Gilbert, Bucknam McPeek, and Frederick Mosteller

Comparisons of Degrees of Control

Although randomized clinical trials are not the only strong form of evidence about therapies in humans, weakly controlled investigations may not give the same results as better controlled ones. Grace, Muench, and Chalmers (1966) and Chalmers, Block, and Lee (1972) have compared views of many investigators who had made studies of a single therapy, with respect to the degree of control used in each investigation. We give the results of one example of such collections of investigations.

Table 4.3 shows the association between degree of enthusiasm and degree of control for the operation of portacaval shunt (slightly revised, by adding two cases, from Grace et al., 1966). The counts in Table 4.3 are not of patients but of investigations. Table 4.3 shows that, among the 53 investigations, only 6 were classified as "well controlled." Among the 34 associated with "marked enthusiasm," none were rated by the investigators as "well controlled." The "poorly controlled" and the "uncontrolled" investigations generated approximately the same distribution of enthusiasm: about 72% "marked," 21% "moderate," and 6% "none." The six "well-controlled" investigations split 50–50 between enthusiasm levels "moderate" and "none." Muench, who participated in collecting these data, has a set of statistical laws (Bearman, Loewenson, and Gullen, 1974), one of which says essentially that nothing improves the performance of an innovation as much as the lack of controls. Because tables for other therapies have given similar results, one must be cautious in accepting results of weakly controlled investigations.

Table 4.3
Degree of Control versus Degree of Investigator Enthusiasm for Portacaval Shunt Operation in Fifty-three Studies with at Least Ten Patients

	Degree of enthusiasm			
Degree of control	Marked	Moderate	None	Total
Well controlled	0	3	3	6
Poorly controlled	10	3	2	15
Uncontrolled	24	7	1	32
Total	34	13	6	53

Source: The table is revised from Grace, Muench, and Chalmers (*Gastroenterology*, 1966: Table 2, p. 685), © Williams and Wilkins, Baltimore. Chalmers advised us of two additional studies to add to the well-controlled–moderate cell, raising the count from 1 to 3.

In Table 4.3, the rows for "poorly controlled" and "uncontrolled" studies suggest that repeated, weakly controlled trials are likely to agree and build up an illusion of strong evidence because of the large count of favorable studies.

Not only may this mislead us into adopting and maintaining an unproven therapy, but it may make proper studies more difficult to mount, as physicians become less and less inclined, for ethical reasons, to subject the issue to a carefully controlled trial lest the "benefits" of a seemingly proven useful therapy be withheld from some patients in the study.

Strengths of Belief

A controlled trial of innovative therapy may sometimes impose a sacrifice on the part of some patients by withholding the more favorable of a pair of treatments. However, prior to the trial we do not know which is the favorable therapy. Only after the trial can the winner be identified. Some will say that the physician must have an initial guess, however ill-founded. It is unlikely that his or her view of the two competing treatments is exactly 50–50. The question then arises: If the physician fails to act on such a preference, is the patient getting responsible care? To help consider this question, let us review information obtained from experiments on incidental information.

Alpert and Raiffa (1969) have performed a number of experiments on guessing behavior. Individuals were asked to estimate quantities about which they might have been expected to have some incidental information, such as the fraction of students in their class having a particular characteristic. Subjects were graduate students in the Faculty of Arts and Sciences and in the Graduate School of Business Administration at Harvard University. In addition to the basic estimate, the graduate students were asked to provide numbers below which various subjective probabilities would lie. If we think of the upper and lower 1% intervals as ones where a responder felt 98% sure that the answer would lie between the chosen 1% and the 99% levels), then these responders were seriously surprised in 42.6% of the guesses or about 21 times as often as they should have been if the subjective estimates matched the true frequencies. Alpert's and Raiffa's work shows that experienced adults are likely to overrate the preciseness of their estimates. These people were too sure of their information. Although these people were not physicians in a patient relation, they were well educated and engaged in thoughtful work. Until we get contrary information from more relevant studies, such data suggest that strong initial preferences for therapies yet to be tested by controlled trials should be viewed with reserve. And, of course, the distribution shown in Figure 4.1 and the results of Table 4.1 also show that, for therapies tested in trials, holding a view not far from 50–50 has some empirical foundation for surgery.

Shapiro (1977) gives examples of wide variation among different physicians' estimates of probabilities in therapeutic situations—data pertinent to this discussion but not the same as the Alpert–Raiffa point. Shapiro shows that physicians differ a great deal in their estimates; Alpert and Raiffa show that people are very frequently much further off than they expect to be.

Do We Owe the Past or Future?

Let us consider the question of whether a present patient should give up something for future patients. We, or our insurance carriers, pay the monetary cost of our care. What we do not pay for is the contribution to the medical system by past patients. These patients, through their suffering and participation in studies, have contributed through their illnesses and treatments to the present state of evidence for all patients. Such contributions cannot be purchased by money but can be repaid in part by making, when appropriate, a contribution to the same system. One good way is through participation in well-designed clinical trials when the patient falls into the limbo of medical knowledge. Other nonmonetary ways are donating blood and organs. So one may feel an obligation to the system of medicine that has reached its present state without his or her assistance, and in addition each person has an interest in its general improvement, as we next explain (for a treatment of this point, see Almy, 1977).

In some circumstances, participation in the trial may turn out to be of help to the patient. Aside from the luck of getting the best therapy of several that are offered, this occurs, for example, when the patient has a disease for which treatments can be readily changed after the trial. Nevertheless, there are circumstances when the treatment is not reversible and when the chances are that the specific trial will be of little individual benefit—that is, when it has but slight chance of being a benefit to the patient, his or her family, or friends.

Under these circumstances, the patient may still be willing to participate in a trial. If the trial is recognized as part of a general system of trials in which patients participate only on such occasions as they qualify and when a trial seems necessary, then the patient may well benefit in the future not so much from the results of the particular trial he or she participates in but from the system that gives rise to it. Findings will come forward on many other diseases, and the patients, or someone dear to them, will be likely to suffer from some of those diseases whose trials will have produced useful findings. It is not so much, then, the direct payoff of this present trial that we should have our eye on, but pooled benefits of the whole system. The longer the patient lives, the more likely it is that he or she will suffer from some other of the diseases being studied by careful trials. And insofar as they are not studied by careful trials, the appropriate conclusions may be slow in coming. By putting off the day when strong evidence is obtained, we reduce the patient's chances of benefiting most fully from modern medicine. Thus the patient has not only an interest in the trial he or she has the opportunity to engage in but also a stake in a whole system that produces improved results that may well offer benefits in the future if the patient survives the present difficulty. Thus, the social system will likely offer benefits through the larger system even when a particular component of the system may fail to pay off directly for a patient, his or her family, friends, or some other social group he or she belongs to.

A further statistical point that may not be much appreciated by potential participants in randomized trials is that the inferences apply primarily to the population sampled in the study. To the extent that individuals or groups decline to participate in studies, and to the extent that their responses may differ from those of the rest of the population (an interaction between participation and response to therapy), the treatments selected may not apply to them as well as to participants and people "like" them. For example, if those in the lower economic status are less likely to participate and if economic status is related to the differential effectiveness of therapies, say, through additional lack of compliance, the study will not properly appreciate the value of the therapy for the nonparticipating group.

The lone individual may seem to have little incentive to participate because one seems so few among many. But the stake is not in any one person appearing in this study; it is in having people from segments of the population that represent that individual being properly represented in this and other studies so that the results of the whole system may be more assuredly applied to this patient when disease strikes. The idea is similar to that of being told not to complain of the system when one does not vote. But the extra feature here is that one gets to vote on certain special occasions, and then only a few are admitted to the booth, and so each opportunity to vote weighs much more heavily than usual.

If certain groups tend not to participate in the evaluative system, then they will find medical evaluations of therapies not as well pointed to their needs as if they did participate. Thus, all individuals have a stake in wanting people like themselves represented. Since it is hard to say what "people like themselves" means, the good solution is to have the whole appropriate population volunteering in all the therapies tested. Participating presumably encourages others like me to participate too, and vice versa.

The main point of this discussion is that if participation seems to the patient to be a sacrifice, it should be noted that others are making similar sacrifices in aid of the patient's future illnesses. So even if the particular trial may not help the patient much, the whole system is being upgraded for his and her benefit. We have a special sort of statistical morality and exchange that needs appreciation.

Responsibility for Research

Much of current popular discussion of the ethical issue takes the position that physicians should use their best judgment in prescribing for a patient. To what extent the physician is responsible for the quality of the judgment is not much discussed, except to say that he or she must keep abreast of the times. Some physicians will feel an obligation to find out what goes beyond the mere holding of an opinion. Such physicians will feel a responsibility to contribute to research. In similar fashion, some current patients may feel a responsibility to contribute to the better care of future patients. The current model of the passive patient and the active ongoing physician is not the most effective one for a society that not only wants cures rather than sympathy but also insists on them—a society that has been willing to pay both in patient cooperation and material resources for the necessary research.

Quality of Life

In addition to a society willing to support medical research through responsible experimentation on human beings, in addition to physicians dedicated to acquiring knowledge on behalf of the sick, we must be certain that controlled trials are designed to seek answers to the appropriate questions. In our survey, we found most concern with near-term outcomes, both mortality and morbidity.

We need additional data about the quality of life of patients. Among our initial sample of 107 papers drawn through the MEDLARS search, quality of life seemed often to be a major consideration, although rarely did papers address more than a few features of that quality (McPeek, Gilbert, and Mosteller, 1977).[3] Because much of medicine and surgery is intended to improve quality rather than to save life, measuring the improvement is important. As we have indicated earlier, different therapies frequently produce about the same mortality and morbidity, and so the ultimate quality of life achieved would bear heavily on the choice. Thus, for proper evaluation of alternatives, we need to assess the patient's residual symptoms, state of restored health, feeling of well-being, limitations, new or restored capabilities, and responses to these advantages or disadvantages.

For surgery, we need long-term follow-up and both objective and subjective appraisals of the patient's quality of life. Frequently, the long-term follow-up is carried out, but overall quality of life is rarely measured. For example, among 16 cancer papers in the initial sample of 107, follow-ups ranged from 2 months to 2 decades. With few exceptions, survival and recurrence data were the principal information given, and because different treatments usually had similar rates, it would be fruitful to report contrasts among the treatments in the quality of life or death experienced by patients with the same disease but having different treatments. This might be especially appropriate because the therapies involved such features as castration, hormones, irradiation, chemotherapy, and various amounts of surgery. Developing and collecting suitable measures for quality of life after surgery requires leadership from surgeons and the cooperation of social scientists. We hope these developments will soon take place.

Summary

Approximately half the surgical innovations tested by randomized clinical trials provide improvements. For those where reduction in percentage of complications was a useful measure, we estimate that

---

[3]The results of the initial sample of 107 are reported in Gilbert et al. (1977). Of these, 36 were randomized and 34 could be used, 11 were nonrandomized controlled trials, and 59 were series (study of one therapy). Our additional sample added 13 randomized trials for use in Table 4.1. McPeek, Gilbert, and Mosteller (1977) discuss quality of life.

about 24% of the innovations gave at least a 20% reduction in complications. Unfortunately, about 12% of the innovations gave at least a 10% increase in complications.

Therefore, keeping gains and discarding losses requires careful trials. Gains of these magnitudes are important but are hard to recognize on the basis of incidental observations. When well-controlled trials have not been used, sometimes data have piled up in a direction contrary to that later found by well-controlled trials. This not only impedes progress but also may make carefully controlled trials harder to organize. Most of the trials we studied did not have large sample groups. To identify dependably gains of the magnitude we found in the discussion on surgery and anesthesia, trials must be designed carefully with sufficient statistical power (large enough sample sizes) and appropriate controls, such as may be provided by randomization and blindness. As Rutstein (1969) suggests

> It may be accepted as a maxim that a poorly or improperly designed study involving human subjects . . . is by definition unethical. Moreover, when a study is in itself scientifically invalid, all other ethical considerations become irrelevant. There is no point in obtaining "informed consent" to perform a useless study.

When we think of the costs of randomized trials, we may mistakenly compare these costs with those of basic research. A more relevant comparison is with the losses that will be sustained by a process that is more likely to choose a less desirable therapy and continue to administer it for years. The cost of trials is part of the development cost of therapy. Sometimes costs of trials are inflated by large factors by including the costs of the therapies that would in any case have been delivered rather than the marginal cost of the management of the trial. This mistake is especially likely to be made when a trial is embedded in a large national program, and this is also the place where trials are highly valuable because their findings can be extended to a whole program.

Surgical treatment frequently trades short-term risk and discomfort for an improved longer term quality of life. Although long-term follow-up is frequently reported, a vigorous effort is needed to develop suitable measures of quality of life.

Table 4.1 gives empirical evidence that, when surgical trials are carried out, the preferable treatments are not known in advance. Although a common situation in a trial would be that the innovation was expected to be a clear winner, the outcome is in grave doubt. Empirical evidence from nonmedical fields suggests that educated "guesses" even by experienced, intelligent adults are way off about half the time. For these reasons, we discount the pretrial expectations or hunches of physicians and other investigators.

Most innovations in surgery and anesthesia, when subjected to careful trial, show gains or losses close to zero when compared to standards, and the occasional marked gains are almost offset by clear losses. The experimental group is neither much better nor much worse off than the control group in most trials, and we have little basis for selecting between them prior to the trial.

The one sure loser in this system is a society whose patients and physicians fail to submit new therapies to careful, unbiased trial and thus fail to exploit the compounding effect over time of the systematic retention of gains and the avoidance of losses. Let us recall that our whole financial industry is based on a continuing return of a few percentage points.

All in all, the record in surgery and anesthesia is encouraging. We regard a finding of 50% or more successes for innovations in surgical and anesthetic experiments as a substantial gain and a clear opportunity for additional future gains. Well-conducted randomized clinical trials are being done. All of us, as potential patients, can be grateful for a system in which new therapeutic ideas are subjected to careful systematic evaluation.

Appendix

ESTIMATING THE DISTRIBUTION OF GAINS

The model of the process of estimating the distribution of gains is that of two-stage sampling. We regard the innovation and its paired standard as drawn from a population of pairs of competing therapies. Let Z be the random variable corresponding to the improvement offered by the innovation (innovation minus standard), with mean M and variance A. For the ith innovation with true gain Z_i, the experiment assesses the gain as W_i, and W_i has mean Z_i and variance D_i.

If we assume as an approximation that the distributions of Z_i and W_i are normal, then the posterior distribution of Z_i has mean

$$Z_i^* = M^* + e_i\,(W_i - M^*)$$

where

$$e_i = A^*/(A^* + D_i)$$

A^* is an estimate of A, and M^* is an estimate of M. The posterior distribution of Z_i is approximately normal with mean Z_i^* and variance $(1 - B_i)W_i$, where

$$B_i = D_i\,/(A^* + D_i)$$

In the current problem the D's are estimated from binomial theory because the W's are the difference between two independent observed proportions. Details of obtaining A^* and M^* are given in Gilbert, McPeek, and Mosteller (1977).

To estimate the cumulative distribution of Z, we compute for each observation W_i

$$c_i = \frac{z - Z_i^*}{(1 - B_i)D_i}$$

Then using normal theory, we compute

$$\phi(c_i) = P(X < c_i),$$

where X is a standard normal random variable. Thus,

$$\Phi(c_i) = [1\sqrt{2\pi}] \int_{-\infty}^{c_i} \exp(-\tfrac{1}{2}x^2)\,dx$$

Finally,

$$\sum_{i=1}^{k} \Phi(c_i)/k$$

estimates $P(Z < z)$ for each value of z. We thus release ourselves from the original normal approximation for Z and get a new distribution that is not normal but should be an improved approximation of the true distribution. When weights were used because one study gave two comparisons, they modified both the estimation of A and W and the estimation of $P(Z < z)$.

Acknowledgments

We appreciate the advice and assistance of A. Bigelow, M. Ettling, M. Gasko-Green, D. Hoaglin, V. Mike, A. Perunak, K. Soper, J. W. Tukey, and G. Wong.

References

Almy, T. P.
   1977   "Meditation on a forest path." *New England Journal of Medicine* 297:165–167.
Alpert, M., and H. Raiffa
   1969   "A progress report on the training of probability assessors." Unpublished manuscript. Harvard University.
Bearman, J. E., R. B. Loewenson, and W. H. Gullen
   1974   "Muench's postulates, laws, and corollaries." *Biometrics Note 4.*
Brehmer, B., and P. O. Madsen
   1972   "Route and prophylexis of ascending bladder infection in male patients with indwelling catheters." *Journal of Urology* 108:719–721.
Brisman, R. C., J. Parks, and J. Haller
   1971   "Dextran prophylaxis in surgery." *Annals of Surgery* 174:137–141.
Chalmers, T. C., J. B. Block, and S. Lee
   1972   "Controlled studies in clinical career research." *New England Journal of Medicine,* 287:75–78.
Day, M.
   1974   "Computer-based retrieval services at the National Library of Medicine." *Federation Proceedings; Federation of American Societies for Experimental Biology,* 33:1717–1718.
Efron, B., and C. Morris
   1973a "Combining possibly related estimation problems." *Journal of the Royal Statistical Society,* ser. B, 35:379–421.
   1973b "Stein's estimation rule and its competitors—Empirical Bayes approach." *Journal of the American Statistical Association* 68:117–130.
   1977   "Stein's paradox in statistics." *Scientific American* 236:119–127.
Gilbert, J. P., B. McPeek, and F. Mosteller
   1977   "Progress in surgery and anesthesia: Benefits and risks of innovative therapy." Pp. 124–169 in J. P. Bunker, B. A. Barnes, and F. Mosteller (eds.), *Costs, Risks, and Benefits of Surgery.* New York: Oxford University Press.
Grace, N. D., H. Muench, and T. C. Chalmers
   1966   "The present status of shunts for portal hypertension in cirrhosis." *Gastroenterology* 50:684–691.
Haller, J. A., *et al.*
   1973   "Peritoneal drainage versus non-drainage for generalized peritonitis from ruptured appendicitis in children." *Annals of Surgery* 177:595–600.
Halverstadt, D. B., and G. W. Leadbetter
   1968   "Internal urethrotomy and recurrent urinary tract infection in female children. I: Results in the management of infection." *Journal of Urology* 100:297–302.
Harris, W. H., *et al.*
   1972   "Prevention of venous thromboembolism following total hip replacement: Warfarin versus dextran 40." *Journal of the American Medical Association* 220:1319–1322.
Lambie, J. M., D. C. Barbier, D. P. Dhall, and N. A. Matheson
   1970   "Dextran 70 in prophylaxis of post-operative venus thrombosis. A controlled trial." *British Medical Journal* 2:144–145.
Laros, R. K., G. I. Zatuchni, and G. G. Andros
   1973   "Puerperal tubal ligation morbidity, histology and bacteriology." *Obstetrics and Gynecology* 41:397–403.

McPeek, B., J. P. Gilbert, and F. Mosteller
1977 "The end result: Quality of life." Pp. 170–175 in J. P. Bunker, B. A. Barnes, and F. Mosteller (eds.), *Costs, Risks and Benefits of Surgery.* New York: Oxford University Press.

Miller, A. B., W. Fox, and R. Tall
1969 "Five year follow-up study of the Medical Research Council: Comparative trial of surgery and radiotherapy for the primary treatment of small-celled or oat-celled carcinoma of the bronchus." *Lancet* 2:501–505.

Nance, F. C., and I. Cohn
1969 "Surgical judgement in the management of stab wounds in the abdomen." *Annals of Surgery* 170:569–580.

Noone, R. B., P. Randell, S. E. Stool, R. Hamilton, and R. A. Winchester
1973 "The effect on middle ear disease with fracture of the pterygoid hamulus during palatoplasty." *Cleft Palate Journal* 10:23–33.

Pinto, D. J.
1972 "Treatment of pyomyositis." *East Africa Medical Journal* 49:643–650.

Roddick, J. W., and R. H. Greenelaw
1971 "Treatment of cervical cancer: A randomized study of operation and radiation." *American Journal of Obstetrics and Gynecology* 109:754–764.

Rosenberg, I. L., N. G. Graham, F. T. DeDombal, and J. C. Goligher
1971 "Preparation of the intestine in patients undergoing major large-bowel surgery, mainly for neoplasm of the colon and rectum." *British Journal of Surgery* 58:266–269.

Rothermel, J. E., J. B. Wessinger, and F. E. Stinchfield
1973 "Dextran 40 and thromboembolism in total hip replacement surgery." *Archives of Surgery* 106:135–137.

Rutstein, D. D.
1969 "The Ethical Design of Human Experiments." *Daedalus* 98:523–541.

Shapiro, A. R.
1977 "The evaluation of clinical prediction: A method of initial application." *New England Journal of Medicine* 296:1509–1514.

Smith, R.
1968 "A comparison between medical and surgical methods of treating glaucoma simplex—results of a prospective study." *Transactions of the Opthomological Society of Australia* 27:17–29.

Ethical Issues in
the Prediction of Criminal Violence

JOHN MONAHAN

Despite William James's well-known admonition that we cannot hope to write biographies in advance, American society spends a great deal of time, energy, and money attempting to identify today the individual who tomorrow will be violent. This identification of persons who reliably can be predicted to engage in violent or dangerous behavior has been called "the greatest unresolved problem the criminal justice system faces [Rector, 1973:186]" and "the paramount consideration in the law–mental health system [Stone, 1975:25]."

The task of identifying violence-prone individuals has been allocated to the criminal justice and mental health systems. In both systems, predictions of violence are variables in decision rules relating to who should be institutionalized and who should be released from an institution—the institution being a jail, prison, civil mental hospital, or hospital for the criminally insane.

In the criminal justice and mental health systems, predictions of violence may be introduced at several stages of the legal process (Shah, 1978:225):

1. Decisions concerning bail or release on personal recognizance for persons accused of crimes, including the level at which the bail is to be set

SOLUTIONS TO ETHICAL
AND LEGAL PROBLEMS
IN SOCIAL RESEARCH

2. Decisions concerning the waiver to adult courts of juveniles charged with serious crimes
3. Sentencing decisions following criminal convictions, including decisions about release on conditions of probation
4. Decisions pertaining to work-release and furlough programs for incarcerated offenders
5. Paroles and other conditional release decisions for offenders
6. Decisions pertaining to the commitment and release of "sexual psychopaths," "sexually dangerous persons," "defective delinquents," and the like
7. Determinations of dangerousness for all indicted felony defendants found incompetent to stand trial (e.g., in New York State)[1]
8. Decisions pertaining to the special handling of and transfer to special prisons of offenders who are disruptive in regular prisons
9. Commitment of drug addicts (because of fears that they will commit violent crimes to support their drug habit)
10. Decisions concerning the emergency and longer-term involuntary commitment of mentally ill persons considered to pose a "danger to self or others"
11. Decisions concerning the "conditional" and "unconditional" release of involuntarily confined mental patients.
12. Decisions concerning the hospitalization (on grounds of continuing mental disorder and dangerousness) of persons acquitted by reason of insanity
13. Decisions regarding the transfer to security hospitals of mental patients found to be too difficult or dangerous to be handled in regular civil mental hospitals
14. Decisions concerning the invocation of special legal proceedings or sentencing provision for "habitual" and "dangerous" offenders
15. Decisions concerning the likelihood of continued dangerousness of persons convicted of capital crimes, as a basis for determination regarding the use of the death sentence

Regarding this last point, the U.S. Supreme Court held that it was not unconstitutional for a state to make the imposition of the death penalty on an offender convicted of certain categories of murder contingent upon a prediction that he or she would be violent in the future: "It is, of

[1]N.Y. Crim. Proc. Law § 730.50 (Consol. 1971). This section is no longer in effect. It was found unconstitutional in 1974 in People ex rel. Anonymous v. Waugh, 76 Misc. 2d 879, 351, N.Y.S. 2d 594 (Sup. Ct. 1974).

Table 5.1
Four Possible Outcomes of Predictive Decisions

	Actual behavior	
Predicted behavior	Yes	No
Yes	True positive	False positive
No	False negative	True negative

course, not easy to predict future behavior. The fact that such a determination is difficult, however, does not mean that it cannot be made."[2]

This chapter will consider the empirical, political, and professional attacks made upon prediction and the moral issues raised by predictive decision making.

The State of Research on Violence Prediction

It is necessary to understand the four possible statistical outcomes that can occur when one is faced with making a prediction of future behavior. Table 5.1 displays these outcomes. One can predict either that the behavior—in this case, violence—*will occur* ("Yes") or that it *will not occur* ("No"). At the end of some specified time period one observes whether the predicted behavior actually *has occurred* ("Yes") or *has not occurred* ("No").

If one predicts that violence will occur and later finds that, indeed, it has occurred, the prediction is called a *true positive*. One has made a positive prediction, and it turned out to be correct or true. Likewise, if one predicts that violence will not occur, and it in fact does not, the prediction is called a *true negative*, since one is making a negative prediction of violence, and it turns out to be true. These, of course, are the two outcomes one wishes to maximize in making predictions.

If one predicts that violence will occur, and it does not, this outcome is called a *false positive*. If one predicts that violence will not occur, and it does occur, it is called a *false negative*. These two outcomes indicate inaccurate predictions and are what predictors of violence try to minimize. A false positive prediction may result in a person's being confined in a prison or a hospital unnecessarily, whereas a false negative may mean that someone goes free to commit a violent act.

[2]Jurek v. Texas, 96 S. Ct. 2950 (1976).

Table 5.2
Validity Studies of the Clinical Prediction of Violent Behavior

Study	Percentage true positive	Percentage false positive	N predicted violent	Follow-up years
Kozol et al. (1972)	34.7	65.3	49	5
Steadman and Cocozza (1974)	20.0	80.0	967	4
Cocozza and Steadman (1976)	14.0	86.0	96	3
Steadman (1977)	41.0	59.0	46	3
Thornberry and Jacoby (1979)	14.0	86.0	438	4

The major research studies that attempted to assess the accuracy of violence prediction by mental health professionals are presented in Table 5.2. A complete description of each of these studies and an evaluation of their strengths and weaknesses is presented in Monahan's (1981) study. For our purposes, it suffices to note that (a) it is possible for mental health professionals to predict violent behavior at greater than chance levels of accuracy; and (b) no study has ever found their predictions to be more accurate than inaccurate.

Criticisms of Prediction in Law

Prediction has always been a part of life and a part of law. Yet one would have to be completely out of touch with recent developments in criminal and mental health law not to notice that the prediction of violent behavior by mental health professionals has been under sustained attack. These criticisms and the issues they raise will be examined here.

The three criticisms are that (a) it is empirically impossible to predict violent behavior; (b) even if such activity could be forecast and averted, it would, as a matter of policy, violate the civil liberties of those being predicted; and (c) even if accurate prediction were possible without violating civil liberties, psychiatrists and psychologists should decline to do so, since it is a social control activity at variance with their professional helping role.

THE EMPIRICAL ATTACK:
ACCURATE PREDICTION
IS IMPOSSIBLE

Rarely have research data been as quickly or as near-universally accepted by the academic and professional communities as are those supporting the proposition that mental health professionals are highly inaccurate at predicting violent behavior.

A task force of the American Psychiatric Association concluded that "the state of the art regarding predictions of violence is very unsatisfactory. The ability of psychiatrists or any other professionals to reliably predict future violence is unproved [1974:30]." In 1978, a task force of the American Psychological Association reached a similar conclusion:

> It does appear from reading the research that the validity of psychological predictions of dangerous behavior, at least in the sentencing and release situation we are considering, is extremely poor, so poor that one could oppose their use on the strictly empirical grounds that psychologists are not professionally competent to make such judgments [p. 1110].

With few exceptions, individual psychiatrists and psychologists prominent in the area have echoed their associations' warnings. Seymour Halleck (1967), for example, noted that "if the psychiatrist or any other behavioral scientist were asked to show proof of his predictive skills, objective data could not be offered [p. 314]." Bernard Diamond (1974) has written

> Neither psychiatrists nor other behavioral scientists are able to predict the occurrence of violent behavior with sufficient reliability to justify the restriction of freedom of persons on the basis of the label of potential dangerousness. Accordingly, it is recommended that courts no longer ask such experts to give their opinion of the potential dangerousness of any person, and that psychiatrists and other behavioral scientists acknowledge their inability to make such prediction when called upon to do so by courts and other legal agencies [p. 452].

Attorneys in the mental health area have shared these conclusions. Alan Dershowitz (1969) concluded that "for every correct psychiatric prediction of violence, there are numerous erroneous predictions [p. 47]." The latest edition of the American Civil Liberties Union Handbook, *The Rights of Mental Patients* (Ennis and Emery, 1978), states that "it now seems beyond dispute that mental health professionals have *no* expertise in predicting future dangerous behavior either to self or others. In fact, predictions of dangerous behavior are wrong about 95 percent of the time [p. 20, italics in original]."

Kahle and Sales (1980) surveyed several hundred practicing psychiatrists, clinical psychologists, and mental health lawyers in a national study of attitudes toward civil commitment. They asked the respondents to estimate the percentage of accurate predictions which are made with current methods of predicting dangerousness to others. The groups did not differ significantly among themselves. The mean estimates of predictive accuracy were between 40 and 46%.

THE POLITICAL ATTACK: PREDICTION VIOLATES CIVIL LIBERTIES

Originally voiced by Thomas Szasz, the position that preventive or therapeutic intervention based upon a prediction of future behavior violates the most fundamental rights guaranteed in a democratic society—punishment for past acts, not detention for future acts—has gained a large number of adherents.

Indeed, the very designation of an act as "dangerous" or "violent" reflects political values that some may find unacceptable.

> Drunken drivers are dangerous both to themselves and to others. They injure and kill many more people than, for example, persons with paranoid delusions of persecution. Yet, people labelled paranoid are readily commitable, while drunken drivers are not.
>
> Some types of dangerous behavior are even rewarded. Race-car drivers, trapeze artists, and astronauts receive admiration and applause. In contrast, the poly-surgical addict and the would-be suicide receive nothing but contempt and aggression. Indeed, the latter type of dangerousness is considered a good cause for commitment. Thus, it is not dangerousness in general that is at issue here, but rather the manner in which one is dangerous [Szasz, 1963:85].

The most recent frontal political assault on the use of predictions of violent behavior has occurred in the context of criminal sentencing. The "just deserts" model of imprisonment, which has been adopted by many states, explicitly eschews reliance upon predictive considerations in determining an offender's release from prison (Twentieth Century Fund, 1976; von Hirsch, 1976). In its place is an explicitly normative and moral judgment of relative harm and the offender's culpability for having committed it.

> Predictive restraint poses special ethical problems. The fact that the person's liberty is at stake reduces the moral acceptability of mistakes of overprediction. Moreover, one may question whether it is ever just to punish someone more severely for what he is expected to do, even if the prediction was accurate [von Hirsch, 1976:26, italics in original].

THE PROFESSIONAL ATTACK: PREDICTION DESTROYS
THE HELPING ROLE OF THE MENTAL HEALTH DISCIPLINES

After years of being blasted as empirically incompetent to predict violent behavior and crypto-fascists if they even tried, some mental health professionals have made a counterattack. They have not only outflanked their critics by *agreeing* that accurate prediction is factually impossible and politically improper but also gone them one better by asserting that the prediction of violence and subsequent interventions to avert it are not—and in fact never were—within the purview of the mental health professions. It was the legal system that asked the psychiatrist and psychologist to give opinions regarding violence potential for use in civil commitment and other proceedings. If mental health professionals naively acquiesced, they have now discovered that this incursion into forecasting the future was a mistake. It was a mistake not simply because research allegedly showed the effort to be fruitless or because political rights were trampled, but because in the process the mental health professional gave up his or her essential role as a healer of psychic pain and became an agent of social control. Engaging in the prediction of violence to others "tends to relegate psychiatry to the very role for which it has been criticized, that of valuing societal rights above those of the individual," whereas "our sole aim should be to ensure the welfare of our patients." Thus "the prediction of danger is not within medical competence and under no circumstances should be [Peszke, 1975:826, 828]."

The professional attack on prediction has been led by Alan Stone, a psychiatrist on the faculties of the Harvard Law and Medical schools. Stone, in his highly influential National Institute of Mental Health monograph, *Mental Health and the Law: A System in Transition* (1975), proposed a new medical model of civil commitment, openly based on paternalistic concern for the patient's welfare rather than for society's protection. His "Thank-you Theory" "divests civil commitment of a police function; dangerous behavior is returned to the province of the criminal law. Only someone who is irrational, treatable, and incidently dangerous would be confined to the mental health system [p. 70]."

Even if accurate prediction could be accomplished with civil liberties safeguarded, many mental health professionals would still be opposed to participating in any scheme that would make them agents of social control rather than benefactors of the welfare of the individual client.

The Moral and Political Issues
Raised by Prediction

The criticisms that have been raised against the use of predictions of violence in criminal and mental health law tend to confound empirical issues with moral and political ones. Even the criticism that violence cannot be predicted accurately enough for use in legal decision making involves a moral and political judgment on the meaning of enough. It may be beneficial, if only to facilitate rational discourse on the topic, to separate empirical and moral–political questions so that each may receive our undivided attention. Since the empirical issues are considered in detail elsewhere (Monahan, 1981), the moral and political ones will be outlined here. The four questions of moral and political value inhering in the prediction of violence appear to concern: (a) the nature of what we are predicting; (b) the factors we use to predict it; (c) the degree of predictability that triggers preventive action; and (d) the nature of the preventive action taken.

THE CRITERION:
WHY SOME FORMS OF VIOLENCE AND NOT OTHERS?

Szasz's (1963) position on the singling out of the mentally ill for preventive confinement based on a prediction of harm has already been noted. The vagaries of how harm is defined do indeed appear to be substantial. Monahan and Hood (1978) surveyed jurors to find how "dangerous" they perceived to be a list of behaviors commonly referred to as such in legal and mental health literature. They found that older persons ranked more behaviors as "dangerous" than did younger persons, females more than males, the less educated more than the more educated, and conservatives more than liberals.

Much of the variation in how a harm comes to be officially perceived and designated as a matter of public concern appears to be produced by social political factors. Monahan, Novaco, and Geis (1979) defined "corporate violence" as "illegal behavior producing an unreasonable risk of physical harm to consumers, employees, or other persons as a result of deliberate decision-making by corporate executives or culpable negligence on their part [p. 120; cf. Megargee, 1976]." They argued that it is responsible for more deaths and injuries than the more mundane forms of crime and suggested that the preoccupation of the law and the behavioral sciences with "street" rather than "suite" violence reflects, in part, political and economic biases operating in American society (see also Geis and Monahan, 1976; Monahan and Novaco, 1980). The very choice of our subject matter, therefore, is a decision laden with moral and political implications.

THE PREDICTORS: WHAT SHALL BE INCLUDED?

As we shall later see, among the principal statistical correlates of future violent behavior are past violence, sex, age, race, socioeconomic status, and heroin or alcohol abuse. Not to take these factors into consideration in making predictions is to doom the effort from the start. Yet many are unwilling to include information that will ineluctably work to the further disadvantage of precisely those they view as most "victimized" in the past by social injustice (Ryan, 1971). As James Q. Wilson (1977) notes with regard to criminal sentencing, "The things that might be taken into account that are most determinative of criminality—the age, sex and race of the offender—are precisely those factors that society, for perfectly commendable reasons, often wishes not to take into account [p. 115]."

Even the use of prior violent behavior as a predictor of future violence raises moral dilemmas. "If an ex-convict has truly 'paid for his crime,' as is so often said, upon his release from custody or supervision, then it would arguably be morally invalid to exact any further payment from him in later years by giving him a greater sentence than a first offender otherwise similarly situated [Wilkins, Kress, Gottfredson, Calpin, and Gelman, 1978:9].

In fact, according to one point of view, racial and economic discrimination, the "diseases" of alcoholism and heroin addiction, and the "macho" demand characteristics of lower-class male subculture can be seen as restricting a person's behavioral options and thereby reducing the moral acceptability of preventive confinement. Clarence Darrow put this position well in a speech to the prisoners of the Cook County Jail in Chicago in 1902:

> Long ago, Mr. Buckle, who was a great philosopher and historian, collected facts, and he showed that the number of people who were arrested increased just as the price of food increased. When they put up the price of gas ten cents a thousand, I do not know who will go to jail, but I do know that a certain number of people will go. When the meat combine raises the price of beef, I do not know who is going to go to jail, but I know that a large number of people are bound to go. Whenever the Standard Oil Company raises the price of oil, I know that a certain number of girls who are seamstresses, and

who work night after night long hours for somebody else, will be compelled
to go out on the streets and ply another trade, and I know that Mr. Rockefel-
ler and his associates are responsible and not the poor girls in the jails
[quoted in Weinberg, 1957:8].

Apropos of Darrow, Brenner (1977) has reported that a 1% increase
in the national unemployment rate generates a 4% increase in the incidence of homicide and a 6% increase in the incidence of robbery.

Ideally, one hopes to develop predictors that "would be based only
upon statistically valid factors and weights which were simultaneously
proper from an ethical standpoint [Wilkins et al., 1978:8]." Yet what
does one do when science and morality are at cross-purposes? And
how does one take into account "justice" to the potential victims of
violent crime, "who, like their offenders and unlike the legislators,
judges, and psychologists making decisions in the criminal justice system, are often poor and nonwhite [American Psychological Association, 1978]"?

THE RELATIONSHIP:
HOW ACCURATE IS ACCURATE ENOUGH?

All a person predicting violence can hope to do is assign a probability figure to the occurrence of violent behavior by a given individual
during a given time period. The figure may be expressed in either
arithmetic (e.g., 75% likely) or prose form (e.g., "substantially likely,"
"more likely than not"). In either case, the question remains, Is this
degree of relationship sufficiently great to justify preventive intervention? whether that intervention is in the form of civil commitment,
denial of parole release, or informing a potential victim. "What represents an acceptable trade-off between the values of public safety and
individual liberty? [Wenk, Robison, and Smith, 1972:402]." (The answer to the trade-off question may be very different depending upon
the intervention to be taken (see following discussion). No one insists
that prediction be perfect. We, after all, require not absolute certainty
for convicting the guilty, only proof beyond a "reasonable doubt." This
means that we are willing to tolerate the conviction of a few innocent
persons to assure the confinement of a much larger number of guilty
criminals. It also means that when there is a doubt, we would much
rather release a guilty person than confine an innocent one.

But how many persons are we willing to hospitalize, or keep imprisoned, to keep the streets safe from one "dangerous" person? Ac-

cording to Dershowitz, "We have not even begun to ask these kinds of questions, or to develop modes of analysis for answering them [p. 60]."

THE CONSEQUENCES: PREDICTION FOR WHAT PURPOSE?

As Shah (1978) has noted, the consequences accruing to a positive prediction of violent behavior range from denying a work-release program to an incarcerated offender to imposing the death penalty. Clearly, the moral issues raised by prediction may vary as a function of the uses to which the predictions are put. If one believes that imposing the death penalty is an intrinsically immoral end, then a prediction of violent behavior, as the means to achieving that end, is likewise tainted (see Dix, 1977a, 1977b). It is not surprising that Szasz (1963), who believes civil commitment to be unethical, also abjures the predictions of harm upon which it is often based.

Most would agree that where the "cost" of predicting too many people to have a condition is negligible and the "benefit" of correctly predicting the true cases is great, prediction is morally acceptable even when extremely inaccurate. Thus, physicians place drops of silver nitrate in the eyes of all newborn infants to prevent blindness resulting from congenital gonorrhea, even though the incidence of congenital gonorrhea is infinitesimal. The erroneously "predicted" babies are not injured, and a great gain—sight—is achieved for the correct predictions (Heller and Monahan, 1977).

As the consequences of prediction vary, so may its moral component. In the case of civil commitment, for example, the consequences of long-term hospitalization to the person committed on the basis of an inaccurate prediction of violence are very great. Yet the situation may be otherwise with predictions of imminent violence that result in "only" several days commitment, after which the person is released. Although such detection is plainly a deprivation of liberty, it is highly disingenuous to compare it to the lifelong confinement so effectively castigated by Szasz (1963) and others. There is reason to believe that short-term predictions may be more accurate than long-term ones (Monahan, 1978b).

> Yet with the costs of each so vastly different, it may be possible ethically to justify short-term commitment even if the predictions of imminent violence on which it is based are *less* accurate than the long-term research indicates. Paraphrasing Blackstone, it may be better that ten "false positives" suffer

commitment *for three days* than that one "false negative" go free to kill someone during that period [Monahan, 1978a:370].

In this regard, it is sometimes noted that the ability of psychologists and psychiatrists to predict violent behavior is not appreciably worse than their ability to predict job performance, school performance, or many other facets of human behavior (Mischel, 1968). The question is whether this observation should make us feel more sanguine about violence prediction or more guarded about prediction in other areas. It may be that the prediction of violence for the purpose of hospitalization or imprisonment is, at its best, no less accurate than the predictions of academic success upon which we base admission to universities and graduate schools, or the predictions of job performance that figure into the hiring of employees for government, industry, and the military. Should this be true, however, it would still not attenuate the urgency of coming to terms with the ethical quandaries of predicting violent behavior. The consequences of erroneous prediction in other areas of life—for example, a career opportunity closed because one failed to score sufficiently high on a test that had low validity to begin with—may indeed be severe. Yet the consequences of erroneous predictions of violence include the injury or death of the victim of the person wrongly predicted to be safe and the extended institutionalization in a prison or mental hospital of the person wrongly predicted to be violent, or even, as we have noted, his or her execution. Although the prediction of violent behavior shares many features with the prediction of other forms of human conduct, the potential consequences of its misapplication give it a priority in professional and ethical concern.

References

American Psychiatry Association
   1974   *Clinical Aspects of the Violent Individual.* Washington, D.C.: American Psychiatric Association.
American Psychological Association
   1978   "Report of the task force on the role of psychology in the criminal justice system." *American Psychologist* 33:1099–1113.
Brenner, M.
   1977   "Does employment cause crime?" *Criminal Justice Newsletter* October 24, 1977:5.
Cocozza, J., and H. Steadman
   1976   "The failure of psychiatric predictions of dangerousness: Clear and convincing evidence." *Rutgers Law Review* 29:1084–1101.

Dershowitz, A.
  1969 "Psychiatrists' power in civil commitment." *Psychology Today* 2:43–47.
  1974 "The origins of preventive confinement in Anglo-American law. Part I: The English experience." *University of Cincinnati Law Review* 43:1–60.
Diamond, B.
  1974 "The psychiatric prediction of dangerousness." *University of Pennsylvania Law Review* 123:439–452.
Dix, G.
  1977a "Administration of the Texas death penalty statutes: Constitutional infirmaties related to the prediction of dangerousness." *Texas Law Review* 55:1343–1414.
  1977b "The death penalty, dangerousness, psychiatric testimony, and professional ethics." *American Journal of Criminal Law* 5:151–204.
Ennis, B., and R. Emery
  1978 *The Rights of Mental Patients—An American Civil Liberties Union Handbook.* New York: Avon.
Geis, G., and J. Monahan
  1976 "The social ecology of violence." Pp. 342–356 in T. Lickona (ed.), *Moral Development and Behavior: Theory, Research, and Social Issues.* New York: Holt, Rinehart & Winston.
Halleck, S.
  1967 *Psychiatry and the Dilemmas of Crime.* New York: Harper & Row.
Heller, K., and J. Monahan
  1977 *Psychology and Community Change.* Homewood, Ill.: Dorsey Press.
James, W.
  1890 *Principles of Psychology.* New York: Holt.
Kahle, L., and B. Sales
  1980 "Due process of law and the attitudes of professionals toward involuntary civil commitment." Pp. 265–292 in P. Lipsitt and B. Sales (eds.), *New Directions in Psycholegal Research.* New York: Van Nostrand Reinhold.
Kozol, H., R. Boucher, and R. Garofalo
  1972 "The diagnosis and treatment of dangerousness." *Crime and Delinquency,* 18:371–392.
Megaree, E.
  1976 "The prediction of dangerous behavior." *Criminal Justice and Behavior* 3:3–21.
Mischel, W.
  1968 *Personality and Assessment.* New York: Wiley.
Monahan, J.
  1978a "Prediction research and the emergency commitment of dangerous mentally ill persons: A reconsideration." *American Journal of Psychiatry* 135:198–201.
  1978b "The prediction of violent criminal behavior: A methodological critique and prospectus." Pp. 244–269 in A. Blumstein, J. Cohen, and D. Nagin (eds.), *Deterrence and Incapacitation: Estimating the Effects of Criminal Sanctions on Crime Rates.* Washington, D.C.: National Academy of Sciences.
  1981 *The Clinical Prediction of Violent Behavior.* Washington, D.C.: U.S. Government Printing Office.
Monahan, J., and G. Hood
  1978 "Ascriptions of dangerousness: The eye (and age, sex, education, location and politics) of the beholder." Pp. 143–151 in R. Simon (ed.), *Research in Law and Sociology.* Greenwich, Conn.: Johnson.

Monahan, J., and R. Novaco
1980 "Corporate violence: A psychological analysis." In P. Lipsitt and B. Sales (eds.), *New Directions in Psycholegal Research.* New York: Van Nostrand Reinhold.
Monahan, J., R. Novaco, and G. Geis
1979 "Corporate violence: Research strategies for community psychology." Pp. 117–141 in T. Sarbin (ed.), *Challenges to the Criminal Justice System.* New York: Human Sciences.
Peszke, M.
1975 "Is dangerousness an issue for physicians in emergency commitment?" *American Journal of Psychiatry* 132:825–828.
Rector, M.
1973 "Who are the dangerous?" *Bulletin of the American Academy of Psychiatry and the Law* 1:186–188.
Ryan, W.
1971 *Blaming the Victim.* New York: Random House.
Shah, S.
1978 "Dangerousness: A paradigm for exploring some issues in law and psychology." *American Psychologist* 33:224–238.
Steadman, H.
1977 "A new look at recidivism among Patuxent inmates." *The Bulletin of the American Academy of Psychiatry and the Law* 5:200–209.
Steadman, H., and J. Cocozza
1974 *Careers of the Criminally Insane.* Lexington, Mass.: Lexington Books.
Stone, A.
1975 *Mental Health and the Law: A System in Transition.* Washington, D.C.: U.S. Government Printing Office.
Szasz, T.
1963 *Law, Liberty and Psychiatry.* New York: Macmillan.
Thornberry, T., and J. Jacoby
1979 *The Criminally Insane: A Community Follow-Up of Mentally Ill Offenders.* Chicago: University of Chicago Press.
Twentieth Century Fund
1976 *Fair and Certain Punishment.* New York: McGraw-Hill.
von Hirsch, A.
1976 *Doing Justice: The Choice of Punishments.* New York: Hill & Wang.
Weinberg, A. (ed.)
1957 *Attorney for the Damned.* New York: Simon & Schuster.
Wenk, E., J. Robison, and G. Smith
1972 "Can violence be predicted?" *Crime and Delinquency* 18:393–402.
Wilkins, L., J. Kress, D. Gottfredson, J. Calpin, and A. Gelman
1978 *Sentencing Guidelines and Structuring Judicial Discretion.* Washington, D.C.: U.S. Government Printing Office.
Wilson, J.
1977 "The political feasibility of punishment." Pp. 107–123 in J. Cederblom and W. Blizek (eds.), *Justice and Punishment.* Cambridge, Mass.: Ballinger.

6

Randomized Social Experiments and the Law[1]

MARSHALL J. BREGER

Government regulation of experimentation on human beings developed out of a concern for the protection of human subjects in medical research. Thus, although social research was never excluded from government regulation, early regulatory activity focused on ethical problems raised by the "biomedical model."[2] Most discussion of the ethics of social research, moreover, has concentrated on problems engendered in regulating psychological or sociological research. Social experimentation, as a type of applied social science research, has as yet received

---

[1]This chapter is based on a paper prepared for the Conference on Ethical and Legal Problems in Applied Social Research, organized by R. F. Boruch and sponsored by the National Science Foundation, in February 1978.

[2]The history of government attempts to regulate social research has been well sketched in Gray (1979b:197, 199–208; see also 1979a:43–49). Early government efforts at regulation were clearly intended to include "investigations in the behavioral and social sciences." See Memorandum from the Surgeon General to Heads of Institutions Receiving Public Health Services Grants, December 12, 1966, cited in Gray (1979a:58). See also U.S. Department of Health, Education and Welfare (1971). There is substantial evidence that social scientists did not focus on the impact of federal regulations until the mid-1970s. See, for example, the contributions of social scientists to the National Commission for the Protection of Human Subjects (1976).

SOLUTIONS TO ETHICAL
AND LEGAL PROBLEMS
IN SOCIAL RESEARCH

little study.[3] This chapter focuses on legal and ethical issues surrounding the experimental testing of public policy through social experiments.[4] It reviews the development of administrative regulations governing social experiments and analyzes the effect of the 1981 regulations amending the Department of Health and Human Services' (HHS) policy for the protection of human subjects as they relate to social experiments.[5]

The avowed purpose of social experimentation is not primarily an increase in the store of human knowledge but the reform of social policy. A social experiment may be defined as "an intentional intervention in an economic or social system designed to yield results useful in the formulation of public policy, where this intervention involves a sample of the human population and sometimes a control group [Brown, 1975:79]."[6] This definition is admittedly imprecise but distinguishes social experiments from the naturalistic observation of behavioral phenomena (see Brandt, 1972; see also Tunnell, 1977), "experiments in nature,"[7] survey research projects (see Singer, 1978), or

[3]The most extensive survey of institutional review boards found that "behavioral research . . . accounted for approximately 30% of the research involving human subjects. About a fifth of this behavioral research entailed the study of an intervention of some kind, such as social or psychological therapy, behavior modification, or educational innovations [University of Michigan Survey Research Center, 1976:1–13]." The number of such interventions that rose to the level of a social experiment is unknown.

[4]The most complete discussion of this problem to date can be found in Rivlin and Timpane (1975). See also C. Fried (1974:143–172).

[5]46 Fed. Reg. 8366–91 (1981) (to be codified at 45 C.F.R. § 46.101). Note that the Department of Health, Education and Welfare was renamed the Department of Health and Human Services in 1980, when the Department of Education was made a separate cabinet department.

[6]Note that this definition excludes both medical and psychological experiments on human beings and is seemingly limited to interventions in the socioeconomic realm. Further, the definition does not include a requirement of a control group and might, therefore, be deemed methodologically faulty or at least be viewed as overinclusive in that it encompasses quasi-experiments and nonexperiments. For a different definition, compare Riecken and Boruch (1974:3). A later definition by the same authors can be found in Riecken and Boruch (1978), where they state, "The essential features of the contemporary model are: the systematic comparison of the effects of a planned program of social intervention either with no intervention or with one or more alternative active treatments [p. 511]."

[7]For an example of an experiment in nature, see Festinger (1956), where fieldworkers studied the behavior of millenarian groups before and after their predicted date for the end of the world. Although the research team was not able to "avoid any influence upon the movement [p. 237]," the millenarian experiment was one the researchers had not created and in which they did not intervene.

laboratory social research experiments[8]—activities that raise their own ethical and legal concerns. Social experiments are not ivory-tower investigations but rather "action-oriented" studies designed to answer the question, How can government make decisions in a more rational way? (Rivlin, 1971:1). This intervention in the social and economic life of citizens is premised on the belief that rational planning can yield a more productive social policy than the hoary model of "muddling through" (Lindblom, 1959:79).

All programmatic decisions ordinarily made by government agencies are experimental in the sense that their consequences are uncertain.[9] Nonetheless, the uncertainty inherent in a program of social reform does not make it a social experiment. It is presumed that government policymakers choose the alternative they believe best for those whom they intend to benefit. In contrast, researchers, by definition, do not attempt to provide all subjects with the best results. Their aim is to develop information that will help formulate better social policy.

Social experiments can be engendered by both the private and the public sector, by both legislative rule and administrative fiat. Indeed, much social innovation has been fueled by private philanthropy (Biderman and Sharp, 1972a:28). Some commentators have suggested that President Johnson's "War on Poverty" was spurred by the Ford Foundation's "gray area" studies (Horowitz and Katz, 1975:8). Many foundations find their raison d'être in funding experiments in areas where government may as yet fear to tread (Bundy, 1974:v–xii). On occasion, these grants might include controlled experiments of the type

[8]See Aronson and Carlsmith (1969:1–79). It is less clear that social experiments can be distinguished from "action research," as practiced by Kurt Lewin and his followers. See Lewin (1951). Such research has been defined as consisting of

> any professional intervention from a social or behavioral science perspective in the ongoing processes of a socially structured entity for the (at least partial) purpose of "the generation of new knowledge of any kind or form that can be incorporated into the preserved and transmitted body of scientific theory, method, and practice [Seashore, 1976:103]."

Action research can be seen as small-scale social experimentations.

[9]See Rivlin and Timpane (1975:5). This is analogous to the argument, often made in discussions of medical experimentation that suggests that every intervention by a physician, even for therapeutic purposes, is in some sense experimental. Thus A. C. Ivy (1948) has noted:

> Even after the therapy of a disease is discovered, its application to the patient remains, in part, experimental. Because of the physiological variations in the response of different patients to the same therapy, the therapy of disease is, and always will be, an experimental aspect of medicine. . . . The patient is always to some extent an experimental subject of the physician [pp. 1, 5]."

discussed here. Historically, of course, social experiments of the most complex sort (albeit lacking rigorous control mechanisms) were funded by private sources. Total communities such as New Harmony and Lanark, as well as migration schemes such as the Jewish Colonization Society, were created by private initiative (Owen, 1921; Cole, 1953; Price, 1969; Lockwood, 1971). Nonetheless, this chapter will center on social experiments funded by the state, since the bulk of existing controlled social experimentation receives its impetus from this source.[10] The large-scale and involuntary character of these experiments makes it unlikely that they would be sponsored by private sources. Furthermore, although moral problems remain, the bulk of the legal issues arise in a state-sponsored context.

As an analytic matter, at least, social experiments can be said to differ from one other form of policy innovation—so-called demonstration projects.[11] These research projects are evaluated on the basis of less rigorous scientific criteria. They are in some sense challenge grants. The utility of a proposed social policy is evaluated by adopting the innovation in a limited context and observing whether the "demonstration" is an improvement over methodologies used in prior programs. Although such evaluations lack a control group or other criteria of scientific rigor, we will view them as equivalent to social experiments.

The last decade has seen increasing interest in government-sponsored or government-funded planned interventions in the social structure. These interventions were part of the ideology of liberalism—the view that the state has both the capacity and the obligation to improve the lot of its citizens. The "Great Society" and its concomitant war on poverty gave rise to an industry devoted to the evaluation of government-funded social programs (see Anderson and Ball, 1978).[12] Such

[10]In 1977 the federal government had social science research obligations totaling an estimated $383 million. See National Science Foundation (1977:24, 29). Although this figure does not isolate expenditures on randomized social experiments, it does suggest the magnitude of the funding involved.

[11]The Department of Health, Education and Welfare defines an experimental project as one "which introduces a new method or approach in an effort to learn whether it is effective," whereas it defines a demonstration project as one "which extends a successful method or approach to a new local or State agency program [1967: § 8432]." In practice, however, the two concepts are often used interchangeably when administratively convenient. The 1981 regulations state that "some 'demonstration' and 'service' programs may include research activities." 46 Fed. Reg. 8387 (1981). 45 CFR § 46.102(e)(1981).

[12]The exact amount of money funneled into program evaluation is unclear. The growth of evaluation activity is discussed in Orlans (1973:118–126). The "knowledge

evaluation took a number of forms. Most often evaluators studied a program's operations through on-site observation and wrote analytic reports about their experiences. On some occasions, participant observation (Webb, Campbell, Schwartz, and Sechrest, 1966) was used or laboratory experiments undertaken (Bonacich and Light, 1978). All these evaluation methods, however, failed to approximate the scientific rigor of the random clinical trial (RCT), a method by which all variables in an experiment except one are controlled, thus ensuring the validity and comparability of test results.[13] The extension of such methods to the world of social reform was seen as a precursor of the "experimenting society."[14]

Examples of randomized social experiments are numerous (see Conner, 1977; Boruch, McSweeny, and Soderstrom, 1978; see also Reicken and Boruch, 1974:279–325). The negative income tax (Watts, 1969; Orr, Hollister, Lefcowitz, and Hester, 1971; Kershaw, 1972; U.S. Congress, 1978a, 1978b), the health copayment schemes,[15] and the welfare "workfare" studies[16] are among the best known. Many others were undertaken in such areas as juvenile delinquency (see, e.g., Powers and Witmer, 1951; Empey and Rabow, 1961; Empey and Erickson, 1972; Empey and Lubeck, 1972; see also McCorkle, Elias, and Bixby, 1958; and Weeks, 1958), crime prevention (Larson, 1972, 1975; Kelling, Pate, Dieckman, and Brown, 1973), public housing (Buchanan and Heinberg, 1972,[17] and education (Bogatz and Ball, 1971; Cook et al., 1976). Each of these experiments had a number of common denominators: They were planned interventions in the social structure;[18] they used randomized distributions of benefits or burdens; they used control groups

---

market" in the United States is discussed in Biderman and Sharp (1972b). As one commentator has pointed out, "Expenditures for research are, after all, cheaper than those for substantive programs [Orlans, 1976:35]."

[13]It has been argued that the only true form of scientific experiment is the random clinical trial. See Cochran (1972:20–66) and Chalmers (1967), cited in Fried (1974:30). Some intellectual problems with RCTs are raised in Cranberg (1979:1265) and Zelen (1979:1242–1245).

[14]The paradigm of this view can be found in Campbell (1970) and Stapleton (1970).

[15]See reviews of the California experience, in Scitovsky and Snyder (1972), Beck (1974), Brian and Gibbons, (1974), and Hopkins et al. (1975).

[16]Aguoyo v. Richardson, 352 F. Supp. 462 (S.D.N.Y. 1972), modified on other grounds, 473 F.2d 1090 (2d Cir. 1973), stay denied, 410 U.S. 921 (1973), cert. denied, 414 U.S. 1146 (1974).

[17]The political background is discussed in Lynn (1978:341, 366–368).

[18]Although not relevant to this argument, it should be remembered that one rationale for a study may be its use as a strategic device to spur legislative reform that Congress did not want to tackle through the legislative process.

as aids for comparative study; they were based on the belief that social experimentation had a significant role to play in the development of social policy in this country.[19]

The social experiment was the high-water mark of the social scientists' effort to make their work applicable to policy formation. Attempting to convert their discipline from a "soft" to a "hard" science, the social scientists' concern for methodological rigor (based on a belief that such rigor was possible) permeated the enterprise. The application of this methodology to the work of social policy raises a variety of legal and ethical problems.

Legal Regulation of Social Experiments

This section will analyze the legal framework regulating social experiments by government agencies prior to the adoption of the 1981 HHS regulations. It will consider the nature of administrative authority to conduct social experiments and review the effect of the institutional review board process mandated by extant federal regulations. It will trace, as well, congressional efforts to reduce or eliminate restraints on social experiments.

ADMINISTRATIVE AUTHORITY
TO CONDUCT SOCIAL EXPERIMENTS

Administrative agencies derive their authority to conduct social experiments from their enabling statutes. Congress may require particular experiments, as it did by authorizing the secretary of the Department of Housing and Urban Development "to undertake on an experimental basis programs to demonstrate the feasibility of providing housing allowance payments to assist families in meeting rental or home ownership expenses."[20] Congress may also grant administrators general au-

---

[19]An example of the sympathy for experimentation by government, even among organizations generally devoted to individual rights, can be found in a letter of July 3, 1979, from Dan Bradley, then president of the Legal Services Corporation, to Congressman Robert W. Kastenmeier, discussing various bills before Congress to encourage alternate dispute resolution methods. In that letter, Bradley made certain complaints from the perspective of a poverty lawyer about the absence of judicial review provisions in these bills and suggested that "the legislation specifically prohibit funding any grantee whose final decision cannot be reviewed by a court. The only exception would be in situations where controlled experimentation is funded."

[20]12 U.S.C. § 1701z–3(a) (1976).

thorization to waive compliance with statutory rules for general experimental purposes. On occasion, administrators may assert their own waiver authority on an informal, and unrecorded, basis. Administrative authority to carry out social experiments depends on the character of their statutory authorization. Where Congress specifically authorizes an experiment, no legal problems constrain administrative action.[21] Where Congress authorizes an agency to waive otherwise applicable statutory requirements, justification for an experiment depends on the nature and extent of that waiver authority.

Waiver authority may take a number of forms. Agencies may be exempted from generally applicable regulations when "necessary for such [experimental] projects to be conducted."[22] On occasion, specific experiments are not identified, but waiver authority is provided for experiments that further the congressional purposes behind a social program. This is the case with the waiver authority authorizing HHS to conduct social welfare experiments.[23]

The statute implementing the Social Security Act provides a case study of the operation of the waiver provision. The act allows the secretary to waive compliance with a variety of social welfare eligibility and payment criteria as well as with general requirements regarding the content of state Aid for Families with Dependent Children (AFDC) and medical assistance programs. These general requirements could be waived only for "experimental, pilot, or demonstration project(s) which [are] likely to assist in promoting the objectives"[24] of various social welfare programs. Similar waiver provisions are available to other social service agencies.[25]

Promoting legislative objectives is an uncommonly broad standard. Thus, for example, the statutory objectives of the AFDC program proclaim the goal of strengthening family life and the attainment of "maximum self-support and personal independence consistent with the maintenance of continuing parental care."[26] Among the objectives of Title XIX of the Social Security Act is the broad mandate that the act

[21]Except, of course, if the statutory authorization or its application should raise constitutional problems.

[22]7 U.S.C. § 2026(b)(1) (Supp. 1977).

[23]42 U.S.C. § 1315 (1976).

[24]Id.

[25]See, for example, Section 222 of the 1972 amendments to the Social Security Act, 42 U.S.C. § 1395b–1 (1976) (Medicare waivers); see also Food Stamp Program Act, 7 U.S.C. § 2026(b)(1) (Supp. 1977); and Housing Allowance Experiment Act, 12 U.S.C. § 1701z–3(a) 1976).

[26]42 U.S.C. § 601 (1976).

enable "each State, as far as practicable under the conditions in such State, to furnish . . . medical assistance on behalf of families with dependent children and of aged, blind or disabled individuals, whose income and resources are insufficient to meet the costs of necessary medical services."[27] It is not difficult to fit a variety of experimental proposals under such broad rubrics. The waiver provision not only provides for the waiver of statutory requirements but also allows the secretary of HHS to waive that department's own regulations, should he or she determine that doing so would meet a program's broader objectives.[28]

The secretary's waiver authority has been broadly interpreted by the courts. In two cases, *Aguayo v. Richardson*[29] and *California Welfare Rights Organization v. Richardson*,[30] federal courts concluded that they could overturn waiver determinations only where they found them "arbitrary and capricious." In *Aguayo v. Richardson*,[31] New York State set up two experimental work programs for employable welfare recipients receiving AFDC assistance, drawing the subject pool along geographical lines. In one experiment AFDC recipients who were officially declared employable but who could not find private employment were assigned public-sector employment. The second experiment was more complex. Participants were assigned full-time jobs under the Federal Emergency Employment Act and could keep a reasonable portion of their AFDC grant. In the first experiment, noncooperation meant that AFDC assistance was cut off; in the second, AFDC grants were reduced by $60 a month. The California case concerned an attempt to study whether participant copayment in a Medicaid health scheme would reduce utilization without affecting the health of participants (Scitovsky and Snyder, 1972; Beck, 1974; Brian and Gibbens, 1974; Hopkins *et al.*, 1975) The experiment was based on the hypothesis that Medicaid participants enjoying a "free ride" would tend to

---

[27]42 U.S.C. § 1396 (1976).

[28]Provisions of the following statutes can be waived by the secretary of HEW under 42 U.S.C. § 1315 (1976): 42 U.S.C. § 302 (1976) (state old-age and medical assistance plan); 42 U.S.C. § 602 (1976) (state plans for aid and services to needy families with children); 42 U.S.C. § 802 (1976) (state plans for services to aged, blind, or disabled); 42 U.S.C. § 1202 (1976) (state plans for aid to blind); 42 U.S.C. § 1352 (1976) (state plans for aid to permanently and totally disabled); 42 U.S.C. § 1382 (1976) (eligibility for benefits—definition of eligible individual); 42 U.S.C. § 1396a (1976) (state plans for medical assistance—reports); 42 U.S.C. § 1397c (1976) (services program planning).

[29]352 F. Supp. 462 (S.D.N.Y. 1972), *modified on other grounds*, 473 F.2d 1090 (1973), *stay denied*, 410 U.S. 921, (1973), *cert. denied* 414 U.S. 1146 (1974).

[30]348 F. Supp. 491 (N.D. Cal. 1972).

[31]*Supra* note 28.

overutilize the system. Selected patients had to pay $1 per visit to a physician and $1.50 per prescription up to a maximum cost of $3 per month for each patient. The proposal contradicted a clear policy in the Social Security Act banning the imposition of copayments on the categorically needy.[32]

Both examples of social experimentation were sustained by federal courts after attacks on constitutional and statutory grounds. In both instances, the government argued that its Section 1315 waiver authority allowed the secretary of the then Department of Health, Education and Welfare (HEW) to authorize projects that departed from otherwise applicable guidelines. These arguments prevailed against the view that it was not an objective of AFDC to make recipients work and that medical copayment requirements for the impoverished violated statutory requirements that charges for services bear a relation to ability to pay. In both cases, the experiments were for a limited duration only and were undertaken to improve the administration of the welfare programs of which they were a part. Thus, in this age of fiscal constraint, cost-effectiveness was deemed a permissible rationale for subjecting the poor to social experimentation.

Both the California and New York courts rejected a number of procedural attacks on these experiments. In *Aguayo v. Richardson* plaintiffs argued that the workfare experiment might adversely affect specific recipients and that the program's "objectives" did not encompass such impositions.[33] The district court, however, determined that slight increases in the weekly expenditures of workfare recipients were valid because "the program may ultimately lead to the removal of recipients from the welfare rolls and thus serve the objectives of the Social Security Act despite any short-term detriment to recipients participating in the project."[34] Whatever the state's *motivation*, the proposed experiment is acceptable if it promotes the act's objectives. The state may wish to save money, yet if that intention results in a proposal that will also serve legitimate objectives of the program, waiver is permissible. This is true, even if the cost of fiscal economy is that "another objective will suffer."[35]

Programmatic objectives are legislative statements of purpose often placed in legislation as part of the boiler plate of statutory draftsman-

[32]Social Security Act Amendments of 1965, Pub. L. No. 89–97, § 1902(a)(14), 79 Stat. 346.
[33]352 F. Supp. at 470.
[34]*Id.* at 470.
[35]*Id.* at 470.

ship. Often "open textured," they are amenable to a wide range of interpretations. Cognizant of this, courts have often shifted the responsibility of specifying and balancing legislative objectives to the administrator. In this sense, Congress entrusted the underlying judgment of whether an experiment serves programmatic objectives to the secretary and not to the courts, thus leaving only a narrow scope for judicial review.

The probable success or failure of an experiment does not impair its status as a Section 1315 experiment. The Senate report on the 1967 Social Security Act Amendments recognized that "not all [Section 1315] demonstrations will be successful."[36] The *California Welfare Rights Organization (CWRO) v. Richardson* court concurred, noting that "it is possible that the Secretary could reasonably conclude that a project was likely to assist in promoting the objectives, only to discover at the completion of the project that nothing of the sort . . . was accomplished."[37]

Even the fact that the *CWRO* copayment scheme suffered "from numerous defects when judged against a scientific model" did not require that approval of the project be withheld.[38] Conflating experiments, demonstration projects, and innovative reform proposals under the same rubric, the California court noted that "'experiment' must be understood as a trial conducted for the purpose of testing a proposition. The Secretary cannot be held to standards of scientific precision in that testing process."[39]

REGULATING SOCIAL EXPERIMENTS THROUGH
INSTITUTIONAL REVIEW BOARDS

Judicial deference to administrative use of waiver authority for social experiments vested practical control of such experiments in the agency funding the research. This lack of external review contrasted sharply with the regulatory approach used to protect human subjects in experiments at institutions that received HEW (now HHS) funding.

The 1974 HEW regulations required research institutions receiving HEW funds to establish local institutional review boards (IRBs) to en-

---

[36]S. Rep. No. 744, 90th Cong., reprinted in *U.S. Code Cong. & Ad. News*, 2834, 3006 (1967).

[37]348 F. Supp. at 497.

[38]*Id.* at 498.

[39]*Id.* at 498. Note that this may be an idiosyncratic definition of an experiment.

sure that experiments funded by the department protect the rights of participating subjects.[40] The IRBs ensured some form of peer review and provided some semblance of lay input into the review of research protocols. Although the extent to which IRBs have affected the content of research is unclear, the boards have permanently changed the procedures for doing research (see Gray and Cooke, 1980).

In 1975, the waiver provision of the Social Security Act provided the occasion for an analysis of the relationship between the HEW regulations and social experiments. In an attempt to devise mechanisms that would reduce the state's Medicaid bills, Georgia proposed a copayment experiment that would require Medicaid recipients to help pay for three mandatory services under the Georgia Medicaid program: physician, outpatient, and inpatient hospital services. Copayments of $2 would be required for office or outpatient visits, and copayments of $5 to $25 would be required for various inpatient hospital services.[41] Although it covered a wider range of services, the Georgia scheme was, in many respects, similar to the California copayment proposal approved in *California Welfare Rights Organization v. Richardson*.[42] However, the Georgia scheme involved the Medicaid population of the entire state. It did not use a control group but instead tested the state's past performance against the new scheme.

In *Crane v. Mathews*[43] Georgia Medicaid patients filed suit to prevent the experiment, arguing that the Georgia copayment scheme was "not a valid experiment under 42 U.S.C. Section 1315" because of its failure to "pass muster under . . . generally accepted experimental standards."[44] They contended that "the articulated purpose (of the 'experiment') was to save the state money and not to promote health care of low-income citizens."[45] This argument was no more successful here than in *California Welfare Rights Organization v. Richardson*. Upholding the secretary's decision to issue a Section 1315 waiver, the

---

[40]45 C.F.R. § 46.102 (1974) (superseded by 46 Fed. Reg. 8387, to be codified at 45 C.F.R. § 46.103(b) (1981)). The development of the review board concept is discussed in Barber, Lally, Makarushka, and Sullivan (1973:145–148).

[41]Exemptions were provided for vital health services and for preventive care. Where numerous visits were necessary, copayment moneys would be refunded. See "The Georgia Section 1315 Waiver Application," in Mullen (1976:259–261).

[42]348 F. Supp. 491 (N.D. Cal. 1972).

[43]417 F. Supp. 532 (N.D. Ga. 1976).

[44]Plaintiffs' Brief in Support of Their Motion for a Temporary Restraining Order at 6, Crane v. Mathews, 417 F. Supp. 532 (N.D. Ga. 1976).

[45]*Id.* at 5.

district court stated that "[i]n the absence of any clear abuses of discretion by the Secretary, the Court will not disturb defendant Mathews' decision in this matter."[46] In their pretrial brief, however, plaintiffs advanced a novel and more successful theory.[47] They contended that even if the copayment scheme were a legitimate Section 1315 experiment, participants were experimental "subjects at risk" within the meaning of the HEW regulations.[48] Therefore, they claimed, the secretary had abused his discretion by granting a Section 1315 waiver before it had been approved by a local IRB.

HEW argued that the social experiment did not involve "human subjects" and was not subject to IRB approval.[49] In HEW's view, counting a controlled copayment trial as an experiment would mean that all social reform policies that do not affect the entire population—for example, busing and affirmative action—would fall within the constraints of the regulations concerning experimentation.[50] The department argued that a program classified as a Section 1315 project was by definition a demonstration program and not a "social experiment." In rejecting the government's position, the court found that the Georgia experiment did involve the participants as "human subjects" in that they were "deliberately and personally imposed upon."[51] It determined that the participants were placed at risk since they were "exposed to some method that is not standard and accepted in meeting the individual's needs."[52] Having determined that human subjects were involved, the federal court required the research protocol to be approved by an IRB.

Enter the Georgia Department of Human Resources Research Review

---

[46]417 F. Supp. at 543 (N.D. Ga. 1976).

[47]Plaintiffs' Pre-Trial Brief, Crane v. Mathews, 417 F. Supp. 532 (N.D. Ga. 1976).

[48]This contention was apparently an afterthought on the part of the plaintiffs. They moved to amend their complaint to include the new theory only 6 days before the commencement of the trial. See Federal Defendant's Memorandum in Opposition to Plaintiff's Second Motion to Amend at 102, Crane v. Mathews, 417 F. Supp. 532 (N.D. Ga. 1976).

[49]The department conceded, however, that one aspect of the project—the surveying of physicians and patients as to the effects of copayment—did involve "human subjects" and was required to be submitted to the IRB. Secretary of HEW, Memorandum, "Application of the Departmental Regulation on Protection of Human Subjects (45 C.F.R. Part 46) to the Georgia Medicaid Co-Payment Project," March 22, 1976, p. 1 (hereinafter Secretary's Memo); Crane v. Mathews, 417 F. Supp. at 546.

[50]Secretary's Memo at 15.

[51]417 F. Supp. at 546. This definition of "human subjects" was offered by Donald Chalkley, director of HEW's Office for Protection from Research Risks. Testimony of Donald Chalkley tr. at 9, Crane v. Mathews (hereinafter Chalkley Testimony).

[52]*Id.* at 547.

Board, which determined that the "imposition of co-payment places human subjects at risk"[53] since, as the district court stated, "requiring a co-payment exposes these individuals to a method which is not standard or accepted in meeting their needs."[54] Rather than considering whether the proposed treatment differed from that of "the experience of the average American in his daily life," the IRB compared the recipients' positions before and after the proposed experiment.[55] Since the Georgia copayment requirement might inhibit a patient from seeking medical care, "such a person may be exposed to the possibility of serious illness, disability or death."[56] The risk to which subjects were placed, it must be stressed, was the risk of not getting needed medical care, and not the risk of financial injury resulting from the proposed copayment. Whether such financial injury was de minimus was not considered.

The board also determined that the risks associated with the copayment project outweighed the benefits that might be derived from the project[57] in that "[t]he project design was judged so seriously inadequate that it would be very unlikely to provide any accurate or reliable information upon which to base policy decisions regarding Medicaid co-payments."[58] Thus, a project based on a flawed design must fail the test of risk–benefit comparison because it cannot provide scientifically legitimate knowledge.

Merely to state this determination is to suggest the difficulty with the underlying reasoning. A social experiment may or may not use a

[53]R. J. Bent, Chair, "Clarification Statement Regarding the Georgia Department of Human Resources Research Review Board's Review of the Proposal Entitled 'Recipient Cost—Participation in Medicare Reform,'" undated, p. 5 (hereinafter Clarification Statement). Note that the 1974 regulations defined "subject at risk" as any individual who may be exposed to the possibility of injury, including physical, psychological, or social injury, as a consequence of participation as a subject in any research, development, or related activity that departs from the application of those established and accepted methods necessary to meet his or her needs, or that increases the ordinary risks of daily life, including the recognized risks inherent in a chosen occupation or field of service. 45 C.F.R. § 46.103(b) (1974) (superseded by 46 Fed. Reg. 8387, to be codified at 45 C.F.R. § 46.102(f), (g) (1981)).

[54]417 F. Supp. at 546. This definition of human subject was also offered by Chalkley, Chalkley Testimony at 54–55, but the court found it more "akin to the meaning of 'subject at risk'." 417 F. Supp. at 546.

[55]Secretary's Memo at 17.

[56]Clarification Statement at 5.

[57]Since this finding was sufficient to render the experiment unacceptable under the the HEW regulations, the board apparently found it unnecessary to consider the issue of the protection of a subject's rights and informed consent.

[58]Clarification Statement at 5.

rigorous scientific methodology. As the CWRO court recognized, loose modeling in the area of demonstration projects may be necessary when studying a large group of citizens.[59] Such studies can provide suggestive solutions, even if these do not qualify as "scientific truth." The demonstration projects approved under Section 1315 waiver authority rarely met standards of strict methodological rigor. Yet an imperfect experimental methodology or flawed research design would prove fatal to its legitimacy under HEW regulations. This tension between Section 1315 and the HEW regulations, although usually submerged, became crucial in the Crane case. Opponents of the experiment argued that "proof of the experiment's scientific validity would seem to be a minimum requirement if due process is to play any part in deciding about social policy experiments [Capron, 1975:152]." Thus, it is the business of administrators, if not of courts,[60] to ensure that a social experiment has scientific rigor.[61] Scientific rigor, it is argued, is important for a variety of reasons. If an experiment is methodologically flawed, it will fail to add to our "public knowledge," no matter how much it reinforces our private experiential truths. Such a flawed experiment is unlikely to pass a risk–benefit test.

After the Georgia court had committed the copayment scheme to IRB review, but before the review board's decision, HEW, in an effort to articulate its view of what kinds of experiments should be subject to IRB review, published the "Secretary's Interpretation of 'Subject at Risk.'"[62] Because the district court had already found the Georgia scheme to be experimental, this interpretation played almost no role in the case. HEW defined "subject at risk" in its regulations as including:

> any individual who may be exposed to the possibility of injury, including physical, psychological or social injury, as a consequence of participation as a subject, in any research development, or related activity which departs from the application of those established and accepted methods necessary to meet his needs, or which increase the ordinary risks of daily life, including the recognized risks inherent in a chosen occupation or field of service.[63]

[59]348 F. Supp. at 498.

[60]Capron (1975:152) criticizes Judge Friendly in Aguoyo v. Richardson, 473 F.2d at 1109, for assuming that the state's experimental purpose was "suitably furthered" by the proposed experiment without seeking or receiving evidence as to the scientific methodology employed.

[61]The fact is that "in the medical model" many IRBs refuse to review scientific methodology, claiming that to do so would be a violation of academic freedom.

[62]Secretary's Interpretation of "Subject at Risk," 41 Fed. Reg. 26,572–73 (June 28, 1976).

[63]45 C.F.R. § 46.103b (1974) (superseded by 46 Fed. Reg. 8387, to be codified at 45 C.F.R. § 46.102(f), (g) (1981)).

The operative phrases are research strategies that depart from *estab-lished and accepted methods* thus *increasing the ordinary risks of daily life.*

> Because, basically, what is being done as we see it is an application of standard and accepted—is an extension of standard and accepted medical care to recipients under the co-payment plan. These are not research meth-ods of medical care. They are standard and accepted medical procedures. The only distinction that is being made is the fiscal arrangements, and fiscal risks are not considered to be risks within the meaning of the regulations. And the question of consent with regard to acceptance of risks which are admittedly inherent in the day-to-day administration of medical care any-way is provided here through essentially the consent of the Government in the selection of their representatives and department of the Executive Branch of the Georgia Government.[64]

The attempted conflation of social reform and social experiments into the same rubric neglects the differences in administrative "intent" that are vital to an understanding of the concepts of "subject" and "risk." In the case of reform, the government chooses a new course in the belief that it is the most efficacious for the policy. In experimentation, the government's research staff will suspend belief as to which option is most efficacious until the "returns" are in.

HEW's position was that the regulations "were not, and have never been intended to protect individuals against the effects of research and development activities directed at social or economic changes, even though those changes might have an impact upon the individual."[65] To stress the point, HEW specifically stated that the regulations were not designed to "protect against possible financial injury" that may result from alteration in the pricing or conditions of eligibility of a govern-ment program. More specifically, copayment or workfare schemes did "not constitute burdens or effects of the nature that the regulations are intended to encompass."[66]

HEW's explanatory gloss cannot be supported by the 1974 regulatory language. The department asserted that exposing persons to the "range of experience of the average American in his daily life" does not place persons at risk. On this view, a hemophiliac subjected to the possibility of a nosebleed is exposed to no greater risk than the average American. The Chicago woman given a placebo instead of a birth control pill is not exposed to unique risks (Bok, 1978:67). This "average risk" theory is clearly incorrect. Individuals on welfare who are forced by an experi-

---

[64]See Chalkley Testimony at 25–26.
[65]41 Fed. Reg. at 26,572.
[66]Id. at 26,573.

ment to work for their welfare checks are in one sense being asked to suffer the same daily indignities as the average American. Still, if they are among the numerous welfare clients with physical or psychological difficulties in responding to the work milieu, they are especially injured. Section 46.104 speaks of increasing the ordinary risks of daily life as the condition triggering IRB reviews. By this it means the daily life of the subject as it would have been without the experiment, not the daily life of the average American. The HEW position fails as a defensible reading of the text because it ignores risks to concrete individuals that may be caused by governmental intervention.

In any event, the secretary's interpretative statement of policy did not establish a binding norm for the courts. Although the distinction between substantive interpretative rules is "fuzzy at best,"[67] an interpretative rule is

> not finally determinative of the issues or rights to which it is addressed. The agency cannot apply or rely upon a general statement of policy as law because a general statement of policy only announces what the agency seeks to establish as policy. A policy statement announces the agency's tentative intentions for the future.[68]

Although deference is always given to an agency's expertise in interpreting its own operative statute, such a regulatory gloss is not dispositive. As one court has suggested, "Although the agency's expertise and experience cannot be ignored, the reviewing court has some leeway to assess the underlying wisdom of the policy and need not affirm a general statement of policy that merely satisfies the test of reasonableness."[69]

Legislative Attempts to Deregulate Social Experiments

Early commentators on *Crane* believed that the decision would result in the termination of those social experiments authorized by Section 1315 waiver provisions.[70] However, the requirement that an IRB

---

[67]National Nutrition Foods Association v. Weinberger, 376 F. Supp. 142, 146 n. 6 (S.D.N.Y. 1974).

[68]Pacific Gas & Electric Company v. Federal Power Commission, 506 F.2d 33, 38 (D.C. Cir., 1974).

[69]*Id.* at 40.

[70]"Future benefit-reducing experiments may prove infeasible," Galblum (1978:375, 382).

approve a Section 1315 experiment changed neither the number of waivers applied for nor granted.[71] Still, when possible, HEW used experimental authority other than Section 1315.[72] Congressional unhappiness with this situation was expressed in the Social Security Act Amendment of 1977,[73] which authorized a state, subject to the secretary's disapproval, to grant a Section 1315 waiver[74] for certain types of demonstration projects related to the AFDC program. By failing to disapprove a waiver determination, HEW allowed it to proceed.[75] The amended language refers specifically to "demonstration projects,"[76] whereas the prior language referred to "experimental, pilot or demonstration projects,"[77] not distinguishing between them. By suggesting

[71]Conversation with Joseph Marches, Office for Protection from Research Risks, National Institute of Health. HEW claims that it keeps no statistics on the number of waivers granted by the secretary so that only impressionistic evidence as to the impact of Crane is available.

[72]In the period between 1972 and 1977, eight Section 222 projects were approved and funded by HEW. See HEW (1977:1). Most proposals were initiated in response to an Request for Proposal (RFP) published in September 1975 requesting proposals in 10 or 11 "priority areas" developed by HEW. See conversation with David Smith, assistant general counsel, HEW. Unsolicited proposals may also be made. No statistics exist as to the number of Section 222 waivers that have been requested. This lacunae may result from the secretary's failure to delegate authority under Section 222 to grant waivers; see U.S. Congress, House (1977:88) and Memorandum on Delegation Authority in id. at 108, which may have resulted in a failure of established lines of authority to be exercised. Id. at 84.

[73]Social Security Act Amendments of 1977; Pub. L. No. 95–216, § 404, 91 Stat. 1562 (codified at 42 U.S.C. § 1315 (Supp. 1977)). The amendment is discussed in S. Rep. No. 612, 95th Cong., 1st Sess. (1977), reprinted in 1977 U.S. Code Cong. & Ad. News 4155, 4322. H.R. 9346 contained no such provision. The Senate amended H.R. 9346, and Congress passed the Social Security Amendments of 1977. Pub. L. No. 95–216, 91 Stat. 1562 (codified at 42 U.S.C. § 1315(b)(2)(A) (Supp. 1977)).

[74]42 U.S.C. § 1315(b)(3) (Supp. 1977).

[75]A state may conduct three such demonstration projects, only one of which may be conducted on a statewide basis. 42 U.S.C. § 1315(b)(1) (Supp. 1977). States must provide public notice of a proposed waiver and invite comments thereon. Id. § 1315(b)(3)(A) (Supp. 1977).

[76]Social Security Amendments of 1962, 41 U.S.C. § 1315 (1962).

[77]The HEW handbook appears to use the term interchangeably, defining the group as follows:

> The basic purpose of experimental, pilot and demonstration projects in the public assistance programs under Section 1115 [42 U.S.C. § 1315] of the Social Security Act is to develop and improve the methods and techniques of administering assistance and related services designed to help needy persons achieve self-support or self-care, or to maintain and strengthen family life [HEW, 1967: Part IV, sec. 8, p. 8431].

Note that "Cooperative Research on Demonstration Projects," 42 U.S.C. § 1310, fails to provide a definition.

that the waiver provision applied only to demonstration projects the statute may have hoped to avoid, by verbal legerdemain, the consequences of *Crane*.[78] Even so, amended Section 1315 gave neither the secretary nor the states power to waive any IRB review requirements notwithstanding the secretary's interpretative gloss on human subject regulations. Innovations considered as "demonstrations" by states could still be classified as "experiments" by courts. More drastic revision was urged in the health care area. Responding directly to *Crane*[79] and spurred by a concern to contain federal spending,[80] legislation to exempt Medicare and Medicaid cost experimentation from IRB review was introduced in the 95th Congress.[81] The proposed exemption was part of a broader Medicare and Medicaid reform act, which passed the Senate[82] but failed to be voted out of conference.

The waiver issue has been raised in another context—an analysis of the secretary's power to initiate experimental health financing programs under the authority of 42 U.S.C. Section 1395.[83] Under this statute, the secretary is authorized to develop and engage in experiments and demonstration projects to determine whether changes in the Medicare reimbursement rates to hospitals could be structured to increase "the efficiency and economy of health services . . . without adversely affecting the quality of such services."[84] In particular, the statute allows the secretary to develop negotiated rates to be paid to "intermediaries," such as Blue Cross programs, for services rendered to patients. An analogous section of the Social Security Act Amendments of 1972 authorizes the secretary to develop prospective payment schemes for a variety of health care providers, including hospitals, in order to stimulate such providers through positive (or negative) financial incentives to use their facilities and personnel more efficiently and thereby reduce the total costs of health programs involved without

[78]Crane v. Mathews, 417 F. Supp. 532 (N.D. Ga. 1978).

[79]See S. Rep. No. 111, 95th Cong. 2d Sess., at 24 (Report to accompany H.R. 5285) (August 11, 1978).

[80]Medicare–Medicaid Administrative and Reimbursement Reform Act, H.R. 5285, 95th Cong., 2d Sess. at 9 (1978).

[81]S. 1470, 95th Cong., 1st Sess. § 43 at p. 66 (1977).

[82]124 *Cong. Rec.* 36079 (1978). Attempts were made to limit the reach of the exemption. Thus, Senator Edward Kennedy amended the bill to require that the secretary, when approving a waiver application, "apply any appropriate requirements" of the human experimentation regulations, including IRB approval, "in making his decision on whether to approve such application." 95th Cong., 2d Sess., 124 *Cong. Rec.* 36079 (1978). See also H.R. 934, 96th Cong. 1st Sess. § 263 (1974), for a later effort to create a special exemption for Medicare and Medicaid.

[83]See 42 U.S.C. §§ 1395b–1, 1395f (1976).

[84]*Id.* at (a)(A).

adversely affecting the quality of care.[85] The point of these experiments, of course, is cost containment of the health care system.

A number of challenges to the secretary's experimental authority were made by Medicare intermediaries, such as Blue Cross, who argued that hospitals should not be coerced into participating in an experimental program (Powers, 1980). These challenges were largely rejected[86] on statutory-interpretation grounds, suggesting that the statute authorizing experimental programs by its very nature overrides statutes detailing programmatic procedures.[87] One court that did reject the secretary's experimental authority, *Blue Cross Association v. Harris*,[88] found that Section 1315 experiment authority does not "authorize noncompliance" with the "statutory right of [health care] providers to choose their own intermediaries."[89] The *Blue Cross v. Harris* reasoning implicitly rejects the entire concept of experimentation (in the reimbursement system at least), arguing that experimental authority cannot be used to override statutory entitlements. If such a position were sustained it would undermine all experimental programs in the context of statutory entitlements.

Administrative Efforts at Deregulation:
The New Health and Human Services Rules
and Randomized Social Experiments

The social science community reacted bitterly to the application of HEW regulations to social science research. Having largely ignored the

---

[85]See 42 U.S.C. 1395b–1 (1976).

[86]See Blue Cross Association v. Califano, 473 F. Supp. 1047 (W.D. Md. 1979); Health Care Service Corporation. v. Califano, 466 F. Supp. 1190 (N.D. Ill. 1979); Blue Cross Association v. Harris, 622 F.2d 972 (8th Cir. 1980). See also the discussion of 42 U.S.C. § 1395b–1 in Daughters of Miriam Center for the Aged v. Mathews, 590 F.2d 1250 (3d Cir. 1978); Rhode Island Hospital v. Califano, 447 F. Supp. 703 (D.R.I. 1978); American Medical Association v. Mathews, 429 F. Supp. 1179 (N.D. Ill. 1977).

[87]Judge Collincon of the Northern District of Illinois resolved this conflict problem in Blue Cross Association v. Califano, *supra* note 85, by developing a reasonable accommodation between the procedure for selecting intermediaries, 42 U.S.C. § 1395h, and the statutory warrant for experimentation, 42 U.S.C. 1395b–1. He decided that the hospitals should be given the opportunity to nominate the intermediaries and the secretary be required to allow them the right of first refusal to a fixed price bid. Only if the nominees reject the bid can the secretary then utilize an open bidding procedure and include nonnominees.

[88]622 F.2d 972 (8th Cir. 1980).

[89]*Id.* at 976–977.

regulation-drafting process in 1974, social scientists produced numerous suggestions for revision, claiming that the 1974 regulations had a debilitating effect on social science research and were, in part, unconstitutional (see, e.g., de Sola Pool, 1980:57, 60–61; Pattulo, 1980:1). The 1979 proposed revisions to the HEW regulations[90] served to remove a significant amount of social research from the reach of the regulatory process. Thus, proposed Section 46.101(C) (1) exempted

> research designed to study on a large scale:
> (A) the effects of proposed social or economic change, or
> (B) methods or systems for the delivery of or payment for social or
>   health services[91]

from the jurisdiction of IRBs. A further proposal insulated "research conducted in established or commonly accepted educational settings, involving normal educational practices" from IRB review.[92] Other types of social science research, including natural observation and deception research, were also exempted.[93]

Unlike exemptions for other categories of social science research, the proposed exemptions for social experiments was total. Thus, the 1979 proposed regulations allowed an IRB to waive the requirements for documentation or informed consent if it found that "the research presents no more than minimal risk of harm to subjects and involves no procedures for which written consent is normally required outside of the research context."[94] "Expedited review procedures" were proposed to handle experiments requiring the routine collection of hair, nail clippings, or excretia.[95] Modification of standard informed consent requirements was proposed for deception experiments if the IRB found that "the research could not reasonably be carried out without the withholding or alteration" of consent and such withholding or altering "will not materially affect the ability of the subject to assess the harm or discomfort of the research."[96] These proposed modifications reflected an effort to balance a variety of risks and benefits to subjects, the research community, and society. The proposed total exemption for

---

[90]44 Fed. Reg. 47,688 (1979).

[91]See 44 Fed. Reg. 46,692 (1979). The proposed regulations list two alternative sets of exemptions. The exemption cited in the text would be operative if either of the alternative lists of exemptions is approved.

[92]44 Fed. Reg. 47,692 (1979).

[93]Id.

[94]Id. at 47,697 (1979).

[95]Id. at 47,696 (1979).

[96]Id. at 47,697 (1979).

large-scale social experiments, however, was a rejection of the need for balancing; it was an implicit claim that social experiments, unlike other kinds of social research, raised no ethical problems whatsoever that require external review.[97] The limitation of the total exemption to large-scale studies was seen as a response to congressional concern that IRB review was frustrating cost-cutting experiments in health and welfare services.[98] Even so, if social experiments were harmless per se, research on individuals and "little men" should be exempt as well (de Sola Pool, 1979:452, 454–455).

One explanation for the special exemption for large-scale studies might be found in the possible parallel between the experimental testing of public policy innovations and the historical interest of government in piecemeal reform. One might argue that restrictions on experiments require, at a theoretical level, equivalent restrictions on proposed reforms that lack scientific control groups. However, this point was nowhere explored.

The final HHS regulations promulgated in 1981 do not contain the total exemption for large-scale social experiments found in the 1979 proposals. Rejecting the demand for total exemption, HHS found that "IRB review of studies of federal, state, or local benefit or service programs is appropriate even where it may be impracticable to obtain the informed consent of the subject."[99] In such cases it would prefer review, allowing the IRB to waive some or all consent requirements. This shift in regulatory philosophy is surprising, given that the 1981 regulations represent a shift toward the deregulation of research, particularly social science research. The final regulations cover only research funded by HHS and not all research at an institution receiving HHS funds.[100] An expedited review procedure was developed.[101] Categories of presumptively low-risk research are exempt from all review including:

> 1. Research conducted in educational settings on commonly accepted educational practices such as institutional strategies and techniques, curricula, or classroom management methods

[97]This claim may go too far. One may argue that social experiments are particularly ill-suited to external review and that the relevant ethical issues can be best resolved by researchers and project administrators themselves. This is tantamount to arguing that although social experiments should be governed by ethical principles, such principles should not be translated into legal regulations.

[98]This point is well made by de Sola Pool (1979:452, 454–455).

[99]46 Fed. Reg. 8383 (1981).

[100]Id. at 8386 (1981) (to be codified at 45 C.F.R. § 46.101(a)).

[101]Id. at 8389 (1981) (to be codified at 45 C.F.R. § 46.110). A list of categories of research activities subject to expedited review procedures can be found at id. at 8392 (1981).

2. Research involving the use of educational tests, if identifiers cannot be linked to subjects
3. Survey or interview research and research involving observation (including participant-observation) of public behavior, except where the subject may be identified and the data pertain to sensitive subject behavior (such as illegal conduct, drug or alcohol use, or sexual behavior), or where the subjects' responses, if they became known outside the research, could place the subjects at risk of criminal or civil liability or be damaging to their financial standing or employability
4. Studies using existing data, documents, records, and pathological or diagnostic specimens, if these materials are publicly available or if the data will not be recorded in a manner that would allow linkage with individuals.[102]

As important, research subject to IRB review under the 1981 regulations may be approved without full informed consent requirements.[103] This flexibility offered the IRB, coupled with the reduction in the IRB's jurisdictional reach, means that "this set of regulations is as suitable as any social researchers could have hoped to receive from the government."[104] Whether this judgment will carry over to the specific area of social experiments will depend, in large part, on the way in which individual IRBs implement the 1981 regulations.

The Structure of Regulations

If decisions concerning the ethics of research ought not be left to researchers themselves, alternative regulatory strategies need to be considered. One such strategy calls for the use of internal review mechanisms by a funding agency. A second strategy would require some form of external review. Internal review strategies generally leave final approval of ethical concerns to the funding agency, believing the agency's interest and expertise in both technical and ethical issues to be equivalent. On some versions of this strategy the government bureaucracy has unfettered approval authority. Other versions attempt to structure the government's internal review process. Exempting social experi-

---

[102]Id. at 8386 (1981) (to be codified at 45 C.F.R. § 46.116(b)).

[103]Id. at 8390 (1981) (to be codified at 45 C.F.R. § 46.116(c)–(d)).

[104]"Response to the 'Final Regulations Amending Basic Policy for the Protection of Human Subject Research,'" memorandum from Murray L. Wax to Judith Jarvis Thomson, chairperson, American Association of University Professors Committee on Institutional Review Boards, February 23, 1981, p. 1.

mentation from IRB review is an implicit acceptance of an internal review approach.

Thus, the Senate version of the Social Security Disability Amendments of 1980 contained provisions that authorized waiver of IRB review for cost-cutting health experiments.[105] Although these provisions were not included in the act as passed, they suggest one approach to the problem of citing ethical review. Under the Senate proposal, the secretary of HHS, although freed from the fetters of IRB review, was still directed to follow IRB standards in approving or disapproving experiments. An agency would be required to determine whether all subjects had provided informed consent to a proposed social experiment and to undertake the equivalent of IRB review of the risks and benefits in a proposed experiment. Even under internal review structures the problem of regulatory standards must be faced.

Although the final version of the 1980 amendments allowed the secretary to waive IRB review, significant statutory controls were placed on cost-cutting social experiments. The act required that:

> (2) With respect to the participation of recipients of supplemental security income benefits in experimental, pilot, or demonstration projects under this subsection—
>
> (A) the Secretary is not authorized to carry out any project that would result in a substantial reduction in any individual's total income and resources as a result of his or her participation in the project;
>
> (B) the Secretary may not require any individual to participate in a project; and he shall assure (i) that the voluntary participation of individuals in any project is obtained through informed written consent which satisfies the requirements for informed consent established by the Secretary for use in any experimental, pilot, or demonstration project in which human subjects are at risk, and (ii) that any individual's voluntary agreement to participate in any project may be revoked by such individual at any time;
>
> (C) the Secretary shall, to the extent feasible and appropriate, include recipients who are under age 18 as well as adult recipients; and
>
> (D) the Secretary shall include in the projects carried out under this section such experimental, pilot, or demonstration projects as may be necessary to ascertain the feasibility of treating alcoholics and drug addicts to prevent the onset of irreversible medical conditions which may result in permanent disability, including programs in residential care treatment centers.[106]

---

[105]H.R. 3236, 96th Cong. 2d Sess. § 505(c) (1980). The Senate version is discussed in S. Rep. No. 408, 96th Cong. 2d Sess. (1979), reprinted in *U.S. Code Cong. & Ad. News* 1277, 1361 (1980).

[106]42 U.S.C. § 1310(b)(2) (Supp. 1980). The deletion of the Senate version in conference is discussed in H.R. Rep. 944, 96th Cong., 2d Sess. (to accompany H.R. 3236), cited in *U.S. Code Cong. & Ad. News* 1392, 1429 (1980).

An alternate mode of internal review is the review process developed in the 1972 amendments to the Medicare provisions of the Social Security Act for various cost-cutting experiments under Medicare. The statute requires that:

> No experiment or demonstration project shall be engaged in or developed . . . until the Secretary obtains the advice and recommendations of specialists who are competent to evaluate the proposed experiment or demonstration project as to the soundness of its objectives, the possibilities of securing productive results, the adequacy of resources to conduct it, and its relationship to other similar experiments and projects already completed or in process.[107]

The purpose of this restriction is to ensure that the proposed experiments are not duplicative and are scientifically sound. It is argued that such advice would "assure that [the suggested] procedures do not cut back on services necessary to quality care."[108] The statutory language does not include provision for an ethical critique of a proposed experiment. Still, the requirement of demonstrated outside consultation is a basic starting point for assuring ethical review.

Internal review strategies allow only one mechanism for review of agency decisions regarding social experimentation—some form of judicial review. The standard of such review is likely to be permissive. Existing judicial deference to agency decisions does not allow the judiciary to analyze research design, the nature of the knowledge to be gained, or the character of the risks involved. As a practical matter, internal review mechanisms vest decision-making power regarding experimental ethics on the very parties sponsoring the experiments. This conflation of roles makes it likely that less than appropriate weight will be given to such ethical considerations as the nature and necessity of the burdens to which subjects will be placed, the indirect effects of the experiment on the general population, or the possibility of alternative means of obtaining the information necessitating the experiment. The structural bias toward policy formulation inherent in internal review mechanisms suggests the need for an effective external review mechanism.

The alternative is to require some form of external check on agency decisions. In the 1972 Medicare amendments, Congress was not pre-

---

[107]42 U.S.C. § 1395b–1(b) (1976).

[108]H.R. Rep. No. 1, 92d Cong., 2d Sess. (1972), reprinted in 3 U.S. Code Cong. & Ad. News 4989, 5087 (1972).

pared to leave its internal review apparatus solely to HEW. As a minimal form of external monitoring, it required that:

> No such experiment or project shall be actually placed in operation unless at least 30 days prior thereto a written report, prepared for the purposes of notification and information only, containing a full and complete description thereof has been transmitted to the Committee on Ways and Means of the House of Representatives and to the Committee on Finance of the Senate.[109]

Congress need only be notified of the secretary's decision. It lacks the power to veto any proposed HEW experiment.[110] Such exposure, like sunlight, is often the best disinfectant (Brandeis, 1933:62). Still, it is unlikely that the congressional scrutiny of individual projects will be rigorous or systematic.[111]

The conventional form of external review, of course, is the IRB. This approach is used for all federally funded research except research specifically exempted under the 1981 regulations. The rationale for such review need not be rehearsed here. The 1981 regulations do, however, articulate a third option—the use by an IRB of a variety of standards for research review and of different regulatory procedures, depending on the form of research and the nature of the risk involved. These regulations recognize the special characteristics of the social experiment as a form of applied research. They do so by allowing for modification of the traditional requirement that experiments must secure the informed consent of participating human subjects before receiving IRB approval.

In requiring IRB review but providing for waiver or alteration of informed consent requirements when the consent process would inhibit experimentation, the 1981 regulations direct IRBs to consider risks and benefits associated with a proposed social experiment. The IRB must attempt to resolve the tension between the scientific aspects of such social experiments and their character as social innovations af-

---

[109]Section 222a(3) of the Social Security Act Amendments of 1972, Pub. L. No. 92–603 (1972). Similar language is included in the Social Security Disability Amendments of 1980, Pub. L. No. 96–265 § 505(a)(3) (1980), noted at 42 U.S.C. §§ 401, 1395 (Supp. 1980).

[110]The veto power has been criticized in other contexts. See generally the Administrative Conference of the United States, ACUS Recommendation 77–1, 1 C.F.R. 305, 77–1; and Bruff and Gellhorn (1977); but see Schwartz (1978:1369–1440).

[111]It should be noted, however, that no congressman has in fact questioned an experimental proposal and indeed that the committee had no records of number and type of waivers submitted to the committee. See conversation with Irving Heitner, House Ways and Means Committee, February 25, 1980.

fecting everyday life. They must focus on the risks that may be carried not only by subjects but also by the general population; the extent to which the choice of subject populations might be inequitable if not illegal; the necessity for a particular experiment, and the availability of less drastic alternatives. These risks should be balanced, according to standard IRB risk–benefit criteria, against possible benefits to subjects and to society.

The 1981 regulations require the IRB to treat social experiments that are part of a government service or benefit schemes more leniently than other social experiments. In these cases, the IRB may waive informed consent requirements without a finding of minimal risk.[112] In the case of other social experiments it must conclude that the risks are minimal and that the rights and welfare of the subject will not be adversely affected.[113] This special exemption for government-sponsored service or benefit schemes is justified on the grounds that these schemes may be likened to a social innovation whose goals are social reform as much as the expansion of research data.

The external review procedures mandated by the 1981 regulations require the IRB to analyze the risks and benefits inherent in a social experiment. This means that the IRB must determine that risks to subjects are minimized,[114] that risks to subjects are reasonable in relation to anticipated benefits, if any, and that selection of subjects is equitable.[115] The IRB must also determine whether the informed consent requirements can be waived and in what manner. This substantive review of the experimental protocol allows the IRB to review issues of equity as well as issues of harm. Nonetheless, the focus is on harm rather than on subject autonomy.

The 1981 regulations view the consent requirements as designed to protect subjects against harm. Where the risk of harm is remote, the necessity for consent diminishes. This is a radically different analysis of informed consent from that which underlay the 1974 regulations. Those regulations based the need for informed consent on the inviolability of personal autonomy and individuals' rights not to have their persons or their personal life-spaces violated without their permission. On this view, the important issue became the definition of subjects. Persuasive arguments were made that observational studies, studies of public documents, or experiments on human waste products do not

---

[112]46 Fed. Reg. 8390 (1981) (to be codified at 45 C.F.R. § 46.116(c)).
[113]Id. (to be codified at 45 C.F.R. § 46.116(d)).
[114]Id. at 8389 (1981) (to be codified at 45 C.F.R. § 46.111(a)(1)).
[115]Id. (to be codified at 45 C.F.R. § 46.111(a)(3)).

intervene in the normal life of participants and thus that they are not subjects in any meaningful sense of the term. This being the case, according to the 1974 regulations, consent was not necessary.

Waiving consent in instances where risk of harm is remote suggests that harm must have physical or observable physiological manifestations. Invasion of privacy and assaults on personal dignity will not suffice. Such a result-oriented approach to harm shows little concern for the subject's amour-propre. Perhaps such concern for autonomy and personal choice is a luxury in the complex world of the twentieth century. The loss, however, should be recognized and not studiously ignored. The wide exemption authority granted IRBs in the 1981 regulations fails to explain this normative transformation on the part of HHS.

The traditional consent requirement raises significant problems for social experiments. For one, voluntary participation may well skew the subject population and affect the legitimacy of the experimental design. The very success of an experiment may depend on a subject's ignorance of being part of an experiment. More important, the voluntary consent requirements, if adhered to, may doom a research proposal. If a subject (or member of a control group) is asked to give up a benefit, as in the Medicaid copayment or the New York workfare schemes, it is unlikely that a rational subject will agree to participate. Unlike the biomedical subject, for whom the prospect of personal benefit is often (if unfairly) held out, the welfare subject is not merely taking a risk, he or she is incurring a clear loss. Indeed, the "major drawback" of all incentive reimbursement health care experiments funded under Section 402 of the 1967 Medicare amendments has been their voluntary character (HEW, 1976:1).

The 1974 HEW regulations required voluntary informed consent by all participants in human experiments. No exemptions were provided. Although the regulations authorized a modified consent procedure, they did not include the waiver of prior consent. In contrast, the 1981 regulations take a far more flexible approach. They allow an IRB to waive the informed consent requirement provided the IRB finds and documents that:

> The research is to be conducted for the purpose of demonstrating or evaluating: (i) Federal, state or local benefit or service programs which are not themselves research programs, (ii) procedures for obtaining benefits or services under these programs, or (iii) possible changes in or alternatives to these programs and procedures and; (2) The research could not practicably be carried out without the waiver or alteration.

Waiver is also permitted in instances where:

(1) The research involves no more than minimal risk to the subjects;
(2) The waiver or alteration will not adversely affect the rights and welfare of the subjects;
(3) The research could not practicably be carried out without the waiver.[116]

Moreover, the regulations background commentary specifically points out that an IRB may waive the consent requirement "where it may be impracticable to obtain the informed consent of the subject."[117]

This flexible approach to informed consent procedures necessitates an analysis of the need for consent in the social experimentation context. The rules make a clear distinction between research growing out of government benefit or service programs and other social experimentation. Such research may be conducted without informed consent if it is impracticable to do so, notwithstanding risks to subjects.

Waiver of informed consent for service or benefit programs can be justified by the implied consent that citizens afford government action in a democratic society. Classification for the purpose of government programs is binding whether participants voluntarily consent and whether the classification places them at risk. Participants in federal benefit or service programs are not subjects in the classic sense. One may challenge the prudence or the ethics of a large-scale government intervention but not the failure to secure unanimous approval from participants.[118]

Waiver of informed consent for other social experiments, however, must be based on different considerations. IRBs have greater discretion to waive consent requirements where the risk to subjects is minimum, where the rights and welfare of subjects will not be altered, and where waiver is necessary to the experiment. Consent requirements may vary depending on whether the individuals involved are subjects, members of a control group, or the general population.

The question of who is a subject was not resolved in the 1974 regulations.[119] The 1981 regulations focus on the definition of a human sub-

---

[116]Id. at 8390 (1981) (to be codified at 45 C.R.F. § 46.116(c)–(d)).

[117]Id. at 8383 (1981).

[118]Morris Abram, chairman of the President's Commission for the Study of Ethical Problems in Medicine and Biomedical and Behavioral Research, advances a similar view when he argues that "social, economic, or health service research conducted under government aegis" may be exempt from IRB review because "the research is *initiated and sponsored*, not merely funded, by the government and involves variations in existing or proposed federal policies and programs." Letter of Morris Abram to Honorable Patricia Harris, September 18, 1980, p. 3 (emphasis added).

[119]See the definition at 45 C.F.R. § 46.103(b) (1980).

ject, separating that question from the concept of risk. A human subject is a living individual about whom an investigator, while conducting research, obtains "(1) data through intervention or interaction with the individual or (2) identifiable private information."[120] The 1981 regulations do not solve the problem of whether all subjects must consent whether or not they are at risk. Some experiments carry no or minimal risk. On other occasions, the risks, however great, are not imposed by the experiment. Thus, participants in work welfare programs, such as the Minnesota Work Equity program (Leyser, 1979:9; see also Minnesota, 1980) are required to participate, or their welfare benefits are terminated. Consent in this context cannot be free or untrammeled. Where subjects are "recipients of a prototypical service delivery system," there seems little reason why consent should be required (Minnesota, 1978:2). In such cases, "subjects" receive treatment identical to that of the general public.[121] The mere denomination of a program as an experiment does not make it one.

Clearly, it is not sufficient to argue that consent is required whenever the introduction of an experimental protocol adversely affects individuals. One report of the negative income tax experiment suggested that "the overall result of the experiment was to increase the role of marital dissolution in the experimenting groups relative to the controls."[122] In that sense, the families who were the subjects of the experiment may be said to have been harmed (assuming that we view marital breakup in itself as harmful to the individual members of the family unit). This result was not intended, nor was it likely that this risk was articulated to the participating families.[123] Nonetheless, the children of these families, although not formally consenting subjects, were clearly harmed.[124] In the Department of Housing and Urban Development experimental housing allowance study poor persons were given rent subsidies to secure housing in middle-income communities (U.S. Department of Housing and Urban Development, 1974, 1976). Although the middle-income families were not considered subjects, they were affected in at least two ways: Their living patterns were changed through

---

[120]46 Fed. Reg. 8387 (1981) (to be codified at 45 C.F.R. § 46.102(f)).

[121]If subjects receive the same treatment as they would absent an experiment, it is unclear how they are placed at risk in any relevant way. Of course, the very act of being studied may mean de facto that treatment will differ.

[122]U.S. Congress, Senate (1978b). The divorce rate was up to 60% higher in the experimental group.

[123]If that were the case, one could not say that the family could have sufficient information as to harm when they signed the consent form.

[124]It is an important causal issue, of course, whether the harm was "induced by the researchers." See Hearings Note 121 supra at 81.

government intervention, and the introduction of new persons into the market for middle-income housing may well have increased housing prices in that rental market (U.S. Department of Housing and Urban Development, 1976:31–33; see also Tropp, 1978:18-4).

To determine who are the subjects of a social experiment requires analysis of the distinctions between intended and unintended consequences and between direct and indirect harm. Researchers cannot be held responsible for unintended consequences of their research so long as they took all reasonable care to discern and prevent harmful outcomes. One cannot anticipate the unexpected, and one can guard against only those dangers about which one knows or can be expected to know. The question of intention, on the other hand, should be distinguished from that of the directness or indirectness of the effect on subjects. This problem, like the issue of "proximate cause," reflects social assessments regarding causation and responsibility. In the negative income tax case, the actual form of the experimental intervention—providing higher incomes to indigents—is not in itself harmful. "Rather it is the participant's response to the treatment that may cause harm."[125] Although one might charge the researchers with lack of foresight in not recognizing the effect that relative affluence will have on family structure, the harm, if any, is not direct. Similarly, in the case of housing allowance experiments, any unfavorable effects suffered by middle-income families were also indirect. It is the intent of the research team and not the fact of injury to the general public that makes an affected person an experimental subject. The decision not to denominate as subjects spouses and children in the negative income tax experiment, or middle-income families in the housing experiment, does not mean that we do not care what happens to them. It means only that we have a duty of care to direct subjects different from that to society at large. One may still decide that the risks to society or to individual nonsubjects are so substantial as to prohibit an experiment whatever the situation of, or the consent provided by, the proposed subject.

One must also be cognizant of the nature of harms to which citizens will be placed at risk. In the medical experiments, the harms are physical and easily ascertainable. In the area of social experiments, harms, especially indirect harms, may be psychological, economic, or purely metaphysical. They may track the risks of everyday life or raise risks of new and unique harms. In the negative income tax experiment, for

[125]U.S. Congress, Senate (1978b: 424 [Letter of Robert Spiegleman to Senator Daniel Moynihan]).

example, the risks that the Senate committee reviewing the study criticized were merely harms that flow from sudden changes in wealth or status. Such harms are not the concern of an agency regulating social research. Alternatively, one might decide that the risk of harm to society or to affected individuals is so substantial as to prohibit an experiment. It is the character of the risk that affects our attitude to a social experiment. One might view the issue differently if the government is allocating a benefit through the experiment rather than a burden. If the risks or burdens are de minimus or no different than the risks raised by ordinary life, consent may be considered less important.

Similar problems are faced when considering the status of control groups. Where a control group is treated in the same way as the general population, it should be clear that group members do not have to consent. Thus, there is "no general obligation to inform controls that they are controls [Riecken and Boruch, 1974:254]" and to secure their consent. They are neither participants nor subjects in any meaningful sense. The counterarguments to this view are not persuasive.[126] They are based on the claim that persons in control groups are being used for the benefit of others—in this instance, research scientists—and that this use is per se improper and results in a violation of the trust necessary between researcher and subject populations. That persons in a social experiment are placed in a control group does not mean that they are unfairly manipulated anymore than are persons whom sociologists observe engaging in public activity. They are merely not singled out for benefits. However seriously one views the necessity of consent in social science research generally, social experiments raise separate and unique issues.

Conclusion

The 1974 HEW regulations effectively resolved the debate over internal or external review in biomedical research. Although debate continued as to the standard of review, the use of IRBs as the primary regulatory review mechanism was accepted by scientists for most areas of research. Not so for social research. Social scientists urged that social research should be exempt from IRB review because the intrusion on personal privacy was so limited that any risks incurred by subjects were merely speculative. For the most part, the 1981 regulations accepted the social scientists' arguments. The vast terrain of social sci-

[126]Capron (1979:16–17) presents this contrary position with characteristic force.

ence research was largely deregulated through exemptions, through expedited review procedures, or through the waiver of otherwise applicable informed consent requirements. Social experiments remained a *tertium quid*. They were not deregulated; however, IRB waiver of informed consent requirements was permitted when necessary to implement social experiments.[127]

The 1981 regulations require that IRBs ensure that the selection of subjects for an experiment take "into account the purposes of the research and the setting in which the research will be conducted."[128] This requirement reflects a concern that the "involvement of hospitalized patients, other institutionalized patients, or disproportionate numbers of racial or ethnic minorities or persons of low socio-economic status should be justified" as necessary to a research design.[129] The root of this concern is that the disadvantaged not be guinea pigs for scientific progress. The legal dimension of the concern for equitable distribution, however, raises questions about the extent to which state-sponsored discriminations between citizens violate the equal protection or due process clauses of the U.S. Constitution.

The "elusive concept[s]"[130] represented by equal protection jurisprudence are difficult to apply in the context of social experimentation. It is easy to imagine courts voiding classifications for experimental purposes when such classifications are based on race or religion and would clearly stigmatize or injure traditionally disadvantaged groups. Beyond such obvious bias in the selection of research subjects, the problem of experimentation is far more complex. Given current standards of judicial review it is unlikely that random selection for experimental purposes will fail to pass judicial muster.[131]

---

[127]46 Fed. Reg. 8383 (1981).

[128]*Id.* at 8389 (1981) (to be codified at 45 C.F.R. § 46.111(a)(3)).

[129]*Id.* at 8378 (1981).

[130]Hannah v. Larche, 363 U.S. 420, 442 (1960).

[131]Courts have traditionally held to the view that discrimination among groups for purposes of differential treatment was constitutional as long as the state had a rational reason for drawing distinctions between groups. A government program rarely failed to pass constitutional muster under this rational basis test. However, when either a fundamental interest or a suspect classification was at stake, judicial scrutiny was rigorous and the attempt at discrimination almost invariably failed. Fundamental interests include the right to travel, Shapiro v. Thompson, 394 U.S. 618 (1969); right to vote, Dunn v. Blumstein, 405 U.S. 330 (1972); right to essential aid in appealing a criminal conviction, Griffin v. Illinois, 351 U.S. 12 (1956). Interests including housing, Lindsey v. Normet, 405 U.S. 56 (1972); education, San Antonio School District v. Rodriguez, 411 U.S. 1 (1973); and welfare, Jefferson v. Hackney, 406 U.S. 535, 546 (1972); Richardson v. Belcher, 404 U.S. 78, 81 (1971), Dandridge v. Williams, 397 U.S. 471 (1970), have been deemed not to be fundamental. Suspect classifications include race, McLaughlin v. Florida, 379 U.S. 184

One might argue that the distribution of goods by lot is, by definition, a methodology that contains significant elements of arbitrariness.[132] However, the view that randomization is the quintessence of the arbitrary is incorrect. The rationality of a random distribution depends on the purpose for its use. In a "tragic choice" context (see Calebresi and Bobbitt, 1978; see also Katz, 1973), for example, a lottery may be a rational response to the need to allocate scarce resources without violating important social values about human equality (Calebresi and Bobbitt, 1978:42).

Although some courts have rejected the claim that random allocation is the preferred way to allocate scarce resources, those decisions were made in contexts where the primary concern was social service and not the search for knowledge. Thus, in *Gordon v. Forsyth County Hospital Authority, Inc.*,[133] where a local hospital planned to comply with its statutory duty to provide indigents with free medical care by providing medical "care on a priority basis to persons categorized as emergency, urgent and elective" cases, a federal court found that the hospital's allocation method was "a more logical and rational basis on which to equitably distribute the limited amount of care available among qualified recipients" than a random distribution method.[134] Here the court apparently considered the reason for the distribution method used—care of the medically ill—and determined that distribution based on need was a rational allocative mechanism. It is the allocative purpose that determines the rationality of an allocative method, not the fact of random allocation itself.

Similarly, the mere fact of partial coverage is not in itself grounds for an equal protection claim. A rigorous analysis of "partial coverage" in

---

(1964); alienage, Examining Board of Engineers, Architects, and Surveyors v. Flores de Otero 426 U.S. 572 (1976), and national origin, Korematsu v. United States, 323 U.S. 214 (1944). Recently, the Supreme Court has moved to a more flexible approach that takes into account the nature of the unequal classification, the nature of the right adversely affected, and the governmental interest urged in support of the classification. This form of intermediate scrutiny requires that a proposed classification "must serve important governmental objectives and must be substantially related to achievement of those objectives." Craig v. Boren, 429 U.S. 190, 197 (1976). The application of these constitutional doctrines to random assignment is reviewed in Capron (1975:127, 152–163). See also Teitelbaum (Chapter 2, this volume).

[132]We can distinguish, then, between a case where a burden is imposed randomly and a case where not all persons receive a benefit. The end result of the distribution might well be the same, but the processes would differ—this is the key point in much of this analysis.

[133]409 F. Supp. 708 (M.D.N.C. 1975), *modified*, 544 F.2d 748 (4th Cir. 1976).

[134]*Id.* at 730.

the social experiment context would yield three types of discriminations. In one example, an agency might start a "new math" program in
Brooklyn, planning over a specified period of time to extend that same
program to Queens. In a second example, an agency is itself not convinced that the "new math" is a good way to teach arithmetic to school
children. It decides to experiment in Brooklyn but cannot with certainty say that the "pilot" program is a special benefit or an added burden
for the school children chosen. In a third example, administrators may
believe that the "new math" is best for fifth-grade students in their area
and yet choose to provide a control group with different teaching techniques so as to secure "scientific" proof of this hypothesis. On that
basis, they start a "new math" program in Brooklyn.

In the first example, partial coverage in no way violates equal protection strictures. The difference in treatment derives from the inescapa-
ble fact that one must start somewhere. As long as the choice of
Brooklyn over Queens was based on defensible administrative grounds,
such geographic discriminations are not in themselves improper. Intrastate discrimination in the provision of services or the administration
of government functions has been sustained even when the avowed
basis for the discrimination is territorial or demographic. In *Missouri v.
Lewis*, for example, the state set up an intermediate court of appeals for
Saint Louis, thus providing two levels of appeal for Saint Louis and one
for the rest of the state.[135] The Saint Louis case might be explained by
virtue of the fact that the right to appeal was provided to all residents of
the state, and only the method of effectuating that right was altered for
Saint Louis. Nonetheless, the *Lewis* holding has been extended to clear
instances of differentiated court systems, such as *Chappell Chemical
and Fertilizer Co. v. Sulphur Mines Co.*, where a Maryland constitutional provision abridging trial by jury in the courts of Baltimore without making similar provisions for the rest of the state was upheld
against an equal protection attack.[136] This demographic distinction
may have been justified on the grounds that Baltimore was the state's
most populous city.[137] Yet when clinical medical laboratories attacked
a New York City Medicaid innovation that planned to jettison, for

---

[135]101 U.S. 22 (1879); see generally Horowitz and Weitring (1968:787–816).

[136]172 U.S. 475 (1899). Other such territorial distinctions in the administration of
justice include Mallet v. North Carolina, 181 U.S. 589 (1901) (state could appeal adverse
decisions of Eastern, but not Western, district); Salsburg v. Maryland, 346 U.S. 545 (1954)
(Anne Arundel County was exempted by state law from a rule making illegally procured
evidence inadmissible in misdemeanor trials).

[137]Salsburg v. Maryland, 346 U.S. 545 (1954).

financial reasons, "freedom of choice" laboratory services in each borough, the district court judge enjoined operation of this programmatic innovation in most of the city, "allowing the city to proceed with its plans in one area if it wish[ed] to do so."[138]

In the second example, the legislators are themselves uncertain which is the best course for the students. Since the decision maker is indifferent between available choices (although, admittedly, the participant might not be), his or her distribution of subjects lacks discriminatory motive. However the actual experiment turns out, its purpose is to try out a new approach to solving social problems. Such a social innovation is in keeping with the view that states should be "laboratories of democracy."[139] It is the paradigm case justifying a social experiment.[140]

Consider the allocation technique used in distributing funds available under the Emergency School Assistance Act.[141] Convinced (as it turned out, wrongly) that "small dollars of unrestricted federal funds could do little in the short run to change the quality of education [Crain and York, 1976:233]," the federal government distributed the available funds randomly. Its justification was that it did not believe that the program would make a difference but wished to innovate and experiment (Crain and York, 1976:236–238). Courts have historically deferred to legislative innovation. This deference extends to distinctions that afford one class of persons benefits denied another class.[142] In a decision upholding Title II of the Narcotic Addict Rehabilitation Act of 1966,[143] which bars defendants convicted of two prior felonies from possible participation in a special rehabilitation program in lieu of incarceration, the Supreme Court noted, "When Congress undertakes to act in areas fraught with medical and scientific uncertainties, legislative options must be especially broad and courts should be cautious not to rewrite legislation, even assuming *arguendo*, that judges with more

[138]Bay Ridge Diagnostic Laboratory v. Dumpson, 400 F.Supp. 1104, 1111 (E.D.N.Y. 1975). This was not a statutorily authorized experimental project under 42 U.S.C. § 1315. In fact, the court suggested that the city secure such formal authorization. The city, however, argued that this was not an experiment at all.

[139]See *New State Ice Co. v. Liebmann*, 285 U.S. 262, 311 (1932); see also Frankfurter (1930:49–51).

[140]This said, it is not the motivating force behind much experimentation. Exploration into that divergence would require an excursus into the sociology of research.

[141]Emergency School Aid, Pub. L. No. 92–318 Title VII, § 702, 86 Stat. 354, 20 U.S.C. § 1601 (1972).

[142]See Maher v. Roe, 432 U.S. 464 (1977).

[143]42 U.S.C. §§ 3411–3426 (Supp. 1977).

direct exposure to the problem might make wise choices."[144] Thus, the "rational basis" for differential treatment becomes the desire to innovate and experiment. On this view, differential treatment for the purpose of increasing a society's store of knowledge may be justified.

In one Massachusetts case,[145] a defendant charged with drunk driving alleged he was dealt with unfairly because the trial court did not participate in an experimental Alcoholism Intervention Project.[146] That project treated defendants found guilty of drunk driving instead of suspending their licenses, but it was available in part of the state only. The Massachusetts court pointed out that because the program was experimental, "there is no constitutional equal protection requirement that such a program be available to all defendants from its inception.[147] Since no invidious means of allocating treatment was used, no unconstitutional burden was placed on persons not provided the possibility of that benefit.

The third example contains the seeds of an equal protection problem. Here it is suspected that treatment A may be better than treatment B or alternatively may be more harmful to the population than no governmental action at all. Yet to gain scientific proof the administrator will treat a segment of the population in a manner he or she believes (based on knowledge and experience) to be adverse to their interests. In this instance an experiment might be described as arbitrarily distributing benefits and burdens. Although the purpose of random selection is to verify scientific hypotheses, the researcher (or authorizing administrator) is consciously placing one segment of the population at risk to secure scientific proof. In some instances, as with juvenile court counsel studies (see Stapleton and Teitelbaum, 1972:63–96; see also Irving,

[144]Marshall v. United States, 414 U.S. 417, 427 (1974). See also People v. Ryals, 420 N.Y.S.2d 257 (1979), in which a 14-year-old juvenile was charged with attempted murder and claimed that a state law denying the protections of the juvenile defender law to juveniles charged with murder had a rational basis and that the special treatment of juveniles "represented a shift in public attitudes and was not the result of any declaration of unconstitutionality." Thus public attitudes can vary by crime committed. See People v. Williams, 410 N.Y.S.2d 978, 985, 97 Misc.2d. 24, 34 (1978).

[145]Healy v. First District Court of Bristol, 367 Mass. 909, 327 N.E.2d 894 (1975). See also McGlothlen v. Department of Motor Vehicles, 71 Cal. App. 3d 1005, 140 Cal. Rptr. 168 (1977). See Commonwealth v. LeRoy, 380 N.E.2d 128 (Mass. 1978) where a Massachusetts court found that the state statute under discussion contained no constitutional defect since an alternative disposition of a drunken driving charge was not available after a defendant chose to have a jury trial. The exercise of that choice deprived the court of its option to grant a continuance and order alternative treatment.

[146]Healy v. First District Court of Bristol, 367 Mass. at 909, 327 N.E.2d at 895.

[147]Id. at 910, 327 N.E.2d at 895.

1968:1, 5–6, and Lefstein, Stapleton, and Teitelbaum, 1969:491, 505–516), the "private hunches" of the investigators were borne out by empirical investigation. In others, the experimental results may contradict a preliminary hunch. In all instances, experimenters hope that success in raising their "private" judgments[148] to the status of "public knowledge"[149] will have sufficient social utility to justify their experimental choices. Although the end results to subjects in this third case may be no different than the results to subjects in the previous examples, the motivation and the intention of the administrator differ radically.

In analyzing the ethical and legal consequences of the third example, one must focus on the type of knowledge gained and balance it against injuries suffered to resolve equal protection concerns. In that context, one would consider issues such as the seriousness of the problem to be solved, the scope or duration of the experimental design, and the quality or efficiency benefits of the knowledge to be gained by society. Experience with the results of social science research has taught us the limited extent to which much research generates new or even "useful knowledge."[150] Such a general claim cannot itself serve as a rational basis for experimental discrimination. Instead, one must look at the concrete project in question and assess whether that specific experiment really requires the proposed discrimination, whether the knowledge sought could be gained by a less discriminatory alternative, and whether that specific experiment will in fact yield socially useful knowledge. The marginal advantages that are to be gained by using random distribution must be balanced against experimental risks.

Our treatment of partial coverage has focused on experiments that propose to benefit the subject population. If the experiment will impose burdens on subjects, equal protection strictures should be stronger. Should the state impose a special burden on a subject or class of subjects, it might be required to make an explicit showing of the specific social benefits that would justify the imposition of the burden. Indeed, some criminal justice researchers have concluded that no crim-

---

[148]One must distinguish here personal preferences from private judgments. A preference is no more than an expression of individual taste. It is subjective only. A private judgment is a personal belief as to knowledge that has the status of truth but lacks the proof necessary to have the claim publically sustained. See, for example, Polanyi (1964).

[149]See Zinman (1968). This point is discussed in Clarke and Cornish (1972:5); see also Fried (1974:141–165).

[150]See Lindblom and Cohen (1979). Of course, the traditional problem of scientific research organized for personal motives, such as employment, prestige, and financial remuneration, rather than for societal benefits still exists.

inal may participate in criminological research until he or she has first received a "just and appropriate" sentence. On this view, experimental variations in treatment may be "no worse than [a convict] would have received in the absence of the experiment," thus ensuring that his or her level of "individual sacrifice is mitigate[d] [Cornell Law Quarterly, 1976:158, 166]."[151] Similarly, congressional authorization for experimental projects designed to "increase the efficiency of the food stamp program and improve the delivery of food stamp benefits" requires "that no project shall be implemented which would lower or further restrict the income or . . . benefit levels [otherwise] provided" in the act.[152] Although limitations might reduce the efficacy of social experiments, they ensure that equity considerations are not violated through the experimental process.

The random character of the distribution of benefits or burdens in a social experiment may also raise ethical questions about the fairness of subjecting specific individuals to the experimental model. This is particularly true for state-supported research. The concern that randomness fails to allow individual attention in allocation decisions reflects tensions inherent in due process jurisprudence. Consider the California copayment scheme. Although most individuals involved in that experiment will be only marginally affected by the copayment requirement, a few extreme hardship cases may be severely affected. These persons may claim that the state's failure (through the experimenter) to take individual needs into account raises a due process issue. By its nature, random classification requires that hardship waivers not be given. The state places a person in a category by lot and does so conclusively. Subjects with special needs may have no recourse but to make a due process claim for individualized attention. Thus, if in a medical experiment making use of marijuana members of the control group required marijuana to ease the symptoms of glaucoma or to counteract the side effects of chemotherapy, they would be severely injured by not receiving the experimental benefit.[153] Such experiments must allow a "safety

---

[151]See also Norval Morris (1966), who notes that experimentation in the pretrial context must be informed by the principle of "less severity [p. 646]."

[152]7 U.S.C. § 2026(b)(1) (Supp. 1977). See also Social Security Disability Amendments of 1980, Pub. L. No. 96–265, § 505(b)(2) (1980), codified as 42 U.S.C. § 1310(b)(2) (Supp. 1980) and cited, supra, in text at note 105.

[153]Due process claims for individual attention based on the defense of medical necessity to criminal charges of marijuana possession have been raised by glaucoma, chemotherapy, and multiple sclerosis patients. The Food and Drug Administration has allowed certain medically needy persons who participate in approved research programs to use marijuana. 21 C.F.R. § 1308.23(a). The state of Washington has also recognized this need.

valve" against the harshness of the classification scheme even if a research design's scientific character is vitiated.

A focus on individualized treatment is a central feature of our criminal justice system. On this model, the punishment that the state metes out to an individual is determined by focusing on the crime committed, the nature and character of the violator's participation in it, the existence of idiosyncratic circumstances, and the possibility of individual rehabilitation.[154] It is in that sense that we must understand Max Gruhut's comment that in the administration of justice no experiments are feasible (Morris, 1957:962, 966). Thus, in a British experiment "juvenile court magistrates, working in the City of Leeds . . . agreed to carry out an investigation, using random allocation, to evaluate two judicial procedures which they normally used with children brought to court" for truancy (Berg, Hullin, and McGuire, 1979:141, 143). Proceedings of this type traditionally use one of four sentencing options. A magistrate might place the child under the supervision of a social worker or probation officer, adjourn the case until a later date, or issue either an "interim" or a "full care" order that would place the child in a residential home. The magistrate agreed randomly either to sentence convicted children to supervision or to adjourn sentencing and not to send them to a home.[155] The study found that this random sentencing

---

1979 Wash. Laws 136. At least two courts have recognized a limited right to possess marijuana based on medical necessity. U.S. v. Randall, 104 Daily Wash. Law Rptr. 2249 (D.C. Super. Ct. November 24, 1976); see also State v. Diana, 24 Wash. App. 908, 604 P.2d 1312 (Ct. App. Wash. 1979), where the appellate court allowed defendant to prove medical necessity. But see Hartz v. Bensinger, 461 F. Supp. 431 (E.D. Pa. 1978). See also *George Washington Law Review* (1978:273–298); similar arguments have been advanced as regards the government's banning of laetrile. Rutherford v. United States, 399 F. Supp. 1208 (W.D. Okla. 1975), *aff'd*, 542 F.2d 1137 (10th Cir. 1976), *cert. denied*, 439 U.S. 1128 (1980). See also Rizzo v. United States, 432 F. Supp. 356 (E.D.N.Y. 1972).

[154]For a discussion of the conflict between general deterrence of crime through mechanical rules of punishment and the theory that the punishment should fit the individual who committed the crime, see Pound (1971:101, 104–105); Menninger (1968:62–71); Andennaes (1966:949–983); Wooton (1963:91–118). See also Thomas and Fitch (1975:61–83); for a discussion of the constitutional issues raised in juvenile court proceedings because of the attempt to relax mechanical rules and to fashion punishment to the juvenile accused of a crime.

[155]There was a sheet of lined paper in each court which was used for the random allocation of children. At the end of each row of the sheet, the procedure to be used, A for *adjournment*, or S for *supervision*, had been typed and then obscured by a stickly [sic] label. All new cases of truancy appearing on any day were listed by the clerk of the court at the start of each session. Children belonging to the same family were put on the same line since they were all given the same treatment. Once the case was proved, the label was removed and the indicated procedure, *adjournment* or *supervision*, was used [Berg, Hullin, and McGuire, 1979:144]."

procedure "inappropriately managed"[156] children by failing to focus on a truant's individual needs,[157] family situation, or psychological reaction to the juvenile justice process. The concern that subjects not be excessively burdened, coupled with the need for random allocation, may well have injured children whose truancy was a symptom of severe adjustment problems.

In two studies of traffic offenders in the United States (Blumenthal and Ross, 1973; Ross, 1974; Ross and Blumenthal, 1975) Ross developed a "safety valve" to ensure that random allocation was not used when the effects would be particularly harsh. He arranged for parking offenders and drunk drivers to receive penalties each month (Ross and Blumenthal, 1975:150, 151–52). Ross allowed the judge to exclude persons on his own authority when he "thought the penalty of the month was grossly inappropriate to the case at hand [Ross and Blumenthal, 1975:152]."[158] Ross further ensured that none of the alternative penalties meted out were hardship punishments, as the term is commonly conceived. Thus, the study "did not consider . . . a jail penalty for the drinking drivers even though this penalty was statutorily available, since it had very rarely been applied to first offenders in the past [Ross and Blumenthal, 1975:152]." By ensuring that experimental burdens were not severe and by providing a "safety valve" for exempting hardship cases, both the English and American experiments sought to protect against claims that individualized attention was not paid to the effect of random allocations. Such protective measures will guard against possible due process problems.

The demand for individualized attention raises analytic problems for the social experiment. In biomedical experiments doctors' concern for their patients' welfare limits experimentation to the narrow range where the physicians cannot select a procedure of choice. At the point when they can do so, experimentation must cease. Social researchers lack the professional responsibility toward experimental subjects that physicians have toward patients. Lacking such fidelity, the need for limiting experimental burdens becomes more acute. This is the underlying ethical problem of the social experiment.

---

[156]From a group perspective, the authors suggest, "the overall improvement in the group hardly justifies the use of this procedure. It is concluded that it would have been best to use the court procedure of adjournment in all instances [Berg, Hullin, and McGuire, 1979:148]."

[157]The state of the art in this area is so primitive that one may well wonder whether the possibility of a "fit," for rehabilitation purposes at least, exists.

[158]The authors "expected such departures to be rare," but this was not the case in practice. Ross and Blumenthal (1975:153–154).

The issues of equitable distribution and individualized attention raise significant philosophical issues concerning the propriety of random assignment in social experiments. Although it is unlikely that legal problems raised by random assignments will reach constitutional proportions, the concerns raised by these issues ought to permeate the deliberations of whatever external review mechanism regulates social experimentation.

As discussed, the 1981 regulations allow IRBs to waive otherwise applicable informed consent requirements when necessary to implement a social experiment. This administrative flexibility should not result in a routinized waiver practice. In taking on waiver responsibilities, the IRBs' concern for the ethical background of social experiments should become more acute. In directing their focus to subject harm rather than subject autonomy, the IRBs cannot ignore the special problems of the random social experiment.

References

Andenaes, J.
   1966 "The general preventive effects of punishment." *University of Pennsylvania Law Review* 114:949–983.
Anderson, S., and S. Ball
   1978 *The Profession and Practice of Program Evaluation.* San Francisco: Jossey-Bass.
Aronson, E., and J. Carlsmith
   1969 "Experimentation in social psychology." Pp. 1–79 in G. Lindzey and E. Aronson (eds.), *Handbook of Social Psychology.* Vol. 2. Reading, Mass.: Addison-Wesley Publishing Company.
Barber, B., J. Lally, J. Makarushka, and D. Sullivan
   1973 *Research on Human Subjects.* New York: Russell Sage Foundation.
Beck, R. G.
   1974 "The effects of co-payment on the poor." *Journal of Human Resources* 9:129–142.
Berg, I., R. Hullin, and R. McGuire
   1979 "A randomly controlled trial of two court procedures in truancy." Pp. 143–151 in D. Farrington, K. Hawkins, and S. Lloyd-Bostock (eds.), *Psychology, Law and Legal Process.* Atlantic Highlands, N.J.: Humanities Press.
Biderman, A. D., and L. M. Sharp
   1972a *The Competitive Evaluation of Research Industry.* Washington, D.C.: Bureau of Social Science Research.
   1972b "Evaluation research: Procurement and method." *Social Science Information* 11:141–170.
Blumenthal, M., and L. Ross
   1973 *Two Experimental Studies of Traffic Law.* Department of Transportation Washington, D.C.: U.S. Government Printing Office.

Bogatz, G. A., and S. Ball
  1971   *The Second Year of Sesame Street: A Continuing Evaluation.* Princeton, N.J.: Educational Testing Service.
Bok, S.
  1978   *Lying: Moral Choice in Public and Private Life.* New York: Vintage Books.
Bonacich, P., and J. Light
  1978   "Laboratory experimentation in sociology." *Annual Review of Sociology* 4:145–170.
Boruch, R., A. McSweeny, and E. Soderstrom
  1978   "Randomized field experiments for program planning, development, and evaluation." *Evaluation Quarterly* 2:655–695.
Brandeis, L. D.
  1933   *Other People's Money and How the Bankers Use It.* New York: Harper and Row.
Brandt, R. M.
  1972   *Studying Behavior in Natural Settings.* New York: Holt, Rhinehart and Winston.
Brian E. W., and S. F. Gibbens
  1974   "California's Medi-Cal co-payment experiment." *Medical Care* 12(Suppl. 12):–303.
Brown, P.
  1975   "Informed consent in social experimentation: Some cautionary notes." Pp. 79–104 in A. Rivlin and P. Timpane (eds.), *Ethical and Legal Issues of Social Experimentation.* Washington, D.C.: Brookings Institution.
Bruff, H. H., and E. Gellhorn
  1977   "Congressional control of administrative regulation: A study of legislative vetoes." *Harvard Law Review* 90:1369–1440.
Buchanan, G., and J. Heinberg
  1972   *Housing Allowance Experiment Design Part 1: Summary and Overview.* Washington, D.C.: Urban Institute.
Bundy, M.
  1974   "The president's review." Pp. V–XIII in *Ford Foundation Annual Report.* New York: Ford Foundation.
Calebresi, G., and P. Bobbitt
  1978   *Tragic Choices.* New York: Norton.
Campbell, D. T.
  1970   "Application for a grant to support research on methods for the experimenting society." Manuscript. Russell Sage Foundation.
Capron, A.
  1975   "Social experimentation and the law." Pp. 127–163 in A. Rivlin and P. Timpane (eds.), *Ethical and Legal Issues of Social Experimentaion.* Washington, D.C.: Brookings Institution.
  1979   "Is consent always necessary to social science research?" Manuscript.
Chalmers, T.
  1967   "The ethics of randomization as a decision-making technique and the problems of informed consent." In *U.S. DHEW Report of the 14th Annual Conference of Cardiovascular Training Grant Program Directors, National Heart Institute.*
Clarke, R. V. G., and D. B. Cornish
  1972   *The Controlled Trial in Institutional Research: Paradigm or Pitfall for Penal Evaluators?* London, HMSO.

Cochrane, A. L.
   1972   *Effectiveness and Efficiency: Random Reflection on Health Services.* London: Nuffield Provincial Hospital Trust.
Cole, M. I.
   1953   *Robert Owen of New Lanark.* New York: Oxford University Press.
Conner, R.
   1977   "Selecting a control group: An analysis of the randomization process in twelve social reform programs." *Evaluation Quarterly* 1:195–244.
Cook, T. D., et al.
   1976   *Sesame Street Revisited: A Case Study in Education Research.* New York: Russell Sage Foundation.
Cornell Law Quarterly
   1976   "Applying the controlled experiment to penal reform." *Cornell Law Quarterly* 62:158–176.
Crain, R. L., and R. L. York
   1976   "Evaluating a successful program: Experimental method and academic bias." *School Review* 84:233–254.
Cranberg, L.
   1979   "Do retrospective controls make clinical trials 'inherently fallacious'?" *British Medical Journal* (November 17): 1265.
de Sola Pool, I.
   1979   "Protecting human subjects of research: An analysis of proposed amendments to HEW policy." *PS* 12:452–455.
   1980   "The new censorship of social research." *The Public Interest*, no. 59 (spring): 57–66.
Empey, L. T., and M. L. Erickson
   1972   *The Provo Experiment: Evaluating Community Control of Delinquency.* Lexington, Mass.: Lexington Books.
Empey, L. T., and S. G. Lubeck
   1972   *The Silverlake Experiment: Testing Delinquency Theory and Community Intervention.* Chicago, Ill.: Aldine Publishing Company.
Empey, L. T., and J. Rabow
   1961   "The Provo experiment in delinquency rehabilitation." *American Sociological Review* 26:679–695.
Festinger, L., et al.
   1956   *When Prophecy Fails.* New York: Harper and Row.
Frankfurter, F.
   1930   *The Public and Its Government.* New Haven: Yale University Press.
Fried, C.
   1974   *Medical Experimentation: Personal Integrity and Social Policy.* New York: Elsevier Publishing Company.
Galblum, T. W.
   1978   "Health care cost containment experiments: Policy, individual rights, and the law." *Journal of Health Politics, Policy, and Law* 3:375–387.
George Washington Law Review
   1978   "Medical Necessity as a Defense to Criminal Liability: U.S. v. Randall." *George Washington Law Review* 46:273–298.
Gray, B. H.
   1979a   "Human subjects review committees and social research." Pp. 43–59 in M. Wax and J. Cassell (eds.), *Federal Regulations: Ethical Issues and Social Research.* Boulder, Colo.: Westview Press.

1979b "The regulatory context of social research: The work of the National Commission for the Protection of Human Subjects." Pp. 197–223 in C. E. Klockars and F. W. O'Connor (eds.), *Deviance and Decency*. Beverly Hills, Calif.: Sage Publications.

Gray, B., and R. Cooke
1980 "The impact of institutional review boards on research." *Hastings Center Report* 10:36–41.

Hopkins, C. E., *et al.*
1975 "Cost-sharing and prior authorization effects on Medicaid services in California." *Medical Care* 13:457–466.

Horowitz, I. L., and J. E. Katz
1975 *Social Science and Public Policy in the United States*. New York: Praeger.

Horowitz, H. W., and D. L. Neitring
1968 "Equal protection aspects of inequalities in public education and public assistance programs from place to place within a state." *UCLA Law Review* 15:787–816.

Irving, J. F. Y.
1968 "Juvenile justice—One year later." *Journal of Family Law* 8:1–12.

Ivy, A. C.
1948 "The history and ethics of the use of human subjects in medical experiments." *Science* 108:1–5.

Katz, A.
1973 "Process design for selection of hemodialysis and organ transplant recipients." *Buffalo Law Review* 22:373–418.

Kelling, G. L., T. Pate, D. Dieckman, and C. E. Brown
1973 *The Kansas City Preventive Patrol Experiment*. Washington, D.C.: Police Foundation.

Kershaw, D.
1972 "A negative income tax experiment." *Scientific American* 227:19–25.

Larson, R.
1972 *Urban Police Patrol Analysis*. Cambridge, Mass.: MIT Press.
1975 "What happened to patrol operations in Kansas City: A review of the Kansas City Preventive Patrol Experiment." *Journal of Criminal Justice* 3:267–297.

Lefstein, N., V. Stapleton, and L. Teitelbaum
1969 "In search of juvenile justice: *Gault* and its implementation." *Law and Society Review* 3:491–562.

Lewin, K.
1951 *Field Theory in Social Science*. New York: Harper and Row.

Leyser, B.
1979 "A summary of the Minnesota Work Equity Project." Unpublished report prepared for the Center on Social Welfare Policy and Law.

Lindblom, C. E.
1959 "The science of muddling through." *Public Administration Review* 19:79–88.

Lindblom, C., and D. K. Cohen
1979 *Usable Knowledge: Social Science and Social Problem Solving*. New Haven: Yale University Press.

Lockwood, G., with C. Prosser
1971 *The New Harmony Movement*. New York: Dover Publications.

Lynn, L. E., Jr.,
1978 "A decade of policy developments in the income maintenance system." Pp.

341–374 in T. Cook et al. (eds.), Evaluation Studies Review Annual. Vol. 3. Beverly Hills, Calif.: Sage Publications.

McCorkle, L., A. Elias, and F. Lovell Bixby
  1958   The Highfields Story: An Experimental Treatment Project for Youthful Offenders. New York: H. Holt & Co.

Menninger, K.
  1968   The Crime of Punishment. New York: Viking Press.

Minnesota Department of Public Welfare
  1978   "Certification of review and special implementation of institutional assurance." Unpublished report of the Institutional Review Board of the Minnesota Work Equity Project.
  1980   "Work equity through meaningful employment: Section 1115 waiver extension application." Report submitted to the Department of Health, Education and Welfare, April 22.

Morris, N.
  1957   "Review of M. Grunhut, Juvenile Offenders before the Courts." Yale Law Journal 66:962–972.
  1966   "Impediments to penal reform." University of Chicago Law Review 33:627–656.

Mullen, L.
  1976   "Human experimentation regulations of HEW bar Georgia Medicaid cutback." Clearinghouse Review 10:259–261.

National Commission for the Protection of Human Subjects
  1978   Appendix to Report and Recommendations: Institutional Review Boards. Washington, D.C.: U.S. Government Printing Office.

National Science Foundation
  1977   Federal Funds for Research, Development, and Other Scientific Activities, Fiscal Years 1975, 1976 and 1977. Washington, D.C.: U.S. Government Printing Office.

Orlans, H.
  1973   Contracting for Knowledge. San Francisco: Jossey-Bass.
  1976   "On social order and orderly knowledge." Pp. 35–58 in E. Crawford and N. Perry (eds.), Demands for Social Knowledge: The Role of Research Organizations. Beverly Hills, Calif.: Sage Publications.

Orr, L., R. G. Hollister, M. J. Lefcowitz, and K. Hester
  1971   Income Maintenance: Interdisciplinary Approaches to Research. Chicago, Ill.: Markham Publishing Co.

Owen, R.
  1821   Report to the County of Lanark of A Plan for Relieving Public Distress and Removing Discontent by Giving Permanent Productive Employment to the Poor and Working Classes. London: Home Colonization Society.

Pattulo, E. L.
  1980   "Who risks what in social research?" IRB: A Review of Human Subject Research 2(3):1–312.

Polanyi, M.
  1964   Personal Knowledge: Toward A Post-Critical Philosophy. New York: Harper and Row.

Pound, R.
  1971   "Criminal justice in the American city." Pp. 101–120 in A. Goldstein and J. Goldstein (eds.), Crime, Law and Society. New York: Free Press.

Powers, E., and H. Witmer
1951 An Experiment in the Prevention of Delinquency: The Cambridge–Somerville Youth Study. New York: Columbia University Press.
Powers, G.
1980 "HEW uses 'demonstration projects' to skirt law." Legal Times 21 (January): 10, 13.
Price, G.
1969 "The Russian Jews in America." Pp. 265–355 in A. Karp (ed.), The Jewish Experience in America. Vol. 4, The Era of Immigration. Waltham, Mass.: American Jewish Historical Society.
Riecken, H. W., and R. F. Boruch (eds.)
1974 Social Experimentation: A Method for Planning and Evaluating Social Intervention. New York: Academic Press.
1978 "Social experiments." Annual Review of Sociology 4:511–532.
Rivlin, A. M.
1971 Systematic Thinking for Social Action. Washington, D.C.: Brookings Institution.
Rivlin, A. M., and P. Timpane (eds.)
1975 Ethical and Legal Issues of Social Experimentation. Washington, D.C.: Brookings Institution.
Ross, L.
1974 "Interrupted time-series methods for the evaluation of traffic law reforms." Proceedings of the North Carolina Symposium on Highway Safety 10:32–67.
Ross, L., and M. Blumenthal
1975 "Some problems in experimentation in a legal setting." American Sociologist 10:150–155.
Schwartz, B.
1978 "The legislative veto and the Constitution—A reexamination." George Washington Law Review 46:351–375.
Scitovsky, A. A., and N. M. Snyder
1972 "Effect of coinsurance on use of physician services." Social Security Bulletin 635 (June): 3–19.
Seashore, S. E.
1976 "The design of action research." Pp. 103–118 in A. Clark (ed.), Experimenting with Organizational Life: The Action Research Approach. New York: Plenum Press.
Singer, E.
1978 "Informed consent: Consequences for response rate and response quality in social surveys." American Sociological Review 43:144–162.
Stapleton, W.
1970 "A social scientist's view of Gault and a plea for the experimenting society." Yale Review of Law and Social Action 1 (winter, No. 2–3): 72–81.
Stapleton, W., and L. Teitelbaum
1972 In Defense of Youth: A Study of the Role of Counsel in American Juvenile Courts. New York: Russell Sage.
Thomas, C. W., and W. A. Fitch
1975 "An inquiry into the association between respondent's personal characteristics and juvenile court dispositions." William and Mary Law Review 17:61–84.

Tropp, R. A.
1978 "What problems are raised when the current DHEW regulation on protection of human subjects is applied to social science research?" Pp. 18:1–17 in The Belmont Report: Ethical Principles and Guidelines for the Protection of Human Subjects of Research. Report of the National Commission for the Protection of Human Subjects of Biomedical and Behavioral Research, appendix vol. 2. Washington, D.C.: U.S. Government Printing Office.

Tunnell, G. B.
1977 "Three dimensions of naturalness: An expanded definition of field research." Psychological Bulletin 84:426–437.

U.S. Congress, House of Representatives
1976 Administration of Medicare Cost Experiments. Hearings before the Ways and Means Committee. Cong., sess. Washington, D.C.: U.S. Government Printing Office.

U.S. Congress, Senate, Committee on Finance
1978a Materials Related to Welfare Research and Experimentation. Washington, D.C.: U.S. Government Printing Office.
1978b Welfare Research and Experimentation. Hearings before the Subcommittee on Public Assistance. 95th Cong., 2d sess. Washington, D.C.: U.S. Government Printing Office.

U.S. Department of Health, Education and Welfare
1967 Handbook of Public Assistance Administration, Part IV. Washington, D.C.: U.S. Government Printing Office.
1971 The Institutional Guide to DHEW Policy on Protection of Human Subjects. Washington, D.C.: U.S. Government Printing Office.
1976 Research in Health Care. Washington, D.C.: U.S. Government Printing Office.
1977 Research in Health Care. Washington, D.C.: U.S. Government Printing Office.

U.S. Department of Housing and Urban Development, Office of Policy Development and Research
1974 Second Annual Report on the Experimental Housing Allowance Program. Washington, D.C.: U.S. Government Printing Office.
1976 Experimental Housing Allowances: The 1976 Report. Washington, D.C.: U.S. Government Printing Office.

University of Michigan Survey Research Center, Institute for Social Research
1976 "A survey of institutional review boards and research involving human subjects." Pp. 1–13 in National Committee for Protection of Human Subjects, Appendix to Report and Recommendations: Institutional Review Boards. Washington, D.C.: U.S. Government Printing Office.

Watts, H. W.
1969 "Graduated work incentives: An experiment in negative taxation." American Economic Review 59:463–472.

Webb, E. J., D. Campbell, R. Schwartz, and L. Sechrest
1966 Unobstrusive Measures: Nonreactive Research in the Social Sciences. Chicago, Ill.: Rand McNally.

Weeks, H.
1958 Youthful Offenders at Highfields. Ann Arbor, Mich.: University of Michigan Press.

Wooton, B.
  1963 *Crime and the Criminal Law: Reflections of a Magistrate and Social Scientists.* London, Stevens.
Zelen, M.
  1979 "A new design for randomized clinical trials." *New England Journal of Medicine* 300:1242–1245.
Zinman, J.
  1968 *Public Knowledge: An Essay Concerning the Social Dimension of Science.* Cambridge, England: Cambridge University Press.

7

The Signed Form— Informed Consent?[1]

CHARLES W. LIDZ
LOREN H. ROTH

In the last 2 decades, the effort to assure ethical behavior by both researchers and professionals has come more and more to depend on the doctrine of informed consent (Katz, 1972, 1978; Meisel, 1977). Researchers and clinical professionals are increasingly being required to disclose to their clients the nature of the research or treatment proposed; its risks, benefits, and purposes; and any possible alternatives. The researcher or clinician must then accept the client's decision.

This approach to ethical behavior is not the only possible one. Traditional ethics for doctors, lawyers, and other professionals have emphasized the fiduciary role of the professional: that the professional should act in the best interests of his or her client (Szasz and Hollander, 1956). Traditional research ethics have emphasized the collective usefulness of science and the need for the researcher to refrain from doing harm to the subject. The conflict between traditional ethics and informed consent is quite marked. The ethics of informed consent require the professional to allow the client to make the decision—a decision that at times

[1]Work on this chapter was supported by PHS Grant No. R12 MH27553, National Institute of Mental Health, Center for Studies of Crime and Delinquency and Mental Health Services Development Branch.

145

SOLUTIONS TO ETHICAL
AND LEGAL PROBLEMS
IN SOCIAL RESEARCH

the professional may believe not to be in the client's best interest. This reflects the intense commitment in our society to individualism. In a broader context, informed consent can be seen as one of the many changes in our thinking about people and their proper behaviors that derive from the Enlightenment commitment to the values of individualism and rationality. There seems to be general agreement in the literature that the primary goals of informed consent are the promotion of individual autonomy and the promotion of rational decision making (Katz, 1972).

However, because current ethical systems enjoin the professional to follow this sort of decision-making procedure does not mean that the procedures that are rationally constructed to implement such a doctrine will actually produce the autonomously made rational decisions that they are supposed to. Despite the ethical desirability of informed consent, a number of studies have raised questions as to whether current procedures can produce the results that the doctrine foresees (Fellner and Marshall, 1970; Gray, 1975; Lidz, 1977).

The purpose of this chapter is to consider what possible role consent forms might have in the informed consent process. The general problem is that for a variety of reasons ranging from protection against legal action to administrative efforts to guarantee that the job gets done, most "informed consent" is obtained through the use of written forms. The patient's or subject's signature on the form is taken organizationally as "standing for" an informed consent.[2] The question that this chapter will ask is to what degree or under what circumstances a signed consent form adequately represents an informed consent as specified in legal and ethical doctrine.

The Doctrine of Informed Consent

Before we can assess consent forms, we must describe what is meant by an informed consent. Perhaps it is not surprising that there is, in both the legal and ethical literature, a great deal of disagreement and even downright confusion over what the term means. However, it is not necessary for us to decide exactly the standards by which everything should be judged, but simply to locate the major elements of the debate.

[2]Organizationally, the form stands for the consent, at least in the setting we studied, in that its completion allows a positive answer to the frequently asked question, Did you get his or her consent? From a legal perspective, however, the signature on the form can be seen only as creating a prima facie case. It transfers the burden of proof from the defendant to the plaintiff.

It is possible to isolate five components of the legal–ethical doctrine of informed consent. These specify that:

1. The consent or refusal must be *voluntary*.
2. The doctor or researcher must provide the patient or subject with all *information* relevant to the decision, including the risks, benefits, alternatives, and the nature and purpose of the procedure.
3. The patient or research subject must be *competent*.
4. The patient or research subject ought to *understand* what he or she has been told, although this is probably not technically a legal requirement.
5. The *decision* should be made by the patient or the research subject, and the doctor or researcher is obligated to respect that decision.

Like most legal and ethical concepts, these have an irreducible vagueness about them that even in the clearest formulations (Meisel, Roth, and Lidz, 1977) cannot be eliminated. We can use them only as what Blumer (1969) has called sensitizing concepts that alert us to the issues and that organize our thinking about the issues. However, a few comments are necessary.

In this chapter we will be primarily concerned with two of these concepts: information and understanding. The law has clearly mandated that information about which the patient or subject needs to decide the proposed treatment or research must be provided by the clinician or researcher.[3] However, the law has been quite vague about the manner in which it is to be presented, and little has been said beyond that the language should be simple[4] and that disclosure should be "full and frank."[5] One is left with the impression that the courts expect a clear, frank, simple factual report of the risks, benefits, nature, and purpose of the procedure and its alternatives. One question this chapter deals with is whether the use of consent forms will produce this type of information.

The other aspect of informed consent that this chapter will discuss is understanding. Whether understanding is a part of the law of informed consent is still a matter of debate. There are differing legal positions on whether the patient must understand for a consent to be valid. However, understanding is a critical issue in evaluating the effectiveness of

[3]See, for example, Natanson v. Kline, 354 P.2d 670 (Kan. 1960); and 39 Fed. Reg. 30, 647–30, 657 (1974), 45 CFR, Pt. 46.
[4]Canterbury v. Spence, 464 F.2d 772 (D.C. Cir. 1972).
[5]Demers v. Gerety, 515 P.2d 645 (N.M. 1973).

the current procedures for implementing the ethical doctrine of informed consent. Unless the procedures for providing information leave the patient or subject with some understanding of the issues in the decision, the whole doctrine seems to make little sense. An individual who does not understand the decision that he or she is making is, by definition, not the rational autonomous decision maker that the doctrine envisions.[6]

Research Methods

The findings reported here are preliminary and partial results of a larger study of informed consent in psychiatry, underway at the Department of Psychiatry of the University of Pittsburgh. It involves nonparticipant observation[7] of informed consent procedures in three different units of a large university-affiliated teaching and research psychiatric hospital. Treatment and/or research decisions about clients are made in each unit. The three units are the admission and referral unit of the hospital, an inpatient clinical research ward, and an outpatient clinic that deals primarily with chronic schizophrenic patients. The study has gathered very detailed ethnographic data on several hundred different treatment and research decisions. The complete process of the decisions we watched ranged from less than an hour to almost 2 months long. The general procedure has been to assign two observers to watch the decisions. One observer's job has been to spend all of her time with the patient or patient–subject in order to understand the decision from the perspective of the patient. The other observer spent his time with the staff and tried to understand the staff perspective on the decision. The quality of the data has been enhanced by the use of speed-writing techniques, which have allowed one of the observers to record almost perfectly the formal interviews and discussions between patients and staff. In general, it has been the observers' task to collect all information that might be relevant to the way in which the decision was made, starting when the patient or patient–subject entered the setting and ending only when he or she left.

This method of research has serious limits for studying patient's understanding of the information. Studying understanding involves trying to assess what is in someone else's mind at a specific time. This

---

[6]This is not by any means to say that understanding should be a requirement written into the law.

[7]By "nonparticipant observation" we mean only that the observer is in the setting only as a researcher and tries not to interfere with the flow of interaction.

is not always obvious from what someone says in their day-to-day interaction. Despite our interest in decision making in its "natural context," we found that enthnographic fieldwork methods did not, by themselves, provide us with adequate data to study understanding. We have been forced to employ more "intrusive" methods. Three different methods were used to try to learn what the patients understood about the treatment decision. First, after the decisions seemed to our patient observer to be complete, she interviewed the patient and asked a series of open-ended questions to ascertain what elements of the information had been understood. The other two methods for assessing understanding were employed only on two specific types of consents that occurred in the inpatient unit: consent to electroconvulsive (ECT) therapy and consent to participate in a drug and sleep research protocol. For 100 patient decisions (57 ECT and 43 research), following a procedure developed by Miller and Willner (1974), we attached a second part to the consent forms. This part consisted of a relatively brief questionnaire about some of the information contained in the first part of the consent form. Finally, after these forms were completed, the psychiatrist on the project did an extended videotaped interview with 42 patients or subjects who agreed to do so. These interviews function to provide a much more detailed and closer look at what the patient or subject understood from the consent forms. They provided us with information on the patient's or subject's "gestalt" of the decision as well as their understanding of the elements of information that they were given.

Information Presentation

The first aspect of consent forms that we will consider is the information presentation through the forms. Of special interest is the way in which the information on the consent form is presented by the staff to the patient. In specific, the discussion that follows focuses on the ways in which the staff can, and sometimes does, evade the restrictions on their power posed by the consent forms.

In order to study this, we focus on the ways in which the staff presented admission forms to voluntary patients. These forms were designed by the Pennsylvania State Department of Public Welfare in order to implement the requirement of the 1976 Pennsylvania Mental Health Procedures Act that informed consent to voluntary admission must be obtained from all voluntary patients.

In designing these forms, the Department of Public Welfare seems to have tried to make use of the advantages that all written forms provide to bureaucratic superiors trying to control their subordinates. In this case, the forms seem to allow the department to regulate the behavior of the mental health workers who admit the patient. These forms seem to ensure that the officially appropriate information will be presented independent of the viewpoint of the particular person presenting the information.

The question that faces us here is whether this mechanism is really effective in the face of the staff hostility to the forms. There is no question that the staff viewed these forms with hostility. Almost every staff member who had to use these forms indicated to us, by both word and deed, that they saw these forms as a well-intentioned bureaucratic mistake that hindered the difficult process of providing the patient much-needed treatment.

We will deal here primarily with two forms. The first involves the consent to voluntary admission. This form contains a place where the patient is allowed to decide how much notice she or he wants to give before being permitted to leave the hospital (between 0 and 72 hours). The staff almost always recommends the maximum notice of 72 hours. The second form is a description of the proposed treatment and should include the doctor's written assessment of the problem, the proposed treatments, and the restrictions on the patient's freedom within the hospital. This form usually contains a total of three sentences written by the doctor, one each to describe his or her assessment, the proposed treatment, and the restrictions.

The staff developed a number of ways of dealing with these forms. Perhaps the most prevalent of these is what can be called "discounting" the forms. The staff conveyed to the patient in a number of ways that the forms were "just paperwork." Thus, they frequently introduced the forms to the patients by saying, "I have to ask you to sign this," or "We are required to tell the patient the general treatment plan and what the restrictions are." Or, when showing the patient a very sparse description of the proposed treatment, the clinician admitted that what was written on the form was vague and general, "but there must be something written here." In another instance, the clinician introduced the admission form to the patient by saying that the patient is "not *officially* admitted until" he or she signs the form. In all of these cases, the clinician conveyed to the patient that he or she did not endorse the form as interesting or relevant. It was "just" paperwork.

The effort to convey this attitude seems to have been fairly successful. As one patient commented, "The paperwork has to be done, I guess, but I can't remember what was in it." Another patient signed herself into the hospital, even though she did not have her glasses with her and could not read the form she was signing.

Of the 48 patients we observed in this setting, 27 signed these forms or a form releasing information to insurance companies so that the insurance would pay for the visit to the hospital—a total of 48 forms. Of these forms, 54% were not read. Of the remaining 46%, only 50% showed any substantial evidence, either from spontaneous comments or from interview answers, that the patients understood any major portions of what was on the form. No evidence either way was obtained from 22%.[8] Thus, one would have to conclude that, for whatever reasons, the patients did not take these forms very seriously.

Another mechanism of controlling what the patient learns from the forms concerns focusing the patient's attention on the "important" parts of the form. This seems to be done not to prevent the patients from gaining information but rather to prevent them from "wasting time" reading nonessential parts of the information. The parts of the forms that the clinicians believe to be important are the parts that require the patient's signature. Thus when one patient started reading a part of the form that did not require the patient's signature, the clinician responded, "It's not necessary to read to the end. We want you to look at this top part." Or in another example, the clinician told the patient, "It's these points 1, 2, 3 and 4 which are the ones you should be reading."

Another mechanism was to inform the patient that although in general what the form says is true, it does not apply to them. For example, one part of the forms that was particularly difficult for the staff to manage was where the patients were given a choice of how many hours notice they want to provide the hospital before leaving. This is supposed to be filled in by the patient. However, it is frequently filled in by the staff with "72 hours" either before or after the patient signs the form. In one case where "72 hours" had already been filled in, the patient questioned this and was told that the patients had that choice when they were only coming in for a few hours to do a specific test but that in her case, since they expected her to be in for a long time, they wanted 72 hours notice before she left. The patient, despite being the most aggressively interested in the admission process of all the patients we saw, accepted this explanation without hesitation even though it contradicted what the form said explicitly.

Finally, at the most illegitimate extreme, one flagrantly psychotic patient who was hesitating over whether to sign himself in was ordered to do so in an authoritative tone by a policeman standing over him.

Although we cannot be sure that any of the mechanisms described

---

[8]It was not always possible for the interviewer to ask explicitly about the forms because of time pressures or other reasons.

here caused it, *of all the patients whom we saw admitted, not one ever changed his or her mind after being presented with the information on the consent form.* Indeed this was true of all the forms we saw signed in all three settings.

The Problem of Understanding

Let us now turn to the question of how much the patient or research subject understood when the consent forms were presented with the intention of making the information as clear as possible. We will consider the consent form for participation in a clinical research project that we studied. This research was a double-blind placebo study in which the investigators endeavored to use sleep electroencephalograph (EEG) studies to predict which patient–subjects would respond positively to a particular drug. It involved the double-blind assignment of patient–subjects to either placebo or drug-receiving categories and nightly monitoring of their sleep with EEG machines. The major risk this involved was that the patient–subjects received for 35 days either no drug therapy or quantities of drugs unadjusted to their particular needs. The benefits were that the project paid all costs not covered by insurance and that the patients received more thorough diagnostic evaluations. Furthermore, the staff on the ward were probably better trained than staff in the rest of the hospital. The patient–subjects for this study tended to be better educated than the average patient in the hospital and rather well oriented although frequently quite depressed.

In general the staff did their best to explain the consent form carefully to the patient–subjects. Following their signing the consent form, the patient–subjects were given the second part of the two-part consent form. Finally, they were interviewed in depth by the psychiatrist on our staff. Interviews were videotaped. They averaged about three-quarters of an hour and included all of the questions on the second part of the consent form as well as a series of other questions designed to uncover the patient's global understanding of the issues in the decision. We will discuss here only the findings from the 19 patient–subjects for whom the entire procedure, including the videotaping, was done.

In brief, the results were not very encouraging. Only 10 of the 19 patient–subjects were able to make a consistent distinction between research on one hand and treatment and diagnosis on the other hand. The 9 that failed seemed to treat the research procedure as part of either treatment or diagnostic testing. When asked what the purpose of the research was, they would respond with some variation of "It's to help make me better." One of the patient–subjects, when it was explained to her that not all patients in the hospital were research subjects, commented that being in the research was clearly an "honor." It is worth commenting that one does not turn down an "honor," nor does one generally question whether an honor would be advantageous to receive. Very few of the patient–subjects saw, prior to the videotaped discussions, that taking the placebo might constitute a risk. Likewise several of the patient–subjects described the sleep studies as helping them to feel better, clearly indicating that they saw this therapeutically neutral research technique as a treatment.

On the other hand, almost half of the patient–subjects seemed to understand fairly well some critical dimensions of the decision that they were making. Except for a few technical aspects of the protocol that were not explained clearly in the consent form, the majority gave answers to our questions that we classified as correct. The key dimension separating this group from the others is some appreciation of the meaning of the concept *research*. Patient–subjects without any such appreciation were not able to understand that their doctors would do something that might not be in their best interests. They showed a good deal of creativity in being able to construct ways in which various nontherapeutic research procedures were really therapeutic and in their own best interests.[9]

Although it is difficult to document, one cannot escape the impression when viewing the videotapes that even the patient–subjects who gave all the proper answers did not really appreciate that being in the research might not be in their own narrowly constructed best interests. With one exception, they seemed to be volunteering not out of altruism but out of some sense that somehow or other it was better to be on this ward, in this research project, than it would be to be treated elsewhere. Uniformly, they seemed to believe that the doctors were there primarily to treat them. Despite their ability to describe the difference between treatment and research, they persisted in believing that the research would make their treatment better. For example, consider the case of a 35-year-old mildly depressed but articulate middle-class woman. We have generally considered her to be one of the two or three most knowledgeable patients, and her score on the two-part consent form was

[9]We are indebted to William Shebar, a Mellon Fellow at Western Psychiatric Institute and Clinic, for his careful analysis of the understanding of the concept of research in these videotaped interviews. This discussion is a summary of a working paper that he wrote while a Mellon Fellow with our project in the summer of 1977.

consistent with that judgment. Yet, when asked what the potential disadvantages of being in the research were, she could not name any. When the interviewer suggested to her that this would delay for 35 days the start of her treatment, she responded that this was an advantage from her point of view, as though the delay in treatment was done so that the diagnosis and appropriate treatment would be better established.

Even these patients did not seem to understand that the research design sometimes forced the doctors to do something that may not have been in the patients' best interests. The patients tended to see the research as an experimental treatment for them—that is, as therapeutic research. Thus the issue for the patients in the decision seems to have been more one of determining whether the doctor was right in trying this experiment with their treatment. Most of the patient–subjects took it for granted that the doctor's greater technical expertise allowed him to decide whether the patient should be in the research. Like the patients in the admission unit, the patient–subjects on the research ward tended to see the consent form as a formality that followed the decision, not as information on which to base a decision.

It must be pointed out that although the research consent form did not say that the research was therapeutic, the wording was ambiguous enough so as to allow most patients to interpret it that way. The researchers had written the consent form themselves under the supervision of the university's Institutional Review Board, which seems not to have been too demanding of the information it required the researchers to disclose. Because the researchers had written the form and generally agreed with the language it contained, they were forthright and clear in their presentation of it to the patient–subjects. They did not use the discounting mechanisms that were used by the hospital staff in presenting the admission forms.

It seems possible, then, to suggest simply that the failure of patients to understand the research consent largely reflects the inadequacies of the consent form. However, our staff psychiatrist's efforts to educate the patient–subjects during the videotape interviews indicate that the misunderstanding is deep-seated and requires a drastic revision of the consent form. The whole notion of double-blind nontherapeutic research and the dual role of the clinician–investigator had to be explained to the patients. They had to be almost forced to understand that what the doctor was proposing to do for them was not necessarily the best or the quickest way in which they could be treated and that the compensations that were proposed—that the research would pay for all the treatment and that a better staffed ward and a more thorough diagnostic workup would possibly provide better care—did not do away with those limitations on the type of treatment they were to receive for the first 35 days. Their trust that the doctor would look out for their best interests had to be substantially challenged in order for them to understand the decision fully. It seems unlikely that most doctors would be willing to present that kind of information to a prospective patient. One might speculate that had such a consent form been written for this study, the doctors presenting the forms would have made use of the same mechanisms to discount the information on the form that the staff in the admission unit used.

Conclusions

If we wish to use consent forms as a major mechanism for ensuring ethical research, we are faced with the problem of how to ensure that consent forms are adequate explanations of the factors involved in the decision and how to prevent the use of informal discounting mechanisms, unfair methods of persuasion, and so on, by doctors or researchers. Like most human problems, these difficulties with consent cannot be solved without notable costs. The requirement of gaining informed consent is a substantial burden on the clinician or researcher and perhaps even on the patient or subject. Any effort to make this a meaningful dialogue will likely prove a greater burden. We should seriously consider whether it is worth the time and effort expended. One must also consider the expenditure of state power necessary to coerce the medical or research staff into disclosing information that they do not want to disclose. The state does not have unlimited support from the citizenry, and this type of coercion can be alienating. On the other hand, the failure of the state to use its power to implement central values such as individualism can also undermine public trust in the government.

If the decision is made that the benefits of such policy are worth the costs, the mechanism to ensure a full and balanced disclosure is still problematic. Probably the central requirement of any such mechanism is that it should abolish the researcher's interest in getting a consent rather than a refusal. Although it would not solve all of the practical problems surrounding informed consent, a procedure that would provide the researcher with some reason not to overlook complete and frank communication in favor of efficient processing would certainly help. One way of doing this would be to assign the researcher a projected number of refusals for each research project. The institutional review board (IRB), on the basis of a careful consideration of the risks, benefits, and alternatives available to the research subject, could assign each research project a number of refusals, with the investigator to report the number actually attained. If the IRB set this minimum number of refusals in a careful and realistic fashion, this should put the investigator in a position where he or she would be encouraged to present fully and accurately both the risks and the benefits accruing to subjects of the research. The potential subject would be both better informed and freer from pressure to participate. Another potential advantage of this system would be that it would encourage investigators to design their research so as to minimize risk and thus reduce the number of IRB proposed refusals. Although it would be a mistake to treat the number of proposed refusals as a rigid quota, failure to obtain such a number might be the basis for assigning a consent auditor or for using other investigatory techniques to determine how consents are being gathered. However, it should be noted that current research on IRBs has not shown them to be extremely vigilant guardians of subjects' rights (Barber, Lally, Markarushka, and Sullivan, 1973; Gray, 1975), and it seems possible that a random selection of the decisions of each IRB would have to be reviewed by another body less closely tied to the institution itself.

This proposal is certainly not without some potential difficulties. The most serious of these is that researchers might use the opportunity to sort out the subjects that they want from those that they do not. This could result in systematically biased samples. Moreover, the IRB's task of assigning an appropriate level of refusals would be difficult. We do not now have the knowledge necessary to determine what factors in a research project govern the level of freely given refusals by research subjects.

Although this proposal is not without flaws, given such current proposals as mandatory consent auditors for some research, it might be worth an experimental test. The alternative seems to be either further rigid controls or a basic rethinking of whether we should continue to use the informed consent doctrine as the basis for regulating research.

Acknowledgments

We wish to thank Eviator Zerubavel, William Shebar, and Roberta Rousseau for help in analysis of the data and Dr. Zerubavel for careful review and criticism of an earlier draft.

References

Barber, B., J. Lally, J. Markarushka, and D. Sullivan
1973 *Research on Human Subjects.* New York: Russell Sage.

Blumer, H.
1969 *Symbolic Interactionism.* Englewood Cliffs, N.J.: Prentice-Hall.

Fellner, C., and J. Marshall
1970 "Kidney donors—the myth of informed consent." *American Journal of Psychiatry* 126:1234–1251.

Gray, B.
1975 *Human Subjects in Medical Experimentation: A Sociological Study of the Conduct and Regulation of Clinical Research.* New York: Wiley-Interscience.

Katz, J.
1972 *Experimentation with Human Beings.* New York: Russell Sage.
1978 "Informed consent: A fairy tale? Law's vision." *University of Pittsburgh Law Review* 37:137–154.

Lidz, C. W.
1977 "The voluntariness of the voluntary patient: The weather report model of informed consent." Paper presented to the VI World Congress of Psychiatry, Honolulu, Hawaii.

Meisel, A.
1977 "The expansion of liability for medical accident: From negligence to strict liability by way of informed consent." *Nebraska Law Review* 56:51–152.

Meisel, A., L. Roth, and C. Lidz
1977 "Towards a model of the legal doctrine of informed consent." *American Journal of Psychiatry* 134:285–289.

Miller, R., and H. Willner
1974 "The two-part consent form: A suggestion for promoting free and informed consent." *New England Journal of Medicine:* 290:964–966.

Szasz, T., and M. Hollander
1956 "A contribution to the philosophy of medicine—the basic models of the doctor–patient relationship." *Archives of Internal Medicine:* 97:575–592.

8

Randomization and Consent in the New Mexico Teleconferencing Experiment: Legal and Ethical Considerations[1]

JEROME R. CORSI

The purpose of this chapter is to examine the procedures concerning randomization and participant consent formed to implement an experimental evaluation of telephone versus in-person administrative appeals hearings in the program areas of unemployment insurance and welfare. The formation of these procedures was integral to research planning and central to negotiations between researchers and the New Mexico state agency personnel who requested the evaluation. Prelimi-

[1]This material is based upon research initially supported by the National Science Foundation under the following grant: Jerome R. Corsi, Principal Investigator, "The Use of Teleconferencing in Administrative Fair Hearings," National Science Foundation Grant No. APR–7715516, starting date July 15, 1977; supplemented by National Science Foundation Grant No. DAR–7715516, awarded February 16, 1979. Additional funding was obtained from the Department of Labor, Employment and Training Administration: initial grant subcontracted through the New Mexico Department of Human Services, September 1978; subsequent grant subcontracted through the Colorado Department of Labor and Employment, August 1979. Funding has also been obtained from the U.S. Department of Health, Education and Welfare, Grant No. 18–P–00114–8–01, September 1979; and from the U.S. Department of Agriculture, Food and Nutrition Service, Grant No. 53–3198–0–23, effective February 1980. Any opinions, findings, and conclusions or recommendations expressed in this chapter are those of the author and do not necessarily reflect the views of the funding agencies. This is a report on research in progress.

159

nary procedures were tested in a pilot study conducted in New Mexico during March and April 1978. Based on this experience, procedures were refined prior to initiating the experiment the following year (Corsi and Hurley, 1979b). Although the reporting in this chapter focuses primarily on this case, care will be taken to reflect when appropriate on larger theoretical concerns.

Legal and Ethical Concerns Relating to Randomization and Consent

Rather than merely adopting the innovation, policymakers in the relevant New Mexico agencies sought first to have teleconferencing evaluated. Although telephone hearings seemed a possible means of reducing costs, saving energy, and providing more timely appeals hearings, questions had been raised concerning the legal adequacy of telephone hearings as well as the effect upon hearing participants and hearing outcome. The Legal Aid Society of Albuquerque (LAS), one of the originators of the concept, was interested in telephone hearings as a means of extending geographically the ability to provide legal assistance to eligible clients. LAS joined with the New Mexico agencies in endorsing a scientific evaluation.[2]

To obtain the least equivocal estimate of treatment effects, researchers sought to implement an experimental design. At a first level, subjects would be randomly assigned to an in-person hearing or a telephone treatment.[3] Of concern here was whether assignment to a tele-

---

[2]The first formal proposal on telephone hearings in New Mexico was written in 1970 by Michael B. Browdie, then executive director of LAS. This document, entitled "Proposal to Provide Statewide Administrative Advocacy in Welfare and Unemployment Cases by Contract with a Law Clinic," called for the establishment of a law clinic at the University of New Mexico Law School to utilize the telephone to represent claimants statewide at appeals hearings. The proposal was submitted to the Legal Services Corporation in response to its 1976 solicitation for demonstration projects in the legal services delivery systems study. The Legal Services Corporation rejected the proposal because of a decision in this solicitation to prefer proposals that did not emphasize technological solutions. With the agreement of the LAS, this idea was shared with National Science Foundation program managers at the NSF RANN–2 Conference in Washington, D.C., November 7–9, 1976. There the concept recast as a research proposal received a more enthusiastic reception given the close relationship between the innovation and NSF/RANN program goals.

[3]For unemployment insurance appeals, two types of telephone hearings have been tested: office telephone hearings (OT), where all parties other than the hearing officer gather at an outlying agency office and the hearing officer teleconferences from the central agency office; and split telephone conference hearings (ST), where parties partici-

phone hearing violated any existing positive legal requirements as specified in controlling statutes, regulations, and/or precedential decisions. Also, previous research experience has indicated that randomization to treatment can be problematic ethically if a detriment is imputed to either the experimental or control condition thus raising important considerations of unequal treatment (Riecken and Boruch, 1974). Finally, even if assignment to a telephone hearing were within the legal prerogative of the state agency and did not raise ethical problems of unequal treatment, obtaining informed subject consent could well compromise the randomization by inviting a self-selection effect.

The initial factorial design called for a second random assignment of all subjects to either a lawyer or nonlawyer mode. The lawyer treatment was specifically designed to test lawyer–telephone interaction effects, that is, the ability of legal representation to function effectively when hearings are teleconferenced. Among the modifications to the design resulting from the pilot study were the decisions to apply the main experiment (i.e., the primary telephone treatment) in a randomized design blocked by geographical area and to implement a factorial design including the lawyer treatment in a separate subexperiment with a smaller number of Albuquerque-only subjects (Corsi and Hurley, 1979b: 505–510). Still, random assignment to a lawyer or nonlawyer mode raised potential legal problems; the impression was easily created that assignment to a nonlawyer mode might suggest a research intervention to deny certain claimants legal representation. Also, given that lawyers were to be provided by the experiment, unequal treatment problems were possible if the offer was not made to all eligible claimants. Finally, until the pilot study was conducted, detailed thought had not been devoted to considering what intervention, if any, would be made by researchers after clients accepted the offered legal representation. For instance, if lawyers were left free to exercise professional judgment in the conduct of an assigned case to the point where some claimants were urged to drop fruitless appeals, then a selective mortality problem could be created.

In designing the experiment, researchers became aware that solutions to potential legal and ethical problems demanded detailed negotiations between researchers, university human subject committee representatives, state agency personnel, and the LAS in full realization

---

pate from locations convenient to each and the hearing officer participates via conference from the central office. For welfare appeals, only office telephone hearings have been held due to the state agency's desire to preserve as much as possible the official nature of the hearing (Corsi and Hurley, 1979b:490–491, 506).

that certain solutions raised important research design concerns. Thus, for instance, even if randomization could be preserved, solutions to specific legal or ethical difficulties could be expected to have important implications concerning validity.

Implementing the Telephone Treatment

Prior to implementing the experiment, the principal investigator had to meet, develop working relationships, and negotiate with actors in two New Mexico state agencies, three federal regional offices, and three national federal agencies. This was in addition to interacting with program managers at the National Science Foundation's Division of Applied Research, which first funded the research and was primarily concerned with the scientific quality of the work.

The first point of substantive inquiry concerned legal due process requirements. Nothing could be found in either federal or state statutes that would prohibit telephone hearings. For instance, regarding welfare Aid for Families with Dependent Children (AFDC) appeals, the pertinent federal regulation leaves the format of the hearing open to the state agencies.[4] Even the requirement that the claimant have an opportunity to confront and cross-examine adverse witnesses[5] does not address the in-person issue, as claimants in teleconferenced hearings would be able to have the opportunity, albeit by telephone. The U.S. Supreme Court has placed standards on AFDC cases that are stricter than those for unemployment insurance cases, distinguishing that only the former fall into the more demanding income maintenance area. However, the landmark *Goldberg v. Kelly* decision, which initially imposed the requirements of a due process hearing in the AFDC context, did not address the question of a face-to-face format being a requirement.[6] The extensive dictum in the majority *Goldberg* opinion specified several procedural requirements that seemed consistent with telephone hearings.[7]

[4]45 C.F.R. 205.10.

[5]*Id.* at (a) (13) (vi).

[6]397 U.S. 254 (1970).

[7]These due process elements included: the necessity of notice regarding adverse action taken on a claim and the opportunity for a hearing, the right to legal counsel if desired by the claimant, that the hearing take place before an unbiased and neutral hearing officer different from and not administratively responsible to the official who took the adverse action from which the appeal arose, the right to confront adverse witnesses and testimony, the right to a decision based solely on the hearing record, and the right to a prompt hearing that is offered prior to the imposition of the proposed benefit reduction or termination.

Since 1970, the California Unemployment Insurance Appeals Board (CUIAB) has been experimenting with telephone hearings: (a) to conduct interstate appeals where California was liable; and (b) to substitute for the intrastate simultaneous-divided in-person procedure. In the 1976 case *Slattery v. California Unemployment Insurance Appeals Board* the California Court of Appeal for the Second District endorsed this innovation.[8] In dictum the court commented that the CUIAB had "devised a pragmatic solution, made possible by modern technology, which attempts to reconcile the problem of geographically separate adversaries with the core elements of a fair adversary hearing."[9] Researchers in the first phase of the project had studied the California innovation and considered its implications for New Mexico. In the latter instance, application of the technology was being investigated as a substitute for travel by hearing officers even when the parties to the appeal were in sufficient geographical proximity to hold a single in-person hearing (Corsi and Hurley, 1979a).

From the beginning of the study, the special need of unemployment insurance to handle split appeals and the court endorsement of the CUIAB innovation led to greater enthusiasm and fewer due process concerns than in the welfare area. Telephone hearings in welfare appeals were always more sensitive given the in-state location of all welfare claimants, the special income maintenance position of welfare programs, and the knowledge that welfare clients to a somewhat larger extent than unemployment insurance claimants would disproportionately include minorities, those with lower standards of living, and those with fewer years of formal education.

That telephone hearings did not violate any established due process requirements was the cornerstone of the research strategy concerning randomization and subject consent. Prior to the pilot study, counsel for the state agencies determined that holding telephone hearings was within agency authority regarding fair hearing format; these attorneys felt they had strict legal justification to adopt the innovation without a social science evaluation. Given this, the agency had no legal difficulty even with an extreme position where telephone hearings would be compulsory as assigned. Still, detailed discussions with various officials were necessary to explain why researchers wanted random assignment. Some administrators initially assumed the test could be conducted merely by trying a few telephone hearings and believed the choice should be left to the client. The discussions became especially difficult when administrators realized that researchers wanted to make

---

[8]131 Ca. Rptr. 422 (1976).
[9]*Id.* at 425.

the assignment to treatment themselves and that this would entail some in-person hearings at distant locations, where the telephone would be more efficient, and some phone hearings reasonably near the central office, where in-person hearings could easily be held. Finally, although administrators felt they had the legal authority to compel telephone hearings, they nevertheless felt uncomfortable about leaving clients no choice whatsoever in an experimental program.[10]

The following compromise position was negotiated: Using a random assignment scheme administered by the researchers as appeal requests were received by the agency, researchers designated cases either for in-person or for telephone hearings. The agency agreed to accept all assignments as specified by the researchers. Hearing participants would receive a telephone or in-person "Notice of Hearing Form" according to assignment. An agency phone number on the hearing notice was listed in case the party receiving the notice had any questions. Any party asking for a change of hearing mode (either from telephone to in-person or vice versa) would be reassigned as requested.

This procedure generated considerable discussion. Objections were voiced that hearing participants would not be aware of a choice. Claimants, some argued, would receive the agency notice without question, never realizing that the telephone hearing was being tested prior to an agency adoption decision. On the other hand, researchers responded that to invite participant choice could lead to a substantial self-selection effect that might compromise internal validity if treatment interaction caused certain types of participants disproportionately to reject telephone assignments (Cook and Campbell, 1979). Researchers relied heavily upon the legal authority of the agency and an affirmative responsibility regarding subject safety, arguing that there was no reason to believe that subjects could be in jeopardy or risk with the experimental treatment (Riecken and Boruch, 1978:521–522). Furthermore, in all cases parties unsuccessful at the hearing level had recourse to further appeals in the courts. Researchers were less confident that fully informed subject consent could be achieved in these program areas (Singer, Chapter 10, this volume).[11]

---

[10]The reader should be aware of the double sense in which the word *experiment* is used here. The innovation of telephone hearings was an *experiment* in that an exploratory application was being made of the technology. At the same time, *experiment* was being used by researchers to refer strictly to a scientific design utilizing random assignment to establish comparisons between treatments. These two meanings tended to complement one another in discussions, but nuances often required reflection and distinction (Lumsdaine and Bennett, 1975:533).

[11]These procedures passed review by the University of New Mexico Human Subjects Committee. However, when the principal investigator moved to the University of Denver

Although the New Mexico Employment Security Department (ESD) accepted these procedures, the Income Support Division of the New Mexico Department of Human Services (ISD) agreed only upon the condition that LAS approved. LAS in New Mexico has been a primary advocate of client rights, and ISD was confident that LAS would agree to nothing that would compromise those rights. The agreement was final when the LAS executive director wrote the director of the New Mexico Department of Human Services that "LAS staff will not raise any legal argument on appeal against the telephone mode of hearing arising out of the Teleconferencing Project in which we participate."[12] This statement resulted from an independent LAS determination that telephone hearings, even in welfare cases, comply with established due process requirements.

During the pilot study, an associate administrator and a lawyer from the Department of Health, Education and Welfare (HEW) regional office in Dallas site-visited in Santa Fe and requested a meeting with researchers and agency staff.[13] The randomization and consent considerations were a primary topic. These issues were raised in virtually all of the many review meetings held with officials of the various agencies prior to the actual implementation of the experiment in the spring of

---

in January 1979, that institution's Human Subjects Committee objected, even though a pilot test in New Mexico had already been conducted on these principles. To secure support of the latter committee, procedures were stressed whereby all parties to a hearing would be read a statement of the study at the conclusion of the hearing and asked to give their consent to being interviewed. If the agreements of the central parties were not obtained, the case was dropped from the study.

[12]Letter of April 12, 1979, from Gary J. Martone, executive director, LAS, to Lawrence B. Ingram, secretary, New Mexico Department of Human Services. Martone carefully added, "This agreement does not mean that other due process issues, e.g., right to confrontation, adequate record, et cetera, might not be raised."

[13]About this time the regional HEW commissioner wrote the secretary of the New Mexico Department of Human Services as follows:

> If our interpretation of your plan not to apprise the person of the experiment prior to his arrival at the hearing is correct, we would hesitate to look upon this exercise favorably in the absence of a forthright explanation to the applicant of the deviation from the established procedure [Letter of April 14, 1978, from Martha A. McSteen, HEW regional administrator, to Fernando E. C. DeBaca, secretary, New Mexico, Department of Human Services].

When researchers were applying for HEW support in March 1979, HEW counsel reviewed the research proposal and could find no specific statute regarding hearing format that teleconferencing violated. Only when researchers requested funding (not during the pilot test) did the New Mexico agency request a waiver under Section 1115(a) of the Social Security Act. This waiver was even then limited to the statewide uniformity provision, which would be violated by applying telephone hearings only to certain claimants.

1979. Ultimately, all agencies accepted these procedures; however, almost always the initial reaction was at least skepticism.

Agreements with Legal Aid regarding the Lawyer Treatment

In order to implement the lawyer experiment, a subsample of Albuquerque-only subjects were first randomly assigned to either an inperson or a telephone treatment and second randomly assigned to a laywer or nonlawyer treatment, thus creating the four cells of the two-by-two factorial design.[14] Establishing the nonlawyer treatment raised important legal and ethical concerns.

To begin with, the agencies administering these programs are not under any legal obligation to provide attorneys to all hearing applicants or even to those who request legal representation. At the same time, the agency cannot deny legal representation to any claimant who obtains legal assistance.[15] For these reasons, the establishment of the lawyer treatment was accomplished by an expansion of the current supply of legal representation. Clients assigned to a lawyer cell were to be contacted by LAS so legal assistance could be offered. To facilitate this, LAS agreed to liberalize substantially the income eligibility requirements, thus permitting more unemployment insurance claimants to qualify.[16]

[14]In the unemployment insurance lawyer subexperiment, only split telephone conferences were utilized since the agency found no implementation likelihood that hearing participants would ever be asked to assemble at an Albuquerque agency office other than the central office, where the appeals referees were stationed. In practice, legal aid lawyers and the clients have assembled at the LAS Albuquerque office for the teleconference with the ESD appeals referee. In the welfare lawyer subexperiment, office telephone hearings have been used since this is the main adoption mode under consideration by the agency. This is facilitated by the location of the ISD central office in Santa Fe; legal aid lawyers and assigned clients met at the designated Albuquerque welfare office with the case-worker–casework supervisor and hearing transcriber to teleconference to the hearing officer in Santa Fe. In selecting these particular configurations from the multiplicity of possibilities, researchers became aware of the extent to which the treatment operationalization "always brings to light the implicit premises and unverbalized assumptions that lurk in the conceptual thickets of intervention programs [Riecken and Boruch, 1978: 514]."

[15]Goldberg v. Kelly, 397 U.S. 254, at 270–271 (1970); United States v. Weller, 509 F. Supp. 50 (N.D. Cal. 1969).

[16]Specifically, during the experiment LAS agreed that the gross annual income (adjusted for family size) eligibility requirements established for welfare claimants would be doubled for unemployment insurance claimants (Letter of January 16, 1979, from Gary J. Martone, executive director, LAS, to Jerome R. Corsi, principal investigator, Fair Hearing Project).

When a subject was assigned to a nonlawyer cell, this was strictly a research determination and was never revealed to the subject. All claimants randomly assigned to a nonlawyer cell received the normal communication from the agency regarding the type of hearing to which they were scheduled. The information provided by both agencies clearly informed the claimants of their right to legal representation. When a person assigned to a nonlawyer cell independently obtained legal representation, that person was dropped from the experiment, data was collected on the case separately, and a new case was randomly assigned as a replacement. By these procedures, researchers sought never to interfere with a claimant's choice to obtain legal counsel.[17]

LAS saw no due process problems with telephone hearings per se but reserved the right to remove any case from a telephone assignment if, in the responsible attorney's professional judgment, the hearing should be held face to face. Also, LAS remained solely responsible for preserving the lawyer–client relationship and for making all necessary legal decisions regarding the provision of representation.[18] Thus, for example, LAS could advise a particular client that there was no basis for the appeal and recommend a withdrawal of the hearing request; or, LAS could continue an appeal beyond the hearing level and into the courts if necessary. All questions of representational strategy were left solely to the domain of LAS. These agreements reflected a determination that the legal rights of claimants were of paramount importance. Conclusions resulting from these determinations were consistent with the research objective to intervene as little as necessary in the dynamics of the legal process under investigation.

Each of the funding agencies in the proposal review process examined in detail these procedures for implementing the lawyer treatment. It was necessary to submit several proposal clarifications, stressing that the lawyer subexperiment was to be implemented via an expansion in the supply of legal representation rather than via a denial of lawyers to those in nonlawyer cells.[19] Some state agency administrators, who un-

[17]Questions were raised about claimants who might hear of the increased legal assistance and as a consequence request LAS representation. A decision was made that such individuals would be treated as any claimant who normally approaches LAS to inquire about services. Those claimants who exceeded normal income eligibility requirements would still be free to obtain private counsel.

[18]Letter of November 27, 1978, from Gary J. Martone, executive director, LAS, to Jerome R. Corsi, principal investigator, Fair Hearing Project.

[19]This solution for implementing the lawyer subexperiment draws upon Zeisel's (1970) suggestion that a test be designed so that the experimental treatment involves an intervention expected to have favorable effects. For example, in testing the relation between cigarette smoking and cancer, Zeisel recommends having subjects *stop* smoking rather than randomly assigning subjects to begin smoking.

derstood this point all too well, expressed concern that increased legal aid involvement would lead to increased litigation against the agency—an unintended and, from their point of view, somewhat mixed benefit.

Discussion

Other solutions to the research problems discussed here are imaginable. For instance, researchers could have agreed at the beginning to inform subjects completely, noting that telephone conferencing was an experimental method of conducting hearings and that researchers would be making repeated observations as well as collecting data on extensive file materials. Subjects could have been asked first to sign agreements indicating their willingness to participate in the study and to accept phone assignments. The population for random assignment could then have been subjects who so consented in writing. This would have eliminated any concern that legal rights would be violated because all subjects in effect would have signed waivers. The state agencies and funding sources would have had few concerns about ethical considerations, adverse participant response, or vocal criticism.

By insisting upon random assignment from the population of all hearing requests in the chosen program areas, researchers opted for a more rigorous test. Self-selection factors would be less likely to present alternative explanations to challenge attribution of outcome to treatment.

Field experimentation inevitably presents researchers with complex ethical problems, often resolvable only through difficult trade-offs. The rigor of design maintained unyieldingly can conflict with important subject rights. At the same time, researchers should not assume that subjects who agree to participate in experiments understand fully all their agreement entails. The phrase *informed consent* involves two concepts logically separate, such that *informed* cannot be assumed simply from an act of *consent*. Thus, a fact of subject consent does not provide researchers with a license to proceed unconcerned about potential adverse consequences. For instance, one can imagine a test where certain subjects who agree to participate later decide to withdraw from the test; in the extreme, some may even contemplate legal action against experimenters for adverse consequences perceived fully only after the test has begun. Subjects in particular instances may argue convincingly that they did not initially understand or appreciate the effects of a treatment; that is, that the treatment as experienced was more objectionable than initially anticipated. If informed consent is conceptualized as a single act entirely consummated before the test begins, then we may be drastically simplifying the situation. The concept of "risk," which at least initially was one of the major motivations for institutionalizing subject consent procedures, must remain a continuing primary concern of researchers throughout a test.

In this instance, the need to evaluate was motivated by the serious questions that had been raised concerning the innovation. Still, the underlying assumptions of the researchers centered upon the realizations that existing law regarding administrative hearings was flexible and that telephone hearings violated no positive rules. Researchers viewed protection of subjects from known risk to be an affirmative responsibility rather than a mechanistic concern in which the researcher bore no responsibility as long as the subject signed a form. At the same time, provisions were made to accommodate the strong wishes of participants who resisted assignments, even if a large number of such objections were to move the test in the direction of becoming a quasi-experiment with self-selection by refusal being a prominent response. Traditionally, legal aid societies have been important defenders of rights for welfare clients; their role regarding unemployment insurance claimants is steadily growing. In New Mexico we could find no other group more concerned with the rights of those likely to be subjects in this test. Thus, the agreement and participation of LAS throughout this test was of major importance to assure agency personnel as well as researchers that client rights were adequately protected.

A second concern underlying informed consent is an implied principle that, in a Kantian sense, subjects should not be treated as objects; that is, researchers should not observe subjects unless subjects authorize the observation. This principle can be defended despite the many contributions to data bases that our societal involvement routinely entails, with or without our full knowledge of how or to what ends such information may ultimately be utilized on either an individual or an aggregate level. Consider, for instance, school records, medical records, employment data, tax information, and so on—all routinely collected and analyzed as personal as well as aggregated data. In this study, subjects at the time they were interviewed were given an additional opportunity to refuse participation, in which instance their records were removed from the test.

Other research questions with other legal or ethical problems associated with the administration of treatment may not be handled in the same way. What is presented here is *not* an argument, for instance, that randomization should be imposed on subjects or that informed prior consent should not be obtained. Rather, the experience of this test argues for examining the legal and ethical obligations not mechanistically but in light of their full behavioral complexity. Given moral restraints, some research problems may be accessible only through the cross-sectional analysis of the quasi-experiment. The larger point sought to be stressed by this example is that the solutions designed should bear a sensitivity to the magnitude and particular configuration of the subject risks and specific legal and ethical concerns evident in each research application.

References

Boruch, R. F.
  1975   "On common contentions about randomized field experiments." Pp. 108–145 in R. F. Boruch and H. W. Riecken (eds.), *Experimental Tests of Public Policy.* Boulder, Colo.: Westview Press; also Pp. 158–194 in G. V. Glass (ed.), *Evaluation Studies Review Annual.* Beverly Hills, Calif.: Sage, 1976.
Campbell, D. T., and J. C. Stanley
  1963   *Experimental and Quasi-Experimental Designs for Research.* Chicago: Rand McNally.
Cook, T. D., and D. T. Campbell
  1979   *Quasi-Experimentation: Design and Analysis Issues for Field Settings.* Chicago: Rand McNally.
Corsi, J. R., and T. L. Hurley
  1979a "Attitudes toward the use of the telephone in administrative hearings: The California experience." *Administrative Law Review* 31:247–283
  1979b "Pilot study report on the use of the telephone in administrative fair hearings." *Administrative Law Review* 31:485–524.
Lumsdaine, A. A., and C. A. Bennett
  1975   "Assessing alternative conceptions of evaluation." Pp. 525–553 in C. A. Bennett and A. A. Lumsdaine (eds.), *Evaluation and Experimentation: Some Critical Issues in Assessing Social Programs.* New York: Academic Press.
Riecken, H. W., and R. F. Boruch
  1974   *Social Experimentation: A Method for Planning and Evaluating Social Intervention.* New York: Academic Press.
  1978   "Social experiments." *Annual Review of Sociology* 4:511–532.
Zeisel, H.
  1970   "Reducing hazards of human experiments through modification in research design." *Annals of the New York Academy of Sciences* 169:475–486.

9

The Efficient Conduct of Social Science Research and Administrative Review Procedures

Some General Principles for Conducting Applied Social Science Research

In conducting applied social research, we operate with a set of assumptions or principles that guide the way we undertake our studies. Some of these principles are designed to ensure the quality of results, whereas others are concerned with ethical issues. Unfortunately, some of the principles are in conflict with others. They frequently lead to costly and time-consuming practices that may not strike a reasonable compromise between the costs and human gains desired.

Listed in Table 9.1 are 10 principles of applied social research. Ideally, we would like to honor them all, but frequently we must accept some middle ground. As the first principle states, we would like to be efficient and cost-effective, yet this goal is frequently frustrated by clearance procedures, requirements for privacy and confidentiality, and problems of informed consent. Similarly, we would like to produce results expeditiously. How can we, though, when government clearance procedures may consume 6 months of a schedule before a field test can be conducted, parents must be contacted before children may

SOLUTIONS TO ETHICAL
AND LEGAL PROBLEMS
IN SOCIAL RESEARCH

Copyright © 1983 by Academic Press, Inc.
All rights of reproduction in any form reserved.
ISBN 0-12-118680-6

Table 9.1
Some Basic Principles of Applied Social Research

---

1. Applied social research should be conducted in an efficient and cost-effective manner.
2. Researchers should conduct studies as expeditiously as possible.
3. Researchers should design and follow proper sampling procedures.
4. Applied social science research should conform to good design and experimental procedures.
5. Researchers should conduct field tests of instruments and revise them before final use.
6. Researchers should be properly respectful of privacy, both individual and institutional.
7. Applied social science researchers should comply with the requirements for informed consent.
8. Researchers should keep response burden as low as consistent with proper investigation of the question being studied.
9. Applied social science researchers should comply with freedom of information requirements.
10. Applied social science researchers should communicate the results of a study to those involved in the study.

---

be administered a simple reading test, or bureaucratic approvals must be obtained at every step of the study?

We all recognize the desirability of proper sampling, be it random or some purposive procedure. Proper sampling can be frustrated, however, by problems of informed consent, the refusal of institutions to participate, or funding considerations. Similarly, we admire good design and experimental procedures. But, perhaps, the treatment is well underway before the evaluation is started. Perhaps the law or considerations of equity make the formation of an appropriate control group impossible. Surely we all want to pretest the instruments used in a study, but this is frequently not done because of time constraints and the lengthy clearance procedures.

We believe in the principles of informed consent, privacy, and confidentiality. However, what price are we willing to pay for these. Does it make sense to read a prepared statement to first-grade students, informing them of the law under which the study is being conducted, of their right to inspect their research record, and that participation is voluntary? No one will disagree with the idea of protecting privacy and the confidentiality of information, but what is a reasonable price to pay? In longitudinal studies, complex identification schemes are often required to maintain confidentiality. But who would want to reveal or know the simple achievement test score of a student? In the realm of applied social research (not credit bureaus or the law enforcement community), are there actual cases where people have been injured because of breaches of privacy? Should we feed back results of studies to all participants, and at what level of detail and cost relative to the gain to the participants?

Lest the point be misunderstood, it must be asserted that there *are* situations where considerations of privacy, confidentiality, and informed consent are paramount. There are cases where clearance and administrative approval at many levels are essential. But because there are situations requiring these procedures, must all research enterprise be made uniformly to follow' the most restrictive procedures? Surely a wise bureaucracy can design regulations and methods that achieve a sensible compromise between concerns for equity, privacy, and cost-effectiveness.

The Clearance Procedures as an Example of the Gain Not Justifying the Cost

In the June 1977 issue of the *Educational Researcher*, I discussed the problems associated with obtaining approval to administer research and evaluation instruments in a study under federal sponsorship. In that article, I described the actual events experienced in obtaining approval of instruments in two different evaluation projects. In this discussion, I will generalize the steps and procedures involved in obtaining clearance for a typical evaluation study. These are the procedures that must be followed under any research or evaluation contract funded by a federal education agency. Some grants to individual researchers are excluded from the clearance process.

In order to illustrate the procedures involved, let us suppose that we have a contract from a federal education agency to evaluate the impact of a particular education program in the public schools and that the evaluation requires collection of data from more than nine cases, be they schools, students, principals, or teachers. Let us also suppose that, in addition to standard published tests, the instruments we will use to collect the data include questionnaires or survey forms. Furthermore, suppose we believe the instruments should be field-tested before being used in the major data collection effort—surely a good practice. There are specific clearance procedures that must be followed before the instruments may be used.[1]

[1]The process described is that existing in 1977. As will be discussed later, there have been some changes since then, but, under a proposed new law, we seem to be going back to the process described here.

A useful way to think of the forms clearance process in education studies is to consider the organizations and schedules involved. Not only the Office of Management and Budget (OMB), as is frequently thought, but also a host of agencies are concerned with instrument clearance. The major organizations and individuals involved are described in the following subsections.

THE CONTRACTOR

Having won a competitive procurement, the contractor must develop the instruments and perform the study. Usually, the contract is awarded several months later than the planned date of award, compressing the schedule. Since the school year during which data are to be collected remains fixed, this late award reduces the time to develop a sampling and analysis plan and to develop instruments, all of which are required for the clearance package.

THE CONTRACT MONITOR

The responsible technical monitor in the customer's organization— the Department of Education (DE), National Institute of Education (NIE), or National Center for Educational Statistics (NCES)—is the person who interacts with the contractor, the educational program office, the agencies' forms clearance offices, the Educational Data Acquisition Council (EDAC), and the OMB. The contract monitor helps in producing the clearance package and getting it cleared.

THE PROGRAM OFFICE

This office is responsible for the administration of the educational program being evaluated, such as the Title I, Emergency School Aid Act (ESAA), Follow Through, or Special Services for the Disadvantaged program offices.

FORMS CLEARANCE OFFICER

Each agency has a person through which all clearance packages must be processed as they go to EDAC or OMB. The forms clearance officer's review may be perfunctory but is often detailed, and he or she frequently requires the package to be modified.

EDUCATIONAL DATA ACQUISITION COUNCIL

EDAC is a legally established review committee operated by the NCES, with membership from the Office of the Assistant Secretary of Education, NCES, the Office of Civil Rights, DE, and NIE and an "observer" from the Committee on Evaluation and Information Systems.

OFFICE OF MANAGEMENT AND BUDGET

By law, the OMB is responsible for clearing all forms, questionnaires, and data collection instruments administered in connection with work done for the federal government and for overseeing the operation of all executive branch agencies. It is thus concerned with the justification for the study and the soundness of its execution.

COMMITTEE ON EVALUATION AND INFORMATION SYSTEMS (CEIS) OF THE COUNCIL OF CHIEF STATE SCHOOL OFFICERS

Each state department of education appoints a staff member as its CEIS representative. Each major DE evaluation study has a CEIS representative on the Policy Advisory Committee for the study and, through an understanding with DE, is to review all instruments. There seems to be a similar understanding with EDAC.

ASSISTANT SECRETARY FOR EDUCATION AND OFFICE OF THE SECRETARY OF HEALTH, EDUCATION AND WELFARE

These are usually channels through which clearance packages must pass. Unless there is some special problem or recent pressure regarding clearances, packages are routinely forwarded.

THE SCHOOLS

Although schools do not become directly involved in the clearance process, their schedules have an important impact. Arrangements for conducting a *field test* must be made while the clearance process is in progress, as must arrangements for full testing in impact studies. Also, notice of intent to collect data must be published in the *Federal Regis-*

ter, and any school or other interested party can ask to review the instruments.

What material must be submitted to these organizations for their consideration? A collection of materials called a "clearance package" must be prepared by the contractor. The content of the package is spelled out by the OMB circular that governs how approval should be obtained. A fairly typical clearance package for a program such as that outlined in our hypothetical example is shown in the following table.

Contents	Number of pages
1. Introduction	2
2. Background and description of study	20
3. Sampling plan, data collection procedures, and analysis plan	30
4. Justification for instruments	170
5. Plans for field test	20
6. Respondent burden	4
7. Confidentiality of data	2
8. Cost	2
9. Appendix containing the instruments, instructions, and procedures	250
	500

Most of the preceding items are self-evident except for "Justification for instruments." In this section, all items serving a similar purpose are grouped together, and the contractor must discuss and defend the reason for asking the items, any literature reference, and any previous use of similar items. Each type of information to be collected must be referenced to the purpose of the study and to the design and analysis plan.

Early in the development of the instruments, the contractor, the contract monitor, and the program officers work with rough drafts. But the agency clearance officer, CEIS, EDAC, and OMB review the formal printed clearance package.

How are all these organizations and people involved in clearing the instrument? Figure 9.1 shows the many activities that are involved from the time a contract is awarded until the instrument can be administered for data collection. It would not be appropriate here to discuss each step, but it is important to emphasize that at each review by the agency clearance officer, EDAC, CEIS, and OMB, the clearance package may well be returned to the contractor for revision and resubmittal. Even a change in wording of a few items or a minor change in procedures means technically that the package must go back to the contractor for revision, retyping, and resubmittal. As can be seen from Figure 9.1, if a contract is awarded in September of a given year (the

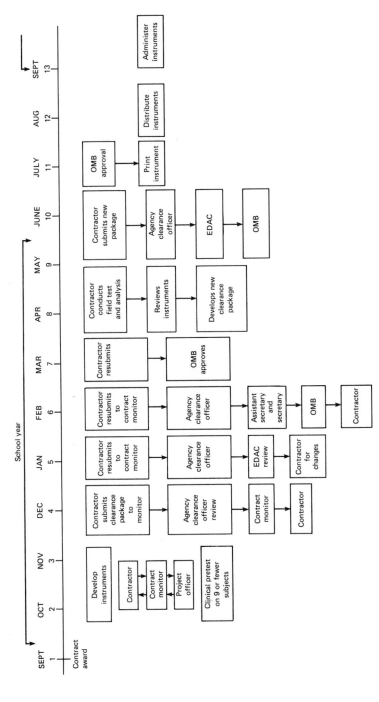

Figure 9.1. Flow chart illustrates the many activities in an instrument review cycle.

beginning of a school year), the contractor will be fortunate to be able to administer instruments early in the next school year.

What are the advantages and disadvantages of the procedures I have just outlined? I believe the following are significant points:

1. The procedures meet the requirements of law. EDAC and OMB are legally required to review and approve instruments. One may question the wisdom of the laws and procedures involved in implementing them, but EDAC and OMB are carrying out their legal responsibilities.

2. The procedures ensure that everyone who should be involved in the development and administration of the instruments has an opportunity to become involved with the instruments' development process. I personally think there are too many people involved, but everyone has the opportunity and may have near or actual veto power.

3. In theory, excellent instruments should result from this expert review. I think this is not the case. Early interaction between the contractor, the program monitor, and the program office is often useful. Beyond that, one can argue that the instruments suffer. Many of the reviewers are expert, but the schedule is usually so tight that the contractor accepts poor suggestions for item revisions simply to move the clearance process forward. This problem is made more difficult because at least currently, some agency clearance officers and the OMB will not meet with the contractor but instead meet only with the agency contract monitor. Although contract monitors are usually conscientious, they cannot defend all the details of the instruments, as the actual instrument developers could.

4. The present procedures are counterproductive in terms of schedules. If an instrument needs to be refined through field-test procedures, the review process ensures that there is at least a year between contract award and collection of data. Some evaluations are using poor instruments because they are foregoing the field test phase of instrument development. A clinical pretest on nine subjects is completely inadequate for the determination of the psychometric qualities of an instrument. Yet that number of cases is all that is allowed without clearance. Applied social researchers are often criticized because our results are often too late for use by senior executives or for use in the legislative process. By its very nature, good research is a slow process. But we are being seriously penalized by the present lengthy clearance process.

5. The present procedures are costly. In the *Educational Researcher* (1977), I estimated that the cost of obtaining clearance for the instruments of a large study of compensatory education was $155,000. Since calculating these costs, I have seen no reason to change them. Indeed,

the procedures are becoming more complicated and expensive. Much of this cost is associated with the serial nature of the clearance process and could be reduced. I will return to this point shortly.

6. Clearance procedures and general management reviews are combined in a confusing and counterproductive manner. OMB has responsibility for the general overview of the operation of the executive branch of government and as part of that responsibility should be concerned that research and evaluation studies are well conceived and executed. The time for OMB involvement, in the requirements for a study and in the general nature of the design, is during the early stages of a project. At present, the clearance package is used as a vehicle for OMB to become involved in the justification for the study, the nature of the sample, and the general design of the study. If OMB should be concerned regarding a study, it should become involved much earlier than at the time of instrument clearance and should separate instrument review from general management review.

The process just described accurately reflects the procedures followed in 1977. In 1978 Congress passed the "Control of Paperwork Amendments of 1978" which changed these procedures for the better. The new law changed OMB and EDAC involvement in the clearance process by establishing a new agency, Federal Educational Data Acquisition Council (FEDAC). In many ways FEDAC operated in the same way that EDAC had previously operated, but with one important exception. FEDAC had final approval authority, and instruments no longer needed review by OMB. This took one review authority out of the link and shortened the procedure. Also, FEDAC was staffed by experts in evaluation methodology and psychometrics and seemed to have a better understanding of instrument development requirements. In addition, under FEDAC the instrument developer met with its staff at the time the instruments were being reviewed. This allowed a much better exchange of information regarding the reasons for the instruments and for the particular items making up an instrument. Generally, FEDAC's procedures, scheduling of reviews, and consideration of the contents of clearance packages were a distinct improvement over the procedure described earlier. Clearance still took too much time and was too costly, but a step in the right direction had been taken.

Now, there has been a regression to the less efficient practices that existed in 1977. Congress passed the "Paperwork Reduction Act of 1980" (H.R. 6410 and S. 1411). The committee report on the House bill says, "H.R. 6410 is based on long and careful study of problems associated with the way the Government manages its information resources.

Different segments of this study were carried out by the Commission of Federal Paperwork, the President's Federal Data Processing Reorganization Project, the General Accounting Office, and others."[2] It is true that the new bill consolidates responsibility and closes loopholes in a number of areas of paperwork control, but as far as education evaluation and research is concerned, it appears to be a step backward. The committee's action regarding education was not taken haphazardly. A complete section of the report is devoted to "Elimination of Division of Clearance Authority with Respect to Education Data Collection." The report says

> In the case of information collections from educational institutions, repeal of the HEW Secretary's authority substitutes the management structure created under H.R. 6410 for one created by amendments to the General Education Provisions Act (GEPA) which were enacted on November 1, 1978. GEPA imposes on the secretary of HEW the responsibility for coordinating the collection of information (1) whenever the respondents are primarily educational agencies or institutions and (2) whenever the purpose of an information collection is to request information for the management of, formulation of policy related to, or evaluation of, Federal education programs. . . .
>
> H.R. 6410 transfers the education information collection approval responsibility back to OMB. GAO and OMB both testified in favor of eliminating the present split authority. The Commission of Federal Paperwork, although it concluded its work before the GEPA amendment, also favored eliminating split authority and central clearance exemptions under the Federal Reports Act.
>
> H.R. 6410 is not the first attempt to repeal the education exemption from central clearance under the Federal Reports Act. The Senate attempted to repeal the exemption by a provision contained in the Senate-passed version of the legislation to create the New Department of Education. The House-passed version did not contain a similar provision. The Senate conferees agreed to the House-passed version on this point, on the understanding that the issue would be dealt with in this legislation. Thus, the provision to repeal the exemption is included in H.R. 6410.
>
> A question has been raised about whether OMB will staff itself to do an effective job of making Government-wide information policy and reviewing and coordinating information collection requests and minimizing the burden imposed by them on the public. The Committee intends that OMB staff itself do an efficient and effective job carrying out all its responsibilities assigned by H.R. 6410. Specific authorization is provided for the Office of Federal Information Policy in this legislation to ensure this.

It is clear that Congress intended to consolidate all paperwork clearance in OMB. Some of the independent regulatory agencies such as the

[2]H. R. Rep. No. 835, 96th Cong., 2d Sess. (1980).

Securities and Exchange Commission and the Federal Communications Commission argued strongly that such consolidation would interfere with their operations. The House committee forcefully rejected their arguments. In the case of education, there have been repeated complaints from the Chief State School Officers that the schools were being overwhelmed with reporting requirements and that at times there had been refusals to supply federally required information. The reversion to OMB clearance authority was not particularly directed toward education research and evaluation but rather was directed to the larger issue of total federal education reporting needs.

The new OMB Office of Federal Information Policy may be staffed with people who understand the problem, and they may develop procedures that expedite forms clearance for evaluation and research projects; but current experience suggest that there is a regression to earlier practices. Again, I repeat the recommendation of my *Educational Researcher* (1977) article:

> I would suggest that serious consideration be given to a different process for obtaining clearance and review. The suggestion is simple: the contractor and the project monitor should work together to develop an instrument package which they believe fulfills the requirements of the study. Once that package has been developed, a meeting should be called which includes the contractor, the government project monitor, a representative from the program office, members of EDAC, representatives from OMB, and a representative from CEIS. This meeting should take as long as required to review the instruments. If revisions need to be made, the contractor should undertake the revisions and submit a revised package; then a second meeting should be called involving the same personnel, and providing the package is satisfactory, approval should be given at that time. In this way, it might be possible to meet the two-month schedule so optimistically stated in the RFP (Request for proposal referred to earlier in the chapter) [p. 12].

Reference

Carter, L. F.
  1977   Federal clearance of educational evaluation instruments: Procedural problems and proposed remedies." *Educational Researcher* 6:7–13.

10

Informed Consent Procedures in Surveys: Some Reasons for Minimal Effects on Response

ELEANOR SINGER

It is generally accepted that the best, if not the only, way to obtain accurate information about the consequences of some hypothesized cause is by means of a randomized experiment. For certain categories of causes—for example, social programs with social consequences—it is sometimes claimed that experiments *in situ*, otherwise known as field trials, are preferable to experiments carried out in the laboratory. In the first place, it is impossible to simulate the complexity of the real world in the laboratory; and second, the artificiality of the laboratory setting may create its own spurious effects (see, for instance, Aronson and Carlsmith, 1969).

In 1976 I carried out such a field experiment to determine the effects of informed consent procedures on response rate and response quality in social surveys (Singer, 1978a, 1978b). The experiment was on a large scale, using as its subjects a probability sample of the adult noninstitutionalized population of the continental United States. The factors were complex, manipulated by means of a classic factorial experimental design, unobtrusively administered as part of a routine survey.

Nevertheless, with the exception of the request for a signature, the experimental variables produced findings that were for the most part unimpressive, indicating little effect on response of the procedures used to secure informed consent.

183

This situation is not uncommon. The question is, Why does it occur? One possibility, of course, is that the hypothesized causal variables really make no difference and that the minimal effects observed are correctly estimated. Another possibility, however, is that conditions in the field attenuate "true" effects, so that the experimental outcomes misrepresent reality. This suspicion is especially likely to arise if findings initially demonstrated in the laboratory fail to be supported in the field. Boruch and Gomez (1977) have proposed what they call a "small theory" to account for such attenuation. Their theory permits one to estimate the decline in power of a field trial as a function of: (a) an imperfect fit between "response" as conceptualized and as measured; and (b) an imperfect fit between "treatment" as intended and as experienced. They list some reasons for what they refer to as the degradation of the treatment variable and advise evaluators, among other things, to measure programs as implemented and received, as well as intended. Related general advice is of course by no means new in the evaluation literature (see, for example, Hyman, Wright, and Hopkins, 1962: 72–86; and Hyman and Wright, 1967).

Fortunately, such information is available for the informed consent study mentioned earlier. Two sorts of supplementary measures were built into the research design. First, I obtained respondents' perceptions of what the interviewer had said. Second, I conceptualized several mechanisms, or intervening variables, by which the experimental variables could affect response and incorporated measures of these into the design as well.

One purpose of the present chapter is to use these supplementary measures to elucidate treatment effects. That is, if we look only at respondents for whom the experimental treatments work as intended, do we get the effects we predict? A related purpose is to examine the implications of this procedure for informed consent in particular and the use of field trials in general.

I begin by briefly describing the design of the informed consent study and the major findings. Then, I report on an "internal analysis" of two of the three experimental variables, in order to see whether such an analysis leads to conclusions different from those based on the experimental treatments themselves. Finally, I turn to the implications of both sets of analyses.

The Informed Consent Study:
Design and Major Findings

The study was funded by a grant from the National Science Foundation and carried out under the auspices of the National Opinion Research Center (NORC). It was designed to investigate the effects of three factors that, together, may be said to constitute "informed consent" procedures in social surveys.

THE CONTROLLED FACTORS

The first of these controlled factors was the amount of information given to respondents ahead of time about the content of the interview. Half the respondents were given a brief, vague description of the survey as a study of leisure time and the way people are feeling. The other half were given a fuller description of the interview, which contained a large number of questions generally considered sensitive. These respondents were told

> We're conducting a national survey about how people are feeling in general and about the kinds of activities people do in their leisure time—that is, their spare time when they are not working. There are questions about your moods, and about the time you spend watching television or going to sports events, about your social activities, and some about your use of alcoholic drinks. We also ask a few questions about sex.

Aside from being shorter, the short introduction is, essentially, a "deceit" condition. The deceit is mild, but the information given to the respondent ahead of time is not consistent with the relatively heavy emphasis on drinking, sex, and mental health in the interview.

The second factor that was experimentally varied in the study was the assurance of confidentiality given to respondents. It has become increasingly clear that although some research organizations, such as NORC, routinely promise to protect confidentiality, such guarantees ordinarily have no legal standing; the relation between researcher and respondent is not recognized as privileged.[1] And although statisticians

---

[1]Current federal law provides examples of several types of protections of research data from compelled disclosure—for example, the statute prohibiting disclosure of Census records and the limited protection enjoyed by the National Center for Health Statistics for all individually identifiable research information it collects (42 U.S.C. 242m, 1970). Patient records maintained in connection with any drug abuse program or research activity conducted, regulated, or directly or indirectly assisted by a federal agency or department enjoy limited protection (42 U.S.C. 4582, 1971; 21 U.S.C. 1175, Supp. 1972). The secretary of the Department of Health and Human Services may authorize researchers engaged in mental health or alcohol or drug abuse research to withhold names or identifying characteristics of subjects; this immunity covers them in any federal, state, or local civil, criminal, administrative, legislative, or other proceeding (42 U.S.C. 4582). But these protections are rarely absolute, and they cover only limited types of data. For a review of these and other problems related to confidentiality, see Committee on Federal Agency Evaluation Research (1975), Nejelski (1976), and Privacy Protection Study Commission (1977: ch. 15).

and other social scientists have devoted considerable attention to developing technological solutions to problems of confidentiality, these often involve analytic complications as well as some compromise with research objectives (see Boruch and Cecil, 1979; and Campbell, Boruch, Schwartz, and Steinberg, 1977).

Unlike the argument for other aspects of informed consent, which is advanced on ethical grounds only, that for confidentiality is advanced on pragmatic grounds as well. That is, not only is breach of confidentiality a risk to which respondents are exposed by virtue of participating in the survey, but, it has also been argued, respondents will not give valid information without a promise that confidentiality will be maintained (Boruch and Cecil, 1979).

In order to investigate the effects of variations in confidentiality, one-third of the respondents in the present study were told nothing at all about the confidentiality of their replies; one-third were given an absolute assurance of confidentiality ("Of course, your answers will remain completely confidential"); and one-third were given a qualified assurance of confidentiality ("Of course, we will do our best to protect the confidentiality of your answers, except as required by law").

The final factor varied in the study was whether a signature was required to document consent, and if so, whether the request for a signature came before or after the interview.

It is generally assumed that requiring a signature to document consent will lower response rate, though the research on anonymity, which also bears indirectly on this problem, suggests that this effect may well be small (e.g., Mason, Dressel, and Bain, 1961; Blumberg, Fuller, and Hare, 1974; Erdos and Reiger, 1977). Deferring a signature until after the interview has been completed has several potential advantages:

1. In some sense, truly "informed" consent can be given only after the respondent has heard the actual questions.
2. Responses, as distinct from response rate, will be unaffected by a request for a signature that is made at the end of the interview.
3. Response rate may be protected to some extent if the respondent, having invested time in giving the interview, is reluctant to see it wasted by refusing to sign the consent form.

Aside from these three factors, which can also be thought of as representing different levels of risk, or cost, to respondents, certain elements of the introduction to the interview were kept constant. All respondents were told that the study was being done by NORC, that the interview would take about half an hour, that after the interview they would be asked to fill out a short self-administered form, that participation was voluntary, and that they could refuse questions within the interview. Every introduction also included a plea for honesty of response if the person decided to participate.

The three factors described above were combined in a two-by-three-by-three factorial design, yielding 18 different introductions to respondents. These introductions were stapled to the household enumeration folders assigned to each interviewer, along with instructions for answering questions and objections, also specifically tailored to each version of the introduction. Interviewers were told to read the introduction in its entirety to the selected respondent and to give standardized replies to questions that might be raised about content, confidentiality, or signature.

THE SAMPLE DESIGN AND INTERVIEWERS

A national probability sample of 2084, drawn within 50 primary sampling units of NORC's master sample, was used for the study.[2] Interviewers were required to list all household members and to select the appropriate respondent according to a sampling table. Each sample line (household) had been assigned in advance to a randomly selected experimental treatment. Every interviewer was assigned 31 sample lines, and every interviewer's assignment included all 18 versions of the introduction.[3]

[2]The universe was defined as the noninstitutionalized population age 18 and over resident in the 48 contiguous states. For a more detailed description of the sample, see the National Data Program for the Social Sciences (1976). In order to detect a difference of 7% or more between extreme levels of a main effect at an alpha level of 5% under the "worst" possible assumption—that is, with proportions symmetrical around 50%—we calculated that a completed sample of 1200 would be necessary. The gross sample size was determined by assuming that 10% of the assigned lines would be lost because of vacancies and other changes in dwelling units and that because of the sensitive nature of the questionnaire and some limitations on follow-up procedures, the completion rate on the remaining cases would average 65%. In fact, the completion rate was 67%.

[3]Interviewer effects were balanced in the design by having each interviewer administer all 18 experimental treatments, with order of administration randomized. A total of 2077 lines was selected in 67 segments (clusters) of 50 primary sampling units. Within each segment, 31 sample lines (households) were assigned to one interviewer, and each of these households was randomly assigned a predesignated experimental treatment. For example, in the first segment, the first 18 lines selected received treatments 1 through 18, randomized to balance order effects. The next 13 lines were assigned a subset of 13 treatments randomly drawn from the complete set of 18. In the next cluster, the remaining 5 treatments were assigned together with a complete set of 18 treatments, plus a randomly drawn set of 8 treatments, for a total of 31 lines. Whenever a subset n of the 18 treatments was assigned to a cluster, leaving a pool of $18 - n$ treatments, the remaining $18 - n$ treatments were assigned to the next cluster. Interviewers were instructed to make initial contact with the assigned households in their segment beginning with the lowest case number and ending with the highest, although we recognized that some deviations from the assigned order were likely to occur.

The interview schedule was substantially the same as that used a year earlier by Bradburn, Sudman, and associates (1979) in a National Science Foundation—supported study of the effects of question threat and question wording on response. Following some questions about conventional leisure activities were sections dealing with emotional well-being and mental health, drinking, marijuana use, and sexual behavior. A number of demographic items, among them income, were also included. The questionnaire was designed to permit investigation of the effect of informed consent procedures on eight types of questions: sensitive and nonsensitive survey-specific and general questions about attitudes and about behavior.

Also measured in the study were respondents' reactions to the interview, ascertained by means of a self-administered questionnaire completed immediately following the interview and handed to the interviewer in a sealed envelope, and interviewers' expectations about and reactions to the study, assessed just prior to and after the completion of field work. After all interviewing had been completed, each respondent was sent a letter thanking him or her for participating, explaining that the study had had a methodological as well as a substantive purpose and briefly describing that purpose. This method was decided on in preference to personal debriefing in order to keep interviewers from receiving feedback that might affect their future performance.

With one exception, only experienced NORC interviewers—almost a third of whom had worked on the Bradburn–Sudman study a year earlier—were used on this survey. They were trained in the special experimental procedures for the study through a combination of written materials, group telephone briefings by area supervisors, and specially developed training exercises that had to be completed before interviewing could begin. Interviews were edited in the New York office, and 20% of each interviewer's cases were validated by means of telephone interviews.

Interviewers were told about the methodological purposes of the study but not about any specific hypotheses, and were urged to keep an open mind about the effects of the experimental variables. Those who felt seriously uncomfortable with either the substantive or the methodological aspects of the study were asked not to take on this particular assignment; about five withdrew for this reason.

PRINCIPAL RESULTS

The primary purpose of the study was to investigate the effect of each of the three experimental variables on three different types of outcome: overall response rate to the survey; response rates to individual questions; and response quality. Major findings, which are reported in detail in Singer (1978a, 1978b), can be summarized as follows:

1. The overall response rate to the survey was 67%; of the three variables investigated, only the request for a signature had a significant effect on the probability of responding. The response rate was 71% for those not asked for a signature, compared with 64% and 65% for those asked to sign before and those asked to sign afterward. Even so, it should be noted that refusals were limited to the signature itself. Only a handful of respondents actually refused to be interviewed; the rest agreed to the interview but refused to sign the consent form, or signed after the interview rather than before.

2. Only the assurance of confidentiality had a significant effect on item nonresponse. Despite the sensitive nature of the interview, nonresponse to individual questions was very low. On those questions to which the nonresponse rate totaled more than 3%—all of them questions about behavior rather than about attitudes—respondents given an assurance of absolute confidentiality had lower nonresponse rates than those in the other two experimental groups, in some cases by a statistically significant margin.

3. None of the three independent variables had either consistent or large effects on the quality of response. However, there are suggestions in the data that asking for a signature before the interview has a sensitization effect, so that better data are obtained if the respondent is asked to sign a consent form afterward rather than before.

Except for the request for a signature, the experimental variables appear to have had little effect. As noted earlier, such an outcome is not uncommon in field experiments. The question is, why does it occur? Are there really strong effects of the experimental variables which we are somehow failing to measure, or are the weak effects which we measure, real?

One way to get at this problem is to conceptualize the processes by which the experimental treatments are supposed to bring about results, and to measure (a) the relationship between the experimental treatments and the hypothesized processes; and (b) the relationship between the processes and the predicted results.[4]

[4]Such an analysis resembles what is sometimes referred to as an internal analysis in social psychological experiments, in which the experimenter eliminates those subjects for whom the treatment failed to have the intended effect. For this purpose, social psychologists normally obtain measures of treatment effectiveness, by which they mean not whether it led to certain hypothesized consequences, but simply whether it aroused the psychological condition hypothesized as the independent variable in the experiment

In the informed consent study, two such sets of processes were conceptualized and measured. One set linked variations in prior information about the content of the study to response patterns; the other did the same for variations in the assurance of confidentiality given to respondents. In the two sections that follow, these processes, which are presumed to underlie treatment effects, are examined. The first section deals with information about content; the second, with variations in the assurance of confidentiality. The material for the analysis is derived from the self-administered questionnaire, completed by respondents immediately following the main interview.[5]

The Effect of Variations in Information about Content

We had predicted that giving respondents more information about the details of the interview should heighten the salience of the topics mentioned in the introduction, and that increased salience should result in responses of better quality among those who decided to participate. The data supported our prediction concerning the behavior of the intervening variable. People who were given more information ahead of time were more likely to anticipate questions about the various topics mentioned in the introduction (Table 10.1), and those who anticipated[6] such questions—that is, those for whom the questions were

---

(Rommetveit and Israel, 1954; Schachter, 1954). Unless an experimental manipulation succeeds in arousing anxiety, for example, there is no use in expecting it to evoke affiliative behavior (Schachter, 1959).

[5]Out of the 1321 respondents to the main interview, 1206, or 91%, completed the self-administered questionnaire; 5% refused; and the remainder claimed they could not read or write well enough to perform the task. Those respondents who had refused to sign the consent form (75 out of the 1321) were also more likely to refuse to fill out the self-administered questionnaire (26% versus about 3% for those who either signed or were not asked to sign; chi-square = 83.75 with 6 degrees of freedom; $p < .01$). Respondents given an absolute assurance of confidentiality and those given a qualified assurance were equally likely to complete the self-administered form (93% and 92%, respectively), whereas respondents to whom confidentiality was not mentioned at all were less likely to do so (88%; chi-square = 9.82 with 4 degrees of freedom; $p < .05$). Prior information about content had no measurable effect on willingness to complete the self-administered questionnaire.

[6]Since "expectations" were ascertained after the interview itself, they are contaminated by its content. This contamination should serve to reduce differences between respondents who heard the more detailed and the vaguer introductions, so that any differences we observe are a conservative measure of effect.

Table 10.1
Expectations about Content by Amount of Information Received Ahead of Time

	Percentage expecting questions		
Topic	Long introduction	Short introduction	Significance[b]
Sports activities	81 (610)[b]	73 (596)	$p < .01$
Gambling with friends	28	24	n.s.
Drinking beer, wine, or liquor	66	47	$p < .01$
Getting drunk	41	29	$p < .01$
Using marijuana	46	32	$p < .01$
Sexual intercourse	51	24	$p < .01$
Masturbation	16	10	$p < .01$
Mental health	58	49	$p < .01$
Education	79	76	n.s.
Income	71	70	n.s.
Religion	70	70	n.s.

[a]Significance levels are based on chi-square.

[b]Percentages are based on all those who filled out the self-administered questionnaire, scoring one point for each "expected" and zero for all other answers (including no, don't know, and no answer). If the last two categories are excluded, so that percentages are based only on those who said either that they expected the question or else that they did not, the percentage expecting increases for both groups and each question, but the pattern of expectations does not change.

Except for the questions on mental health, which were asked much earlier in the interview, the ordering of topics in Table 10.1 parallels their ordering on the questionnaire. Hence, differences in the percentage expecting each topic cannot be accounted for by differential forgetting due to differences in the elapsed time since the introduction was read.

Table 10.2
Nonresponse[a] by Whether Respondent Expected Questions about Topic (percentage)[b]

	Nonresponse			
Question	Expected	Did not expect	Don't know or no answer	Significance[c]
1. Ever smoked marijuana 3 times a week	8 (154)	7 (135)	6 (17)	n.s.
2. Number of pipes or joints smoked	5 (154)	6 (135)	12 (17)	n.s.
3. Intercourse during past month	5 (453)	10 (627)	12 (126)	$p < .01$
4. Frequency of intercourse	5 (339)	13 (382)	17 (58)	$p < .01$
5. Intercourse in last day	2 (339)	6 (382)	7 (58)	$p < .05$
6. Masturbated in past month	6 (160)	9 (892)	14 (154)	$p = .05$
7. Frequency of masturbation	7 (15)	9 (68)	0 (8)	n.s.
8. Masturbated in last day	7 (15)	6 (68)	0 (8)	n.s.
9. Amount of earned income	7 (851)	14 (246)	15 (109)	$p < .01$

[a]"Nonresponse" includes don't know, refused, and not asked.

[b]All topics asked about on the self-administered form to which the nonresponse rate on the main interview totaled more than 3% are included in this table.

[c]Significance levels are based on chi-square.

more salient—had a lower rate of item nonresponse (Table 10.2). They also tended to give responses of better quality[7] to sensitive questions (Table 10.3).[8] Expectations significantly affected responses to 8 of the 15 questions shown in Table 10.3, and on all but 1 of the 15, those who expected the question were more likely to acknowledge the behavior, even though most of the behaviors can be construed as sensitive.[9]

But all of these relationships were modest. Only half of the respondents in the "informed" condition, for example, expected questions about sexual intercourse, even though they had been told explicitly to expect them, and as many as a quarter of the respondents in the "uninformed" condition expected such questions as well. *In consequence, differences in response between information conditions (that is, the experimental treatment as intended) are less clear-cut than differences between expectation conditions (that is, the experimental treatment as perceived).*

We had also predicted that giving respondents more information about the content of the interview ahead of time would result in less upset or embarrassment at sensitive questions, and that this, too, would enhance the quality of response.

Again, predictions concerning the relationship of advance information to self-reported upset or embarrassment were supported (Table

[7]Previous research has indicated that for sensitive or threatening questions, more reporting is better reporting. For a citation of studies, see Blair *et al.* (1977).

For attitudes and behaviors that are positively valued in a society, on the other hand—for example, voting, owning a library card, holding liberal racial views—less reporting may be considered better reporting. For evidence on reports of voting and voter turnout, see, for example, Parry and Crossley (1950), Freeman (1953), Cahalan (1968), Clausen (1968), and Weiss (1968).

[8]Accuracy with respect to expectations does not enhance the quality of response. That is, those who accurately expect certain questions do not give better replies than those who expect such questions in the absence of prior warning by the interviewer. Putting it a different way, expectations have a significant independent effect on response, but the interaction between experimental condition and expectations is not significant.

[9]The column headed "eta/partial beta" in Table 10.3 indicates that a substantial portion of the correlation between expectations and reported behavior derives from the relationship of expectations to the three covariates of age, sex, and education (i.e., is spurious) and to their intercorrelation with four other independent variables controlled simultaneously—social desirability, upset at a particular question, concern with honesty, and concern with confidentiality. In general, about half the reduction in eta is accounted for by the other independent variables, and half by the covariates.

The net effect of expectations is, thus, often considerably smaller than that shown in Table 10.3, but the effect is nevertheless to elicit better data from respondents who expected a question than from those who did not. This is true even though most of the questions concern sensitive behavior, where one might suppose that respondents who are forewarned would alter their replies in a socially desirable direction.

Table 10.3
Responses to Selected Questions[a] by Respondents' Expectation of Question Topic

Question	Eta/partial beta	Responses (mean scores)[b]			Significance[c]
		Expected	Did not expect	Don't know or no answer	
1. Probability of walking in past month	.06/.05	.58 (928)	.49 (178)	.53 (100)	n.s.
2. Probability of watching sports event in past month	.06/.04	.20 (928)	.14 (178)	.17 (100)	n.s.
3. Probability of bowling in past year	.07/.02	.32 (928)	.27 (178)	.20 (100)	n.s.
4. Gambling Scale score	.11/.07	1.14 (313)	.85 (746)	.80 (142)	p(F) < .01
5. Probability of drinking liquor	.21/.14	.91 (677)	.76 (408)	.73 (121)	p(F) < .01
6. Number of 3 closest friends drunk in past year	.15/.04	1.16 (413)	.87 (629)	.59 (141)	p(F) < .01
7. Probability of smoking marijuana	.15/.06	.33 (468)	.22 (606)	.13 (132)	p(F) < .01
8. Number of 3 closest friends who smoke	.15/.06	.86 (461)	.55 (598)	.44 (129)	p(F) < .01
9. Probability of intercourse in past month	.19/.09	.75 (453)	.61 (627)	.46 (126)	p(F) < .01
10. Probability of masturbating in past month	.04/.05	.10 (160)	.08 (892)	.06 (154)	n.s.
11. Positive Affect	.05/.07	13.68 (647)	13.98 (429)	13.88 (130)	p(F) < .05
12. Negative Affect	.02/.04	9.96 (647)	9.90 (429)	10.16 (130)	n.s.
13. Langner Scale	.07/.07	3.28 (645)	3.01 (429)	3.71 (128)	n.s.
14. Years of school	.18/.06	12.34 (933)	12.26 (158)	10.72 (114)	p(F) < .05
15. Income[d]	.11/.02	8.07 (791)	7.69 (211)	6.38 (93)	n.s.

[a]Table 10.3 includes virtually all questions asked of the total sample about the more threatening of the 11 topics included on the self-administered form but, for economy, only a sampling of items on sports, drinking, and mental health.

[b]Mean scores are based on unadjusted deviations. Deviations adjusted for the other independent variables (social desirability, upset, importance of truth telling, and certainty of confidentiality) and for the covariates of sex, education, and age are usually, but not always, smaller than those shown here, the reduction being due about equally to the independents and the covariates.

[c]Significance levels are based on an F test among the means, adjusted for the effect of the other independent variables.

[d]The analysis here is based on numbered response categories rather than dollar amounts. "8" corresponds to an earned income of $7500–8900; "5," to an earned income of $4000–4999.

Table 10.4
Respondents Reporting Upset by Different Question Topics and Amount of Prior
Information about Content (percentage)

	Respondents very or somewhat upset	
Question topic	Long introduction	Short introduction
Sports activities	1	2
Gambling with friends	5	6
Drinking beer, wine, or liquor	7	8
Getting drunk	14	19
Using marijuana	14	19
Sexual intercourse	42	50
Masturbation	48	53
Mental health	8	10
Education	2	4
Income	13	14
Religion	3	3

10.4),[10] as were those concerning the relationship of upset to item
nonresponse (Table 10.5). But, as with salience, differences in reported
upset between information conditions were not large, and so the effect
on response tendencies between experimental conditions is very small.
Furthermore, the relationship of upset to response quality is complex.
On the most sensitive questions in the interview schedule, both those
respondents who were very upset and those who were not at all upset
tended to acknowledge less of the behavior asked about than respondents experiencing an intermediate degree of threat (data not shown; cf.
Bradburn, Sudman, Blair, and Stocking, 1978; Singer 1978b: ch. 7).

For these and perhaps other reasons, I found no significant or consistent differences in item nonresponse rates or response quality by
information condition. In large part, this appears to be true because of
the modest relationships between the experimental treatment and the
hypothesized intervening variables of salience and upset. In the con-

[10]This effect appears to be mediated by the role of expectations. As we have just seen,
respondents who were given the more detailed introduction were more likely to expect
questions about such sensitive topics as drinking and sex. At the same time, those who
said they expected questions about a topic invariably reported having been less upset by
the questions. For all topics except sports, differences in reported upset between those
who did and those who did not expect the questions are statistically significant, and in
some cases substantial: 11% versus 23% upset by questions about income, for example;
24% versus 57% by questions on masturbation; and 32% versus 57% by questions on
intercourse.

Table 10.5
Nonresponse,[a] by Self-Reported Upset with Question Topic (percentage)[b]

	Nonresponse				
Question	Not upset	Somewhat upset	Very upset	Don't know, no answer	Significance[c]
Ever smoked marijuana 3 times per week	9 (213)	4 (70)	8 (13)	0 (10)	n.s.
Number of pipes, joints smoked	7 (213)	4 (70)	0 (13)	0 (10)	n.s.
Intercourse during past month	3 (612)	7 (403)	25 (119)	31 (72)	p < .01
Frequency of intercourse	5 (404)	11 (290)	30 (61)	25 (24)	p < .01
Intercourse in last day	2 (404)	6 (290)	15 (61)	4 (24)	p < .01
Masturbated in past month	5 (553)	6 (371)	22 (191)	28 (91)	p < .01
Frequency of masturbation	3 (34)	8 (40)	13 (15)	50 (2)	p < .10
Masturbation in last day	0 (34)	8 (40)	7 (15)	50 (2)	p < .05
Amount of earned income	6 (972)	15 (109)	43 (47)	21 (78)	p < .01

[a]"Nonresponse" includes don't know, refused, and not asked.
[b]All topics asked about on the self-administered form to which the nonresponse rate on the main interview totaled more than 3% are included in this table.
[c]Significance levels are based on chi-square.

cluding section, I return to the question of whether or not such modest relationships are to be regarded as "attenuated."

The Effect of Varying Assurances of Confidentiality

Reviewing prior research on the effects of anonymity and confidentiality, Boruch and Cecil (1976) concluded that, for sensitive information, "strong" assurances of confidentiality (by which they mean technical, in addition to verbal, guarantees) improve response rate as well as quality. However, their review of the literature, as well as that by Singer (1978a), suggests that verbal assurances, and assurances attached to innocuous information, produce little difference in response. For example, variations in a verbal assurance of confidentiality had trivial effects on overall response rates in a field experiment by Goldfield, Turner, Cowan, and Scott (1977), and none in the present study. Item nonresponse rates, however, were consistently and sometimes significantly lower in the present study when respondents received an absolute verbal assurance of confidentialty, and such an assurance may have improved the quality of response to the most sensitive items on the questionnaire.

Table 10.6
Respondents' Perception of Confidentiality, by Confidentiality Condition (percentage)

	Confidentiality condition		
Perception of confidentiality	No mention	Qualified	Absolute
No mention	20	3	6
Confidential except as required by law	17	63	29
Results public, answers confidential	26	21	49
Do not remember	33	10	12
Other	4	3	4
Total	100 (403)	100 (397)	100 (404)

It was hypothesized that the effects associated with variations in the assurance of confidentiality might be weak for one or more of three reasons: Respondents might not hear or understand what the interviewer had said about confidentiality; even if they heard, they might not believe; and even if they believed, they might not care. The hypotheses were tested by examining the effect of the experimental variations in confidentiality on these intervening variables, and the effect of the intervening variables on response.

EFFECTS ON UNDERSTANDING

In fact, we found that misunderstanding was widespread, but that correct understanding resulted in effects no stronger than misunderstanding did. As can be seen from Table 10.6, less than half of those given an absolute assurance of confidentiality correctly perceived the assurance they had been given,[11] and only 20% of those in the "no mention" condition correctly reported this fact after the interview.[12] However, the respondent's perception of the amount of confidentiality

[11]The question was, "What did the interviewer say about who would find out the answers you gave in the interview?" with the following response alternatives provided: "The results would be made public but my answers would be confidential; the interview would be a matter of public record and anyone who wanted could find out the answers I gave; the research organization would try to keep my answers confidential except as required by law; the interviewer didn't say anything about this; I don't remember."

[12]Goldfield and his colleagues (1977) concluded, on the basis of questions asked after the interview, that most respondents had accurately understood what the interviewer had said to them about confidentiality. However, the probabilities of perfect understanding, conditional on response, vary from .76 for the condition in which the respondent was promised confidentiality forever, to .14 for the condition in which no mention was made of confidentiality at all.

Cognitions Concerning Confidentiality and Responses to Selected Questions[a]

Question	Eta/partial beta	Responses (mean scores)[b]					Significance[d]
		Answers confidential (N = 386)[c]	Answers public (N = 14)	Confidential except by law (N = 434)	Interviewer did not say (N = 118)	Does not recall (N = 223)	
1. Probability of walking in past month	.03/.01	.56	.58	.54	.57	.58	n.s.
2. Probability of watching sports event in past month	.01/.02	.20	.17	.20	.19	.21	n.s.
3. Probability of bowling in past year	.05/.05	.28	.34	.32	.30	.34	n.s.
4. Gambling Scale score	.04/.05	.89	.50	.95	.93	.98	n.s.
5. Probability of drinking liquor	.06/.07	.85	.67	.86	.87	.83	n.s.
6. Number of 3 closest friends drunk in past year	.08/.06	.89	.67	.91	1.12	1.12	n.s.
7. Probability of smoking marijuana	.08/.04	.25	.25	.23	.30	.32	n.s.
8. Number of 3 closest friends who smoke	.08/.04	.62	.92	.62	.84	.80	n.s.
9. Probability of intercourse in past month	.06/.06	.67	.84	.65	.71	.62	n.s.
10. Probability of masturbating in past month	.05/.05	.10	.00	.08	.07	.07	n.s.
11. Positive Affect	.05/.05	13.82	14.75	13.88	13.47	13.74	n.s.
12. Negative Affect	.05/.03	10.01	10.09	9.73	9.85	10.06	n.s.
13. Langner Scale	.07/.08	3.29	2.42	2.93	3.16	3.48	n.s.
14. Years of school	.05/.06	12.27	11.50	12.50	12.47	12.12	n.s.
15. Income	.10/.10	8.17	6.09	8.10	8.03	7.20	p(F) < .05

[a]Questions are identical to those in Table 10.3.

[b]Mean scores are based on unadjusted deviations. Deviations adjusted for the other independent variables (confidentiality condition, certainty of confidentiality, and worry about confidentiality) and for the covariates of age, sex, and education are usually, but not always, smaller than those shown here, changes being due in part to the other independent variables and in part to the covariates.

[c]Numbers shown are for all 1175 respondents who answered the self-administered form and the question about perceptions of confidentiality and may vary somewhat from question to question because of nonresponse.

[d]Significance levels are based on an F test among the means, adjusted for the effect of the other independent variables.

197

the interviewer had promised appears to have little effect on response (Table 10.7). Only with respect to income do these perceptions make a significant difference, and in only 2 of 15 comparisons is the perception that one's answer will remain confidential associated with the highest estimates of the behavior or characteristic.

On the assumption that it might be the *accurate* perception of confidentiality which makes the difference, we examined the responses of those who both perceived that their answers would be held in confidence and were in fact given an assurance of absolute confidentiality, and contrasted them with those of respondents who accurately perceived that their responses would be accorded lesser protection. However, this comparison provides no more evidence for the effect of cognitions about confidentiality than the analysis immediately preceding.

EFFECTS ON CERTAINTY

We also found that some people believed the assurance of confidentiality they had been given, whereas others did not. Asked to indicate, on a 5-point scale, how certain they were that answers would remain confidential, some 27% of the sample professed a great deal of certainty; at the other extreme, 22% said they were "not sure at all" (Table 10.8). Those who were assured of absolute confidentiality professed the highest level of certainty, but although the difference among confidentiality conditions was significant, in absolute terms it was not very large.[13] Less than half a point on the 5-point scale, or 11 percentage points in Table 10.8, separates those who had been given an absolute assurance of confidentiality from those to whom the matter had not been mentioned at all, suggesting that respondents either did not hear, or else did not believe, very much of what the interviewer had told them about the confidentiality of their replies.

Turning now to the *effects* of certainty, we note that, with one exception, item nonresponse rates of those who were certain about the confidentiality of their answers are lower than those of respondents who were not certain (Table 10.9). Four of the comparisons reach statistical significance, though the relationship is linear only for those items asked of the total sample. This finding is consistent with the conclusion drawn on the basis of the experimental treatments themselves— namely, that an assurance of confidentiality has a modest but con-

[13]Of the five demographic variables we examined, only two—sex and race—proved to be significantly related to the respondent's certainty that confidentiality would be maintained. Men were more skeptical than women, and black respondents more skeptical than those of other races, most of whom were, of course, white.

Table 10.8
Respondents' Certainty of Confidentiality, by Confidentiality Condition (percentage)

| | Confidentiality condition | | | |
Degree of certainty	No mention of confidentiality	Qualified confidentiality	Absolute confidentiality	Total
1 (not at all)	26	21	18	22
2	9	12	8	10
3	24	27	22	24
4	13	17	15	15
5 (very)	24	22	35	27
Don't know; not answered	4	2	3	3
Total	100 (403)	101 (397)	101 (406)	101 (1206)

sistent effect on response rates to sensitive questions—but offers no stronger support for it. Differences between those who claimed to have been certain, and those who said they were not, averaged 4.2 percentage points on the nine questions with the highest nonresponse rates; differences on the same nine questions between those given an absolute assurance of confidentiality and the average of the other two experimental groups averaged 4.3 percentage points.

The relationship between certainty and response quality is more complex. On theoretical grounds, one might expect those who are very

Table 10.9
Item[a] Nonresponse[b] by Certainty of Confidentiality (percentage)

| | Nonresponse | | | |
Question	Not certain (1, 2)	(3)	Certain (4, 5)	Significance[c]
Ever smoked marijuana 3 times a week	9 (104)	7 (77)	7 (121)	n.s.
Number of pipes or joints smoked	4 (104)	8 (77)	6 (121)	n.s.
Intercourse during past month	11 (380)	7 (292)	6 (503)	$p < .05$
Frequency of intercourse	10 (229)	15 (200)	6 (338)	n.s.
Intercourse in last day	4 (229)	9 (200)	2 (338)	$p < .01$
Masturbated in past month	13 (380)	9 (292)	7 (503)	$p < .05$
Frequency of masturbation	11 (18)	4 (26)	9 (47)	n.s.
Masturbation in last day	11 (18)	0 (26)	6 (47)	n.s.
Amount of earned income	15 (380)	9 (292)	5 (503)	$p < .01$

[a]All topics asked about on the self-administered form to which the nonresponse rate on the main interview totaled more than 3% are included in this table.
[b]"Nonresponse" includes refused, don't know, and not asked.
[c]Significance levels are based on chi-square.

certain of the confidentiality of their replies to be more likely to acknowledge engaging in sensitive or threatening behavior than other
respondents, and those who are not at all certain of confidentiality to be
less likely to do so. Differences in response, by certainty of confidentiality, are shown in Table 10.10. Differences were significant on 6 of
the 15 items: the probability of having gone bowling in the past year; of
ever having smoked marijuana; the number of three close friends who
smoke; the probability of having had intercourse during the past
month; the number of years of schooling; and the amount of earned
income. On all of these, however, both those who are very certain about
confidentiality, and those who are not at all certain, give lower estimates than intermediate groups. This curvilinear pattern, which is not
confined either to the most sensitive items or to those asked about
behavior rather than attitudes, characterizes the responses to two-
thirds of the items in Table 10.10, and suggests that, whereas skepticism about confidentiality may lead to underreporting, certainty is not
necessarily associated with the reporting of high levels of sensitive
behavior. Thus, the failure of variations in the assurance of confidentiality to affect the quality of response cannot be attributed to disbelief,
any more than it can be attributed to misunderstanding.

EFFECTS ON IMPORTANCE

Finally, we found that some people cared whether or not their answers remained confidential, whereas others did not. Asked to indicate, on a 5-point scale, how much they would care if anyone knew the
answers they gave, 36% of the respondents claimed they "would not
care at all," but 21% said they "would care very much." Asked to judge
how uneasy "most people" would be made by the various topics included on the questionnaire, 56% of a similar sample said most people
would be made very uneasy by questions about masturbation; 41%, by
questions about intercourse; and 42%, by questions about marijuana
(Bradburn et al., 1978). In short, although many questions were considered innocuous, others were regarded as sensitive; and although some
respondents were indifferent to the disclosure of their answers, others
clearly were not. Those people who refused to sign the consent form
were significantly more concerned about confidentiality than others,
but the assurance of confidentiality given to respondents had no effect
on the importance they attached to it.[14]

[14]It is entirely possible, of course, that different survey topics would arouse greater
levels of concern, and that under certain conditions the assurance of confidentiality
might affect the concern expressed.

Table 10.10
Certainty of Confidentiality and Responses to Selected Questions[a]

Question	Responses (mean scores)[b]					Eta/partial beta	Significance[d]
	Not at all certain (1) (N = 262)[c]	(2) (N = 118)	(3) (N = 292)	(4) (N = 178)	Very certain (5) (N = 325)		
1. Probability of walking in past month	.56	.56	.52	.63	.56	.07/.06	n.s.
2. Probability of watching sports event in past month	.21	.27	.16	.21	.20	.08/.07	n.s.
3. Probability of bowling in past year	.25	.39	.32	.34	.31	.09/.06	$p(F) < .05$
4. Gambling Scale score	.92	1.08	.93	1.00	.84	.06/.02	n.s.
5. Probability of drinking liquor	.82	.87	.86	.86	.85	.05/.04	n.s.
6. Number of 3 closest friends drunk in past year	.98	1.13	.98	.97	.86	.06/.06	n.s.
7. Probability of smoking marijuana last year	.24	.35	.27	.31	.21	.11/.01	$p(F) < .01$
8. Number of 3 closest friends who smoke	.66	1.00	.67	.78	.53	.12/.04	$p(F) < .01$
9. Probability of intercourse in past month	.59	.67	.69	.78	.62	.13/.09	$p(F) < .01$
10. Probability of masturbating in past month	.04	.07	.09	.10	.09	.08/.08	n.s.
11. Positive Affect	14.01	13.64	13.45	13.84	13.98	.08/.09	n.s.
12. Negative Affect	9.91	10.06	9.95	9.70	9.90	.03/.04	n.s.
13. Langner Scale	3.35	2.95	3.14	2.79	3.34	.07/.06	n.s.
14. Years of school	12.02	12.66	12.52	12.83	12.06	.09/.06	$p(F) < .05$
15. Amount of earned income	7.53	8.18	8.16	8.58	7.56	.10/.05	$p(F) < .05$

[a]Questions are identical to those in Table 10.3.
[b]Mean scores are based on unadjusted deviations. Deviations adjusted for the other independent variables (confidentiality condition, perceptions of confidentiality, and worry about confidentiality) and for the covariates of age, sex, and education are usually smaller than those shown here, the reduction being due almost entirely to the effect of the covariates.
[c]Numbers shown are for all 1175 respondents who answered the self-administered form and the question about certainty of confidentiality and may vary somewhat from question to question because of nonresponse.
[d]Significance levels are based on an F test among the means, adjusted for the effect of the other independent variables.

The effects of the importance attached to confidentiality resemble those reported for certainty. Item nonresponse shows a trend in the expected direction (Table 10.11): That is, those who would care very much if their answers were disclosed generally have nonresponse rates higher than those of respondents attaching less importance to confidentiality, but the relationship is weak and generally nonsignificant. The relationship between importance and quality of response is more complex, defying ready interpretation. Those to whom confidentiality is not important at all tend to give the lowest estimates of sensitive behavior (Table 10.12), perhaps because they engage in little of it and hence are unconcerned about disclosure. Those to whom confidentiality is very important, on the other hand, sometimes give the lowest and sometimes the highest estimates, suggesting that concern with confidentiality may function as both cause and effect. Some respondents are concerned with confidentiality and therefore reveal very little about themselves; others reveal a great deal and hence are concerned about the protection of their answers. As with item nonresponse, however, the effects are weak and generally nonsignificant, and thus provide no evidence for the hypothesis that if confidentiality had mattered more, the experimental treatments would have produced a stronger effect.

Table 10.11
Item[a] Nonresponse[b] by Importance of Confidentiality (percentage)

Question	Would not care (1, 2)	(3)	Would care (4, 5)	Significance[c]
1. Ever smoked marijuana 3 times a week	6 (146)	10 (63)	7 (94)	n.s.
2. Number of pipes or joints smoked	3 (146)	13 (63)	4 (94)	p < .05
3. Intercourse during past month	8 (585)	6 (244)	10 (346)	n.s.
4. Frequency of intercourse	7 (363)	11 (180)	11 (223)	n.s.
5. Intercourse in last day	3 (363)	4 (180)	7 (223)	n.s.
6. Masturbation in past month	9 (585)	7 (244)	12 (346)	n.s.
7. Frequency of masturbation	5 (39)	6 (17)	9 (34)	n.s.
8. Masturbation in last day	5 (39)	6 (17)	6 (34)	n.s.
9. Amount of earned income	9 (585)	7 (244)	12 (346)	p < .05

Nonresponse header spans "Would not care (1, 2)", "(3)", "Would care (4, 5)".

[a]All topics asked about on the self-administered form to which the nonresponse rate on the main interview totaled more than 3% are included in this table.
[b]"Nonresponse" includes refused, don't know, and not asked.
[c]Significance levels are based on chi-square.

To summarize this section: It was hypothesized that the observed effects of confidentiality on item nonresponse rates and response quality might be weak for one or more of three reasons: People might not hear; they might not believe; or they might not care. Although it is true that relatively few people heard correctly, believed implicitly, or cared very much, the effects of confidentiality would have been no stronger had the numbers been larger. This is true for several reasons. First, there is no relation between correct perception and response. Second, the relationships between certainty and importance, on the one hand, and response quality, on the other, are not linear. Finally, the effects of certainty and importance on item nonresponse rates are no greater than those of the confidentiality conditions themselves—that is, the treatments as perceived have effects no greater than the treatments as intended.

Conclusions and Implications

In this concluding section I would like to stress certain limitations on the findings derived from the informed consent study and consider some more general issues in drawing inferences from field trials.

First, of course, there are the conventional caveats. All of the findings reported here concerning the effects of informed consent procedures derive from one type of survey only. It is entirely possible that certain types of questions, asked of certain specialized categories of respondents, might interact with the independent variables to produce results other than those reported here. For example, if welfare clients were asked about their income, refusals under several of the experimental conditions might be higher than those in the present study; the same is true if we asked employees of a large corporation about their drinking habits. One study cannot hope to answer all such questions; the present one specifies what is likely to happen in a general population survey dealing with generally sensitive content. Studies of more specialized problems and groups—for example, the effect of General Accounting Office audits of social experiments—would usefully supplement the present findings.

Furthermore, although this study provides information about the effects of informing (or failing to inform) respondents about the content of the interview in advance, it says nothing about the effects of other kinds of deception. For example, respondents to the present survey

Table 10.12

Importance of Confidentiality and Responses to Selected Questions[a]

Question	Responses (mean scores)[b]					Eta/partial beta	Significance[d]
	Would not care at all (1) (N = 427)[c]	(2) (N = 158)	(3) (N = 244)	(4) (N = 93)	Would care very much (5) (N = 253)		
1. Probability of walking in past month	.55	.64	.58	.55	.52	.09/.07	n.s.
2. Probability of watching sports event in past month	.19	.19	.19	.22	.19	.04/.04	n.s.
3. Probability of bowling in past year	.30	.37	.29	.36	.26	.10/.06	n.s.
4. Gambling scale score	.89	.96	.99	1.18	.86	.09/.04	n.s.
5. Probability of drinking liquor	.80	.86	.88	.92	.84	.12.05	n.s.
6. Number of 3 closest friends drunk in past year	.85	1.11	1.03	1.18	.87	.12/.02	n.s.

7. Probability of smoking marijuana last year	.21	.34	.25	.33	.25	.12/.04	n.s.
8. Number of 3 closest friends who smoke	.58	.89	.65	.83	.65	.12/.06	n.s.
9. Probability of intercourse in past month	.58	.74	.74	.74	.62	.17/.10	$p < .01$
10. Probability of masturbating in past month	.05	.12	.07	.12	.10	.10/.07	n.s.
11. Positive Affect	14.06	13.90	13.38	13.67	13.88	.08/.08	n.s.
12. Negative Affect	9.53	9.98	9.97	9.85	10.49	.14/.11	$p(F) < .05$
13. Langner Scale	3.06	3.17	3.34	2.84	3.48	.08/.04	n.s.
14. Years of school	11.93	12.65	12.38	13.00	12.03	.18/.07	$p(F) < .05$
15. Amount of earned income	7.41	8.70	8.09	8.25	7.82	.12/.08	n.s.

[a] Questions are identical to those in Table 10.3.

[b] Mean scores are based on unadjusted deviations. Deviations adjusted for the other independent variables (social desirability, upset, expectations, and certainty of confidentiality) and for the covariates of age, sex, and education are usually smaller than those shown here, the reduction being due almost entirely to the other independent variables.

[c] Numbers shown are for all respondents who answered the self-administered form and the question about the importance of confidentiality and may vary somewhat from question to question because of nonresponse.

[d] Significance levels are based on an F test among the means, adjusted for the effects of the other independent variables.

were not told about its methodological purpose until after the completion of fieldwork, and, ironically, the study could not have been carried out successfully without this deception. More research to specify the conditions under which responses are affected by disclosure, and those under which they are not, is clearly needed. This includes work on the effects of disclosing information about purpose and sponsorship, for instance. Note, however, that any research designed to get at this question is bound to use deception in one or more experimental conditions.

Aside from these limitations on generalizability, however, there are those imposed by the weakening of the experimental variables demonstrated in the present chapter. At the outset, I posed the question, do the findings of minimal effects deserve to be treated as real, or do they, as some might maintain, reflect the inevitable attenuation of experimental variables in the field? From the data presented, it seems reasonably clear that the findings concerning both information about content and the assurance of confidentiality would have been stronger if there had been a better fit between the experimental treatments as intended and the treatments as perceived or believed by the respondent. The relationships between response and the concepts underlying the experimental treatments—that is, expectations, on the one hand, and certainty, on the other—are stronger than the relationships between the treatments embodying those concepts and response. The conventional caveats apply here, of course, as well: Expectations and certainty may have different consequences in more specialized populations and with respect to different types of subject matter.

But what conclusions are to be drawn from these findings? At least two sorts of questions can be addressed to the data that have been presented. First, since the introduction to the interview was designed to provide respondents with sufficient information on which to base a decision about participating, how adequately were they in fact informed? That is, how adequately were the ethical imperatives of informed consent met by the procedures employed? Second, which set of findings—those based on the experimental treatments, or those based on the internal analyses reported here—should be used in drawing inferences about the consequences of these procedures for survey research?

So far as alerting respondents to potential risks in the interview is concerned, the evidence presented is not very reassuring. Although people who were told to expect certain kinds of questions did in fact expect such questions more often than other respondents, by absolute standards they were not especially well informed. Only two-thirds of those who had received the detailed introduction said they had expected questions about drinking alcoholic beverages, and only 50% expected to be asked about sexual intercourse, despite the explicit mention of these topics in the introduction to the interview.

Nor were respondents especially well informed about the degree of confidentiality their answers would be accorded. Overall, only 44% of the sample correctly heard or recalled what the interviewer had said about confidentiality. Those who received a qualified assurance were most likely to be accurate, followed by those to whom an absolute assurance had been given and, finally, by those to whom confidentiality had not been mentioned at all. Thus, when we talk about the "effect of informed consent procedures" in this study, it ought to be clearly understood that many—perhaps most—of the respondents were not accurately informed with respect to at least some elements of the interview and in that sense certainly cannot be said to have given their informed consent. This is true despite the fact that between 80% and 90% of those who completed the self-administered form claimed they had not found the introduction unclear or confusing in any way.[15] The only element of the introduction remembered correctly by the overwhelming majority—93% of those who completed the self-administered form—was the interviewer's statement concerning the voluntary nature of the interview. (Age and education were significantly related to accuracy concerning expectations about content, with older and less well-educated respondents less likely to harbor accurate anticipations. Only race had a significant effect on accuracy concerning confidentiality, with black respondents being significantly less accurate than those of other races.)

These findings indicate a need for research in order to discover how best to inform respondents about the risks and benefits associated with their participation in research. The findings also raise the question of

---

[15]Some 31% of respondents with less than 4 years of high school found the introduction unclear or confusing in some respect, compared with 19% of high school graduates or those with some college and 16% of college graduates; 19% of those with less than 4 years of high school failed to answer the question. Similarly, as many as 35% of the oldest (66 and over) group had some trouble with the introduction, compared with 14% of the youngest (18–25). It would have been desirable to explore the reasons for the lack of understanding, perhaps by means of unstructured interviews with a subsample of respondents, but we did not do this.

how far the researcher's responsibility for informing subjects extends. It is one thing to misinform those participating in research; it is another to inform and be misunderstood. All this suggests that exclusive reliance on informed consent may be relatively ineffective in protecting the subjects of research against harm.

But what should one conclude about the effects of the procedures used in the present study? Is the attenuation of treatment effects that is observed in the field, in this study and in others, to be "corrected for," like attenuated correlation coefficients, or is this attenuation an integral part of the phenomenon we are trying to appraise, so that it is the corrected estimate that is misleading?

The answer depends on one's purpose. If one is trying to demonstrate certain conceptual or theoretical linkages—for example, if one is trying to establish the precise relationship between salience and accuracy of recall—then obviously one wants to refine these concepts as much as possible, stripping away all extraneous influences. Or, if one is trying to pinpoint the reasons for program failure, one would pay particular attention to the linkages among the concepts and mechanisms postulated by the theory underlying the program and to the relationship between the program and those concepts. That is the message of the Boruch–Gomez (1977) article.

But is this the situation we are dealing with here, and in many other field trials? It seems to me that it is not. So far as informed consent is concerned, it seems clear that there will always be a less than perfect fit between what is said and what is understood or believed, just as different procedures for informing subjects are bound to have different utility for subgroups varying in age, education, and perhaps other characteristics. The finding that the procedures used in the present study have little discernible net effect on response, therefore, deserves to be treated as real, not as a mishap of measurement. Whether one regards it optimistically, concluding that because effects are small, practical considerations do not conflict with ethical imperatives, or pessimistically, concluding that even the procedures used in this survey fail to ensure truly informed consent, is a separate question.

The same argument probably applies to most social programs. In the real world, teachers lose motivation and children interrupt their television viewing to play with a friend, go the the bathroom, have a snack.

---

[16]It has been suggested that the low response rate—67% if those for whom a signature is available are counted, or 71% if all those interviewed are—vitiates the conclusions that can be drawn from the study. But this response rate, too, is part of the real world,

Respondents trust interviewers even in the face of a weak guarantee of confidentiality.[16] For these and other reasons, the effects of social programs are weakened in the field. This does not mean that the theories linking concept to concept, or proposition to proposition, are incorrect. It does mean that theories about effects in the real world will have to be much more complex, including many more variables, than theories about what happens in the laboratory. It also means that many simplified theories, translated into programs in the real world, will fail to produce effects. Often that is a misfortune, but sometimes, perhaps, it is, on the whole, a good thing.

References

Aronson, E., and Carlsmith, J. M.
  1969   "Experimentation in social psychology." In G. Lindzey and E. Aronson (eds.), *Handbook of Social Psychology.* 2d ed., vol. 2. Reading Mass.: Addison-Wesley.
Blair, E., *et al.*
  1977   "How to ask questions about drinking and sex." *Journal of Marketing Research* 14:316–321.
Blumberg, H. H., C. Fuller, and A. P. Hare
  1974   "Response rates in postal surveys." *Public Opinion Quarterly* 38:113–123.
Boruch, R. F.
  1976   "Methodological techniques for assuring personal integrity in social research." Photocopy. Evaluation Research Program, Northwestern University.
Boruch, R. F., and J. S. Cecil
  1979   "On the need to assure confidentiality." Chap. 3 in *Assuring Confidentiality of Social Research Data.* Philadelphia: University of Pennsylvania Press.
Boruch, R. F., and H. Gomez
  1977   "Sensitivity, bias, and theory in impact evaluations." *Professional Psychology,* November: 411–434.
Bradburn, N. M., S. Sudman, E. Blair, and C. Stocking
  1978   "Question threat and response bias." *Public Opinion Quarterly* 42:221–234.
Bradburn, Norman M., Seymour Sudman, and Associates.
  1979   *Improving Interview Method and Questionnaire Design.* San Francisco: Jossey-Bass.
Cahalan, D.
  1968   "Correlates of respondent accuracy in the Denver validity survey." *Public Opinion Quarterly* 32:607–621.

---

reflecting response rates currently being obtained by NORC and other survey organizations. Since only the request for a signature affects overall response rate, and since those who refused to sign the consent form are *included* in the analyses of the effects of the other two independent variables, it is entirely reasonable to regard the findings reported here as accurately reflecting the real-world effects of confidentiality and information about content on the quality of response.

Campbell, D. T., R. F. Boruch, R. D. Schwartz, and J. Steinberg
  1977 "Confidentiality-preserving modes of access to files and to interfile exchange for useful statistical analysis. *Evaluation Quarterly* 1:269–299.
Clausen, A. R.
  1968 "Response, validity: Vote report." *Public Opinion Quarterly* 32:588–606.
Committee on Federal Agency Evaluation Research
  1975 *Protecting Individual Privacy in Evaluation Research.* Assembly of Behavioral and Social Sciences, National Research Council, National Academy of Sciences, Washington, D.C.
Erdos, P. L., and J. Regier
  1977 "Visible vs disguised keying on questionnaires." *Journal of Advertising Research* 17:13.
Freeman, H. E.
  1953 "A note on the prediction of who votes." *Public Opinion Quarterly* 17: 288–292.
Goldfield, E. D., A. G. Turner, C. D. Cowan, and J. C. Scott
  1977 "Privacy and confidentiality as factors in survey response." *Proceedings of the American Statistical Association.* Washington, D.C.: ASA.
Hyman, H. H., and C. R. Wright
  1967 "Evaluating social action programs." Pp. 741–782 in P. F. Lazarsfeld, W. H. Sewell, and H. Wilensky (eds.), *The Uses of Sociology.* New York: Basic Books.
Hyman, H. H., C. R. Wright, and T. K. Hopkins
  1962 *Applications of Methods of Evaluation.* Berkeley: University of California.
Mason, W. S., R. J. Dressel, and R. K. Bain
  1961 "An experimental study of factors affecting response to a mail survey of beginning teachers." *Public Opinion Quarterly* 25:296–299.
National Data Program for the Social Sciences
  1976 Codebook for the Spring 1976 General Social Survey. New York: National Opinion Research Center.
Nejelski, Paul (ed).
  1976 Social Research in Conflict with Law and Ethics. Cambridge, Ma.: Ballinger.
Parry, H. J., and H. M. Crossley
  1950 "Validity of responses to survey questions." *Public Opinion Quarterly* 14: 61–80.
Privacy Protection Study Commission
  1977 *Personal Privacy in an Information Society.* Washington, D.C., U.S.G.P.O.
Rommetveit, R., and J. Israel
  1954 "Notes on the standardization of experimental manipulations and measurements in cross-national research." *Journal of Social Issues* 4:61–68.
Schachter, S. S.
  1954 "Interpretative and methodological problems of replicated research." *Journal of Social Issues* 4:52–60.
  1959 *The Psychology of Affiliation.* Stanford, Calif.: Stanford University Press.
Singer, E.
  1976 "Self-fulfilling prophecies: A proposal to study the effect of interviewers' expectations and experimenter effects in survey research." Photocopy. New York: National Opinion Research Center.
  1978a "Informed consent: Consequences for response rate and response quality in social surveys." *American Sociological Review* 43: 144–162.

1978b "Informed consent: Consequences for response rate and response response quality in social surveys." Photocopy. New York: National Opinion Research Center.
Sudman, S., and N. M. Bradburn
1974 *Response Effects in Surveys: A Review and Synthesis.* Chicago: Aldine.
Weiss, C. H.
1968 "Validity of welfare mothers' interview responses." *Public Opinion Quarterly* 32:622–633.

11

The Statutory Protection of Confidential Research Data: Synthesis and Evaluation

ROBERT L. NELSON
TERRY E. HEDRICK

The last decade produced unprecedented debate about what is and what should be the status of legal protection for confidential research information. Three voices were heard most loudly during the debate. One was the voice of the research community, which, with the surge in evaluation research in public and private sectors, began to claim need for testimonial privileges immunizing researchers from legal process (Boness and Cordes, 1973; Nejelski and Peyser, 1975). Another was the voice of research participants and their representatives. The prospect of an "experimenting society," or at least an "information society," led them to articulate concern for the privacy of participants apart from the legal protection of researchers. Their concern was in part translated into federal law protecting individuals about whom information had been collected.[1] The third voice—that of interested third parties to research: police, prosecutors, private plaintiffs, government committees, and the like—often spoke with the force of formal legal process.[2]

[1]The most fundamental of these is the Privacy Act of 1974, 5 U.S.C. § 522(a) (1977). See also the Family Educational Rights and Privacy Act of 1974, 20 U.S.C. § 1232(g) (1977). For legislation establishing human subjects review panels, see 42 U.S.C. § 289 (1) (3) (a) (1977).
[2]For a more comprehensive analysis of such incidents, see Knerr (1976).

Their demands for access to putatively confidential data underscored the very real consequences of the debate over rights in the research relationship.

Legislation enacted during this period resulted in a set of partial and ill-defined compromises among the interests of researchers, research participants, and third parties. The Public Health Services Act,[3] the Drug Abuse Office and Treatment Act,[4] the Controlled Substances Act,[5] and the Crime Control Act,[6] among others,[7] provided some form of statutory protection for research information identifying individuals. The statutes presented a number of legal questions concerning their scope and interrelationship. And it is only with the publication of implementing regulations and a scholarly analysis[8] that the pieces of the legal puzzle have begun to come together. Despite the beginnings of a convergence of law and administrative policy with respect to these statutes, the issue of the most appropriate policy for the statutory protection of research data, in drug abuse and other fields, remains unresolved. Much of the debate about appropriate statutory policy, and indeed much of the judicial doctrine on the protected status of research communications, revolves around empirical questions about confidentiality in research. Given the salience of the empirical questions, it is curious that the evaluation community has not applied its methods to study the statutory innovations as experiments in legal protection.[9]

---

[3]Publ. L. No. 91–513, § 303(a), amended by Pub. L. No. 93–282 (1974) (codified at 42 U.S.C. § 242(a) (1977)).

[4]Pub. L. No. 92–255, § 408, amended by Publ. L. No. 93–282, § 303 (1974) (codified at 21 U.S.C. § 1175(a) (1977)). See also Pub. L. No. 93–282 (codified at 42 U.S.C. § 4582(a) (1977)), which provides similar protection for alcohol-abuse research.

[5]Pub. L. No. 91–513, § 502(c) (codified at 21 U.S.C. § 872(c) 1977)).

[6]Pub. L. No. 93–83, § 524(a) (codified at 42 U.S.C. § 3771 (1977)).

[7]In addition to long-standing protection of Census data, 13 U.S.C. §§ 8,9 (1977), and Social Security data, 42 U.S.C. § 1306 (1977), other specific forms of data are protected. See 42 U.S.C. § 242(m) (d) (1977) (subpoena immunity for the National Center for Health Statistics' evaluation research data); id. § 247 (c) (d) (5) (1977) (veneral disease records); and, id. § 5732 (1977) (statistical survey of runaway youth).

[8]See 44 Fed. Reg. 20,384 (April 4, 1979); 42 Fed. Reg. 54,946 (Oct. 12, 1977); and Boruch and Cecil (1979: 240–261).

[9]Other researchers have investigated practices concerning confidentiality in research, but none have focused on the use of these statutory innovations. McNamara and Starr (1973) surveyed the directors of drug abuse treatment centers about their record-keeping practices and whether they had been approached by authorities seeking records. The human subjects review process has been studied rather extensively. See, for example, Barber, Lally, Makaruska, and Sullivan (1973) and University of Michigan Survey Research Center (1978:1-67–1-69). The impact of informed consent procedures on research results has also been surveyed. See Sudman and Bradburn (1974) and Singer (1978).

Because the policy issues presented by statutory protection of social data remain very much alive—as witnessed by the proposals of the Privacy Protection Study Commission (1977:580–581) and pending congressional legislation (U.S. Congress, House, 1979:35–41)—it is a critical time for the research community to begin an empirical assessment of the present statutory schema.

This chapter begins the assessment process by studying two statutes, Section 303(a) of the Public Health Services Act[10] and Section 502(c) of the Controlled Substances Act.[11] The analysis combines a legal and an empirical approach. It reviews the law of confidential research records by examining the common law of privileged communications, the text and legislative history of Sections 303(a) and 502(c), and the cases interpreting Sections 303(a) and 502(c). The impact and operation of these new statutes is then assessed on the basis of results from a survey of researchers receiving protection under Section 502(c) from 1971 to 1976. Following a review of final implementing regulations issued after the survey was conducted, some recommendations for developing statutory protection of research data are proposed. By analyzing the current state of the law and the empirical evidence produced by the survey, the chapter describes what the law is and asserts what the law should become with respect to the statutory protection of confidential research information.

The Legal Context

THE COMMON LAW OF PRIVILEGES: PAST AND PRESENT

Statutes protecting the confidentiality of research data are in large part designed to meet the inadequacies of safeguards under constitutional law and common law doctrine.[12] Nonetheless, a brief consideration of the criteria by which the courts have traditionally judged whether information is privileged is warranted. Regardless of the legal consequences attending the judicial rules, the traditional principles are a historically rich set of policy considerations that may well appeal to

---

[10]See *supra* note 3.

[11]See *supra* note 5.

[12]See, for example, United States v. Doe (Appeal of Samuel Popkin), 460 F.2d 328 (1st Cir. 1972), and Branzburg v. Hayes, 408 U.S. 665 (1972). The limitations of constitutional theories are discussed by Knerr (1976), Nejelski and Peyser (1975), Boruch and Cecil (1979), and *Valparaiso University Law Review* (1970).

legislatures and administrative agencies. As such, they are useful criteria from which to evaluate the new statutes. Moreover, the traditional principles are still legally operative in some respects. Two of the new protective statutes seem to incorporate the common law test of balancing competing interests in determining whether confidential data should be released in court.[13] And Rule 501 of the recently adopted Federal Rules of Evidence dictates that the "privilege of a witness . . . shall be governed by the principles of common law as they may be interpreted by the courts of the United States in the light of reason and experience."[14] This has led to a resurgence of interest by federal courts in the classical doctrine of evidentiary privilege.[15]

The discussion of privileged communications in Wigmore's classic treatise on evidence is still authoritative on what protection research data may enjoy at common law. Wigmore outlined four conditions a communication must meet to be privileged in the courts.[16] First, the communication must originate in confidence. Second, confidentiality must be an essential element to satisfactory maintenance of the relationship. Third, the relationship must be one the community wishes strongly to foster. Fourth, injury to the relationship caused by disclosure must be greater than the benefit gained from its contribution to the disposition of the litigation. The first three of these criteria are not generally problematic for research in which confidentiality is a concern. Courts have recognized the importance of confidentiality in research,[17] and often there is a congressional mandate for research into a problem area.[18] Consequently, the decision to order the production of

[13]21 U.S.C. § 1175(b)(2)(c) (1977) and 42 U.S.C. § 4582(b)(2)(c) (1977) (see supra note 4) allow the disclosure of confidential records "if authorized by an appropriate order of a court of competent jurisdiction granted after application showing good cause therefor. In assessing good cause the court shall weigh the public interest and the need for disclosure against the injury to the patient, to the physician–patient relationship, and to the treatment services."

[14]Fed. R. Evid. 501.

[15]See, for example, Lora v. Board of Education of City of New York, 74 F.R.D. 565 (E.D.N.Y. 1977), discussed infra at pp. 218–219, and United States v. King, 73 F.R.D. 103 (E.D.N.Y. 1976).

[16]J. Wigmore, Evidence § 2285 (McNaughton Rev. 1961).

[17]"Much of the raw data on which reserach is based simply is not made available except upon a pledge of confidentiality. Compelled disclosure of confidential information would without question severely stifle research into questions of public policy, the very subjects in which the public interest is the greatest." Richards of Rockford v. Pacific Gas & Electric Company, 71 F.R.D. 388, 390 (N.D. Cal. 1976).

[18]See, for example, the introduction to the Comprehensive Drug Abuse Prevention and Control Act, 1970 U.S. Code Congr. & Ad. News, at 4566; Pub. L. 90–513, Oct. 27, 1970, 84 Stat. 1236.

research information will usually hinge on the balancing test contained in the fourth of Wigmore's conditions: Does the benefit of disclosure to the legal process outweigh the harm caused by breaching the confidentiality of the relationship? Once the issue is cast in these terms, the outcome will depend on the particular facts of the case before the court. A brief review of cases adjudicating the confidentiality of research data will illustrate some of the relevant considerations.

The balancing test has resulted in the protection of research information in cases where researchers or news reporters have not been parties to the litigation and the requesting parties have not demonstrated the relevance of the research records. *Richards of Rockford v. Pacific Gas & Electric Company* is the only case in which a social scientist successfully resisted the disclosure of research documents on other than statutory grounds.[19] The plaintiff in *Richards* sought the notes and testimony of a researcher to substantiate charges of breach of contract and defamation against the defendant utility. Although the court conceded that information from interview notes may have been relevant to the charge of defamation, it exercised its supervisory authority over discovery to deny the plaintiff's request.[20] The court was persuaded by the facts that the researcher was not a party to the suit, that the research was not initiated for purposes of the suit, and that the central focus of the study was not directly relevant to issues at stake. It held that it would not order production of the research materials unless the plaintiff made a prima facie showing of their relevance.[21]

Similar reasoning is found in *Apicella v. McNeil Laboratories*,[22] which involved the confidentiality of newspaper sources rather than of research records. In *Apicella*, both plaintiffs and defendants sought the disclosure of confidential sources used by a medical newsletter in publishing a report on the potentially harmful effects of a drug that plaintiff alleged had been improperly sold by defendant. Although the court recognized the difficulty of obtaining medical testimony on the administration of drugs and the public interest in obtaining a full hearing about a potentially dangerous drug,[23] it found these considerations outweighed by the harm to the future flow of medical information.

[19]71 F.R.D. 388 (N.D. Cal. 1976).
[20]Although the court ruled on the basis of its supervisory power rather than on grounds of testimonial privilege, it explicitly balanced the public interest in maintaining the confidentiality of the relationship between an academic researcher and his or her sources. *Id.* at 389.
[21]*Id.* at 390. For a critique of *Richards*, see *Northwestern Law Review* (1976:651).
[22]66 F.R.D. 78 (E.D.N.Y. 1975).
[23]*Id.* at 82.

Also, the court was not persuaded that the same information could not be obtained elsewhere.

Parties to litigation have not fared so well in protecting information from disclosure. For example, in *Lora v. Board of Education of the City of New York*,[24] a plaintiff class of black and Hispanic students enrolled in schools for the emotionally disturbed alleged discrimination in the selection of students for the special schools. They sought to support their claim with an analysis of a random sample of the files of students considered for the remedial schools, with all individual identifiers removed from the files. Over the school board's objection, the court ordered the discovery. It cited that because individuals would remain anonymous, there was a minimal intrusion into individual privacy. The court questioned the school board's representation of students' rights to privacy, in that most of the information sought concerned the plaintiff class itself. And the court emphasized the importance of the *expectation* of confidentiality in determining the legal protection of a communication.

> Any argument that permitting the plaintiffs' experts to examine redacted files will adversely affect future diagnosis and treatment of disturbed school children must rely on the premise that such communications are made in conscious reliance on legal or professional guarantees of strict confidentiality. Defendants have, however, furnished the court with no evidence that students are promised such confidentiality prior to screening and counseling sessions, or are informed that their communications are privileged under state law.[25]

The school board's failure to demonstrate an expectation of privacy by students was fatal to their argument to prevent disclosure.[26]

A similar concern for the expectations of research participants is articulated by the Privacy Protection Study Commission. Their recommendations for virtually complete protection of research participants against the risks of disclosure are in large part aimed at fulfilling the expectations of participants about the confidentiality of research records (1977:567–578).

These cases reflect a well-reasoned, case-by-case approach to the issue of confidentiality. The results are somewhat encouraging to the research community. It would appear that nonparty researchers are not likely to be compelled to release information unless the information is

[24]474 F.R.D. 565 (E.D.N.Y. 1977).
[25]*Id.* at 583.
[26]*Id.* at 586.

not available from other sources. And even then, the benefits of disclosure must outweigh the costs of disclosure. The major defect with such common law protections of research data is that the balancing of interests is a highly subjective process. As other commentators have pointed out, common law privileges are not a reliable source of legal protection (Boness and Cordes, 1973; Boruch and Cecil, 1979). The two statutes reviewed in this chapter were designed to broaden and simplify legal assurances of confidentiality in the sensitive area of drug abuse research. Before turning to an empirical assessment of how well they have performed that function, a brief legal analysis of the statutes is necessary.

THE STATUTORY RESPONSE

Sections 303(a) and 502(c) were enacted as provisions of the Comprehensive Drug Abuse Prevention and Control Act of 1970.[27] The statutes were constructed as grants of authority to the secretary of the Department of Health, Education and Welfare (HEW) and the attorney general, respectively. Section 303(a) permits the secretary to:

> authorize persons engaged in research on mental health, including research on the use and effect of alcohol and other psychoactive drugs, to protect the privacy of individuals who are the subjects of such research by withholding from all persons not connected with the conduct of such research the names or other identifying characteristics of such individuals. Persons so authorized to protect the privacy of such individuals may not be compelled in any Federal, State, or local civil, criminal, administrative, legislative, or other proceedings to identify such individuals.[28]

Section 502(c) consists of a similar delegation of authority to the attorney general to protect individuals who participate in drug abuse research.[29]

Among the recently enacted statutes protecting research information, these two provisions seem particularly appropriate for study. In some sense they offer the broadest form of protection for data. Unlike

[27]Pub. L. No. 91–513 (codified in scattered sections of Titles 21 and 42 of U.S.C.) (hereinafter referred to as the 1970 Act). To prevent confusion, we should point out that Sections 303(a) and 502(c) are also referred to herein under the titles of acts that make up the Comprehensive Drug Abuse Protection and Control Act: Section 303(a) under the Public Health Services Act, *supra* note 3, and, Section 502(c) under the Controlled Substance Act, *supra* note 5.

[28]See *supra* note 3.

[29]See *supra* note 5.

other statutes,[30] these provisions offer unqualified protection of names
and identifying characteristics. Such a strict guarantee is an interesting
parallel to the absolute nature of some common law privileges, such as
the attorney–client privilege. The statutes also have some other pecu-
liarities that warrant investigation. Rather than offering automatic protection, the statutes allow the authorization of immunity on a case-by-
case (researcher-by-researcher) basis. Hence, there is some question
about how the authorization is administered. There are also questions
about the scope of protection afforded by the statutes. The ambiguity
revolves around the language in the statute: "names or other identifying characteristics of such individuals." The main question is whether
the statutes authorize a researcher to refuse to disclose information
other than names or identifying characteristics, such as the research
records of persons the police identify by name. The cases interpreting
the statute have not provided a direct test of this issue, but they may
give an indication of how courts will address it in the future.

The leading cases on the statutes were decided by state courts in
New York; one case stands for a broad interpretation of the scope of the
statutes, whereas the other stands for a more narrow interpretation. In
People v. Newman the director of the New York City Methadone Maintenance Treatment Program refused to comply with a subpoena requiring him to produce unnamed photographs of patients treated at one of
the program's units, citing a grant of confidentiality received under
Section 502(c).[31] The central issue decided by the *Newman* court was
whether the unqualified protection under 502(c) was qualified by Section 408(b)(2)(c), passed after Section 502(c) as part of the Drug Abuse
Office and Treatment Act of 1972.[32] Section 408(b)(2)(c) allowed for
disclosure of "records of the identity, diagnosis, prognosis, or treatment" of patients in drug abuse programs to "a court of competent
jurisdiction" after "application showing good cause."[33] In holding that

---

[30]See *supra* notes 4, 6, and 7. Although the authorization to protect information is
drafted with identical language in the statutes, their statutory contexts are slightly different. These differences are discussed in Boruch and Cecil (1979:249–253). Final implementing regulations emphasize the different roles the DEA and the Department of Health
and Human Services will play in the future granting of protection. See the discussion
infra pp. 231–233. Despite the divergence in implementing regulations, our empirical
assessment of Section 502(c) can be generalized to Section 303(a). The operation of 502(c)
during the period surveyed raised questions about administration, legal protection, impact on research, and interpretation by researchers that are relevant to 303(a).

[31]32 N.Y.2d 379, 298 N.E.2d 502 (1973).

[32]21 U.S.C. § 1175(b)(2)(c) (1977), quoted *supra* note 13.

[33]*Id.*

the statutes provided cumulative rather than exclusive coverage, the court cited the congressional intent to provide broad protection to research data. It quoted from the amicus brief submitted by HEW.

> The United States Congress has enacted legislation over the last few years to encourage research into [the] causes and cures [of narcotics addiction]. In order to induce those suffering from drug addiction . . . to participate in these research programs, Congress enacted [in 1970] a statute granting *absolute* confidentiality to such participants, upon proper authorization. . . . This federal statute is in full force and effect and is fully applicable to Methadone Maintenance Treatment Programs.[34]

The *Newman* court was not directly dealing with the protection of research records other than identifying information because the subpoena sought nothing more than photographs. Nonetheless, its construction of the 1970 and 1972 acts adopts the view that the 1970 Act provided protection for all forms of research records.

People v. Still distinguishes *Newman* and confines it to its facts.[35] The defendant in *Still* attempted to defend against a charge of illegal possession of methadone with a letter from a clinic saying he had been given a legal "weekend dose," while at the same time claiming that the records of the clinic were protected from disclosure by the 1970 statutes. The court rejected the claim and distinguished between the absolute protection of *identifying information* in the 1970 statutes and the qualified protection of *research records* under the 1972 statute.[36] But the court also indicated that the defendant's disclosure that he was under treatment "obviated" analysis under the 1970 Act, because he had waived whatever protection the statutes offered.[37]

The facts of the *Still* case can be distinguished from the hypothetical situation discussed earlier as the chief ambiguity in the 1970 statutes. Because the defendant waived protection under the 1970 statutes, there was no need for the court to determine the scope of coverage beyond mere identifiers. Putting aside the factual distinction, however, *Still*

---

[34]298 N.E.2d at 508–509.

[35]369 N.Y.S.2d 759 (1975).

[36]*Id.* at 764.

[37]*Id.* at 765. See also Anastasi v. Morgenthau, 373 N.Y.S.2d 751 (1975) [confession to drug treatment program officials, later supplied to police at request of defendant, not protected by 21 U.S.C. § 1175(b)(c)(c) (1977)]; and, State v. White, 363 A.2d 143, 169 Conn. 223 (1977) [defendant accused of violating probation by leaving a drug treatment facility cannot invoke privilege for treatment records under 212 U.S.C. § 1175(b)(c) (1977)].

stands for the interpretation that identifying information can be absolutely protected under a grant of confidentiality from HEW or the Department of Justice, whereas the research records of an already identified individual might be disclosed if they meet the balancing test in Section 408(b)(2)(c). The commentators thus far have agreed with that interpretation of the 1970 Act (see Knerr, 1976:41; Boruch and Cecil, 1979:250). Researchers are therefore advised to beware that the coverage of the 1970 Act may be limited to identifying information.

The present authors argue that the narrow interpretation of the 1970 provisions is incorrect. The legislative history of the 1970 Act describes the purpose of the confidentiality provisions in broad terms:

> Section 3(a) of this title grants the Secretary of Health, Education, and Welfare a much needed authority to protect the privacy of drug research subjects by nondisclosure of identification data of such individuals. It enables the researcher, when authorized by the Secretary, to assure research subjects complete anonymity, with immunity from prosecution for withholding this identifying information.[38]

To construe the statutes literally, and limit coverage to identifying information alone, could make a sham of the statutory protection. Given the reasonable likelihood that participants in drug abuse programs have had some kind of identifying contact with law enforcement, and given the relative ease with which program participants could be observed, protection under the statute could evaporate. If the law is interpreted to allow the disclosure of research records pertaining to already identified individuals, it encourages researchers to devise "see no evil, hear no evil" procedures to avoid the identities of research participants.[39] Not only would such procedures be awkward for researchers and possibly anxiety arousing for research participants, but they also might limit the opportunities for longitudinal research. Finally, as the survey evidence reported later in the chapter demonstrates, a narrow interpretation is unjust because it departs from the understanding of the vast majority of researchers about the scope of the protection of a grant of confidentiality.

Having described the legal context out of which the 1970 statutes grew, and having raised ongoing legal issues concerning the statutes, the next section summarizes the results of a survey that studied the impact, operation, and researcher understanding of the statutes.

[38]1970 U.S. Code Congr. & Ad. News, 4594–4595.
[39]For a discussion and bibliography of various approaches, see Campbell, Boruch, Schwartz, and Steinberg (1977).

An Empirical Evaluation: Method and Results

The common law of evidentiary privileges and conflicting judicial interpretations of the new statutes raised empirical questions requiring a survey of researchers who had received protection under the new statutes. The common law test for whether information is protected suggested some broad questions about the value and understanding of the new statutory schema: Was legal protection necessary or beneficial to the research process? What were the expectations of researchers and participants about the legal protection afforded by the statutes? The novelty of the legislation prompted additional inquiries: How widely were the statutes used? How were they administered? Did they provide effective legal protection? Did they have any unintended consequences, such as reducing the possibility for secondary analysis of data or supplanting other safeguards for confidentiality?

SURVEY DESIGN

The findings reported here are based largely on telephone interviews (one interview was completed by mail) conducted in 1976 and 1977 with researchers receiving grants of confidentiality from the Drug Enforcement Administration (DEA) under the authority granted the attorney general.[40] Analogous protection was available from the secretary of HEW, but because only a small number of researchers had received authorization in this manner prior to the time of the survey, the survey was confined to recipients of grants of confidentiality from the DEA.[41]

The list of grant recipients was compiled by Robert Boruch and Joe Cecil after lengthy negotiations with the DEA and an appeal to the provisions of the Freedom of Information Act.[42] A total of 84 individuals received grants of confidentiality between 1971 and 1976. Because these 84 individuals included both subcontractors and research collaborators, the original list was pared down to 47 separate research projects. Attempts to interview researchers associated with these proj-

[40]See supra note 5.
[41]See supra note 3. Notices concerning the protection of projects under HEW authority were published in the Federal Register during 1971–1979. The small number of projects approved by the HEW apparently resulted from rather cumbersome procedures for review in the Federal Register. These procedures have been streamlined under final implementing regulations. 44 Fed. 20,382 (Apr. 4, 1979).
[42]The procedure used to obtain the list is an interesting example of the creative use of law in social research. For a discussion of the procedure, see Cecil and Boruch (1977).

ects yielded information on protected research for 37 projects (78.7% of the total projects). Attrition was a function of difficulties in locating researchers who had completed research projects several years previously and changed institutional affiliations.

The interview schedule covered a range of issues relevant to the receipt and use of the grant of confidentiality. Researchers were asked to describe how they learned about the grant, how they acquired it, how they used it, its usefulness in securing cooperation from research participants, and its effectiveness in resisting requests for disclosure. When appropriate, researchers were also asked to provide documentation of correspondence with the DEA, informed consent waivers, instructions to interviewers, survey protocols, and descriptions of their research. The combination of survey responses and documentation provided a rich data set from which to evaluate the statutory protection administered by DEA.[43]

SURVEY RESULTS

Administration of the Grants of Confidentiality

In many respects the administration of grants of confidentiality by the DEA was a success. The disclosures from the DEA obtained by Cecil and Boruch indicated that no applications were actually denied (1977). The only exception was a researcher whom DEA officials believed to be sufficiently protected by other statutes. Contrary to the fear expressed by some commentators that administered confidentiality privileges might lead to the censoring of research (Nejelski and Peyser, 1975; Knerr, 1976; Boruch and Cecil, 1979:252), the substance of research proposals apparently received only cursory review by the DEA. A broad range of research projects, consistent with the legislative mandate for research into drug use and abuse, were authorized to receive grants of confidentiality. Of the 37 authorized projects, 22% (8) involved experimental studies; 11% (4) were counseling or drug therapy programs. The majority of projects were surveys (62%, or 23 projects). These surveys included highly focused research into drug use as well as more global investigations into a variety of areas besides drug use. In one case it was obvious that researchers had obtained the grant primarily to protect personal but non-drug-related data. One study involved participant observation as a data collection technique; another consisted largely of the collection of breath samples.

---

[43]For a copy of the interview protocol and related materials, contact Robert F. Boruch, Division of Methodology and Evaluation Research, Department of Psychology, Northwestern University, Evanston, Illinois 60201.

One administrative weakness that was identified during the interviews with grant recipients was the absence of an effective system for disseminating information about the availability and scope of grants of confidentiality. Most of the recipients "happened upon it," either by word of mouth from other researchers (43%, or 16), reading in professional publications (22%, or 8), information from research sponsors (19%, or 7), or, on one occasion, from the advice of a local city attorney. One extremely well connected researcher heard about the grant from three sources: a colleague, a professional publication, and the research sponsor. The remainder of researchers were not sure how they learned of the grant. Although it was not possible to assess the general level of awareness of the grants in the research community, the clear inference is that information on the availability of the grants must be disseminated more widely and reliably if they are to become a recognized device for assisting drug-related research.

The Quality of Legal Protection under Grants of Confidentiality

The crucial issue in evaluating the worth of the DEA's grants of confidentiality is whether the legal protection offered is effective in thwarting requests for disclosure. The responses to the survey reaffirmed previous findings that confidential data are quite frequently sought after (McNamara and Starr, 1973: 1588; Knerr, 1976). Seven of the survey's respondents reported being approached for confidential information. Three of the respondents reported such experiences in the course of research projects for which they had not received an authorization of confidentiality; four of the respondents were covered by a grant at the time they were approached. The three cases occurring prior to receipt of statutory protection did not result in flagrant violations of confidentiality, but the researchers judged that the grant would have been useful for protection of their data. For example, one researcher had his research records subpoenaed by Treasury agents investigating criminal drug dealings. It was only after negotiations through counsel that the government request was narrowed. A compromise was reached whereby the researcher testified about the dates of research operations without releasing any individually identified information.

The four cases involving projects covered by the grants of confidentiality attest to the convenience, if not the necessity, of the formal legal safeguard. In one case, the wife of a research participant sought information from a survey data set to establish her husband's alcoholism. No information was released, and the matter was dropped. The other incidents involved state and local law enforcement officials requesting information on specific individuals. With the exception of one instance in which a researcher voluntarily honored an arrest warrant for an armed robbery suspect on the premises of a drug abuse program, law enforcement officials withdrew their requests for information after being informed of the grant. The experiences of New York City's Methadone Maintenance Treatment Program, one case of which was adjudicated in *People v. Newman*,[44] are the most dramatic we encountered. In 1977 Newman reported that the New York City program frequently received up to five requests a month for information from such parties as child welfare officers, immigration officials, the FBI, district attorneys, the state education department, and even fire marshals (Newman, 1977). None of these requests resulted in the compelled disclosure of information on program participants.

These descriptions of attempted access indicate the need for the legal protection of research records. Despite potential legal problems in preventing the disclosure of information about named individuals,[45] grants of confidentiality have thus far been effective in meeting the need for legal protection.

Impact on Research Operations

The grants of confidentiality were also assessed with respect to their impact on research operations. One section of the survey asked researchers whether they would have conducted their research if a grant of confidentiality had not been available. Their responses, shown in Table 11.1, demonstrate that research into drug abuse would have suffered without statutory protection:

Table 11.1
Researcher Responses to Question, "Would You Have Done the Research if the Grant of Confidentiality Had Not Been Available?"

Response	N	Percentage
Yes	13	35
No	9	24
Do not know	8	22
No information	7	19
Total	37	100

Of those researchers possessing information directly relevant to this question, almost one-third indicated they would not have gone ahead

[44]See *supra* note 31.
[45]See the discussion *supra* at pp. 220–222.

without statutory authorization. Another 27% were not sure. Of the respondents answering this question, 43% indicated that they would have proceeded without statutory protection, but one of these researchers indicated that it would have been necessary to make major changes in the study design. According to these results, six surveys, two experiments, and the participant observation study would not have been carried out in the absence of the grant. The reasons given included the reluctance of the researcher to collect sensitive information without some assurance of immunity, the reluctance of institutions to give cooperation for the collection of sensitive data, and the failure to obtain clearance from human subjects review boards without legal guarantees of protection.

Besides assessing the impact of the grants on the ability to carry out research, the survey explored the role legal protection played in the research process. Statutory protection was described as having had an impact on obtaining cooperation from participants, on getting access to participants, and on the morale of the research staff.

Impact on obtaining the cooperation of participants

It is a long-standing tenet of research and treatment in drug abuse that confidentiality is critical to obtaining the full participation of subjects. The practices followed by our respondents were consistent with that tenet. Almost 90% of the projects made explicit assurances of confidentiality to research participants. Two exceptions to this practice involved hospital patients, who may have presumed that their communications were confidential, as between physician and patient. No information was available on the procedures followed by another two projects.

One of the primary focuses of the survey was the impact of statutory protection on the informed consent of research participants. Of the 39 researchers offering assurances of confidentiality, 36.4% (12) mentioned the grant explicitly, either by oral communications or by actually showing potential participants a copy of the award letter from the DEA. Another 48.4% (16) kept information about the grant in reserve to prod reluctant participants. Only 15% (5) did not recall using information about the grant to obtain consent. Somewhat surprising was the finding that even though most researchers used information about the grant in some way during their communications with potential participants, a relatively small proportion felt it was helpful in obtaining their cooperation. Twenty-four percent (8) of the researchers reported the grant to be specifically valuable for this purpose, whereas 58% (19) said people were already cooperative, so that the grant could not have had an additional impact. This finding is consistent with the findings of other studies that subjects are surprisingly willing to accept the re-searcher's definition of the research situation (see, e.g., Milgram, 1973). It should not be assumed, however, that the impact of formal legal protection on obtaining the cooperation of research participants is un-important. Those researchers who found the grant helpful in obtaining cooperation were those working with populations facing high risks from disclosure: noncollege drug-using youth, other users, drug ad-dicts, and drug dealers.

Impact on access

Although information was not specifically solicited on the role the statutory protection played in securing institutional cooperation, ap-proximately one-third of the investigators spontaneously volunteered that the grant had served to benefit their research in this way (32%, or 12). This was especially true for studies of noncollege drug-using youth, hospital patients, prisoners, and other users, as well as persons facing obvious legal risks—drug dealers. In some cases, physicians would have refused to cooperate with the researchers without such protection. School principals, in particular, were reported to be much more cooperative when told that records of a survey of drug use among students would be legally safeguarded. One researcher told of a case in which state officials who had recently been involved in legislative debates over confidentiality would not have cooperated with the re-search but for the grant of confidentiality.[46] Research requiring follow-up data collection, such as the follow-up of incarcerated persons, was thought impossible without statutory protection. And three researchers mentioned that their institutions' human subjects review boards would not have approved the research proposals without formal legal protec-tion for participants. As institutional authorities become more sophisti-cated about exposing their charges to legal risks, the need for legal assurances to gain access to potential respondents can be expected to increase.

Impact on research staff

In addition to increasing institutional cooperation, grant recipients volunteered that possession of the protection sometimes served to bol-ster staff morale and decrease staff anxiety (24%, or 9). Some investiga-tors said they would not have been comfortable doing the research with only conventional confidentiality precautions, and others stressed that the authorization was instrumental in developing and maintaining a

[46]Letter from S. B. Sells, Dec. 16, 1976.

motivated research staff. For example, one study using community-based interviewers to survey drug use found the statutory protection helpful in developing trust between the interviewers and the research staff. Although it was anticipated that grants of confidentiality would be most important in increasing the cooperation of research subjects, it appears that they may be equally important in obtaining cooperation from institutions and research personnel. Since the interview format did not seek to assess these impacts directly, but only allowed for coding them when volunteered, it is likely that statutory protection is even more useful in this respect than the percentages indicate.

Impact on Use of Alternative Safeguards for Confidentiality

Boruch and Cecil (1979:261) suggest that formal legal privileges should not be viewed as sufficient protection for confidential research information. A variety of dangers to confidentiality exist outside the courtroom, ranging from inadvertent disclosure to theft. Therefore, it was important to assess whether receipt of a grant of confidentiality led researchers to relax and dispense with other safeguards for protecting data. Apparently it did not. The overwhelming majority of grant recipients employed additional mechanisms to ensure confidentiality (89%, or 33). The precautions taken consisted largely of physical separation of identifying information and the remaining data. Of those using extra measures, 79% (26) used the mechanism of a name–identification link list,[47] with 9% (3) initially refraining from collecting any type of identifying information. Two respondents reported that they not only kept their link list under lock and key but also sent it to Canada to remove it further from the possibility of subpoena.[48]

Impact on Secondary Analysis

A subsidiary interest in the survey was whether researchers obtaining statutory protection for their data would be hesitant to allow secondary analysis of the data by others. It is not unreasonable to speculate that the formalization of data protection makes some researchers even more reluctant than usual to release data to other legitimately interested researchers. Such an outcome would be a negative effect of a

---

[47]For a discussion of the terminology of the means by which data and identifiers are separated, consult Campbell et al. (1977).

[48]For a discussion of the law on whether various forms of linked systems will protect data from compelled disclosure see Teitelbaum (Chapter 2, this volume).

statutory privilege, since it would discourage alternative analyses of potentially rare and valuable data sets. Only 7 (19%) of the survey respondents had a written policy on secondary analysis; 16 (43%) researchers responded that they would release data for secondary analysis only after identifiers had been removed. One respondent said that he would release data without qualification. Seven (19%) researchers said that they would not release information for further analysis; the rest of the respondents did not know what their policy would be or did not respond to the inquiry. Cross-tabulations indicated that projects employing addicts, dealers, and users as participants were almost unanimously opposed to releasing data, with or without identifying information. The same finding holds for research involving counseling and drug therapy. The reluctance of these researchers to release data to others is more likely explained by the risks their participants face than by the effect of receiving a grant of confidentiality.

Researcher Interpretations of the Scope of the Coverage

At this point in the presentation of results it is well to recall two conclusions from the analysis of the common law and the new statutes. First, in the absence of a confidentiality statute, whether a court orders the disclosure of research information will depend in part on the expectations of parties about the confidentiality of their communications.[49] The expectation of privacy is a factor tending to make a communication legally confidential. Second, the 1970 Act and the cases interpreting it are ambiguous concerning whether a grant of confidentiality covers anything more than names and similar identifying information about participants.[50] Indeed, even though this chapter has argued that a narrow interpretation is wrong, at least one case suggests that the grants do not protect information beyond identifiers.[51] In the light of this ambiguity, it was important to assess how researchers receiving grants interpreted the scope of protection offered.

It is clear from the responses received that most researchers had a dangerously exaggerated expectation of coverage under the grant that did not appreciate the ambiguity in the language of the authorizing statute or the potential effect of cases decided before the time of the survey. When asked if they interpreted the grant to cover more than

[49]See discussion supra at p. 218.
[50]See discussion supra at pp. 220–222.
[51]People v. Still, 369 N.Y.S.2d. 759 (1977). See discussion supra at p. 221.

identifying information, 81% (30) said yes, 14% (5) said they were not sure, and only 1 said he did not think so. Their perceptions were further explored by asking if they thought general operating records (such as sites and dates of data collection) were covered by the authorization. Again the majority took the broad view, with 65% (24) answering yes, 19% (7) not sure, and 11% (4) answering no. Moreover, it seems reasonable to conclude from the comments of researchers about the effectiveness of the statutory authorization in obtaining cooperation from institutional authorities that the broad interpretation of legal coverage was conveyed to participating institutions. In fact, it may have been the perception of a blanket coverage that was instrumental in obtaining institutional cooperation, even though that perception may have been unwarranted.

The broad interpretation held by the researchers contains several messages. One message is for legislators and agency administrators: Even sophisticated groups of nonlawyers are not sufficiently aware of potential complexities in formal legal safeguards. Another message is for researchers: Beware of barristers bearing gifts. It is important to scrutinize carefully the language used to define the legal protection, to inquire of the administering agency what that language means, and to be cautious about its effectiveness. Finally, and perhaps more importantly, policymakers in the area of research privacy should take note that the most common interpretation of statutory protection by researchers is that it is legally safe to participate in research that has received statutory protection. Consistent with the expectancy interest that is recognized in common law, statutory protection should be drafted to conform to the expectations of participants that all records and communications pertaining to the research are legally protected from disclosure.

The Latest Developments: Final Regulations

Since this survey was conducted, the two agencies charged with the administration of the 1970 Act have promulgated final implementing regulations concerning grants of confidentiality.[52] The regulations are of direct practical interest because they describe the procedures and requirements for obtaining authorizations protecting confidentiality. The regulations may also be legally significant. The interpretation of a statute by the agency charged with its administration is entitled to

[52]See *supra* note 8.

considerable weight in the deliberations of a court over the statute's meaning.[53] The final regulations, therefore, may be a consideration for future courts interpreting the scope of the confidentiality provisions of the 1970 Act.

DEA regulations indicate a realignment between HEW and DEA for the future authorization of confidentiality protection for research data. Previously, HEW followed rather cumbersome procedures for granting an authorization, including a public notice in the *Federal Register* for each project. Most researchers, therefore, turned to the DEA for a grant of confidentiality. The new DEA regulations, however, may discourage applicants by a more selective stance; authorization is limited to "research project[s] directly related to the enforcement of the laws under the jurisdiction of the Attorney General concerning drugs or other [controlled] substances"[54] Thus it will be increasingly difficult to acquire a grant from DEA to protect research data indirectly related to drug use. Because HEW has streamlined its procedures and has a broader mandate for research authorizations than does DEA, researchers may find it a more favorable source of protection than in the past.

The issuance of the regulations puts to rest some questions about the administrative policy under the 1970 Act. The coverage provided to participants in protected projects is permanent. It does not lapse when the authorization for the project ends. Also, HEW regulations prescribe some objective criteria for reviewing applications; these criteria do not include reviewing the merits of a research proposal. If an application is denied, the reason for the denial must be stated in writing. These rules should operate to minimize the potential for abuse in administration of the protection mechanism.

The regulations say little, however, about what kinds of research records are covered by the authorization. The DEA regulations do not attempt to define the operative language in the 1970 Act. The HEW regulations define "identifying characteristics" as "the name, address, any identifying number, fingerprints, voiceprints, photographs or any other item or combination of data about a research subject which could reasonably lead directly or indirectly by reference to other information to identification of that research subject."[55] Although this definition is broad and could be interpreted to include virtually all kinds of infor-

---

[53]See, for example, Red Lion Broadcasting v. F.C.C., 395 U.S. 367 (1969); and Zemel v. Rusk, 381 U.S. 1 (1965).

[54]42 Fed. Reg. 54,946 (Oct. 12, 1977).

[55]44 Fed. Reg. 20,384 (Apr. 12, 1979).

mation, it does not put HEW clearly on record as to whether all information that could be used to identify individuals is given absolute protection, or whether the information is protected only insofar as it is intended to be used to identify an individual. Until additional guidelines are published or a pattern of practice emerges in the course of HEW's administration of the grants, the scope of the coverage remains ambiguous.

Conclusion

The preceding analysis of a statutory innovation leads to several recommendations. The law of confidential research data, even in spheres of statutory protection, remains unclear. Research projects falling outside the purview of confidentiality legislation must deal with the uncertainties of the common law of privileged communications. Although the legal protection of data at common law is not as consistent or reliable as researchers desire, researchers should be encouraged to contest requests for data in courts. If the researcher fails to obtain a complete bar to disclosure of research information, disclosure might be supervised by the judge presiding over the case. The state of the law may not be different for researchers receiving statutory authorizations of confidentiality. The provisions of the 1970 Act may not provide coverage for anything beyond identifying information. It has been argued here, and researchers and their lawyers are encouraged to argue similarly, that to fulfill the congressional purpose for granting confidentiality to drug abuse research and to fulfill an expectation of confidentiality by researcher and participant alike, the 1970 Act should be read broadly to protect any information that could be identified with an individual. Until clarification is received, however, researchers would be well advised to be cautious in their reliance on statutory authorizations of confidentiality.

The survey to assess the effectiveness of the confidentiality provisions of the 1970 Act indicated that federally administered statutory protection has promise. Grants of confidentiality were well administered by the DEA. Of fundamental importance, authorization provided effective protection for research data in the field. No researcher with an authorization was forced to disclose information, and requesters usually retreated when informed of the authorization. Moreover, the added protection had a salutory effect on participants, institutional access, research staff, and even the inclination of researchers to initiate studies. These benefits of the grants were observed to occur without simultaneous negative side effects, such as decreasing reliance on other confidentiality safeguards or diminishing prospects for the secondary analysis of data.

Survey results indicate that some disturbing problems remain, however. The findings suggest a failure to disseminate information about the existence and scope of statutory protection. It is doubtful that the majority of qualified researchers have knowledge of or have applied for grants. The responsible agencies should seek to inform funding sources, in government and out, of the availability of the statutory protection.

Among the most disturbing of the survey results is the tendency for researchers to give the broadest reading possible to the scope of protection offered by the statutes. Although this can be taken as an indicator of the naiveté of the research community, it is a matter for serious consideration by courts, legislators, and administrative agencies. Courts should consider the expectations of researchers when adjudicating the scope of protection under the 1970 Act. Legislators should be advised to draft legislation with enough precision to provide clear signals to researchers about what is and what is not protected. After 10 years on the books, the confidentiality provisions examined are still not clearly defined. Because of the difficulty of granting clearly understandable coverage in piecemeal fashion, it is advisable to draft protective statutes as simply and broadly as possible. The proposals of the Privacy Protection Study Commission (1977:580–581) and the Privacy of Research Records Act (U.S. Congress, House, 1979:35–41) are good examples of such simplicity and breadth. Finally, the agencies administering authorizations under the 1970 Act should clarify their policies on the kinds of research information that is protected. It would be appropriate for these agencies to take the lead in carrying out the congressional intent of the legislation by defining the coverage broadly. At a minimum, they should alert the research community to potential legal risks stemming from the ambiguities of coverage.

Acknowledgments

An earlier version of this chapter was published with Joe S. Cecil as a co-author in *Proceedings and Background Papers: Conference on Ethical and Legal Problems in Applied Social Research* (Evanston, Ill.: Department of Psychology, Northwestern University, 1979). This final product would not have been possible without Joe's efforts or those of Robert F. Boruch. At various times during the preparation of this chapter the authors and their colleagues were supported by National Science Foundation Grant DAR–7820374. The second author is now at the Institute for Program Evaluation, U.S. General Accounting Office.

References

Barber, B., J. Lally, J. Makaruska, and D. Sullivan
    1973   *Research on Human Subjects.* New York: Russell Sage.
Boness, F. H., and J. F. Cordes
    1973   "The researcher–subject relationship: The need for protection and a model statute." *Georgetown Law Review* 62:243–272.
Boruch, R. F., and J. S. Cecil
    1979   *Assuring Confidentiality of Social Research Data.* Philadelphia: University of Pennsylvania Press.
Campbell, D. T., R. F. Boruch, R. D. Schwartz, and J. Steinberg
    1977   "Confidentiality-preserving modes of access to files and to interfile exchange for useful statistical analysis." *Evaluation Quarterly* 1:269–299.
Cecil, J. S., and R. F. Boruch
    1977   "A note on the deductive disclosure of confidentiality grantees." Research memorandum. Department of Psychology, Northwestern University.
Knerr, C.
    1976   "Compulsory disclosure to the courts of research sources and data." Paper presented to the Annual Meeting of the American Psychological Association, Washington, D.C., September 7.
McNamara, R. M., Jr., and J. R. Starr
    1973   "Confidentiality of narcotic addict treatment records: A legal and statistical analysis." *Columbia Law Review* 73:1579–1612.
Milgram, S.
    1973   *Obedience to Authority: An Experimental View.* New York: Harper & Row.
Nejelski, P., and H. Peyser
    1975   *A Researcher's Shield Statute: Guarding against the Compulsory Disclosure of Research Data, in Protecting Individual Privacy in Evaluation Research.* Washington, D.C.: National Academy of Sciences.
Newman, R. G.
    1977   *Methadone Treatment in Narcotic Addiction.* New York: Academic Press.
Northwestern Law Review
    1976   "Note: In light of reason and experience: Rule 501" *Northwestern Law Review* 71:645–654.
Privacy Protection Study Commission
    1977   *Personal Privacy in an Information Society.* Washington, D.C.: U.S. Government Printing Office.
Singer, E.
    1978   "Informed consent: Consequences for response rate and response quality in social surveys." *American Sociological Review* 43:144–162.
Sudman, S., and N. Bradburn
    1974   *Response Effects in Surveys: A Review and Synthesis.* Chicago: Aldine.

U.S. Congress, House of Representatives
  1979   *Privacy policy, message from the president: The proposed "privacy of research records act."* House document no. 96–84. 96th Cong., 1st sess., April 2. Washington, D.C.: U.S. Government Printing Office
University of Michigan Survey Research Center, Institute for Social Research
  1978   "A survey of institutional review boards and research subjects of biomedical research." Pp. 1.67–1.69 in *Appendix to Report and Recommendations: Institutional Review Boards.* DHEW Pub. no. (OS) 78–0009. Washington, D.C.: U.S. Government Printing Office.
Valparaiso University Law Review
  1970   "Comment: Social research and privileged data." *Valparaiso University Law Review* 4:368–399.

12

Randomized Response

TORE DALENIUS

During the past 10 years, spirited and sometimes heated debates have taken place in most Western democracies about the invasion of privacy problem in general, and especially about threats to individual privacy in the context of surveys and censuses. It is worth emphasizing that these debates have focused on *potential* rather than realized threats. It is also worth emphasizing that alleged cases of realized threats typically have not been validated in the past except in very rare cases. By and large, statisticians, social researchers, and others have a most satisfactory record of *not* encroaching upon citizens' privacy. Moreover, the professionals just mentioned have devoted considerable effort to the development of new "privacy-protection" tools for data collection, especially tools for collecting data about sensitive characteristics.

Collecting Data about Sensitive Characteristics

What constitutes a sensitive characteristic is to some extent relative. What is sensitive in the United States, for instance, is not necessarily sensitive in Sweden, and vice versa; what is sensitive to women may

237

SOLUTIONS TO ETHICAL
AND LEGAL PROBLEMS
IN SOCIAL RESEARCH

not be sensitive to men. By the same token, a certain characteristic may be more sensitive in the United States than in Sweden: Salary is no doubt an example in kind.

The degree of sensitivity associated with a certain characteristic is reflected in various ways in the course of a survey, and especially in the data collection operation; it is not uncommon that individuals selected for a survey show reluctance to provide answers to some questions. Based on their experiences, most survey practitioners would presumably agree that such sensitive areas would include induced abortion, drunken driving, income tax evasion, and sexual practices, at least when it comes to reporting *personal* experiences. The choice of method for collecting data on such topics may then become crucial.

DIRECT METHODS FOR DATA COLLECTION

In order to clarify the notion of "*direct* methods," let us consider the area of income tax evasion. In an interview survey for the purpose of estimating the proportion of taxpayers who failed to report *all* income in their income tax returns ("tax cheaters"), asking the question Did you fail to report all income in the 1978 income tax return? is an example of the use of a direct method.

Survey statisticians have made two important observations when using direct methods to collect sensitive data. First, there are often sizable *nonresponse rates:* Some people refuse to answer questions concerning the sensitive characteristics or may even flatly refuse to cooperate at all. Second, some people who cooperate in responding to the questions may deliberately give *untruthful answers.*

In recent years there has been a marked increase in the nonresponse rates in many parts of the world; in some important surveys (such as the monthly labor force survey in Sweden), these rates have trebled or quadrupled! It is plausible to expect that a similar development has taken place in the extent of untruthful answering; this phenomenon is naturally more difficult to measure.

The change that has thus taken place is a source of grave concern to survey statisticians: Nonresponse and untruthful answering may seriously distort ("bias") the results of surveys.[1]

---

[1]As a consequence, it may not be satisfactory to measure the accuracy of a sample estimate by its variance; the proper measure is the mean-square error: MSE = Variance + Bias². If the bias-term is equal to zero, the variance measures both the precision and the accuracy.

NEW DEMANDS ON SURVEY STATISTICIANS

These developments have served as a challenge to survey takers to improve traditional methods and to develop new ones. I will make special mention of two related endeavors: the development of new criteria for taking surveys; and the development of survey methods that take into account the need for "privacy protection."

In traditional survey practice, the design of a survey reflected an effort to balance the cost of the survey against some measure of the accuracy of its results, as reflected in the criterion of "minimizing the cost of taking the survey for a fixed level of variance." Such criteria, although still important, may in specific instances have to be replaced by one that involves not only cost and accuracy but also the degree of protection given to the individual respondents. Significant progress has in fact been made in developing such a criterion.

Moreover, methods that take into account the need for "privacy protection" have been developed on a very broad front: with respect to methods for data collection, processing, and storage and methods for disclosure control. A signal innovation in the realm of methods for data collection is the randomized response method, the subject of the next section.

Randomized Response

The basic idea of randomized response, or randomized inquiry, is to introduce *by design*— that is, deliberately—an element of uncertainty into the responses collected from the respondents. This uncertainty serves to protect the respondents by concealing their true status with respect to the sensitive characteristic, while still making it possible to make statistically sound statements ("estimates") for the population from which the respondents have been selected. Technically, using the randomized response method means trading off the elimination (or at least reduction) of the bias associated with some direct method for a measurable increase in the variance of the estimate.

WARNER'S METHOD

Randomized response is a recent development: The idea was first presented by Stanley Warner (1965). I provide a nontechnical presentation of the basic idea here.

An interview survey is to be carried out to estimate the unknown *relative* frequency F (or equivalently, the percentage) of "tax cheaters" in a specific population. We will refer to F as a proportion. An individual is classified as a tax cheater if he or she failed to report all income in the 1977 income tax return. For the purpose of the survey, a simple random sample of n individuals is selected.

Each interviewer is equipped with a deck of cards[2] of two types: In *Type 1*, $100P\%$ of the cards in the deck have the statement "I failed to report all income in 1977." In *Type 2*, the remaining $100(1 - P)\%$ of the cards in the deck have the complementary statement "I did report all income in 1977." Thus, one statement is technically the negation of the other statement.

It is of critical importance that the choice of the P value be made by the statistician. In an application, he or she may choose $P = .7$. Thus, 7 out of 10 cards are Type 1 cards.

Each respondent is then asked to shuffle the deck of cards thoroughly and then select one card "at random" and silently read the statement on the card so selected, without revealing to the interviewer the type of card selected. In technical language, the deck of cards serves as a "randomizer." Then the interviewer asks the question, "Is the statement on your card true or false with respect to you?" and instructs the respondent to answer by "true" or "false" as the case may be. The interviewer records the answer as: $X = 1$, if it is "true"; and $X = 0$, if it is "false."

In an individual case, $X = 1$ will be recorded in two cases: The respondent is a tax cheater and happened to select a Type 1 card; or the respondent is not a tax cheater and happened to select a Type 2 card.

By the same token, $X = 0$ will be recorded in two cases: The respondent is a tax cheater and happened to select a Type 2 card; or the respondent is not a tax cheater and happened to select a Type 1 card. In other words, $X = 1$ will be recorded for both some tax cheaters and some others, as will $X = 0$, as summarized by the following table:

	Respondent's true status	
Choice of card	Tax cheater	Not a tax cheater
Type 1	1	0
Type 2	0	1

[2]In Warner (1965), a roulette wheel is used instead of a deck of cards.

Thus, whatever the recorded response is—$X = 1$ or $X = 0$—it does not reveal the respondent's true status.

The survey will therefore result in a string of 1s and 0s, say n_1 cases of 1s and n_0 cases of 0s, with $n_1 + n_0 = n$.

It can be shown[3] that the proportion of tax cheaters, F, may be estimated by:

$$\hat{F} = \frac{1}{2P - 1}\left(P - 1 + \frac{n_1}{n}\right)$$

from which formula it follows that the statistician must not choose $P = .5$, as this makes $2P - 1 = 0$.

The estimate $\hat{F}$ has an important property: It is "unbiased," that is, not distorted by systematic errors, under two assumptions. The first is that reporting is truthful. This assumption is reasonable in this case, as the use of the randomized response method makes it unnecessary to lie to conceal any wrongdoing. The second assumption is adherence to the instructions for the interviewing. As indicated earlier, an estimate of F based on some direct method is likely not to be unbiased.

The elimination of the bias is not without cost, however. The price paid is an increase in the variance of the estimated proportion, $\hat{F}$, in comparison with the variance of the estimate $\tilde{F}$ one might have obtained if all had responded truthfully to a direct question. More specifically:

$$\text{Var } \hat{F} = \frac{F(1 - F)}{N} + \frac{P(1 - P)}{N}\frac{1}{(2P - 1)^2}$$

But the first term on the right-hand side of the equation is the *variance* of $\tilde{F}$ (assuming n responses). Thus,

$$\text{Var } \hat{F} = \text{Var } \tilde{F} + \frac{P(1 - P)}{N}\frac{1}{(2P - 1)^2}$$

that is,

$$\text{Var } \hat{F} - \text{Var } \tilde{F} = \frac{P(1 - P)}{N}\frac{1}{(2P - 1)^2}$$

Thus, as a rule, $\text{Var } \hat{F} > \text{Var } \tilde{F}$. But, as mentioned earlier, the proper comparison is between $\text{Var } \hat{F}$ and $\text{MSE } \tilde{F}$. If the bias of $\tilde{F}$ exceeds the

---

[3]The rest of this section is semitechnical and may be skipped by the lay reader.

difference Var $\hat{F}$ − $Var\ \tilde{F}$, then $\hat{F}$ may be considered superior to $\tilde{F}$ in the following sense: It may be possible to achieve a preassigned accuracy in the estimate of F with a smaller sample using the randomized response than that necessary when using the direct method; the randomized response method is cost-effective. And $\hat{F}$ has an additional, very important advantage relative to $\tilde{F}$: It is by far simpler to estimate Var $\hat{F}$ using only the sample data than it is to estimate MSE $\tilde{F}$—in fact, it may not be possible to compute a meaningful estimate of MSE $\tilde{F}$.

SOME NEW METHODS

Since the appearance of Warner's pioneering paper in 1965, the method of randomized response has undergone a remarkable development in various ways. Some of the advances are discussed in the following sections.

Choice of Randomizer

Warner proposed that a roulette wheel be used as a randomizer. The use of a deck of cards is an example of an alternative randomizer. In addition, boxes with beans, bottles with balls, and a great many other devices have been developed.

The Unrelated Question Method

In Warner's method, the statement on one type of card is the negation of the statement on the other type of card, that is, the statements are *related*.

An alternative is to use unrelated statements. This method is usually referred to as the "unrelated question method" and is typically designed as follows: I relate, as earlier, the discussion to a survey to estimate the proportion of tax cheaters. Thus, the deck of cards comprises two types of cards with questions: Cards of Type 1 have the question "Did you report all income in 1977?" Cards of Type 2 have the question "Was your mother born in July?" These questions are now to be answered with "Yes" or "No," as the case may be. Clearly, the choice of the unrelated question, in this case "Was your mother born in July?" must be made with care; the true answer must not be known to (or derivable by) the interviewer or the statistician.

Estimating More Than Two Proportions

Warner's method is designed to estimate two proportions: the proportion F and its complement $1 − F$. Methods are now available that permit the estimation of any number of proportions, say $F_0, F_1, F_2, \ldots$ F_R, with $F_0 + F_1 + F_2 + \ldots = F_R = 1$. As an example, consider the case where F_0 equals the proportion of women who have had no induced abortions, F_1 equals the proportion of women who have had one induced abortion, and F_2 equals the proportion of women who have had two or more induced abortions. Application in the field can be a simple variation on the Warner approach. The product in the ideal case is unbiased estimates of the relative frequencies in each category.

Estimating Magnitudes

The preceding discussion has concerned "qualitative" data. The idea of randomized response may also be used to estimate "magnitudes," for example, the amount of money concealed by tax cheaters.

APPLICATIONS

The randomized response method is, as indicated earlier, a recent addition to the kit of tools available to the survey statistician. As a consequence, it has not as yet found widespread use.

Some of the applications made have been undertaken as a means of "testing" the method, such as by comparing its performance with some direct method in instances where the true result is known (for example, on a set of individuals with known characteristics). For some examples of tests, see Brown (1975) on drug usage, Eriksson (1973) on public relief, Folsom (1974) on drunken driving, Krotki and Fox (1975) on fertility control, and Boruch and Cecil (1979) more generally.

The Illinois Law Enforcement Commission's study of illegal gambling is one of the few large-scale attempts to use the method in a routine way rather than in an experimental test (IIT Research Institute and Chicago Crime Commission, 1971). Their report suggests no unusual problems in application and that respondents did not have any notable difficulty in understanding the method.

A Special Application: Data Banks

The idea underlying the randomized response method may be used to develop a method for encryption, "privacy transformation," for the purpose of protecting data in a data bank. I will give a simple example that elucidates the basic idea. For a detailed presentation of the scheme, refer to Dalenius (1977).

Consider a survey of N individuals. For these individuals, observations have been made with respect to some sensitive characteristic S.

The observations are of the dichotomous type: $S = 0$ or $S = 1$, as the case may be. To subject the data to a privacy transformation, we proceed as follows: For each individual, we generate a Z value, where $Z = 0$ with probability P, and $Z = 1$ with probability $1 - p$. This operation yields a set of N pairs of data:

$$S: 1, 0, 0, 0, 1, \ldots 0, 0$$
$$Z: 1, 1, 0, 1, 1, \ldots 1, 0.$$

The next operation calls for comparing S and Z for each individual. If $S = Z$, the outcome is recorded as $X = 1$, but if S differs from Z, it is recorded as $X = 0$. The outcome will be:

$$X: 1, 0, 1, 0, 1, \ldots 0, 1.$$

These X values represent the privacy transformation of the S values. It can be shown that it is possible to estimate F, the proportion of individuals with $S = 1$, on the basis of these X values and knowledge about the P value used to generate the Z values. In the interest of protecting the individuals, we get rid of the S and the Z values (for example, by burning the questionnaires). The resulting data bank now comprises only X values, and as in the case of the use of the randomized response method, the true status of an individual cannot be deduced on the basis of his or her X value. An individual with $X = 0$ may have $S = 0$ or 1, and an individual with $X = 1$ may have $S = 0$ or 1.

Some Ethical and Legal Issues in Brief

In a discussion of ethical issues in the context of a review of some method for data collection—in this instance, randomized response—it seems desirable to make a distinction between *general* ethical issues, that is, issues that apply irrespective of the method for data collection under consideration, and *specific* ethical issues. I will limit my discussion to the latter.

The randomized response approach helps to satisfy two ethical concerns. First, the interviewer or researcher with no ethical claim to identified information on individuals can avoid the needless exercise of the claim. Necessary statistical information is obtained without obtaining information about specific individuals. Second, to the extent that the approach reduces the respondent's embarrassment—and there is some evidence that it does—the researcher meets an ethical obligation to avoid the respondent's discomfort.

Irrespective of the choice of randomizer (roulette wheel, deck of cards, etc.), the randomized response method may be beyond the comprehension of some respondents. It is reasonable to argue that the statistician nonetheless has a responsibility to protect the respondent. The situation is in a way analogous to the situation facing a physician who must protect patient interests in experimental surgery even though the patient does not understand the surgery. There is as yet too little information available and too little debate about this ethical problem.

The legal issues must, of course, refer to the law in some specific country. Here I will refer first to Swedish law and then to American law.

Consider Section 8 of the Swedish Data Act, which dates to 1973:

> If there is reason to suspect that personal information in a personal register is incorrect, the responsible keeper of the register shall, without delay, take the necessary steps to ascertain the correctness of the information and, if needed, to correct it or exclude it from the register.[4]

As discussed at some length in Dalenius (1978), Section 8 may be interpreted to mean that the use of the randomized response method is *not* compatible with the spirit of the Swedish Data Act. If the Data Inspection Board were to implement that interpretation, the survey statistician would have two options, both of which are unsatisfactory: (a) to process the data collected by manual methods, as the Data Act applies only to computerized data; or (b) to use some direct method instead of the randomized response method.

THE CASE OF A SUBPOENA

In some countries—for example, the United States—data collected in a survey may be subpoenaed. Subpoenaing data collected by the randomized response method would, however, be useless: The respondents are perfectly safe.

Consider, for example, data collected by Warner's (1965) method for the purpose of estimating the proportion of tax cheaters. The data would—as already discussed—appear as a string of 1s and 0s, where 1 would be associated with some tax cheaters and some others, and 0 would be associated with some tax cheaters and some others. Thus, no *certain* statement could be made about any individual represented in a survey. Clearly, the possibility of making an *uncertain* statement (for

---

[4]The translation is that appearing in a document used by the Swedish Data Inspection Board (Datainspektionen), Stockholm, Sweden.

example, claiming that an individual for whom the datum is $X = 1$ is "likely" to be a tax cheater) is present, but this possibility may effectively be controlled by the statistician's choice of the parameter P associated with the randomizer.

The Future of Randomized Response

There is a Swedish saying to the effect that "it is difficult to make forecasts, especially about the future." But in the case of randomized response, it is easy. The basic rationale for using randomized response today is the high level of public concern about invasion of privacy and the corresponding strong resistance to surveys. This resistance may be stronger in the next few years—1984 is just a few years ahead! As a consequence, the case for using randomized response will be stronger in the (near) future than it is today. Randomized response is here to stay.

THE NEED FOR FURTHER
METHODOLOGICAL DEVELOPMENT

Despite the quantitatively and qualitatively impressive methodological development that has taken place since 1965, there is ample room for further development. I will give two examples of potential research topics.

First, there is some need for the development of theory for dealing with "multivariate data analysis." In most surveys, statisticians observe not a single characteristic X but several, or often many, characteristics $X, Y, \ldots T, V$, and try to estimate their associations. Although a beginning has been made, much remains, however, to do.

Second, there is a need for the design of randomizers that are operationally "sturdy" yet simple to use. A deck of cards is vulnerable—it cannot be disregarded that the cards may get sticky or that a card may be lost, thus changing the parameter P.

THE NEED TO EDUCATE THE PUBLIC

Two kinds of public education are called for. In the first place, the public must be educated to appreciate various methods that have been developed to enhance privacy protection, especially the randomized response method. Second, the public must learn to view the issue of invasion of privacy in the context of striking a reasonable balance between the right to privacy and the need to know. Some ways that may be used to provide this education would involve workshops for journalists on social statistics in general and privacy issues in particular, articles in the popular press rather than in the scientific media, and television and radio programs on the topic. These examples do not exhaust the options, of course.

THE NEED FOR IMPROVED LEGISLATION

Most, if not all, privacy acts that have come into force have been developed in haste. As a consequence, they are by no means perfect instruments for privacy protection. There is a need for an evaluation of the performance of these acts, in order to provide a basis not for criticism of those who developed them but for better legislation in the future.

We will point to two means of improving legislation. First, it may be possible to subject a proposed privacy act to experimental tests in the spirit of social experiments, as discussed in Riecken and Boruch (1974). A second approach is to initiate cross-national research and international exchange of experiences.

References

Boruch, R. F., and J. S. Cecil
    1979   Assuring the Confidentiality of Social Research Data. Philadelphia: University of Pennsylvania Press.
Brown, G.
    1975   "Randomized inquiry vs. conventional questionnaire method in estimating drug usage rates through mail surveys." HUMRO Technical Report 75–14. Arlington, Va.: Human Resources Research Organization.
Dalenius, T.
    1977   "Privacy transformations for statistical information systems." Journal of Statistical Planning and Inference 1:73–86.
    1978   "The Swedish Data Act and statistical data." Statistisk Tidskrift: 37–45.
Eriksson, S.
    1973   "Randomized interviews for sensitive questions." Ph.D. dissertation, Department of Statistics, University of Göteborg, Göteborg, Sweden.
Folsom, R. E.
    1974   "A randomized response validation study: Comparison of direct and randomized reporting of DUI arrests." Report 25U–807, prepared for U.S. Bureau of the Census. Research Triangle Institute, Research Triangle Park, N.C..

IIT Research Institute and the Chicago Crime Commission
  1971   "A study of organized crime in Illinois." Report prepared for the Illinois Law
         Enforcement Commission, Chicago.
Krotki, K. J., and B. Fox
  1975   "The randomized response technique, the interview, and the self-administered
         questionnaire: An empirical comparison of fertility reports." Pp. 367–371 in
         *Proceedings of the American Statistical Association: Social Statistics Section,
         1974.* Washington, D.C.: ASA.
Riecken, H. W., and R. F. Boruch (eds.)
  1974   *Social Experimentation: A Method for Planning and Evaluating Social Inter-
         vention.* New York: Academic Press.
Warner, S. L.
  1965   "Randomized response: A survey technique for eliminating evasive answer
         bias." *Journal of the American Statistical Association* 60:63–69.

13

Social Research Use of Archival Records: Procedural Solutions to Privacy Problems

JOSEPH STEINBERG

Data archives are valuable resources. They may exist as a result of program administration in government, business, or nonprofit organizations. They may stem from sample surveys or complete enumerations of defined populations.

Whatever their nature, it is in the social researcher's interest to capitalize on these resources whenever possible. Tabulations and analyses based on archival data can help advance research economically. The linkage of new data with existing archival records can enrich the research considerably and in some cases—notably, program evaluation—may be essential for achieving a study's objective.

The researcher's use of archival records may, however, pose some ethical and legal problems. This chapter reviews some procedural solutions to these problems that have been developed over the past 30 years.[1] The solutions proposed are applicable both to situations in which outside researchers are concerned with only one archival system

---

[1] A number of papers and reports discuss procedural solutions to problems in this area and provide extensive bibliographies. The reader may wish to start with Campbell, Boruch, Schwartz, and Steinberg (1977). Boruch and Cecil (1979) update earlier work, consider alternative approaches, and furnish a large number of examples.

(intrafile analysis) and to situations in which multiple archives must be used without violating confidentiality regulations governing each (interfile analysis). The procedures outlined are also relevant for long-term longitudinal surveys of groups.

The chapter closes with a brief review of recommendations by a federal interagency committee for dealing with problems of statistical disclosure and of one federal agency's guidelines illustrating an operational approach.

Social Research Publications and Statistical Disclosure

Social research is customarily published in the form of tables and related analyses. Special tabulations of surveys and censuses made available for reanalysis also are the basis of additional publications. With the advent of the computer age, the need for access to information has also been served by "public use" files and the availability of information in other than tabular form. This increased access to data in all forms has exacerbated some of the problems of social research. Nevertheless, the problems have existed since the first appearance of statistical tables and analyses.

The problems themselves can be summarized under the rubric of "statistical disclosure." I adapt a useful definition of statistical disclosure proposed by Tore Dalenius (Office of Federal Statistical Policy and Standards, 1978): If the releases of certain statistics makes it possible to determine a particular value relating to a known individual more accurately than is possible without access to those statistics, then a disclosure has taken place. In the simplest case, for example, a particular physician's income might be deduced easily from a table that contains no clear identification of individuals but that shows a distribution of income, by occupation, for each city ward.

Types of Data and Access Policies and Procedures

Social research makes use of both original and archived data. Original data may be collected solely for a one-time study, or it may involve repeated surveys of the same group and the longitudinal linkage of data to serve the study objectives. The use of stored data by external researchers may involve simply intrafile analysis by the outsider. In order to meet some study objectives, however, interfile linkage of confidential data may be needed.

To deal with any of these types of data use, the data archive must develop appropriate policies, procedures, and record linkage strategies that would prevent statistical disclosure. Moreover, it is necessary for the agency to consider carefully the character of the problem so as to arrive at solutions that will provide adequate safeguards against all forms of statistical disclosure, including subpoena.

An important aspect of the matter is the archive's willingness to deal with the problems that require solution. The policies and procedures may be codified in guidelines so that both the agency staff and the social research group interested in data access know the character of the policies and the suggested solutions. When operational prototypes are developed, these should become part of the research literature. The agency personnel will then have models to follow in order to provide the necessary information and the researcher will have models to obtain it. An important aspect of the operational characteristics of an archive is the development of procedures for internal disclosure analysis. This implies that a set of rules of behavior are developed to establish when a disclosure is likely and when it is not. In addition, appropriate clearance procedures must be developed so that all data archive accesses may be reviewed by appropriate levels of agency personnel.

Apart from these operational aspects, staff and equipment must be available to service requests. This includes ensuring that the costs of services are returned to the cooperating agency. When staff and equipment to service requests are available, this facilitates timely cooperation—a necessary ingredient in dealing with record access by outsiders.

Internal Archive Protection

One of the primary and traditional ways in which agencies protect data has been to require that the information, when used solely for a one-time purpose, should be depersonalized. This requires that in one form or another there be a break in the linkage between the collected data and any personal identification that might permit disclosure. Of course, the availability of information on a multitude of characteristics about individuals even in the absence of personal identifiers may permit a breach of confidentiality. Information in publicly available sources, when collated with data on the identical variables in the data collection, may in fact lead to disclosure concerning the nonpublic information available from the archive. Some of the methods that are discussed later can be used to ensure that data, when retained beyond a one-time use, are in fact not subject to this type of disclosure.

There are a number of situations in which a data collection agency must require that data be accessible over a period of time. This kind of access, for example, is required whenever there is need for an internal longitudinal tabulation and analysis. Tracking the same employees over a long period of time to assay employment rates, absenteeism, and so on, is a typical illustration. The need for some kind of method for permitting the longitudinal linkage to serve this purpose is obvious. One of the approaches that merits consideration is the use of alias identifiers. It is now customary for some organizations to use an alias identifier for purposes other than statistical research. For example, many banks now make use of a personal identification number (PIN) so that depositors may access their accounts solely through the use of a single known identifier. The same approach is potentially useful for statistical research if a proper methodology can be established. One way of creating this is to provide each interviewer at the start of the entire process with a set of appropriate randomized identifiers. When the respondent has agreed to the process, he or she is permitted to select any one of the available random identifiers and to record it separately for retention for subsequent visits by the interviewer. Once a given identifier has been selected by a respondent, that identifier should be removed from the list that the interviewer retains for use by subsequent respondents. One means of ensuring that personal identification numbers are used is to provide an incentive payment to respondents. This payment would be given at the final interview, at which time the identification number would be destroyed.

Two forms of use of alias identifiers for internal longitudinal linkage have been used. In the first, the alias is assigned by the social scientist and provided to the respondent for subsequent uses. With this approach the interviewer would in a sense know the personal identification number. That the interviewer retains knowledge is a potential problem if, for example, a subpoena is used in an attempt to access information or if the personal identification number is retained inadvertently in a place where unauthorized access is possible. In any event, the alias identifier needs to be carefully protected and purged from the file once the internal longitudinal linkage has been accomplished. A second form of alias identifier involves creation of an identifier by a neutral entity; the identifier is then supplied to the respondent. After its use, the identifier would be purged from the researcher's file as well as from the neutral's and respondent's records.

Alias identifiers may be either numeric or nominal aliases. In either event, it is necessary that a high proportion of the respondents cooperate for this process to be successful. Thus, researchers should carefully consider the use of incentive payments or other rewards as ways of ensuring success.

Intrafile Analysis by Outsiders

Analysis of data contained in a single data file is often the only way to examine whether a prior analytic result is accurate or is the most proper. Reanalysis is an important function of an independent reviewer. Such research efforts require procedural solutions to the problems of data confidentiality. This section discusses a number of them.

One of the simplest approaches to permitting intrafile analysis by outsiders is the deletion of all personal identifiers from a set of records. It is true that this approach may not be sufficient to protect against deductive disclosure if the data are also coded to small geographical areas. The problem arises when there are a number of items that are publicly identifiable. In this event, the data may need additional protection even after deletion of identifiers.

CRUDE REPORT CATEGORIES

One significant approach to data protection in this context is the use of crude report categories and the restriction of publicly identifiable variables even when there is to be only intrafile analysis by outsiders. In this approach, the data that are obtained by an archival agency are then coded to cruder categories. For instance, geographical groups may be coded to larger geographical areas. Age, instead of being coded in terms of single years, may be coded to age groups. Instead of specific four-digit occupational information, the data on occupation may be coded to two- or three-digit levels. Education, instead of being provided on a single-year-of-schooling basis, may be grouped into cruder categories.

Using crude report categories requires a bit of research in order to determine the combinations that will preclude inadvertent disclosure. Occasionally, the archival agency will need to delete specific publicly available variables from the file to prevent disclosure of identifiable information about individuals.

PUBLIC-USE DATA TAPES

Making available public-use tapes is another strategy to permit intrafile analysis by outsiders. The general strategy, employed prior to release of the tape, is to delete all identifiers, to make existing report categories more crude where necessary, and to analyze the possibilities of inadvertent disclosure by examining the kinds of combinations of information that would be available to the researcher. Public-use tapes are generally made available when only a small percentage of a defined population is involved. For large-scale data collection, public-use tapes are often based on different random subsamples of the original survey sample. In this approach, each outside group that requests access is provided access only to a separate random subset of the data collected originally.

MICROAGGREGATION

A second approach, microaggregation, involves releasing data not for single individuals but for synthesized persons; any one data set or record is for, say, an average of five persons per group. One of the possibilities here is the release of not only the arithmetic mean for each group but also a summary measure of dispersion—the within-group variance. If tests verify that no disclosure would occur, then covariances can and should be released. In this way, more of the data would become available to the outside researcher. It is true that aggregation of variables may result in a loss of statistical efficiency. Thus, the problem of "ecological correlation" must be considered when a microaggregated data set is analyzed by an outside researcher. The archive performing the microaggregation must test that the variables used in the aggregation are independent of sampling variation so as to ensure that an estimate based on the aggregated data is unbiased. When multiple accesses to data through microaggregation are likely to occur, one of the strategies for preventing disclosure is the random deletion of individuals from each microaggregated group. This helps to ensure that there will not be inadvertent disclosure when comparisons are made across groups that are formed and required for different kinds of statistical reanalysis.

ERROR INOCULATION

Error inoculation requires that at least one publicly available variable in each individual's record be changed arbitrarily. The unique variables in a record are spared from error inoculation. When this approach is used, it is crucial that outside users are aware that errors have been introduced deliberately. The character of the error inoculation must be identified only in a general way, permitting the analyst to adjust for the average error but providing too little information about the precise character of the inoculation to lead to disclosure.

In one approach to error inoculation, errors are introduced in such a way that the mean of the random errors over the set of records is zero and the dispersion of the error is modest. The purpose of restricting dispersion of the error is to avoid major contamination of the analyses when this strategy is used. The process is set up so that the extent of the dispersion of the added random error is known and restricted to be small relative to the original dispersion of the data set. There is, of course, no need to add random error when high frequency variables are involved—for example, sex of the respondent.

A second approach to error inoculation involves random score substitution. In this method, a pair of random processes is involved. A determination is first made at random to decide whether the particular respondent is to be assigned a substitute response. Once the determination is made that a substitute response is required, a second random process determines what the nature of the substitute response will be. The two random processes are designed so that the original overall distribution for a given variable is maintained.

These strategies may be used one at a time or in combination. Thus, for example, the idea of using a random subsample in the release of a public-use tape may be combined with the addition of random error in some of the public variables to prevent disclosure.

IN-HOUSE CAPACITY FOR ANALYSIS

Creating an in-house capacity for an archive to run outsiders' statistical analyses is the preferred method for expediting intrafile analysis. Of course, this requires that there be a sufficient staff for this approach at the archive. If there are multiple releases of information to outsiders, it is desirable to consider using random subsets. For instance, the archive may delete one or more persons at random from the subsets of the file in each of the multiple releases. In addition, random modification of tabulated data is sometimes carried out to prevent disclosure when tabulations are run for outsiders. That is, the tabulated data are modified so that the tabulations from one outside analysis to the next are not identical. In this way, inadvertent disclosure is precluded. Differences between data sets obtained at different times, rather than the characteristics of any one individual, represent the random modification differences.

Random rounding has also been used in order to avoid disclosure when comparisons are made across data sets obtained at different times. In addition, the idea of using cruder categories in the initial file seems to be the best method if there is in fact a potential problem with the use of this approach.

Interfile Linkage of Confidential Data

Meaningful statistical analysis sometimes requires that different files, each containing confidential data on the same individuals, be linked. To carry out such interfile linkage without generating privacy problems, one of several strategies can be important.

CROSS CLASSIFICATION

Parallel use of the same criteria of classification is a simple method for executing interfile linkage of data while preventing disclosure. In this procedure, microaggregated data are cross classified by available public criteria then combined after microaggregation. Thus, criteria that are publicly available, such as the zip code, the Standard Industrial Classification (SIC) code, or tract code, are possible kinds of classifiers for carrying out interfile linkage.

SYNTHETIC LINKAGE

Another type of interfile linkage that has been used but engenders a number of statistical problems is synthetic linkage by matching. In this procedure, the final outcome is a one-to-one matching of individual cases from two files. Usually, the two files are not necessarily of the same individuals. However, each file has a number of variables shared; then the matching makes use of the identity or near identity of shared variables between individuals in each of the files for creating a linked file. This linked file is then analyzed as though all of the data came from the same person. If the shared variable in each set and the other variables in each set are independent, the relationship between the nonshared variables across the set will be subject to an attenuated or underestimated association. A number of other statistical problems exist when the two files differ widely on the means of the common variables.

LINK-FILE BROKERAGE

Link-file brokerage is another technique for the interfile linkage of confidential data. In this approach, a double alias is used. A broker that is either protected by confidentiality statute, such as the U.S. Bureau of the Census, or otherwise not subject to the normal subpoena process, such as one located in another country, is the vehicle by which the linkage is created. The broker has access to a list of names or other individual identifiers from each of the files and also the corresponding file-specific codes. The broker then creates a matched list that links the two file-specific identifiers. After this has been created, the base data from each of the files are merged through the collated file-specific codes. At no time would the merged file contain either the individual identifier or the file-specific code when it is in use by either of the agencies that have contributed to the merged file. In addition, where the confidential data may lead to disclosure, it is necessary for the broker to protect the data by error inoculation or by the use of crude categories before releasing the file for analysis.

INSULATED FILE LINKAGE

Mutually insulated file linkage is the preferred strategy when inter-file linkage of data is required. In this process, the linkage occurs without merging. The two agencies involved would need to have a shared identifier available for each of the lists that are to be linked. Consider Figure 13.1, which illustrates the procedural aspects of subdivision of study respondents to permit the use of mutually insulated file linkage. Each of the elements of a total population for agency one has been classified into two study groups. In each study group, subsets of individuals have been identified so that each subset pertains to a particular variable value. Suppose further that each subset is made up of at least eight individuals. The subsets are randomly coded so that there is no relationship between the coded letters and the category of the subset or the study group. The first agency provides a list of the shared identifiers by subset to the second agency. The second agency takes its information for the individuals in each of the subsets and creates a microaggregated set of information for each subset. One of the processes that may be used is for the second agency to delete at random one or more individuals from each set. In this way, when the values of means or variances are available from the second agency's file, they are not necessarily for any identifiable subset that has been supplied by the first agency.

On occasion, when the first agency is interested in information from the second, it must identify whether the individuals in its list are in fact members of the second agency's file. This may be required when absence from a file, in itself, may create inadvertent disclosure concerning the characteristic of an individual. For example, if the second agency is the Internal Revenue Service, the presence of an individual in a list supplied by an agency may lead to the greater likelihood of audit of

Study group I:

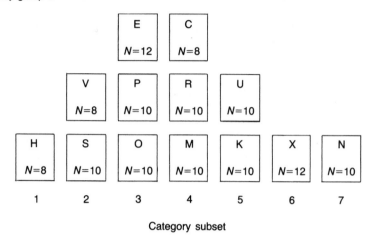

Category subset

Study group II:

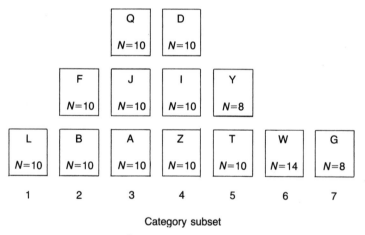

Category subset

Figure 13.1. This hypothetical distribution of sample persons in two study groups in a social research project, grouped by study category subset, shows randomly assigned coded interfile list designators.

that individual by the IRS if the individual does not exist in IRS files. Thus, by using the IRS index, the first agency weeds out those individuals from each of its subsets that are not found in the IRS files and prevents the possibility of inadvertent disclosure to the IRS of something that may lead to a problem for the individuals thus involved. Once this process has been carried out, the determination of means and dispersions by the second agency (e.g., the IRS) and the supply of only such information to the first agency does not create disclosure of individually identifiable information to either agency. In Figure 13.1, the original agency would have the data for each of the 26 subsets. When it receives the means and dispersions for each of the subsets, the analyzing agency combines the data from the two groups of data into tabulations. In order to avoid disclosure to the supplying agency, it is incumbent on the user agency to combine subsets so that no single set is in a tabulation by itself.

A number of strategies previously discussed can provide additional protection against disclosure. For example, if the researcher supplies data with random error inoculation, the supplying agency is denied exact access through any kind of detailed analysis. If the supplier also uses error inoculation of some type, further protection against disclosure is provided. Of importance here is the need to use either a random deletion or some other technique to make sure that neither the researcher nor the supplier are able to get data concerning individuals involved in the mutually linked file.

IMBEDDING GROUPS TO PREVENT DISCLOSURE

There are some occasions when the nature of the study population requires that it be imbedded in a much larger one in order to avoid disclosure concerning membership in a group. So, for example, a particular study population might be of interest to a supplier, for example, individuals who participate in a given income maintenance program. The individuals who are in the program need to be imbedded within a larger set of individuals in the list provided to the supplier. The category subsets, in this way, would not disclose which persons are members and which are not members of the population. This imbedding would be an important way to achieve the mutually insulated file linkage without disclosure.

Putting the Tools to Use:
An Illustration at the Federal Level

Over the years, there has been recognition at the federal level of the need to address these issues. An interagency subcommittee was created to examine the matter more closely. It has prepared a report and recommendations emphasizing the need for agencies to adopt policies and practices that avoid statistical disclosure (Jabine, Michael, and Mugge,

1977). The Social Security Administration is one agency that has long sought to respond to such concerns.

Under Regulation 1 of the Social Security Administration, statistical data may be used for research purposes provided that there is reasonable protection against disclosure. In setting forth its guidelines for preventing disclosures, the Social Security Administration (1977) research staff examined the character of the data set under its control and decided that there is need for separate standards for counts and for amounts. Thus, in dealing with counts such as the number by age of beneficiaries, the guidelines require that data be shown in at least 5-year intervals. When frequency distributions of earnings are being provided, the guidelines require that the information be provided in intervals of $1000 or more. When benefit data are involved, the intervals must be $50 or more. The guidelines also require that there must be two or more nonempty cells in a given distribution. For sensitive data, such as race, medical condition, and program entitlement, these requirements are especially important. It is further required that there be no one-person cells involved in any of the tabulations that are provided.

When dollar amounts are involved in tabulations, then the guidelines require that: (a) there be no one-person cells; (b) no average value be equal to the upper or the lower benefit limits; (c) restriction on two-person cells be applied when necessary; and (d) no average value be presented if there is a restricted range of information possible.

When consideration is given to merging Social Security Administration data with user data, another set of guidelines become pertinent. For example, there is a requirement that cells include five or more persons and that the data merged with Social Security Administration data be subject to the same restrictions on counts and dollar amounts, discussed earlier.

The methods employed by the Social Security Administration for preventing disclosure include suppression and grouping of data and the examination of resulting tables to be sure that disclosure cannot occur. The general rules require that there be a minimum number of beneficiaries involved in a tabulation and that when data are made available on small geographical areas, groupings must be made so that the number involved in any one tabulation is above this minimum number of beneficiaries.

Finally, the Social Security Administration staff recommends the introduction of error either in the individual records or in the tabulations, or random rounding of cells in tabulations and control of the rounding to mimimize distortion in the totals. Thus, the general guidelines that are in use at the Social Security Administration make use of the general principles and the specific details that have been discussed in this chapter.

References

Boruch, R. F., and J. S. Cecil
  1979 *Assuring the Confidentiality of Social Research Data.* Philadelphia: University of Pennsylvania Press.
Campbell, D. T., R. F. Boruch, R. D. Schwartz, and J. Steinberg
  1977 "Confidentiality-preserving modes of access to files and to interfile exchange for useful statistical analysis." *Evaluation Quarterly* 1:269–300.
Jabine, T. B., J. A. Michael, and R. H. Mugge
  1977 "Federal agency practices for avoiding statistical disclosure: Findings and recommendations." In *Proceedings of the American Statistical Association's Social Statistics Section.* Washington, D.C.: ASA.
Social Security Administration, Office of Research and Statistics
  1977 *Guidelines for Preventing Disclosure in Tabulations of Program Data.* Washington, D.C.: SSA.
U.S. Department of Commerce, Office of Federal Statistical Policy and Standards
  1978 *Report on Statistical Disclosure and Disclosure-Avoidance Techniques.* Statistical Policy Working Paper 2, Washington D.C.: OFSPS

14

Statutory Approaches to Ensuring the Privacy and Confidentiality of Social Science Research Information: The Law Enforcement Assistance Administration Experience

THOMAS J. MADDEN
HELEN S. LESSIN

Introduction: Protection Statutes

Privacy and confidentiality are issues that are often at the forefront of public concern as society's capacity to gather and utilize data increases. Wide-scale use of computers in the last 20 years has enabled society to gather, analyze, and, most significantly, link massive amounts of data. The development of microprocessors daily puts that knowledge and ability in the hands of literally hundreds of thousands of new users. A major theater of concern for privacy and confidentiality is data gathered by the federal government and under federal government sponsorship. Each year, tens of billions of dollars of federal funds are being invested in research. In 1979 alone, the federal Office of Management and Budget (OMB) estimates that over $3.5 billion in federal funds were used to support basic research and that the National Institutes of Health spent over $1.5 billion on biomedical and behavioral studies.

One mechanism for dealing with the concern for privacy in research is through the introduction and enactment of statutes designed to protect research and statistical information identifiable to a specific individual. Among the earliest statutes dealing with confidentiality of re-

SOLUTIONS TO ETHICAL
AND LEGAL PROBLEMS
IN SOCIAL RESEARCH

search information was a federal statute dealing with Bureau of the Census records. By law, data collected by the Bureau of the Census may not be revealed to anyone outside of the bureau in a form in which an individual respondent is identifiable. There is no discretion for any bureau official with respect to disclosure, and there are criminal penalties for disclosure. The prohibition against disclosure serves to defeat legal process. If a respondent retains a copy of a report made to the bureau, the copy, like the original, is immune from compulsory disclosure.[1]

A second statutory approach to privacy is found in legislation such as the Alcohol Abuse and Alcoholism Prevention, Treatment and Rehabilitation Act.[2] This law authorizes federal officials to authorize others to protect the privacy of individuals who are the subject of research by withholding from all persons not connected with the research the names and other identifying characteristics of such individuals. Those who obtain the authorization may not be compelled by legal process to disclose the information. The prohibition is not absolute since the researcher with the authorization may voluntarily disclose the information.

In our view, a statute dealing with privacy and research should address three major goals:

1. Protection of privacy of research subjects, by requiring that identifiable information on a private person, obtained in a research or statistical program, may be used and/or revealed only for the purpose for which it is obtained
2. Assurance of an appropriate balance between individual privacy and essential needs of the research community for data to advance the state of knowledge in the area of the research
3. Assurance that research information shall not, without the consent of the person to whom the information pertains, be admitted as evidence or used for any purpose in any judicial or administrative proceedings

Section 818(a) of the Omnibus Crime Control and Safe Streets Act, as amended, provides:

1. Unqualified prohibition against disclosure of research information for other than research purposes unless authorized by federal law or unless the individual to whom a record pertains consents to disclosure

[1] 13 U.S.C. § 9214.
[2] 42 U.S.C. § 4582.

2. Prohibition against compulsory disclosure of research information by judicial, legislative, or administrative process
3. Authority to issue regulations reasonably designed to achieve statutory intent

We believe Section 818(a) of the Omnibus Crime Control and Safe Streets Act meets the three major goals set out earlier. It ensures confidentiality by providing that research and statistical information identifiable to a private person may be used only for the purpose for which it was obtained. Furthermore, the information is immune from legal process and cannot be admitted as evidence or used for any purpose in any judicial, legislative, or administrative proceeding without the consent of the individual to whom the information relates. Section 818(a) reads as follows:

> Sec. 818. (a) Except as provided by Federal law other than this title, no officer or employee of the Federal Government, nor any recipient of assistance under the provisions of this title shall use or reveal any research or statistical information furnished under this title by any person and identifiable to any specific *private person* for any purpose other than the purpose for which it was obtained in accordance with this title. Such information and copies thereof shall be immune from legal process, and shall not, without the consent of the person furnishing such information, be admitted as evidence or used for any purpose in any action, suit, or other judicial, legislative, or administrative proceedings.

Regulations to Implement Section 818(a)

The process used by the Law Enforcement Assistance Administration (LEAA) in drafting and finalizing its regulations to implement Section 818(a) included the assembling of a reactor panel for two daylong working sessions to review the proposed draft regulations prior to publication in draft form and in final form. Those who attended these working sessions included, among others, the chairman of the Sociology Department at Yale University, the counsel to the Vera Institute of Criminal Justice and Criminology, a noted criminologist from the University of Chicago, representatives of research grantees involved in the operation of the criminal justice system, and individuals from the Bureau of the Census involved in the collection of statistical data for LEAA. These prepublication meetings were open to the public. A number of public representatives were observers at the meetings. The assembled researchers and statisticians provided considerable "real-world" comments that materially assisted us in formulating the final regulations. These sessions were recorded and the record made available to the public.

The researchers and statisticians were quite eager to be part of the drafting process since they were aware that well-drawn regulations would not only protect the privacy of individuals but also provide needed guidance to persons engaged in research and statistical activities by clarifying the purposes for which information identifiable to an individual may be used or revealed.

APPLICABILITY

The LEAA regulations provide that the statute governs the use and revelation of research and statistical information obtained, collected, or produced either directly by LEAA or under any interagency agreement, grant, contract, or subgrant awarded under the Omnibus Crime Control and Safe Streets Act. The regulations state, however, that the statute provides no confidentiality for information gained regarding future criminal conduct.

DEFINITIONS

By defining *private person* as used in the statute to include public officials, the regulations specifically cover the public officials whose "on-duty" activities are the subject of a research or statistical activity. Applying the confidentiality protections of the statute to activities of public officials was necessary since a research project may involve exposure of these individuals to potential civil or disciplinary actions. The research deals with subjects such as police assault or direct-recorded observations of street activities or court-observer activities.

The regulations define a *research* or *statistical project*, covered by the statute, to mean any program, project, or component whose purpose is to develop, measure, evaluate, or otherwise advance the state of knowledge in a particular area. Because LEAA funds were used to prevent and reduce crime as well as to conduct research, we specifically provided that the term does not include information-gathering activities in which data are obtained for purposes directly related to enforcement of the criminal laws.

ESTABLISHING APPROPRIATE USES AND DISCLOSURES

One of the most important issues defined by the regulations concerns establishing proper limits for the disclosure of individually-identifiable information. The principle established is that research or statistical information identifiable to a private person can be used only for research or statistical purposes.

Information in identifiable form can thus be transferred to other researchers not related to the original project in compliance with a transfer agreement that would prescribe uses of the information. For example, the transfer agreement must include physical and administrative precautions to ensure the security of the information. The agreement must provide that project plans will be designed to preserve the anonymity of private persons to whom information relates and that records of identifiable information received will be returned without copies retained upon completion of the project. There is a provision in the regulations allowing retention of the identifiable information under extraordinary circumstances.

Where objectives of subsequent research or statistical projects (such as longitudinal studies) can be obtained through the use of records that are stripped of individual names or coded data, release of information in indentifiable form would be precluded.

PRIVACY CERTIFICATE

Prior to the approval of an application for a research or statistical activity, the LEAA-funded researcher is required by the regulations to submit what we have denominated as a "privacy certificate." The privacy certificate must briefly describe the project and contain assurances that access to data will be limited as authorized by the regulations, that all employees having a need for the information will be advised and will agree in writing to comply with the regulations, and that adequate precautions will be taken to ensure administrative and physical security of identifiable data. This would include designing the project plans to preserve anonymity, such as where appropriate, stripping the names of individuals from records, coding data, and other procedures designed to prevent identification of individuals. Project findings and reports prepared for dissemination cannot contain information that can reasonably be expected to be identifiable to a private person without the private person's authorization. Of course, there are situations where, because of sample size or uniqueness of the subject (number of inmates on death row in a certain state, for example), total concealment of subject identity may not be possible. This kind of situation is provided for under the regulations. What is required in such circumstances is that the individual, when information is obtained directly, be advised that because of sample size, or other unique factors, his or her identity may conceivably be discovered.

Requiring a privacy certificate of the researcher prior to embarking upon the project is designed to ensure that researchers explicitly consider the status of research data and provide adequate safeguards for physical security and, most importantly, to alert and sensitize the research grant applicant at the outset of a research endeavor regarding the areas that must be considered to ensure confidentiality of such material.

NOTIFICATION

The regulations set out specific notification procedures that must be followed prior to collecting information directly from an individual. First, the notification procedures requires that the individual be advised that the information will be used or revealed only for research or statistical purposes. The original draft regulations provided that the specific research or statistical purpose must be given. However, LEAA was persuaded by the research reactor panel that such specific disclosure could inhibit the individual or direct the individual to provide a certain kind of response and that subsequent use of information for a different but valid research purpose—a purpose that was within the general scope of the project—would not be possible without prior consent by the individual.

Second, the individual must be notified that his or her agreement to provide the requested information is entirely voluntary and can be terminated at any time. We felt that because of the criminal justice aspects of such research, it was important for an individual to be made aware at the beginning of the voluntary nature of such information giving.

The original draft regulations proposed that the individual be advised that the information provided would be immune from legal process. Again, LEAA was persuaded by the researcher panel that such a notification might be inhibiting in nature since, in most circumstances, an individual would be unlikely to be concerned about such a situation and for him or her to be advised routinely of "legal process" considerations would create a fear that would not normally be present.

The regulations, therefore, leave to the discretion of the researcher whether to advise the individual regarding the immunity provisions. The immunity protection, as discussed later, would, of course, still be there, whether disclosed to the individual subject or not.

IMMUNITY

As noted earlier, identifiable data collected by the researcher, whether collected directly from the individual, from other records (except public records), or through third parties, are immune from judicial or administrative process and cannot be admitted as evidence without the consent of the individual concerned.

This is by far one of the most important protections offered to the individual by the Section 818(a) amendment. In the criminal justice research field, much information collected could have an adverse effect upon the individual if revelation in a judicial or administrative proceeding were permitted.

The researcher must be assured of the immunity when he or she is subpoenaed into court. Normally, there is no time to turn to the federal agency and request that the immunity be conferred. If a request is made at the beginning of the project, at the application stage, the time-element problem can be eliminated. However, the request for immunity would not protect information collected by a researcher who did not have the foresight at the beginning of a project to ask for such immunity. One of the more important guarantees of protection is that information collected for one purpose cannot be used for another purpose without the consent of the person to whom the information pertains. An immunity provision that is self-executing, as distinguished from the administrative approach, is clearly preferable. The potential danger to the individual is great in the area of criminal justice research, and the concern that such information could be admitted as evidence in a judicial, legislative, or administrative proceeding is quite legitimate. Strong safeguards should be provided.

A deficiency found in the original provision has since been corrected. Prior to the latest amendment, a researcher could not invoke the provision where he or she might be required to testify from memory. An example of a problem that could occur because of this limited immunity was provided to LEAA by a researcher from a West Coast university. The research he was conducting dealt with defendant attitudes toward the criminal courts. The research design involved interviews with defendants charged with felonies shortly after their arrests and reinterviews with the same defendants shortly after the disposition of their cases.

The district attorney's office advised the researcher that should a defendant who had been interviewed shortly after arrest enter a plea of not guilty by reason of insanity, his office would subpoena the questionnaire and the interviewer. The questionnaire responses and interviewer reports as to the apparent mental state of the respondent– defendant would, the district attorney asserted, be material to the question of the validity of an insanity defense. Under such conditions, the actual questionnaire itself would be immune. However, no protection would be given to the observations made by the interviewer as to the general mental state of a defendant during the interview, and if questioned, the researcher would be required to respond to such questioning regarding his or her unrecorded recollections. Without complete immunity, sufficient protection is not provided. In the latest reauthorization of the Omnibus Crime Control and Safe Streets Act (Justice System Improvement Act of 1979), the provision was broadened to provide protection not only to copies but also to all information, including observations.

Lastly, a question may be raised regarding the effect of a federal immunity statute upon a state court proceeding. Is a state court bound by such a statute? This issue has been raised and addressed by the Supreme Court in a different context in *Adams v. Maryland,* where the Court held that a federal immunity statute was binding on a state court.[3] In *Murphy v. Water Front Commission,* the Court held that a state immunity statute protects state witnesses against incrimination under federal as well as state law and protects federal witnesses against incrimination under state as well as federal law.[4] These cases involved substantive guarantees of the Bill of Rights (Fifth Amendment) and not a privilege created by statute, such as the confidentiality of research data. However, there appears to be language in these decisions that is broad enough to bring this statutory immunity within their coverage.

Although this is the state of the law, it should not be taken to imply that the issue of immunity will not be challenged. A few years ago, a state court held two women employees of a local Rape Crisis Center in contempt for refusal to comply with a court subpoena for their records. The matter arose out of a prosecution of several minors in Colorado juvenile court for rape. The two alleged rape victims had been interviewed by the Rape Crisis Center in Pueblo, Colorado, which was partially funded by LEAA grant funds. The project involved a research component dealing with rape victims' reactions during and after the incident. At the state court proceeding to prosecute the alleged offenders, the presiding judge issued a subpoena to the two employees of the center, requiring them to appear with any center records concerning the rapes. The two employees appeared before the court but without the records, offering the explanation that their grant contract with LEAA prohibited the production of the records. The judge found them in civil contempt and ordered them to jail. The women were released from custody when the rape victims gave consent to have their records given to the court. Needless to say, this incident should never have occurred. LEAA became aware of the situation only after the fact, and

[3]347 U.S. 179 (1954).
[4]378 U.S. 52 (1964).

we were ready to take appropriate action. However, after we indicated our concerns with the judge's action, the contempt findings and confinement of the two women were expunged upon their release from custody. Therefore, the issue became moot, and the state attorney general has taken steps to ensure that this will not happen again.

Concluding Remarks

The preceding discussion illustrates the process by which a government agency can implement regulations to deal with privacy and confidentiality concerns. A number of states have in the last few years come to recognize the need to provide some privacy protection for research data.[5] We expect more such legislation in coming years, as the public becomes increasingly aware of and concerned about these critical issues. It is our hope that this discussion can provide guidance to legislators on the issues such laws must address, to agencies on the mechanisms by which legislation can be implemented, and to practitioners on the valuable role that they might play in the formation process.

Reference

Knerr, C.
    1978   *Confidentiality of Research and Statistical Data: A Compendium of State Legislation*. Washington, D.C.: National Criminal Justice Information and Statistics Service, Law Enforcement Assistance Administration, U.S. Department of Justice.

[5]In 1978, the National Criminal Justice Information and Statistics Service of LEAA published a compendium of state legislation on confidentiality of research and statistical data. The compendium shows that a number of states have recognized the need to provide some privacy protections for research data. States have enacted statutes granting special access rights for researchers to nonpublic administrative record systems. Most statutes deal with mental health, alcohol, and drug records. A number of states have also enacted laws providing that research information gathered from state records may be revealed only in nonidentifiable form. See Knerr (1978), for the complete list.

15

Proposed Legislation to Improve Statistical and Research Access to Federal Records[1]

LOIS ALEXANDER

Development of Federal Privacy and Confidentiality Laws Affecting Research

Prior to the passage of privacy legislation in the mid-1970s, there were several avenues open to federal agencies for obtaining access to identifiable federal records for research purposes.[2] In general, it was assumed that an agency could routinely have research access to records collected in its own program administration. Occasionally an agency had access to records collected by other agencies that shared responsi-

---

[1]This chapter is based on the author's work in the Office of Research and Statistics, Social Security Administration, but the opinions expressed are her own and do not represent the views of the agency.

[2]Among these research purposes are the preparation of statistical summaries and analyses of agency program operations, economic and social policy research, use of program records as sampling frames for surveys, and use of individual data extracted from administrative records on an individual basis. Epidemiologists combine data such as work history, morbidity, and mortality data about a known study group from separate sources, or use tax records to locate persons or the records of their deaths. Human subjects' research involving intervention with research subjects, or contact other than interviews or similar data gathering contacts, is not generally included in the present discussion.

273

SOLUTIONS TO ETHICAL
AND LEGAL PROBLEMS
IN SOCIAL RESEARCH

bility for administering particular programs. The general rule for disclosure of information collected by federal agencies was contained in the Federal Reports Act of 1950.[3] When transfers were made under that authority, information collected in confidence could be released only in the form of statistical totals or summaries, with consent of the person who provided the information, or to a federal agency that itself had legal authority to compel a reply from the person who was the source of the information.

Additional procedures for interagency exchange were possible under agency law. For example, with a demonstration of need, a series of executive orders allowed access to tax return information by agencies such as the Social Security Administration (SSA), Federal Trade Commission (FTC), and others, and this access was understood to include use for agencies' statistical activities. The linking of individual records from agency files on a sample basis to records maintained by the Bureau of Census was possible for projects in which the Bureau participated, and for which it would swear in agency personnel as temporary Bureau of the Census employees.[4] Within the Department of Health, Education and Welfare (now the Department of Health and Human Services; HHS), epidemiologists and other researchers in the Public Health Service were given access to Social Security Administration records under a special *ad hoc* authority formerly available to the Commissioner of Social Security, exercised in a formal "Commissioner's Decision" process.[5]

Certain other limited access was possible for researchers not regularly employed by federal agencies. An agency might contract with a private organization to perform its research study, and provide the contractor with the temporary use of information from its program files necessary for performing the contractual duties (e.g., a sample listing of names and addresses to conduct a survey, or a compilation of program data for analysis). In certain activities, cooperative federal–state arrangements were made whereby researchers might have reciprocal access to data for research, such as the Cooperative Health Statistics System (CHSS) program undertaken by the Public Health Service in cooperation with state health agencies. The Freedom of Information

[3] 44 U.S.C. § 3508.

[4] 13 U.S.C § 9 (1976), authorizes the use of special sworn Census employees.

[5] 20 C.F.R. 401 (1980), implementing 42 U.S.C. § 1306, which contains SSA's record confidentiality provisions. The "*ad hoc*" discretion of the commissioner was eliminated in the 1980 revision of the regulation conforming with changes in law enacted in the Privacy Act, Tax Reform Act of 1976, and "Sunshine" amendments to the Freedom of Information Act.

Act (FOIA) amendments liberalized access by outside users to "sanitized" data (i.e., data purged of names and other obvious identifiers). However, FOIA did not ordinarily allow access to information that could be individually identified.

THE PRIVACY ACT OF 1974

The Privacy Act of 1974[6] constituted a more general approach to sharing information among federal agencies by specifying the purposes and conditions for disclosure of records, and in some instances, by limiting the disclosure to particular agencies. This act was a records management statute that applied generally to information about natural persons (as distinguished from information about businesses and other entities), and that held federal agencies strictly accountable for their collection, use, and disclosure of records covered by the act. The act grew principally out of concerns about administrative or law enforcement abuses of information about private persons, and out of some generalized fears of large computer data banks. Although no reported misuse of statistical or research data was at issue, there was concern about potential abuse of sensitive personal information used in research and statistics, or the possibility of unwarranted reliance on incorrect, outdated, or irrelevant data. The remedies that the act provided were especially restrictive with respect to statistical use of data.

The act created a new system of notification and access, through which individuals were to be given a measure of control over the government's use of information about them. Its method was to prohibit any disclosure of information in scope of the act unless the subject consented, or unless 1 of 11 express exceptions applied.

Those exceptions were generally concerned with disclosure for carrying out necessary functions of government—such as transfers among employees within an agency, release to agencies and courts for law enforcement purposes, or release to designated recipients such as the Bureau of the Census for its work, or to the National Archives for evaluation or permanent maintenance and storage. To meet the regular needs of agencies to conduct interagency business or release information outside the government, a special "routine use" exemption provided for miscellaneous kinds of disclosure not otherwise categorized.

The act established a Privacy Protection Study Commission (PPSC), whose 2-year task was to study public and private data banks and to

[6]5 U.S.C. § 552a (1974).

recommend changes in law that would extend or better carry out the purposes of the Privacy Act. One of the important concerns of the PPSC was to seek a balance between individual privacy and the legitimate needs of government for an accurate fund of information about individuals for research as a base for informed public policy. The commission in its final report (Privacy Protection Study Commission, 1977) prepared a model revision of the Privacy Act incorporating all of its formal recommendations. A number of those recommendations related to statistical and research information.

In developing its recommendations the PPSC gave special attention to providing a way to make administrative data (information that agencies acquire in administering their programs) more generally available among agencies for research and statistical analysis, when identifiers are needed for that research.

As the Privacy Act was enacted, treatment of data for statistical use was essentially tailored to the needs of the Bureau of the Census; little attention was given to the activities of other statistical agencies, or to the manner in which their practices differed from those of the Bureau. No restrictions were placed on disclosure of identifiable data, including statistical data, to the Bureau of the Census for conducting its censuses and intercensal surveys. Otherwise, the only provision that the act made for disclosure of statistical data was an exception permitting its release in unidentifiable form.

As a practical matter, agencies that found interagency transfers of identifiable statistical data necessary for conducting their statistical and research activities authorized those releases as "routine use" disclosures.[7] A routine use disclosure is required by the statute to be "compatible with" the purpose for which the information was collected. There have been significant differences in the way various agencies have applied this compatibility constraint with respect to data exchanges for research and statistical purposes. At one extreme, nearly any federal research might be regarded as compatible with a collection purpose, and at the other, studies might require direct relationship to the mission of the collecting agency in order to be considered compatible.

The PPSC took a narrow view that the provision for disclosure of statistical data in unidentifiable form[8] was the only authority which

[7]5 U.S.C. § 552a(a) (7).
[8]5 U.S.C. § 552a(b) (5). The Privacy Act does not define "disclosure," but § 552a(b) prohibits disclosure of a record "by any means of communications to any person" unless allowed by one of 11 express exemptions, including disclosure in a form that is not

the statute provided for releasing statistical data, except to the Bureau of the Census, and did not consider that the "routine use" exception applied to this type of data. However, the PPSC conducted extensive study and hearings, during which producers and users of statistical data presented their positions on the needs of the statistical and research community. Out of these studies, the PPSC concluded that the narrow authority of the provision for release of unidentifiable statistical data needed to be expanded, provided that safeguards be strengthened, and that various protections and immunities be added. PPSC recommended the replacement of the section limiting statistical transfers to unidentifiable form, proposing that a new set of conditions be enacted as a substitute, under which transfers of identifiable data could be made with adequate protection against further release for nonstatistical uses. Its proposal for remedial legislation established principles for transfer of statistical data under procedures that would adequately safeguard personal information in the complex conditions of the research and statistical environment, which is different from the area of program management, and also provide consistency in the criteria and methods applicable to data sharing.

THE TAX REFORM ACT OF 1976

The subsequent passage of the Tax Reform Act,[9] following soon after the Privacy Act, amended the Internal Revenue Code with a confidentiality provision that had substantial effect on federal statistical work. Unlike the Privacy Act, which had general applicability to federal records, the Tax Reform Act provided new confidentiality rules exclusively for those records which it defined as "returns" and "return information." The statistical and research uses of information from these classes of records by federal agencies had been extensive in the past, and the act made major reductions in those uses.

For example, epidemiologists in the Public Health Service formerly made use of addresses provided by the Internal Revenue Service (IRS) from income tax returns in order to perform follow-up studies of persons in their study populations. The Federal Trade Commission and

---

individually identifiable. This language highlights the conceptual difference between disclosure as a legal term connoting transfer of information, and "statistical disclosure" which conveys a meaning to the statistician that the identity of a data subject can be linked to the information, usually for a nonstatistical purpose.

[9]26 U.S.C. § 6103 (1976) contains the record confidentiality provisions of the Internal Revenue Code, as amended by the Tax Reform Act of 1976.

the Social Security Administration research staffs have made use of tax return information in their statistical studies for financial analysis of business organizations. In the past, the Department of Agriculture conducted surveys using names of farm employers stratified by geography and number of workers, drawn from employer returns in the Social Security Administration records. The Bureau of Labor Statistics has relied on SSA's earnings data for studies in its unemployment insurance program. Most of these uses have been curtailed as a consequence of the 1976 Tax Reform Act, since no express provisions were made for these purposes.

Before that act, returns (including information returns) filed with the Commissioner of Internal Revenue and transmitted to the SSA were protected by the SSA's confidentiality statute and subject to its disclosure regulations. Disclosure of returns by the IRS was controlled by a collection of executive orders and Treasury regulations. In the 1976 law, the earnings reports of the Social Security Administration for administering its Old Age and Survivors Insurance program became subject to the Internal Revenue Code and applicable Treasury regulations as well as to the Social Security Act and the SSA's Regulation No. 1.[10] IRS also classified the Form SS-4 Application for an Employer Identification Number (EIN) as an information return subject to its provisions. (The Application for an Employer Identification Number must be filed by every employer prior to filing wage and FICA reports for employees.)

Like the Privacy Act, the Tax Reform Act of 1976 prohibits all disclosure of information in its scope except as expressly provided by it. For statistical use, the Tax Reform Act allows disclosure of returns and return information with identifiers to the Bureau of the Census and the Bureau of Economic Analysis in the Department of Commerce, the Federal Trade Commission, and the Treasury Department's Office of Tax Analysis, with redisclosure only in unidentifiable form.[11] Agencies such as the Social Security Administration and the Department of Labor are not named in this provision as recipients of return information for statistical uses. These agencies have been provided access, however, to certain tax information to carry out specified laws that they administer.[12] Although the act is silent on the use of these records for

[10]Op. cit. fn. 5.
[11]26 U.S.C. § 6103(j) (1976).
[12]26 U.S.C. § 6103(l) (1) (1976) provides for release of information related to chapters 2, 21, and 24 of the Internal Revenue Code (employment and survivors insurance, self-

statistical purposes, the IRS has interpreted it to permit these agencies to use tax information in statistical activities which are their statutory responsibility. The act gave the IRS authority to prepare statistical studies and compilations based on return information, on a reimbursable basis, as requested in writing by anyone.[13] These statistics, however, may be released by the IRS only in anonymous form. This restriction precludes interagency transfers of identifiable or potentially identifiable return information in processing data for research purposes. In addition, the IRS regards the provision as the only authorization permitting the preparation of reimbursable statistical work based on return information. Thus, when statistical users request reimbursable work from agencies other than the IRS, which have the use of return information for their own purposes (such as the SSA or the Department of Labor), the IRS takes the position that the users must obtain authorization from it for each such statistical project. The output approved by the IRS for these reimbursable projects has been limited to summary information with no release of microdata.

Epidemiologists in particular have complained about the combined effect of these limitations. A simple illustration of this is the potential use of SSA's work history data to study work-place exposures to harmful substances. Epidemiologists in the Department of Health and Human Services would like to identify occupations of individuals in study and comparison groups, and measure the length of time in particular work environments associated with exposure to substances causing cancer and other conditions. There are two impediments to linkage of this sort under the present view of the tax law. First, SSA does not have current access to occupational information from the income tax returns of workers. Second, the SSA has not been authorized by the IRS to release individual records to epidemiologists in the National Cancer Institute of the HHS Public Health Service even with identifiers removed.

Outside the statistical community, there is an impression that statistical data comprise data only in the forms of summaries or tables, or less generally, a perception of microdata records in an entirely anonymous form. (The term *microdata* is used in this discussion to mean files containing records with information about individual data subjects

---

employment, and withholding), to SSA for administering the Social Security Act; § 6103(l) (2) allows release to the Department of Labor for administering titles I and IV of the Employee Retirement Income Security Act of 1974 (ERISA).

[13]26 U.S.C. § 6108(b) (1976).

from a defined study population.) These concepts suitably describe the usual end product of most statistical and research work in the form which is disseminated for public use. They are the perceptions which shaped the treatment of statistical data in the Federal Reports Act, the Privacy Act, and the Tax Reform Act.[14]

This view disregards, however, the important intermediate stages of the statistical process, which may involve a series of transfers among programmers and analysts when they perform specialized steps in the whole process. Use of identifiers is often needed for editing and linkage, even when the work is performed by one person in one place. For much statistical work, which the agencies perform, disclosure of identifiers is necessary during the collecting and processing stages; this may involve transfers among component agencies and organizations; and may also be necessary for historical linkage. The recommendations of the Privacy Commission and several recent legislative proposals have attempted to resolve these difficulties. These proposals would allow identifiers to remain with the individual data as long as necessary while use and transfer of the data are in stages of a statistical process. If liberalized rules of data access were to be provided for a statistical purpose, however, the process must remove identifiers as its final step. Removal of identifiers or preparation of summary data would be required before the data could be released to policymakers, administrators, law enforcement personnel, or the general public.

Major Recent Proposed Legislation for Research and Statistical Use of Records

During the past 5 years, a number of legislative proposals dealing with privacy and confidentiality were discussed both in the executive branch and in Congress. Some had significant potential for improving statistical and research access to information collected by federal agen-

---

[14]The Federal Reports Act recognized the authority to release information "only—(1) in the form of statistical totals or summaries; . . ." 44 U.S.C. § 3508(b) (1) (1976). In this same tradition, the Privacy Act permitted disclosure "to a recipient who has provided the agency with advance adequate written assurance that the record will be used solely as a statistical research or reporting record, and the record is to be transferred in a form that is not individually identifiable." 5 U.S.C. § 552a(b) (5). The Tax Reform Act permits release of return information to named statistical agencies with the proviso that such information cannot be redisclosed except to the subject of the information "except in a form which cannot be associated with or otherwise identify, directly or indirectly, a particular taxpayer." 26 U.S.C. § 6103(j) (4) (1976).

cies. Among these was a bill for "Privacy of Research Records," endorsed by the administration and introduced in both houses.[15] Another proposal for protecting "Confidentiality of Statistical Records" grew out of the work of the Carter administration's Statistical Reorganization Project. Some thought that this proposal might be introduced either as an independent piece of legislation, or as a part of the "Federal Paperwork Reduction" bill.[16] There was considerable discussion among agencies and support in the private statistical community for this proposal. Attention was also given to fitting its provisions together in a consistent way with those of the proposed bill for privacy of research records. However, the confidentiality of statistical records proposal was not formally introduced as a bill. A bill for privacy of medical records was introduced in both houses, but was eventually defeated.[17] That bill was prinicpally concerned with preventing misuse of medical information in records maintained by medical care facilities; several provisions dealt with permissible use of medical records for health research purposes. A fourth important proposal, discussed publicly for several years, but also not formally introduced, would have provided broader statistical access to the Standard Statistical Establishment List (SSEL), a comprehensive listing of business establishments maintained by the Commerce Department (U.S. Department of Commerce, 1978). Other proposals to meet conditions encountered by particular federal agencies were more parochial in their purposes, and would have provided in a limited way certain of the protections advanced in the more general proposals.

The thrust of these proposals was to increase the scope of permissible sharing of research and statistical information, principally among federal agencies. In addition, the common purpose was to offer a degree of generalized availability among federal agencies of data drawn from administrative records—that is, from those records that agencies generate in administering their programs and in making determinations or decisions about individuals. Some consideration was given to permitting access by nonfederal researchers to certain types of identifiable data for the performance of research which would meet particular standards for federal sponsorship or approval.

The bills and other proposals varied significantly in their scope,

---

[15]Privacy of Research Records, introduced in the House as H.R. 3409, 96th Cong. 1st Sess. (1979), and in the Senate as S. 867, 96th Cong., 1st Sess. (1979)

[16]Paperwork Reduction Act of 1980, P.L. No. 96–511.

[17]Privacy of Medical Information Act. S. 865, 96th Cong. 1st Sess. (1979) and Federal Privacy of Medical Information Act, H.R. 5435, 96th Cong. 1st Sess. (1979).

types of records covered, and the circumstances and procedures associated with data sharing. Implicit in all, however, was the underlying principle of "functional separation." That principle was first articulated as a formal rule in the Report of the Privacy Protection Study Commission in 1977, with respect to records about natural persons. Some aspects of this principle were discussed in a general way in earlier work by writers such as Boruch; the more rigorous principle has been implicit in subsequent initiatives to enhance access to information about individuals. In some instances, the concept has even been applied to information about business entities. In its work, the PPSC defined this term to mean separating the use of information about an individual for a research and statistical purpose from its use in arriving at an administrative or other decision about that individual (Privacy Protection Study Commission, 1977, p. 572).

In essence, the concept developed two basic classifications for records about reporting entities, according to the function the records perform—either the function of providing the basis for individual decisions, determinations, or treatments affecting individuals (administrative function), or that of providing a study base for defining groups and producing summary information about them (statistical–research function). Applying this principle, the statistical–research function can be performed using records from any source—including records that originate in administrative files, as well as those obtained directly from persons through surveys and similar contacts. Once a decision has been made that these are to be treated as statistical records and assigned to perform a statistical function, however, final output from the designated records must remain statistical. This means that files and reports must be anonymous, regardless of whether the records are collected exclusively for research purposes through personal contact, or whether they are obtained by researchers indirectly by extraction from program files originally collected for administrative purposes. Of course, intermediate transfers of statistical records often need to be made in forms that are not anonymous, and one of the underlying problems dealt with in these various proposals is to provide for necessary disclosures among researchers and statisticians of identifiable records, while guarding those records from inappropriate use for nonstatistical purposes.

The rationale for the principle of functional separation is based on two important assumptions. First, as an equitable matter, it is considered that individual research subjects whose records are selected should not be singled out for differential treatment or placed in special jeopardy merely because of their chance inclusion in a research study. Second, there is an intuitive belief, with some empirical support, that the quality and completeness of information available for statistical and research purposes is directly related to the confidence respondents have in the confidential treatment of information they provide.

Despite their diversity in method and coverage, in short, the legislative proposals developed two common themes: first, to protect statistical–research data from nonstatistical uses resulting from disclosures, either voluntary or compulsory, that would individually affect or harm data subjects; and second, to liberalize research access to data from surveys and administrative record files so protected.

PRIVACY OF RESEARCH RECORDS

A bill that incorporated many of the recommendations of the Privacy Protection Study Commission for access and disclosure of statistical and research data was introduced in 1979[18] as the Privacy of Research Records bill.

The proposal was developed in the Commerce Department, through the principal efforts of the National Telecommunications and Information Administration (NTIA). It grew out of the Carter administration's Privacy Initiative, whose research task group was headed by HEW. That initiative was charged with the task of reviewing and evaluating the PPSC report and recommendations, and if it found a change in the privacy law to be indicated, to endorse or initiate legislative proposals.

The privacy rules proposed in this bill would apply to records containing confidential information about natural persons, collected or compiled for research performed under federal sponsorship. To be eligible for the protections provided in the bill, proposed data collections would be named by an agency head as a research project. The action of designating the proposed data collection as research data would generate an "expectation of confidentiality." Given that expectation, certain statutory rights would then accrue to data subjects when the data collection began.

With a few limited exceptions required by other law, prior consent of the individual subject was to be required for disclosure of identifiable information for nonresearch purposes. The collecting agency would have the authority to use the data for its statistical–research purposes, and to disclose identifiable information to other specified classes of

[18]Note 15, *supra.*

recipients exclusively for research purposes under defined conditions and safeguards.

In sharing identifiable data with other research organizations, the agency would have to determine that the disclosure would be consistent with the conditions offered at the time of collection, that release of identifiers would be both necessary and justifiable in the circumstances of secondary use, and that the secondary user could and would maintain acceptable safeguards. In addition, the agency would have to inform the individual at the time of collection about anticipated uses for secondary research and nonresearch purposes, avoid nonconsensual recontact, and require its contractors or grantees to assume comparable duties when they collected or used research data.

Thus the operative mechanism would be the formal selective process by which planned sets of records would be named as research records before they were collected or assembled. The "research" character of the records would be indelibly assigned. That is, once designated for a research purpose, research records could not then ever be voluntarily or mandatorily used for a nonstatistical purpose except in an anonymous form, subject to a few special exceptions (e.g., for a medical emergency, to comply with a judicial order in connection with alleged abuse of records by researchers, or for audit purposes not affecting the research subjects).

CONFIDENTIALITY OF STATISTICAL RECORDS

A proposal that might have become a companion bill to the Privacy of Research Records bill grew out of the studies of the Carter administration's Statistical Reorganization Project (U.S. Department of Commerce, 1981). That project had a broad mandate to perform a critical evaluation of the decentralized federal statistical system and to make recommendations with respect to planning and coordination for the improvement of quality, policy relevance, and timeliness of statistical information, as well as reduction in excessive paperwork burden. The project also was charged to offer recommendations and prepare a legislative proposal for confidentiality of statistical data.

The resulting Confidentiality of Statistical Records proposal was to protect federal files created or maintained exclusively for statistical purposes. Since the proposed bill for Confidentiality of Statistical Records made no distinction between information about natural persons and about business entities, there was some overlap with the Privacy of

Research Records bill in potential coverage of information about individuals.

The Confidentiality of Statistical Records proposal provided for an official, to be known as the Chief Statistician of the United States, who would determine whether particular files nominated by federal agencies would be entitled to protections under the bill. In addition, the proposed bill provided for the establishment of "protected statistical centers" and named those federal statistical units or agencies which both elected to become protected centers and were able to meet the strict eligibility criteria. The legislative proposal also provided that statistical agencies or units not named in the draft bill could, if they chose, ask to be named by the Chief Statistician as protected centers and demonstrate to that official that they adequately met the eligibility requirements. The right of an approved center to retain its protected status depended on its continued ability to maintain the required standards. An important element in those eligibility requirements was that the center not be subject to any law requiring disclosure under conditions which were inconsistent with those set forth in the proposed bill, in particular that the record be subject to no mandatory disclosure for nonstatistical purposes.

To become a protected statistical center, an agency or its statistical component would have to meet the safeguard standards specified in the proposed bill to assure the integrity, confidentiality, and security of protected files. Except for internal management records, all files of each statistical center would become protected statistical files. In contrast, an agency might not choose or qualify to become a protected statistical center. Nevertheless, it might have certain collections of data accepted by the Chief Statistician as eligible to become protected statistical files. The effect of becoming a "protected statistical center" would be to insulate the records and all of the work of the center's staff from that of other agencies, as well as from other offices and components of a center's parent agency, in situations where the center might be a statistical unit within an agency.

A protected statistical center, under the proposed legislation, would use individually identifiable information exclusively for statistical purposes, and as a general rule could disclose it without consent of the subject only to another protected center. Certain express exceptions would permit disclosure for important governmental processes (audit, or judicial order, or special circumstances involving health and safety). In addition, specified classes of recipients, including statistical units of state and local governments, which were not protected statistical centers, could be authorized to receive name and address listings for statistical surveys, provided they could give adequate assurance to satisfy the Chief Statistician that they would not voluntarily disclose the list information, and that they could not be compelled to do so.

The principal benefits to an agency becoming a protected statistical center are twofold: (a) The statistical center would have the authority for discretionary transfers of identifiable statistical information to or from another protected statistical center on a showing of need for identifiable information; and (b) the statistical center concept provides a mechanism whereby one center could appeal to the Chief Statistician if it was refused information by another. That official could order the release if the need was found to warrant such action.

A section in the proposed legislation would provide a general authorization for agencies to disclose confidential data for statistical purposes. That provision would apply to data held by agencies that were not protected statistical centers, in files which did not have the status of protected statistical files, but were subject to other legal restrictions. For a file containing identifiable information subject to the Privacy Act, for instance, this provision would perform a function similar to that proposed in the Privacy of Research Records bill. That is, the authorization would overcome the restriction of the Privacy Act provision allowing transfer of statistical data only in identifiable form, and it would overcome the test of "compatability" associated with the "routine use" disclosure. For a file containing confidential information obtained from a business or other reporting entity, the provision would overcome the Federal Reports Act rule limiting release to anonymous statistics.

The principal benefit to research subjects would be that exchange of their identifiable information among federal and certain other approved statistical agencies would not appreciably increase the risk of having information about them disclosed or used to affect them individually. The information would be immune from most mandatory process, and available only in limited circumstances to government auditors. This protection was to avoid selective audit of persons merely because they were included in a project that was being audited. It was thought that selection for audit should be related to the reason for audit, and not be based on random inclusion of individuals in a research sample. Significant sanctions were provided for violation of the confidentiality protection. The sanctions included civil and criminal penalties for persons who made unauthorized disclosure. Special standing to sue would be given to a person whose confidentiality was violated. Administrative sanctions included fines and debarment of contractors or grantees. Moreover, the Chief Statistician could revoke the protected status of a protected statistical center, or the authorization of a recipient to hold a protected statistical file. Protected files themselves, of course, would keep their protections regardless of changes in status of the center that produced them.

PRIVACY OF MEDICAL INFORMATION

A bill that was introduced in 1979 but was not enacted into law was the Privacy of Medical Information bill, which provided for protection of medical information maintained by hospitals and other inpatient medical facilities.[19] The protection would be independent of whether the institution received federal or other sources of funding, and would establish special confidentiality rules for availability and use of medical information for research.

The proposal was similar in several respects to the bill for privacy of research information discussed earlier, in that it would permit research access where need could be demonstrated and safeguards provided, and where restrictions could be assured that the information would not (with narrow exceptions) be disclosed except for research. As applied to federal facilities, its provisions would supersede those of the Federal Privacy Act with respect to access and disclosure. It was meant also to overcome the Freedom of Information Act (FOIA) rules on disclosure, for mandatory release of information (i.e., it would relieve the institution of the burden of proving that the release of a medical or similar record would be a clearly unwarranted invasion of personal privacy in order to justify its withholding).

There were some differences between this bill and the privacy of research records bill. For medical information, the access and safeguard provisions would be carried out at the institutional level by the administrator, rather than by an official of a statistical agency (or by the Chief Statistician as provided by the statistical confidentiality bill). The recipient of research data—including the private researcher—could make disclosures for research on his own authority. Although the history of this legislation made reference to disclosure for related social research, the bill did not make access available to general-purpose research and statistical users, but rather limited release to health-related research, such as biomedical research, epidemiological research, or health services and statistical projects. (The practical consequence of this limitation appeared to be slight, since most potential users seemed to be health-related researchers.) Accountability was to be provided

[19]Note 17, supra.

through the mechanism of institutional review boards, both before initial access by the researcher, and before any redisclosure to other researchers, rather than through agency regulations.

STANDARD STATISTICAL ESTABLISHMENT LIST

An important area in which legislation has been considered deals with access to the Standard Statistical Establishment List (SSEL) by Federal Statistical units. In its development phase, that list has been generated and maintained by the Bureau of the Census and is available for exclusive use of Census employees under the strict prohibitions on disclosure of Census data provided by Title 13 of the United States Code.

SSEL was designed as a computerized list with comprehensive coverage of U.S. business establishments, the establishment being the basic reporting unit. For each establishment, the minimum intended file content includes name and address information, Employer Identification Number (EIN), as well as codes for industry and product, geography, employment and business receipts, and legal form of organization. The list permits aggregation of establishments on a firm, subfirm or other ownership basis. The comprehensive nature of its coverage and the relatively high quality of the information make it valuable as a sampling frame for surveys and other statistical compilations. Because of the underlying Bureau of the Census presumption against use of its data for investigatory, regulatory, or enforcement purposes, the question of providing access to other federal statistical organizations has raised many complex issues, and discussion of extending the availability to nonfederal users has been controversial.

For several years legislative proposals have been discussed to resolve some of the difficulties encountered in making the SSEL available to federal agencies. The effort to develop a central list and achieve consensus among agencies as to the appropriate form of legislation has been led by the unit in the Office of Management and Budget (OMB), which is responsible for developing statistical policy (for a time the Office of Statistical Policy and Standards in the Department of Commerce, and now once again a component of OMB). To date, however, no SSEL legislation has actually been introduced, despite the considerable agency support for the general principle of making the list available.

This brief review is based principally on the legislative proposal presented in 1977 and reported in a 1978 Department of Commerce working paper on the SSEL (U.S. Department of Commerce, 1978), which would have amended Title 13 of the United States Code to permit access by agencies other than the Bureau of the Census. Subsequent proposals have differed in detail rather than in general approach. These proposals include interactions with the Internal Revenue Code arising out of the Tax Reform Act of 1976, which attached new legal restrictions on confidentiality of tax return information used in compiling and validating the list information. The Employer Identification Number (EIN) for instance, an important element in the SSEL, is treated by the IRS as tax information under this new statute.

The main thrust of legislative proposals to make SSEL more widely available is to permit expanded use for statistical purposes by federal statistical agencies. The various information codes (e.g., industry, size, employment, geography, etc.) are used in drawing stratified samples of firms and in assigning sampling weights. In comparing and integrating business unit information from various sources, the codes assigned in SSEL may be used as reference guides for validating or correcting information from other sources. For instance, the Social Security Administration has at times compared Standard Industrial Classification (SIC) codes assigned by its coders to particular business firms with the SIC codes in SSEL to obtain current information on those firms' business activity, since its own codes are assigned on the basis of information supplied at the time of the business birth.

The 1979 proposal would prohibit any voluntary or compulsory disclosure of information identifying particular business entities except to authorized statistical recipients. That restriction would apply to information compiled from other sources with respect to establishments selected from the list, as well as information from the list itself. Some unresolved questions have to do with possible access by nonfederal statistical organizations associated with federal agencies—their contractors or state agencies in cooperative functions.

Summary

Important laws were enacted in the 1970s to protect the privacy and confidentiality of the administrative records that federal agencies collect and develop in carrying out their programs. The Privacy Act of 1974 established strict limitations to be imposed by all federal agencies on disclosure of information about individuals. The Tax Reform Act of 1976 placed even more stringent prohibitions on redisclosure by federal agencies of the limited amount of information about taxpaying entities to which the law gave them access. These laws had more serious consequences for research users than for nonresearch users of individual records.

In the mid and late 1970s, Federal attention was focused on the changes in record keeping and disclosure practices of agencies made in carrying out the Privacy Act. The Privacy Protection Study Commission, the Commission on Paperwork Reduction, the government-wide Privacy Initiative, whose research and statistical inquiries were headed by the Department of Health, Education and Welfare, and the Statistical Reorganization Project headed by the Office of Management and Budget, all studied the impact of privacy and confidentiality on the use and sharing of information in federal statistical and research activities. These studies systematically examined the experience of agencies and articulated two important aspects of the new treatment of records. First, the processes in which researchers use records are quite different—even opposite—from the processes by which administrators perform their functions, because of the inherent difference in purpose—the one to study the attributes and behavior of defined groups, and the other to take actions affecting individuals. Second, because the statistical and nonstatistical processes differ so greatly, but the record-keeping rules are the same, the laws impinge differently and impose far more hardship for the research user than for the program administrator. Moreover, the disadvantageous consequence for research is, in the view of many, without corresponding benefit to the individuals whom researchers study. It is ordinarily the concern of researchers to protect the confidentiality of their information from nonresearchers even without any legal requirement that they do so, and they generally express support for the principle of reinforcing this protection by statute. However, the new laws prevent researchers from making necessary transfers of data within the statistical processes of the research itself, and many researchers have urged remedial legislation to facilitate research transfers of identifiable data with strict safeguards from nonresearch use.

The government study groups arrived at a common view that the principles and practices for protecting research records need to be different from the rules for protecting administrative records. The term which the Privacy Commission devised for that difference was *functional separation*—by which the commission meant separating the use of information about an individual for a research and statistical purpose from its use in arriving at an administrative or other decision about that individual, with sanctions to keep the record uses separate. The assumption underlying functional separation is that the societal benefits of research warrant liberal access to individual records by researchers, but that the individual subjects of information have a special claim to protection of their privacy in information about them used by researchers, considering that the research purposes do not usually confer direct benefit on the persons whose information is used.

Four important approaches based on functional separation were discussed and given serious consideration as potential legislation. The proposal to protect privacy of research records focused on the records themselves and on the particular information content to be protected. The approach set up a formal process which would authorize specified classes of research users to have access to identifiable data thus protected. Records in the scope of the proposal were research records containing information about natural persons. The criteria governing the process of protecting designated files and releasing them to authorized users were carefully designed to meet the Freedom of Information Act test for statutory exemption from compulsory disclosure.

The proposal for confidentiality of statistical records was distinguished in two ways from that described above for privacy of research records. This approach was to establish a set of organizational units (protected statistical centers) essentially all of whose statistical data would be files protected by a proposed statute, disclosable only to another protected statistical unit. The proposal made no distinction between records containing information about natural persons and those containing information about business and other nonindividual entities.

The approach taken in the bill to protect privacy of medical records used in research had both similarities and differences with respect to the proposal for privacy of federal research records. Medical records used for research were to be protected regardless of whether the medical facility that maintained them was federal or nonfederal. The scope of coverage and the restrictions on disclosure resembled those of the proposal to protect privacy of federal research records. There was an important difference in the accountability structure, however, since in the bill for medical data, a research recipient could redisclose to others whom he or she considered to be authentic researchers, where the other proposals required that a federal official make that determination.

Legislation has been proposed for several years to make access to the Standard Statistical Establishment List more readily available to statistical agencies. This valuable resource contains extensive current data about business firms and establishments. Under the Title 13 U.S. Code rules which govern its use and disclosure, the list can be used in microdata form only by Bureau of the Census employees. Anonymity of information about businesses is substantially more complex and difficult to achieve than anonymity of information about natural persons in research based on microdata. As long as the suppression rules used for microdata about individuals are also applied to data about businesses, requiring anonymity, the difficulty in providing wider availability of the SSEL will probably persist.

To summarize, although expressed in various ways, the concept of functional separation has been a central assumption in the important proposals for legislative improvement for research use of records. Thus, in all the proposals, records used for research–statistical purposes would be characterized as research–statistical records, even when the information originated in and duplicated information in administrative records. Furthermore, once records had been characterized as research–statistical records, they could not be reused for nonstatistical purposes in identifiable form, subject to sanction.

References

Privacy Protection Study Commission
  1977   *Personal Privacy in an Information Society.* Washington, D.C.: U.S. Government Printing Office.
U.S. Department of Commerce
  1978   *Department of Commerce Working Paper on the Standard Statistical Establishment List.* Washington, D.C.: U.S. Government Printing Office.
  1981   *Statistical Reporter.* "Improving the Federal Statistical System: Issues and Options." Prepared by the President's Reorganization Project for the Federal Statistical System, February 1981.

16

Solutions to Legal and Ethical Problems in Applied Social Research: Perspective and Prospects[1]

ROBERT F. BORUCH

The authors of chapters in this volume consider a variety of approaches to resolving legal and ethical problems in applied research. Three areas were targeted for examination: experimentation and prediction, informed consent and clearance, and individual privacy and confidentiality of research data. This concluding chapter is dedicated to summarizing and integrating the solutions that have been proposed, to reviewing gaps and shortcomings, and to identifying related work.

The Choice of Targets and Themes

The choice of problems here is based on their fundamental importance and persistence. For instance, the tension between public in-

[1]Research on topics considered here has been supported by the National Science Foundation. The support implies neither endorsement nor rejection of our views, only that the problems are in the opinion of our peers worth addressing. Earlier versions of this chapter and most of the chapters in the volume were presented in a meeting on resolving ethical and legal problems in social problems in social research, organized in February 1978, under the auspices of Northwestern University's Division of Methodology and Evaluation Research (psychology department) and the Center for Statistics and Probability (mathematics and other departments).

SOLUTIONS TO ETHICAL
AND LEGAL PROBLEMS
IN SOCIAL RESEARCH

terests in information and public interests in individual privacy is traceable to the Old Testament books of Samuel and Exodus, where censuses are the subject of both support and opposition, from both God and man. Conflict that is not dissimilar reemerges periodically, sometimes ritualistically, in censuses and surveys designed to understand social problems. Considering social experiments, one finds in Paul's letters to the Thessalonians the advice "to try all things, and hold fast that which is good." This advice can be used to oppose social experiments as well as to advocate them. The ambiguity of the advice and the polarity it may create are reflected as well in current challenges to experiments on ethical and legal grounds.

Our choice of problems is also based on an assessment of their tractability, and we take as a first the idea of *resolving* certain problems rather than explicating them. Explication, articulation, and the like are important to understanding a problem, and this understanding provides some leverage to handle conflicts. Still, the concrete solutions of different kinds are rarely given much attention in the professional literature. A further justification for stressing solutions here is that a variety of able examinations of problems themselves are already available in the professional literature on the ethics of research. These works, often international in their scope, include disquisitions by Barnes (1979), Diener and Crandall (1978), and Reynolds (1982), edited monographs by Bulmer (1979), Bermant, Kelman, and Warwick (1978), Sieber (1982), and Beauchamp, Faden, Wallace, and Walters (1982) and others cited by the authors of chapters in this volume.

A second major theme concerns the multiplicity of solutions and the limits on any particular solution's utility. That is, there are statutory, procedural, technical, and empirical approaches to resolving conflicts between research interests and legal or ethical standards. The presumption is that we cannot expect a single approach to be satisfactory for all disciplines in this context, any more than we expect singular solutions to suffice in engineering, medicine, or literature. The statistical approaches to ensuring privacy and confidentiality, for instance, are most appropriate for large-scale surveys rather than for individual case studies, and for numerical rather than for narrative records. Similarly, statutory approaches to ensuring legitimacy of experiments may accommodate legal demands but may fail to satisfy social custom or individual preference.

A third underlying theme is that the solutions are relatively new and still under development, partly because the conflicts they are designed to resolve are relatively new. The idea of large-scale controlled experiments in planning and evaluating social programs, for instance, was not actualized vigorously by government until the 1960s. The dilemmas that this approach engenders appeared only gradually. Though privacy and confidentiality have been matters of concern since the early censuses, the use of large-scale special surveys to clarify controversial social problems did not become common until the 1930s and 1940s. Not until the 1960s were innovative technical solutions such as Warner's randomized response methods developed to resolve some privacy problems. Even the value of these failed to be recognized until the 1970s, to judge from the published research literature. More important, we can expect that as research attention is dedicated to this area, as solutions are tested in the field and reexamined, as some approaches become obsolete, better solutions will emerge.

The stress on solutions, even admittedly imperfect ones, will doubtless offend some academic scientists. Indeed, this volume presents much more engineering of various kinds than it does science. It does not address fundamental questions about how privacy is viewed by the philosopher or the general population, for instance; nor does it present coherent theory about the matter. We chose not to explore theory as solution simply because current theory is not sufficiently strong. In any case, it is reasonable to suppose that solutions of the kind discussed here will illuminate problems in ways that will eventually inform fundamental theory. We accept, rather than question, the public and professional values attached to privacy, information, reforms as experiments, and related concepts since others, such as Kelman (1968), have questioned them ably.

Experimentation and Prediction

Our special interest here lies in randomized experiments, settings in which individuals or institutions are *randomly* assigned to one of two or more program variations in the interest of gauging the relative effectiveness of the variations. Such experiments have been undertaken in education, welfare, law and criminal justice, health, and other fields. They are politically important in that they can inform decisions about initiating, operating, or terminating public programs. They are scientifically important insofar as they confirm, disconfirm, or sharpen theory and add to our understanding, as the negative income tax experiments appear to have done for economists and sociologists. When executed well, they can reduce chronic biases in estimating the effects of social programs (see Campbell and Stanley, 1963; and Riecken and Boruch, 1974). They present ethical problems and the opportunity to resolve them, as the chapters discussed next and others, such as Rossi, Boeckmann, and Berk (1978), do.

The first major focus of this volume is on issues in experimentation and prediction. Teitelbaum's chapter, the first of the set with this focus, capitalizes on his experience in field tests of innovations in juvenile justice (Stapleton and Teitelbaum, 1972), administrative law (Corsi and Hurley, 1979), and on his legal research. He reiterates the need to distinguish between legal problems and difficulties of judging moral correctness of activities, since little can be gained by combining the two, and, at worst, we may confuse matters. Asking certain questions, for instance, may be legal, but the act may be unethical in the sense that there is grave discomfort for a respondent—discomfort that can be anticipated—or in the sense that responses cannot be protected from uses that harm the respondent.

The need for this separation is clear in other examinations of randomized experiments. These include a report by the Federal Judicial Center (FJC) (1981), a research arm of the federal courts, whose Committee on Experimentation in Law focused on *ethical* issues rather than on law. That the two frames of reference often need not differ appreciably in their implications, despite the need to distinguish them, must also be kept in mind. That graduate courses that address either law or ethics are few is clear from academic catalogs that describe training requirements and from research such as Warwick's (1980). This is true despite work on the matter by conscientious academics, bureaucrats, lawyers, and statisticians, not to mention the public-interest groups that give momentum to that work.

Teitelbaum's positivist approach to legal issues involves educing judicial consequences and liabilities from the rules of law that apply to the researcher's actions and discriminating among problems that are tractable, intractable, and specious. The law that he uses as a basis for prediction and discrimination is constitutional, especially the due process and equal protection clauses.[2] To reason from these, he separates privately supported experiments from those sponsored by government and separates projects that confer benefits from those that involve burdens to participants.

---

[2]The Fourteenth Amendment to the Constitution took effect in 1868 and provided that no state shall "deprive any person of life, liberty, or property without due process of law." Its guarantee runs parallel in intent and wording to the Fifth Amendment's provision of protection against an arbitrary federal government. The First Amendment, guaranteeing freedom of speech and press, is historically associated with the Fourteenth Amendment. Its guarantee has been viewed by the courts as being reinforced by the Fourteenth. See, for instance, Kelly and Harbison (1963).

The privately sponsored experiment is generally immaterial to the Fifth and Fourteenth Amendments, since they bear only on government action, though in a few cases a private institution's violation of other laws may bring research to the court's attention. For publicly supported experiments, the due process clause is pertinent in requiring that rights established under the law cannot be denied. In some cases, the clause may present a clear obstacle and an intractable legal problem in supporting the entitlement of individuals to benefits that program offers and supporting a prohibition against downward adjustment of those benefits. Entitlement laws ordinarily specify only a few conditions for denial of benefits, and experimental tests that require manipulation of benefits within those constraints constitute an intractable problem. The remarkable exceptions involve laws, such as the demonstration project provisions of the Social Security Act, that permit adjustment of benefits within limits in the interest of improving the laws themselves. Experiments falling into this category appear to present more tractable problems, the solutions being part of law itself.

The equal protection clause requires, roughly speaking, that persons who are similarly situated with respect to law must be similarly treated. For example, a participant in a publicly supported test of an existing program may claim that the regimen to which he or she has been assigned constitutes a burden or deprivation of benefit relative to others who are similarly situated. Teitelbaum reminds us that the clause does not mean individuals must be treated the *same*, for the law also implies that differentiation is acceptable, as in the case of disparate sentences, for example. The differentiation must be compatible with a legitimate state purpose however. Apart from this, the problems of mounting randomized tests are reduced to the extent that law is explicitly tentative and permits waiver of existing or future benefits in the interest of satisfying the purpose of law.

Zeisel's classic chapter shifts our attention from legal resolution of problems to strategies for tailoring experimental designs so as to avoid legal and ethical problems. A variety of practical suggestions are provided. For example, one obvious tactic that is nevertheless frequently ignored is to ensure that the number of people exposed to potentially burdensome treatments should be kept to a minimum, by choosing the appropriate sample size with statistical advice and by coordination of efforts to avoid unnecessary redundancy in risk-laden studies. The suggestion is as pertinent for surveys as it is for experiments in that we must often reduce to a minimum the number of individuals who must be asked offensive, disturbing, or otherwise upsetting questions. The technology for minimizing the number of questions that must be asked and minimizing sample size under a variety of constraints is adaptable from sample design technology, developed to reduce costs without appreciably reducing precision in research (e.g., Sudman, 1976). Zeisel further maintains that, wherever possible, the experimental treatment should be that which will have a desired effect. Thus, one would evaluate the impact of smoking on health not by encouraging a nonsmoking experimental group to begin smoking but rather by having a smoking experimental group either stop or reduce smoking. At times, it may be necessary to restrict experiments to a limited socially acceptable range on some variable. So, for instance, when evaluating the effect of college scholarships, the benefit may not be randomly assigned for the whole applicant group but may be randomly assigned within a range of equally needy or deserving applicants if the resource, scholarship support, is scarce and it makes no sense to spread it thinly. Zeisel examines several other specific design modifications that can be made in the interest of meeting ethical or legal requirements, including mock features, regression discontinuity designs, and indirect experiments.

This list of tactics can be lengthened. Testing components of programs rather than full programs, for example, is often warranted on management grounds, since full-blown tests are expensive and may not be worth the effort, as well as on ethical or legal grounds. That is, procedures or operations that are not known to be essential but may be useful become the target for testing. Similarly, variations in program intensity may be compared. For instance, several durations of a program designed to influence serious traffic offenders may be testable, under the assumption that the outcome of a no-program condition can be extrapolated or that the condition is meaningless since "no program" is not a realistic political option. One may alter the units of analysis, randomizing institutions where that process is legal and ethical, but where randomization of individuals is not, this being in the interest of indirectly estimating impact on institutions. Graduated introduction or withdrawal of benefits whose effect is not clear can be tailored to designs that capitalize on the stagewise character of the process. See Riecken and Boruch (1974) for a description of these and other tactics.

Zeisel's first two suggestions for solving ethical or legal problems through design are related to more general guidelines that have been developed to help in making decisions about the ethical appropriateness of randomized trials. Warwick (1978), for instance, endorsed the principle that the conditions under which experiments are carried out should approximate the full-blown program. The FJC (1981) proposes in its guidelines that the innovation tested must constitute a realistic prospect, providing a choice that one might adopt instead of retaining the status quo. And indeed, the advice seems to have been met in many social experiments, at least to the extent that we can judge what is realistic despite political or social uncertainty. Still, there is considerable room for debate. A program regimen that seems unrealistic now—such as expensive training, support, and maintenance of families who have been persistently unable to be self-supporting—may be realistic in the future; narrowly realistic tests may be ethically unacceptable to some on that account (see Riecken and Boruch, 1974).

Zeisel's chapter first appeared in 1969, and he stressed then that there appeared to have been little support for randomized trials. The same is less true today. But whether experiments are supported depends considerably on the state of the knowledge in the particular substantive area and perhaps more heavily on government and private interest in understanding what works and how well it works. To the extent that these interests shape social ethics and law, the acceptability of experiments will vary. It is only in the last 15 years, for instance, that educational intervention strategies have been mounted systematically by the federal government, much less tested conscientiously. During the 1970s, similarly vigorous attempts to assess new programs that improve on the status quo have been supported in health services delivery by the National Center for Health Services Research, in criminal and administrative justice and the courts by the National Institute of Justice and the National Science Foundation, in accident prevention by the federal and state departments of transportation, and in employment and income subsidy by the U.S. Department of Labor and others. They are not common, but the increase in number over the past 10 years is remarkable (see Boruch, McSweeny, and Soderstrom, 1978, for a bibliography). Political and public acceptance of randomized trials appears then to have changed, though progress has been slow.

Gilbert, McPeek, and Mosteller's chapter bears on a criterion that ought to be taken into account in any decision about whether a randomized trial ought to be undertaken. As the FJC's Committee on Experimentation in Law puts it, there must be significant uncertainty about the value of the proposed innovation to justify an experiment. The same criterion has been reiterated elsewhere, for example, by Robert Levine (1981) in discussing ethical aspects of medical experimentation, by Warwick (1978) in proposing guidelines for determining ethical acceptability of experimental tests of social interventions, and by Boruch, Anderson, Rindskopf, Amidjaya, and Jansson (1978) in appraising appropriateness of social experiments. The point is that if there is certainty about a program's value, then the need for an experiment and the need to meet the ethical or legal problems it engenders are much less clear.

Obtaining evidence that can be brought to bear on the criterion can, however, be difficult. The Gilbert et al. assessment of the likelihood of success of a medical innovation is direct in focusing on the dilemma of whether individuals in experimental or control conditions are put at risk of hazard or benefit. It is indirect insofar as it concerns a sample of innovations rather than the one on which a decision to experiment has to be made. Indeed, if one looks at carefully designed studies of primary and secondary medical therapies, notably new surgical and anesthetic treatments, one finds the new treatment labeled as successful about half the time. In about 20% of the cases the innovation performs more poorly than standard treatment; in about 30%, far better. The implication is that the ethical dilemma of depriving people of benefit randomly is gratuitous to the extent that available information does not justify confidence in one or the other candidate treatments.

Originally written for the medical research community, the chapter is relevant for experimental tests of social interventions. Evidence of the kind developed by Gilbert, McPeek, and Mosteller has generated for other fields. For instance, Smith and Glass's (1977) quantitative integrations of results from different studies also provide numerical estimates about how often innovations work in mental health and other areas. The "meta-analysis" approach has become fashionable in both basic and applied social sciences primarily because synthesis is important. But one incidental benefit—empirical understanding that bears on ethical acceptability of randomized trials—is often unrecognized (e.g., Rosenthal, 1980). Gordon and Morse's (1975) work is similar in spirit. They review the published reports of high quality evaluations of social interventions and find that 35% of new programs succeed notably but that just over 20% are clearly failures relative to control conditions.

Gilbert and his colleagues also argue that evidence is available to show that people are far too confident of the assumption that a regimen "works." They provide evidence for an old scientific rule of thumb that nothing so improves the chances of apparently successful innovation as lack of experimental controls, thus extending work by Thomas Chalmers and others. They find, for example, that marked enthusiasm for an innovation is negligible in reports on controlled trials and typical in uncontrolled or poorly controlled trials; enthusiasm is considerably more evident in the latter. No identical analysis appears to have been done in the social arena. But Gordon and Morse's (1975) work is pertinent in showing that declarations that a program is successful are about four times more likely in research based on poor or questionable evaluation designs as in that based on adequate ones.

The weight of the evidence then supports a more general point, made by Zeisel in considering criminal justice research and by Rutstein (1969) in considering medical research, that badly designed research can yield misleading results and is ethically unacceptable on that account. The same point is an integral part too of another criterion proposed often to assist in decisions as to whether controlled experiments are warranted. For the FJC's Committee on Experimentation in Law, the criterion is that there must be no practical means to resolve uncertainty about the value of alternative regimens in justice-related work *other* than the experimental design. A similar message is given by Boruch, Anderson, *et al.* (1978) for different reasons: A randomized test may be inappropriate on management grounds, since it is difficult to mount, especially if estimates of relative effectiveness of programs that are as valid can be generated using other designs.

Judgments as to whether designs other than randomized tests yield fair results are difficult partly because we do not fully understand the kinds of biases that can be generated in nonrandomized trials. At one extreme, the situation is clear. As Levine (1981) suggests for medical research, historical controls can be useful and are sensible when the time series implied by such controls are uncomplicated and stable, with deaths occurring soon after onset of a particular disease being a clear example. This regularity in cause and consequence is what makes assessing interventions in some areas, such as behavioral modification and certain industrial changes, particularly useful. The other extreme usually involves fragmentary data, instability, and little coherent theory; this is much more typical in social, medical, and health services field research. The possible sources of bias identified in reports such as that of the FJC (1981) and in texts such as Campbell and Stanley's (1963) are identifiable. But estimating them is difficult or impossible. The work of Chalmers, Block, and Lee (1972) in special areas of medicine and that of Gordon and Morse (1975) on published reports of the effectiveness of sociological interventions, for example, suggest that poorer designs will yield estimates of effect that are inflated, exaggerating the value of the intervention. Still other studies, however, show that the bias may be positive, negative, or negligible, depending on the particular evaluation design, and that the bias often cannot be predicted in public health, educational, or medical trials (Meier, 1972; Gilbert, Light, and Mosteller, 1975; Boruch, 1976). The main point is that differences in quality of research design produce differences in results and that evidence on the matter is available. That evidence can be used in the social as well as medical sectors to illuminate decisions about the ethical acceptability of randomized trials. The information can constitute an empirical resolution to conflict between one ethical standard that argues against randomized trials on grounds that an innovation will benefit or harm and a second standard that implies alternative designs are less ethically acceptable because they produce results that cannot be interpreted with much confidence. In other cases, one may have to rely on abstract standards of quality in design of research to make judgments.

The conflicts between research and law that require statutory or judicial resolution command Breger's attention. His special focus is on administrative authority for conducting social experiments, Congress's role in specifying statutes that avoid problems, and the courts' interpretation of each.

The administrative authority stems from the enabling statutes of the various federal agencies. The statutes may be specific, as in the case of law that directs the Department of Housing and Urban Development to undertake housing allowance experiments. Or the laws may be general, as in the case of statutory provisions that an agency head may waive compliance with other statutes for purposes of experimentation or demonstration projects, as, for example, the waiver authority of the secretary of the Department of Health and Human Services permits social experimentation, within limits. It is the latter approach that Teitelbaum identifies as something of a model in understanding how to facilitate social experiments without abridging the rights or participants. It is this and a hierarchy of authority that are also important to the JFC's Committee on Experimentation in Law, higher authority being regarded as necessary to justify burdens entailed by demonstration projects that are approved at lower levels.

Federal authority for randomized field tests of social programs has been challenged in the courts on at least two occasions. The courts have interpreted the authority broadly, rejecting the challenges in *Aguoyo v. Richardson* and *California Welfare Rights Organization (CWRO) v. Richardson*. It is worth remembering in this respect that the legal history of experimentation—*experimentation* being defined broadly—is long and compatible with contemporary court decisions. In the *Truax v. Corrigan* decision of 1914, for example, Justice Holmes rendered a dissenting opinion that "there is nothing I more deprecate than the use of the Fourteenth Amendment beyond the absolute compulsion of its words to prevent the making of social experiments . . . in the insulated chambers of the several states, even though the experiments may seem futile or even noxious to me and to those whose judgment I most respect." A similar spirit was reflected nearly 20 years later by Justice Brandeis in *New York State Ice v. Liebmann*. He applauded a state's ability to experiment without risk to the rest of the country, cautioning that the Court might "erect our prejudices into legal principles."

Institutional review boards (IRBs) are a procedural vehicle for establishing propriety of research and for resolving conflicts. The construction of regulations that govern IRBs constitutes an administrative effort to solve the problems engendered by restrictive rules. The federal regulations governing the boards, notably those issued in 1981 by the Department of Health and Human Services, are crucial in principle, though Breger and the FJC's (1981) Committee on Experimentation in Law are reserved in speculating about how much impact these can have. For Breger, it is clear that recent regulations recognize the generally low risks attached to social research—by expedited review procedures, for instance—and this is to the good. But they keep social experiments within the purview of the IRBs on account of the potentially serious consequences of this type of research. He takes pains to identify conflicts, such as those between court rulings that recognize field experiments can be flawed but legitimate, on one hand, and IRB rulings that reject experiments on technical grounds, on the other hand, as in *CWRO v. Richardson* and *Crane v. Mathews*, respectively. The general issue remains of how able, much less willing, IRBs can be in judging *technical* quality of projects, apart from their responsibility to judge ethical propriety.[3] It is a matter of concern for IRB members, to judge from workshops on the topic by Boston's Project on Responsibility in Medicine and the University of Illinois Medical Center, for instance; and the stress on technical criteria is likely to vary considerably across IRBs.

Breger reiterates Teitelbaum's theme in stressing that the legal dimension of concern for equitable distribution of resources generates questions about the extent to which discrimination or the appearance of it in experiments may violate the due process and equal protection guarantees of the Constitution. He extends the examination in a different direction, using *Gordon v. Forsythe* to illustrate that when service delivery must be allocated rationally on grounds other than randomization, the court will approve the alternative and that in cases involving pilot or demonstration projects, the court will sustain the use of randomization. He suggests that in balancing potential injuries or burdens against benefits, one should consider criteria such as seriousness of the problem and scope and duration of the experiment. This seems compatible with criteria proposed, for instance, by the FJC's (1981) Committee on Experimentation in Law. Breger's emphasis on stringent review when burdens rather than benefits are at issue is also compatible with the views of some ethicists on experimentation, such as Warwick

---

[3]There is a good deal of variability in the extent to which IRBs have attended to quality, if we may judge from work by Goldman and Katz (1982) and others.

(1978), and the views of the FJC committee. Breger emphasizes that this does not mean that burden is unacceptable. Finally, Breger, like Teitelbaum and Zeisel, recognizes research design solutions to some problems in this arena. The use of a safety-valve category in randomized tests has been a device to ensure that unfairly harsh or severe burdens are not imposed as a consequence of blind randomization in traffic-offender experiments. It is one of an array of such devices that can reconcile institutional responsibility to take action on the basis of special needs or conditions of the individual in law, medicine, and elsewhere with the need for fair assessments of innovative practices.

One kind of research on randomized experiments that has *not* been considered in this volume but is pertinent involves the study of attitudes toward the randomization process. Do individuals involved in such trials find randomized assignment objectionable or demeaning, as some have claimed? What do we know about attitudes, preferences, and opinions, or about the accuracy of information on which the opinions are based? In fact, we know too little, but evidence is accumulating. The evidence from actual field experiments is indirect—individuals have participated, being randomly assigned to alternative regimens and knowing in many cases that assignment is a matter of chance. Still, research on refusal rate for field experiments is sparse: We know of no pertinent work on the range of social experiments that have been mounted.

Laboratory studies on attitudes rather than on behavior are just beginning. In Australia, for instance, J. M. Innes (1979) has executed small studies to understand how individuals view random assignment to new family therapy programs when various justifications for such assignment are stressed to the eligible families: scientific need for evidence on the program's effect, the equity of randomization when resources are scarce, and the possible negative effects of innovative treatment. The results suggest that the appeals to scientific or equity arguments do not appreciably affect a favorable attitude toward randomization but that the possibility of negative program effects on participants does. This conflicts in some respects with studies by Hillis and Wortman (1976) in the United States on medical research. These studies suggest that randomization is indeed viewed in a more favorable light when scientific merit of the design is emphasized and that it is viewed in a less favorable light than are alternatives when resources are scarce. Subsequent unpublished work by Wortman suggests that in the absence of self-interest randomization is, on the average, preferred as a method of allocation of scarce educational resources by individuals eligible to receive them.

Small-scale studies such as these use samples of college students, whose preferences are not clearly material to preferences of individuals who are actually involved in social ameliorative programs. Nonetheless, the studies are an important vehicle for understanding the role that attitudes might play in field research, how the randomization process can be described to individuals, and how attitudes might be assessed. As Innes points out, small studies of similar design should be mounted for target groups actually involved in social experiments if we believe that attitudes are important.

Fallible information must often be used to make administrative decisions in a variety of contexts. For example, judgments by parole boards, psychiatrists and psychologists, police, and others about probable violent conduct are employed at various stages in both the criminal justice and mental health systems. Monahan provides an analysis of the use of such predictions in his chapter, focusing on three major attacks that have been launched against predictions of violence in the last few years. First, the record of empirical accuracy of such predictions is weak, to judge from evidence he summarizes from conscientious and massive studies of how well violent criminal behavior is predicted from psychometric, psychiatric, demographic, and other information. A second fundamental critique concerns those decisions that are based on prediction—to withhold bail or extend a prison sentence, for example—despite the inaccuracy; these decisions often violate ethical standards and involve intractable legal problems. Punishing individuals for acts they might commit in the future violates many tenets of our democratic society. The third, more recent criticism suggests that prediction of violence is an improper role for mental health professionals, whose primary objective should be assistance and rehabilitation. Monahan then provides an analysis of ethical issues raised by prediction, including why some forms of violence and not others are sanctioned, what are acceptable predictions, what level of accuracy is sufficient, and what the consequences of such predictions may be. The ultimate use of the prediction is obviously critical. When the costs are negligible and the benefits great, prediction will be ethically acceptable even when extremely inaccurate. Monahan argues, however, that the potential for misuse of prediction of violent behavior gives it high priority as a professional and ethical concern.

Monahan's approach, seeking evidence that bears on an ethical concern, is not new, of course, though it is applied sensibly to a new target. His conscientious empiricism is a solution here in that the result verifies that our ability to predict is poor despite advertisements to the contrary. And it obviates other problems, those generated by an erroneous presumption that prediction is adequate. It is a reiteration of the lesson that some practices that are adopted routinely for administrative purposes and labeled as administrative can be properly regarded as having been mislabeled, that is, a better target for research than for immediate exploitation by management. If indeed they are identified as a matter for research, other problems, notably legal and ethical ones engendered by a poor prediction system, become moot. In *Merriken v. Cressman*, for instance, a prediction system was installed in a school district to identify routinely children who were likely to become troublesome. Actions were taken on the basis of the prediction, despite the meager evidence for quality of the system. Legal challenges to the system were eventually upheld. The important point is that the court battle and discomfort and embarrassment for the individuals involved could have been avoided had pertinent evidence on quality of prediction been collected first as part of research (Boruch and Cecil, 1979). Similar approaches and resolution have been relevant to postdiction, including polygraph tests, voice stress analysis, and the like. The history of these and similar shortcuts to identifying liars and thieves is long, as Daniel Defoe advised in the eighteenth century to monitor the miscreant's pulse; ignoring evidence that runs counter to the advice seems to have been chronic. The problems apply to the commercial sector as well as to the public, to judge from Lykken's (1981) list of organizations that have naively adopted polygraph tests. These are no less important than simplistic attempts by private political groups to use simple dossiers routinely for prediction and post facto explanation (see Donner, 1980, for instance).

Informed Consent and Clearance

The second section of this volume deals with informed consent and clearance procedures. The concerns of a variety of interest groups that Riecken identifies has increased government emphasis on ensuring that prospective participants in research be able to provide voluntary and informed consent to their involvement. The administrative vehicle for ensuring that opportunities to consent or refuse exist and for waiving consent requirements is often the institutional review board, discussed by Breger in a legal context. Other clearance processes exist, generated by concerns that research is a burden to participants and should be minimized. These involve screening of federally supported work by the U.S. Office of Management and Budget and, in education, by the Federal Educational Data Acquisition Council as well.

Both requirements for informed consent and clearance procedures, more generally, are important in reducing burdens on the research participant. Despite this and despite 10 years in developing government regulations for medical research, we are just beginning to learn how to make such procedures efficient. For instance, the absence of information on how informed consent was actually obtained in clinical trials has prompted formal recommendations that journal editors include such information in published reports of results (Mosteller, Gilbert, and McPeek, 1980).

The chapter in this volume by Launor Carter concerns a class of procedures for clearing federally supported field research, that is, determining appropriateness of the research relative to statistical, bureaucratic, ethical, and legal standards. An element of such procedures involves acquisition of informed consent. The chapters that focus more narrowly on informed consent do so in different ways. Those by Lidz and Roth and by Singer stress an empirical approach, determining how well consent procedures are followed, on one hand, and the degree to which "informed" consent affects research findings, on the other. The fourth chapter, by Corsi, is negotiative in perspective and discusses how compromises were reached in designing research so as to ensure the propriety of an experiment. Each focuses on what appear to be problems and offers options for solutions.

Carter argues that although insufficient care has been devoted to issues of respondent burden and propriety of questions in the past, such procedures have been carried too far in some instances. They demand considerable time and resources of the researcher and inflate the costs to the public of doing research. He supports the argument with a case study of clearance procedures for questionnaires and tests used in the national evaluation of an education program in public schools, establishing that procedures ended up costing over $150,000 and taking months to complete.

Carter's chapter is exceptional in that although researchers complain often about clearance procedures, they rarely produce evidence needed to sustain their claims. Carter has indeed generated evidence that can, in principle, be verified. The publication of his views here and elsewhere is remarkable in that such data are embarrassing to government and could have jeopardized his research. That it does not appear to have been damaging is some credit to the relevant bureaucrats and managers. His procedural solution to the problem of sequential clearance arrangements and the time they entail is to make reviews by the four reviewing agencies simultaneous.

To this case we may add another, stemming from research undertaken over a 9-month period to meet congressional demands for a review of federal program evaluations. This work, the Holtzman Project, was executed by Northwestern University. Because the effort was federally funded, approval for surveys involved two organizations that review work such as that planned by the project (Boruch, Cordray, Pion, and Leviton, 1981). The first, the Federal Educational Data Acquisition Council, is required by law to examine survey designs with respect to propriety and respondent burden. It bases its judgments partly on review by a second group, the Committee on Evaluation and Information Systems of the Council of Chief State School Officers. The aim of both groups seems sensible in that coordination of research efforts is warranted. In practice, the groups serve often as gatekeepers. For the Holtzman Project, the gate was opened only after the researchers had jumped the fence. That is, the surveys were executed before they were actually approved; approval took 6 months and came a week or so before the final report was due. The disappointment here is that limits on expertise and resources prevent either group from being a helpful facilitator of field studies, at least at times, and prejudice against any clearance procedure can prevent the contractor from viewing the groups as such.

The activity of each clearance organization raises larger questions. Screening of surveys can be productive, but it can prevent on political grounds important questions from being asked and jeopardize the timeliness of research. The performance record of such groups needs to be open to professional scrutiny if these risks are to be reduced.

Requiring informed consent is a device to ensure that subjects' rights are not abused in experiments, surveys, and other kinds of research. Lidz and Roth, in detailing their research on informed consent in psychiatric treatment, note that many of the factors appear to be widely applicable in applied social science. They contend that there is a gap between the elements required to ensure informed consent and our ability to actualize them. The first of these elements is that information should be provided; and the second, that the research participant should understand the issues involved. To the extent that researchers are indifferent or hostile to the process of informed consent or too busy to attend to it, the consent procedure will be distorted. The distortion, in Lidz and Roth's clinical studies, seems to take a variety of forms. In some instances, the staff appear to have "discounted" the importance of the informed consent form. In other cases, the research participants' attention was directed to the part of the form that was said to be important for the researcher—the signature blank. Even when patients were involved with staff who were vigorous in explaining the experimental situation, Lidz and Roth observed that many patients still did not comprehend that the research project might not further their interests. The implication is that if effective informed consent is the objective, we must overcome the researchers' stress on obtaining only consent in lieu of an informed refusal and the participating individuals' lack of comprehension. They suggest that one means of doing so is to have institutional review boards establish refusal ratios. A research team would then have to show that a fraction of subjects did indeed select themselves out of the experiment. Lidz and Roth recognize problems in assigning such ratios and the damage to research that it might produce, but the procedure is at least subject to experimental testing. Whether a test is worth the effort remains to be explored.

Corsi's field tests of telephone conferences against in-person hearings in unemployment and other public assistance programs are remarkable on several counts. They are the first to assay effectiveness of the two modes of communication at the state level and to use well-designed field experiments in administrative law. The experiment involves random assignment of individuals to either in-person hearings or telephone conferences. A second randomization of appointed counsel versus conventional conditions in which no counsel is appointed is designed to assess the influence of lawyers on the proceedings.

Corsi discusses legal and ethical problems that might be engendered by such an exercise and takes an eclectic attitude toward negotiated solutions. If ignored, the problems he discusses could have destroyed the experiment or damaged it badly enough to make results uninterpretable in his research, as they have in other settings (e.g., Conner, 1977). On the other hand, the research could violate law or ethical standards regardless of its technical quality. To handle the problem of clients who are assigned to phone hearings but insist on in-person hearings, Corsi and the agencies involved agreed to treat the innovation as a legitimate management procedure, equal in administrative appropriateness to in-person hearings. That is, the judgment about appropriateness does fall within the legitimate authority of the agencies involved. Lawyers involved in the project were concerned, however, that despite the absence of legal obligation to serve control group members there was an ethical one. Corsi appealed to arguments that the teleconferencing approach needed to be tested fairly to extend the reach of existing programs. Clients who were not assigned lawyers but who hired them fell into a special category, since it would have been unethical and illegal to deprive them of the right to counsel. They were identified as a distinct target for research, and the implications of not conforming to the expected regimen were treated as matters for empirical and analytical research.

The idea of negotiated solutions to consent and related problems in randomized tests is not new. What is new is the detail, context, and policy import of the exercise, and this is why negotiation of the kind Corsi discusses is worth studying. Other research on how agreements are reached in randomized tests and on the failure of agreements exists, such as Conner's (1977) examination of tests of 12 reform programs. Goldman's (1979) description of field tests of pretrial settlement and ordered scheduling for the Appellate Court also is instructive in emphasizing incremental problem solving through negotiation with the host institution—the courts—and legal staff. Most such efforts focus on negotiated agreement about what particular features of a new program can be tested, as Corsi and Goldman suggest, and on tailoring randomization procedures in accord with ethical, legal, and other constraints on the research (e.g., Goldman, 1977).

Singer takes a survey sample approach to shed light on two kinds of questions—whether government-required consent procedures and various confidentiality assurances have any effect on respondents' behavior in surveys, and whether respondents even remember the procedures and assurances. Strong critics of the relevant government regulations maintain that good research may be rendered impossible by such rules and carry protection to easy extremes that offend common sense. Level of confidentiality assurance is a plausible influence on cooperation rate in research, but data on the matter have been scarce. Singer chose to examine the influence by presenting some potential respondents with no information at all, some with absolute guarantees that the information would remain completely confidential, and some with the assurance that information would remain confidential except as required by law. She also questioned respondents after completing the formal interview to determine if indeed respondents are able to be informed, under the presumption that if they are not, then rules regarding "informed" consent warrant more skepticism. Singer took an empirical and analytic approach to determining if there are issues worth worrying about here.

To put Singer's findings briefly, the amount of information given to prospective respondents and the level of assurance of confidentiality have remarkably little effect on willingness to cooperate in responding to questions, even notably sensitive ones. Well-trained interviewers from a legitimate survey organization did, in a national probabilty sample, elicit good-quality data whether they provided a great deal of information about the survey or little and whether they provided limited or absolute guarantees of confidentiality. Respondents' attitudes, rather than behavior, are, however, affected remarkably by efforts to provide information that helps them anticipate the sensitivity of questions and by emphatic confidentiality assurance.

One exception to these generalizations about behavior is that requiring signatures of respondents does have a clear effect—people often do not want to sign questionnaires, though they are willing to respond to questions. Furthermore, an assurance of absolute confidentiality has a small but significant effect on willingness to respond to questions about behavior.

Singer found that the fraction of respondents who recalled the level of confidentiality assurances ranged from one-third to two-thirds, depending on the character of the assurance. This is true despite that following interviews better than 90% of respondents said they found nothing obscure or confusing about introductions to the process. The relatively low fraction is important, considering the ethicists' stress on informing research participants (e.g., Warwick, 1978) and that the target here is a well-designed national sample.[4] The finding is compatible with work by the U.S. Census Bureau, and the National Research Council's Panel on Privacy and Confidentiality as Factors in Survey Response (1979), and others (see Boruch and Cecil's review, 1979). The related research suggests that individuals generally trust interviewers—perhaps more than they should, but trust nonetheless—when interviewers are skilled and auspices for survey appear legitimate. A fair proportion of respondents fail to recall with any precision the information that is provided to them.

The effects of varying levels of effort dedicated to research participants' rights then may, as in this study, have negligible effects on behavior except for extreme conditions and do appear to affect attitudes. The dynamics underlying this are still unclear but appear to depend on factors such as age, sex, and education and whether the individual cares about the information.

If we take seriously the adjective in the phrase *informed consent*, the research suggests that we will have to overcome our own ignorance *and* that of respondents and respondents' indifference. More generally, it becomes reasonable to regard any requirement for informed consent as having a probabilistic character—not everyone can be informed in

---

[4]Current federal regulations (45 C.F.R.46, Jan. 26, 1981) require that information "be in language understandable to the subject." What is understandable is ambiguous, of course, given contemporary evidence that people vary a great deal in what is understood, regardless of what they say they understand. What is remembered about the information is not mentioned by regulations. Still, it is important, to judge from Singer's research on recollection of respondents in surveys. Riecken and Ravich's (1982) work on patients in Veterans Administration hospitals illuminates this further, suggesting that readability of consent forms used in that research requires a college-level education. Perhaps as a consequence, over a quarter of the patients did not realize they were participants in research despite their signature on consent forms.

equal measure—a character that may complicate the tasks of the ethi-
cist, lawyer, researcher, or bureaucrat with an interest in simple solutions to problems in this arena. A second implication is that some of the
researcher's concerns about the damaging effects of government requirements are unjustified at times if the standard is evidence: The
effect of only the stringent requirement of signatures has a remarkable
effect on behavior for at least surveys of this type. In other kinds of
research, however, laboratory work on the effects of noise stress
(Gardner, 1978), such as the effects of new regulations on behavior,
have been substantial.

Some later work, based partly on Gray's (1975, 1978) pioneering
efforts, is promising at least with respect to reducing participants' ignorance. Grabowski, O'Brien, and Mintz (1979) actually test the knowl-
edgeability of individuals after they have been informed but before they
are permitted to sign consent forms. The authors ask individuals directly about the investigator's willingness to answer questions and provide instruction when it is clear that individuals' understanding is low
despite earlier information. Their small follow-up studies during the
course of experiments suggest that individuals do indeed retain the
information.

Individual Privacy and Confidentiality

The interest in individual privacy with respect to government can be
traced to colonial times in the United States. The more general interest
reemerges as a public issue periodically, especially when applied social research, government supported or otherwise, must address sensitive questions. As an ethical matter, avoiding diminution of privacy
and abiding by assurances that information collected for research will
be used only for research purposes have been stressed in the codes of
professional organizations, including most recently by the American
Statistical Association and the International Statistical Institute
(Jowell, 1981), and in codes developed by ethicists such as Warwick
(1978). Its import has been reiterated and examined in detail by private
organizations, such as the Social Science Research Council (Riecken
and Boruch, 1974), by government agencies with responsibility for support and execution of research, such as the FJC's (1981) Committee on
Experimentation in Law, as well as by individual researchers. That the
interest is not confined within U.S. borders is clear from the products
of work in England, Germany, Norway, Canada, Sweden, and elsewhere (Boruch and Cecil, 1979; Mochmann and Müller, 1979; Flaherty,

1980). Nor is the interest confined to any specific discipline, for the anthropologist, sociologist, economist, archivist, psychologist, political scientist, and medical and educational researcher have to cope with similar problems.

The chapters presented in the last section of this volume discuss several approaches to resolving the problem of ensuring privacy of the research participant and confidentiality of the information obtained. They cover legal, procedural, statistical, and empirical research techniques for achieving this end without needlessly limiting the researcher's ability to conduct good field studies.

Teitelbaum's chapter sets the stage for these in providing one framework for analysis of researchers' legal liability, an analysis that turns partly on the researcher's providing a promise of confidentiality to the research participant. During the course of a study, the researcher comes to possess evidence of a criminal activity. Does the researcher have an obligation to disclose this knowledge on his or her own initiative? Theories of accessorial liability, misprision of a felony, and obstruction of justice are examined. But as a matter of fact only rarely does a genuine legal problem arise. These chapters also examine the issue of compelled disclosure, and here the legal problems are greater. Grand jury subpoena powers are broad, as are those of a congressional committee. Clearly, if mechanical solutions to eliminating identifiers, of the kind that Steinberg discusses, are to be used, they must be employed before a subpoena is issued. By the same token, some have suggested keeping data or identifiers lists overseas to defeat subpoena. The central issue is not the locale but the extent of the researcher's control over records. Finally, assuming that data are subpoenaed, is there a researcher liability for disclosure pursuant to public duty? From an examination of legal doctrine of invasion of privacy, breach of contract, and misrepresentation and deceit, Teitelbaum concludes that at times there will be. To avoid such liability, some care should be taken in constructing the promise of confidentiality given to research participants. Also, attempts have to be made to design the study so as to eliminate or minimize the value of the collected information to investigative agencies.

Steinberg describes a variety of procedural approaches for maintaining the confidentiality of social science data that are used in a number of agencies. If the data are to be analyzed only once, the obvious approach is immediately to depersonalize the data, and if longitudinal analyses will be required, substituting an identification number for the individual's name is an simple first step in ensuring confidentiality. Problems can arise, however, even if names are removed. For example, the number and kind of data elements and the nature of the sample may make it possible to link data to individual respondents. Among the potential solutions to this problem are using crude report categories, microaggregation of data, and error inoculation or random contamination of data elements. In-house capacity for analysis will, of course, improve the prospects for maintaining data confidentiality, although such analysis may also need to employ some of the confidentiality-ensuring procedures. When two or more files are to be merged, link-file brokerage and mutually insulated file linkage procedures are appropriate. Embedding target groups in larger groups on which data are disclosed can also reduce or eliminate the possibility of deductive disclosure.

Dalenius reviews some statistical approaches to ensuring confidentiality of information by ensuring the privacy of individuals in field surveys. Traditionally, those concerned with conducting survey research have focused on obtaining estimates of population parameters that are precise, in the sense of having low sample-to-sample variance. However, surveys often suffer from both high nonresponse rate and bias introduced by untruthful responses. Dalenius suggests that we need to be willing to accept more random variance in analysis, with which we know how to cope, in the place of less bias, which is often impossible to deal with. This is the trade-off offered by the randomized response method, a procedure in which random error is in effect introduced by the respondent when he or she answers questions. Invented by Stanley Warner, the approach was designed originally to ensure higher response rate and a reduction in response bias. In particular, the approach guarantees that even in face-to-face interviews the interviewer cannot know the state of the individual from his or her response to a question. Yet, the statistician can still undertake reasonable analyses. The guarantee presumably fosters a higher cooperation rate. But whether it does or not, it provides clear protection to the respondent. These methods have been implemented in a variety of countries, including the United States, Canada, and Taiwan, for research on sensitive topics, such as alcohol use, drug abuse, fertility control, and child abuse. The Boruch–Cecil (1979) review suggests that the method works well in the sense of providing protection and often generating higher cooperation rates. They can be applied to not only questionnaire surveys but also data banks (e.g., the error-inoculation described by Steinberg). Steinberg suggests that the public must also be informed to understand and appreciate how such methods work and that because these solutions are limited in utility, we need legislation on privacy and confidentiality issues. The limits on utility are being removed slowly, partly through mathematical–statistical work that is then tested in the field (e.g., Tamhane, 1981).

Nelson and Hedrick undertake an analysis of statutory protection of confidential research data. They argue from a common law perspective, using Wigmore's treatment of privileged communication, that the key element here is the balance between the benefit of disclosure to the legal process and the harm caused by breaching the confidentiality of the relationship. Common law provides some direction on these issues, but court cases suggest that common law privileges are not a reliable source of legal protection. Nelson and Hedrick also assess the results of a statute enacted to protect the research participant from having research records appropriated for more research purposes, including use in court cases against the recipient.

This statute permits the researcher to apply to the government for a grant of confidentiality, which will prevent forced disclosure of research participants' identities in federal, state, or local criminal, civil, administrative, or legislative proceedings. Nelson and Hedrick's survey of researchers who received grants suggests that the grants were relatively easy to obtain and that researchers found them useful, although only a minority believed grants were helpful in obtaining cooperation from research participants. Rather, the primary benefit of such grants appears to be that they assist in obtaining access to institutions. Most of the researchers surveyed reported that other safeguards to ensure confidentiality were also employed. The Supreme Court has recognized the legality of the confidentiality grant in *People v. Newman*, a conflict involving research in a methadone maintenance clinic. But as the scope of the coverage of this and similar grants is clarified further, researchers should be cautious in their reliance on statutory authorizations.

Madden and Lessin discuss the development of a statute to protect research data: Section 524(a) of the Omnibus Crime Control and Safe Streets Act. The statute provides that the use of research records on identifiable research participants is restricted to the purpose for which it was obtained, that is, statistical research. Furthermore, the information is immune from the judicial and administrative process and cannot be admitted as evidence in proceedings without the consent of the individual to whom the information relates. Unlike related statutes, Section 524(a) provides automatic protection for criminal justice research assisted under the act—that is, the protection is not a matter of discretion of the attorney general or other executive officer. Moreover, it covers both identification of and information about the individual. The drug statute examined by Nelson and Hedrick, for example, covers only identification.

One important element of the statute development process that Madden and Lessin describe is the inclusion of information from researchers and statisticians who would be subject to these regulations. Vigorously obtaining evidence and reactions from researchers with experience in criminal justice research appears to have helped substantially in both constructing a clear statute and generating awareness of and support for the law among researchers. Other statutes with similar functions are not as familiar to researchers.

Finally, Alexander's chapter discusses bills developed after the 1974 Privacy Act. The act's restrictions on access to records grew partly from fear of misuse of identifiable information maintained in large data banks. One of its unanticipated consequences was that statistical uses of identifiable records were also restricted. The changes made in law since the act's passage recognize a principle of functional separation; that is, separating the use of information about an individual for a research and statistical purpose from its use in arriving at administrative or other decisions about that individual. Several of the new legislative proposals have two common themes: liberalizing research access to data from surveys and administrative record files, and protecting statistical research data from nonstatistical uses resulting from disclosures that would affect or harm research subjects. Alexander also discusses several new proposals regarding data access.

Federal laws and regulations governing access to institutional records for research purposes are influential. They may be copied by states, for example, to regulate state information systems. Their translation into state or local agency rules may be required by law, as, for example, when the agency activity is supported partly by federal grants. To the extent that this happens, the law is a solution to the legal problem of ensuring legitimate access. Within this framework, state law may be more restrictive, or authority may be vested in offices that differ across states.

Reliable information on how federal rule is translated into state and local rule and on invention of state or local rules is sparse. Two studies illuminate special areas, however. The first, by Sasfy et al. (1982), was supported by the National Institute of Justice and concerns criminal justice records. The second, by Alice Robbin at the University of Wisconsin, is unpublished and concerns Wisconsin state record systems. Both have antecedents in research on general public access to records, such as that by Flaherty (1980).

Sasfy's survey suggests that about half the central state repositories maintaining criminal justice records are empowered to provide access to legitimate researchers and that about 90% of the state correctional agencies do so. Nearly all have received some form of federal assistance for developing record systems, and as a consequence they are constrained by federal law (e.g., Section 524 of the Crime Control Act of 1973) or regulations governing records. Both the laws and the regulations permit researchers access to confidential criminal records but do not require states or local agencies to provide it. In fact, of the 12 states that Sasfy studied intensively, 5 of the central state repositories were governed by state regulations that matched the federal ones. Some agencies, such as local police departments, had more variable rules partly because they are less directly influenced by federal or even state rules. Prosecutors' offices differ, too, in that separating records that could be accessible to the researcher from inaccessible records (i.e., those that cannot be disclosed under the law) may be time-consuming: consequently, release of any records is difficult.

Several of the prosecutors' offices in the Sasfy et al. study were interesting because staff members were unaware of state laws or rules that provided for researcher access to records. The unfamiliarity is predictable, given the workload and turnover of staff and the poor or nonexistent relations between the research community and such offices. Still, it suggests that researchers must know the law better than attorneys do in this arena.

The thoughtful reader will recognize that none of the chapters treats commercial or administrative applications of the approaches discussed. Like most technologies, these can be applied in other sectors, and so a few examples are worth discussing.

Stanley Warner (1979) of Toronto's York University, for instance, has managed to develop new applications of his invention, the randomized response technique. His idea is to apply the method to voting by ballots in small groups—boards of trustees, promotion committees, and the like—to ensure that ballots advertised as secret indeed remain so. The "secret" votes of each member of a two-member committee can ordinarily be deduced by the opposing member, for instance, and any unanimous or nearly unanimous vote permits one to infer how identifiable individuals voted. Warner recognized that procedural solutions can be employed to avoid such deductions by observers, such as announcing only the final decision, not enumerating the vote count publicly. But this is not possible in some cases and in any event may not prevent deductive disclosure within the committee. He proposes a modification of randomized response that increases the privacy of individuals within the group—a method that amounts to destroying or reversing one vote randomly and in such a way as to sustain the final outcome of a yes or no decision. If a five-person committee is customary, for example, the approach may require six to accomplish its objective. This addition or the technical complications introduced are the cost of furnishing privacy in such settings and will be justified at least occasionally to committee members and to the extent that the increased secrecy in balloting also increases truthfulness in voting.

Potential applications of other techniques are not hard to find. Methods for reducing the likelihood of deductive disclosure can be applied to data shared by companies in order to accommodate the need to protect proprietary interests. Some of the methods discussed here may be useful for estimating rates of petty theft, drunkenness, absences without leave, and so on, in organizations that need such estimates. The laws are pertinent here, too, in that candor in reporting disease incidence, accident rates, and so on, to a government may require that institutional privacy be preserved. The statutes that apply to confidentiality of records on individuals are likely to be pertinent in at least a few respects to bills developed to ensure privacy of institutions involved in research.

Finally, applications are possible in audits of contracted social research, to judge from the U.S. General Accounting Office (GAO) experience. Both technical and procedural devices are options in conflicts between the need for government to audit research and the researcher's need to abide by promises of confidentiality made to research participants (Marvin, 1978; U.S. GAO, 1979; Havens, 1981). The GAO work itself appears to be pertinent to state-supported research as well as federally supported research and to at least some privately sponsored investigations.

References

Barnes, J. A.
   1979   Who Should Know What? Cambridge: Cambridge University Press.
Beauchamp, T. L., R. R. Faden, R. J. Wallace, and L. Walters (eds.)
   1982   Ethical Issues in Social Science Research. Baltimore: Johns Hopkins University Press.
Bermant, G., H. Kelman, and D. P. Warwick (eds.)
   1978   The Ethics of Social Intervention. Washington, D.C.: Hemisphere.
Boruch, R. F.
   1976   "On common contentions about randomized field experiments." Pp. 158–194 in G. V. Glass (ed.), Evaluation Studies Review Annual Vol. 1. Beverly Hills, Calif.: Sage.

Boruch, R. F., P. S. Anderson, D. Rindskopf, I. R. Amidjaya, and D. Jansson
  1978   "Randomized experiments for evaluating and planning local programs: A summary on appropriateness and feasibility." *Public Administration Review* 4: 655–695.
Boruch, R. F., and J. S. Cecil
  1979   *Assuring the Confidentiality of Social Research Data.* Philadelphia: University of Pennsylvania Press.
Boruch, R. F., D. S. Cordray, G. M. Pion, and L. Leviton
  1981   "A mandated appraisal of evaluation practices: Digest of recommendations to the Congress and the Department of Education." *Educational Researcher* 10(4): 10–13, 31.
Boruch, R. F., A. J. McSweeny, and E. J. Soderstrom
  1978   "Randomized field experiments for program planning, development, and evaluation: An illustrative bibliography." *Evaluation Quarterly (Evaluation Review)* 2(4):655–695.
Bulmer, M. (ed.)
  1979   *Census, Surveys, and Privacy.* London: Macmillan.
Campbell, D. T., and J. S. Cecil
  1979   "Protection of the rights and interests of human subjects in the areas of program evaluation, social experimentation, social indicators, survey research, secondary analysis of research data, and statistical analysis of data from administrative records." Pp. 23.1–23.23 in R. F. Boruch, J. Ross, and J. S. Cecil (eds.), *Proceedings and Background Papers: Conference on Ethical and Legal Problems in Applied Social Research.* Evanston, Ill.: Northwestern University.
Campbell, D. T., and J. C. Stanley
  1963   "Experimental and quasi-experimental designs for research on teaching." Pp. 171–246 in N. L. Gage (ed.), *Handbook of Research on Teaching.* Chicago: Rand-McNally.
Chalmers, T. C., J. B. Block, and S. Lee
  1972   "Controlled studies in clinical cancer research." *New England Journal of Medicine* 287:75–78.
Conner, R. F.
  1977   "Selecting a control group: An analysis of the randomization process in twelve social reform programs." *Evaluation Quarterly* 1(2):195–244.
Corsi, J. R., and T. L. Hurley
  1979   "Pilot study report on the use of the telephone in administrative fair hearings." *Administrative Law Review* 31:485–524.
Diener, E., and R. Crandall
  1978   *Ethics in Social and Behavioral Research.* Chicago: University of Chicago Press.
Donner, F. J.
  1980   *The Age of Surveillance.* New York. Alfred Knopf.
Federal Judicial Center
  1981   *Experimentation in the Law: Report of the Federal Judicial Center Advisory Committee on Experimentation in the Law.* USGPO No. 027–000–01148–9. Washington, D.C.: U.S. Government Printing Office.
Flaherty, D. H.
  1980   *Privacy and Government Data Banks: An International Perspective.* London: Mansell.
Gardner, G.
  1978   "Effects of federal human subjects regulations on data obtained in environmen-

tal stressor research." *Journal of Personality and Social Psychology* 36: 628–634.

Gilbert, J. P., R. J. Light, and F. Mosteller
  1975 "Assessing social innovations: An empirical base for policy." In A. Lumsdaine and C. A. Bennett (eds.), *Central Issues in Social Program Evaluation.* New York: Academic Press.

Goldman, J.
  1977 "A randomization procedure in 'trickle-process' evaluations." *Evaluation Quarterly* 1:493–498.
  1979 "Experimenting with appellate reform: The second circuit experience." Pp. 13.1–13.13 in R. F. Boruch, J. Ross, and J. S. Cecil (eds.), *Proceedings and Background Papers: Conference on Ethical and Legal Problems in Applied Social Research.* Evanston, Ill.: Northwestern University.

Goldman, J., and M. D. Katz
  1982 "Inconsistency in decision-making by institutional review boards." *Journal of the American Medical Association,* in press.

Gordon, G., and E. V. Morse
  1975 "Evaluation research." *Annual Review of Sociology* 1:339–361.

Grabowski, J., C. P. O'Brien, and J. Mintz
  1979 "Increasing the likelihood that consent is informed." *Journal of Applied Behavior Analysis* 12:283–284.

Gray, B. H.
  1975 *Human Subjects in Medical Experimentation: A Sociological Study of the Conduct and Regulation of Clinical Research.* New York: Wiley.
  1978 "Complexities of informed consent." *Annals of the American Academy of Political and Social Sciences* 437:37–48.

Havens, H. S.
  1981 "The U.S. General Accounting Office: Role of reanalysis in an oversight agency." Pp. 50–56 in R. F. Boruch et al. (eds.), *Reanalyzing Program Evaluations.* San Francisco: Jossey-Bass.

Hendricks, M.
  1982 "Oral policy briefings." In N. L. Smith (ed.), *Alternative Forms of Representation in Evaluation.* Beverly Hills, Calif.: Sage.

Hillis, J. W., and C. M. Wortman
  1976 "Some determinants of public acceptance of randomized control group experimental designs." *Sociometry* 39:91–96.

Innes, J. M.
  1979 "Attitudes toward randomized control group experimental designs in the field of community welfare." *Psychological Reports* 44:1207–1213.

Jowell, R.
  1981 "A professional code for statisticians?" Paper presented to the Plenary Session of the International Statistical Institute's 43rd Biennial Meeting, Buenos Aires, December 1.

Kelly, A. H., and W. A. Harbison
  1963 *The American Constitution: Its Origins and Development.* New York: W. W. Norton.

Kelman, H. C.
  1968 *A Time to Speak: Human Values and Social Research.* San Francisco: Jossey-Bass.

Levine, R. J.
1981   *Ethics and Regulation of Clinical Research.* Baltimore and Munich: Urban and Schwarzenberg.

Lykken, D. T.
1981   *A Tremor in the Blood: Uses and Abuses of the Lie Detector.* New York: McGraw-Hill.

Marvin, K. E.
1978   "Statement on access to social research data for audit and reanalysis by the General Accounting Office before the conference on solutions to ethical and legal problems in social research." Unpublished transcript. U.S. General Accounting Office, Washington, D.C.

Meier, P.
1972   "The biggest public health experiment ever: The 1954 field trial of Salk poliomyelitis vaccine." In J. M. Tanur, F. Mosteller, W. Kruskal, R. F. Link, R. S. Pieters, and G. Rising (eds.), *Statistics: A Guide to the Unknown.* San Francisco: Holden-Day.

Mochmann, E., and P. J. Müller (eds.)
1979   *Data Protection and Social Science Research.* Frankfurt: Campus Verlag.

Mosteller, F., J. Gilbert, and B. McPeek
1980   "Reporting standards and research strategies for controlled trials: Agenda for the editor." *Controlled Clinical Trials* 1:37–58.

National Research Council, Panel on Privacy and Confidentiality as Factors in Survey Response, Committee on National Statistics
1979   *Privacy and Confidentiality as Factors in Survey Response.* Washington, D.C.: National Academy of Sciences.

Reynolds, P. D.
1982   *Ethics and Social Science Research.* Englewood Cliffs, N.J.: Prentice-Hall.

Riecken, H. W., and R. F. Boruch (eds.)
1974   *Social Experimentation: A Method for Planning and Evaluating Social Intervention.* New York: Academic Press.

Riecken, H. W., and R. Ravich
1982   "Informed consent to biomedical research in Veterans Administration hospitals." *Journal of the American Medical Association,* 248:344–348.

Rosenthal, R. (ed.)
1980   "Editor's Notes: Quantitative assessment of research domains." *New Directions for Methodology of Social and Behavioral Science* 5:vii–ix.

Rossi, P. H., M. Boeckman, and R. A. Berk
1978   "Some ethical implications of the New Jersey–Pennsylvania income maintenance experiment." Pp. 245–266 in G. Bermant, H. C. Kelman, and D. P. Warwick (eds.), *The Ethics of Social Intervention.* New York: Halsted.

Rutstein, D. D.
1969   "The ethical design of human experiments." *Daedalus* 98:523–541.

Sasfy, J., et al.
1982   *Report to the National Institute of Justice.* McLean, Va.: Mitre Corp.

Sieber, J.
1982   *Ethical Decision Making in Social Science Research.* Munich: Verlag.

Smith, M. L., and G. V. Glass
1977   "Meta-analysis of psychotherapy outcome studies." *American Psychologist* 32: 752–760.

Stapleton, W., and L. Teitelbaum
  1972   In Defense of Youth: A Study of the Role of Counsel in American Juvenile
         Courts. New York: Russell Sage.
Sudman, S.
  1976   Applied Sampling. New York: Academic Press.
Takeuchi, J. S., F. Solomon, and W. W. Menninger
  1981   Behavioral Science and the Secret Service: Toward the Prevention of As-
         sassination. Report of the Planning Committee for the Institute of Medicine
         Workshop on Behavioral Research and the Secret Service. Washington, D.C.:
         National Academy of Sciences.
Tamhane, A. C.
  1981   "Randomized response techniques for multiple sensitive attributes." Journal of
         the American Statistical Association 76:916–923.
U.S. General Accounting Office
  1979   A Framework for Balancing Privacy and Accountability Needs Evaluations of
         Social Research. PAD–70–33. Washington, D.C.: U.S. GAO.
Warner, S. L.
  1971   "The linear randomized response model." Journal of the American Statistical
         Association 66:884–888.
  1979   "Extended randomized response applications." Pp. 7.1–7.10 in R. F. Boruch,
         J. S. Cecil, and J. Ross (eds.), Proceedings and Background Papers: Conference
         on Ethical and Legal Problems in Applied Social Research. Evanston, Ill.:
         Northwestern University.
Warwick, D. P.
  1978   "Ethical guidelines for social experiments." Pp. 267–288 in G. Bermant, H. C.
         Kelman, and D. P. Warwick (eds.), The Ethics of Social Intervention. New York:
         Halsted.
  1980   The Teaching of Ethics in the Social Sciences. Hastings-on-Hudson, N.Y.: Hast-
         ings Institute.

Author Index

Numbers in italics refer to the pages on which the complete references are listed.

A

Administrative Conference of the United States, 121n
Almy, T. P., 74, 81
Alpert, M., 73, 74, 81
American Psychiatry Association, 87, 94
American Psychological Association, 87, 92, 94
Amidjaya, I. R., 299, 319
Andenaes, J., 135, 137
Anderson, P. S., 299, 301, 319
Anderson, S., 100, 137
Andros, G. G., 66, 81
Aronson, E., 99, 137, 183, 209
Astin, A. W., 20, 25, 26, 47

B

Bain, R. K., 186, 210
Ball, S., 100, 101, 137, 138
Barber, B., 107, 137, 156, 157, 214, 235
Barbier, D. C., 66, 81

Barnes, J. A., 294, 318
Bearman, J. E., 72, 81
Beauchamp, T. L., 294, 318
Beck, R. G., 101, 104, 137
Bennett, C. A., 164, 170
Berg, I., 135, 136, 137
Berk, R. A., 296, 321
Bermant, G., 294, 318
Biderman, A., 99, 101, 137
Bixby, F. L., 101, 141
Blair, E., 192, 194, 209
Block, J. B., 72, 81, 301, 319
Blumberg, H. H., 186, 209
Blumenthal, M., 136, 137, 142
Blumer, H., 147, 157
Bobbitt, P., 129, 138
Boeckmann, M., 296, 321
Bogart, L., 209
Bogatz, G. A., 101, 138
Bok, S., 111, 138
Bonacich, P., 101, 138
Boness, F. H., 213, 219, 235

323

Subject Index

QUANTITATIVE STUDIES IN SOCIAL RELATIONS
(Continued from page ii)

QUANTITATIVE STUDIES IN SOCIAL RELATIONS